Russia in Asia

This edited volume presents new research on Russian-Asian connections by historians, art historians, literary scholars, and linguists. Of particular interest are imagined communities, social networks, and the legacy of colonialism in this important arena of global exchanges within the imperial, Soviet, and post-Soviet eras. Individual chapters investigate how Russians imagined Asia and its inhabitants, how these different populations interacted across political and cultural divides, and how people in Siberia, China, and other parts of Asia reacted to Russian imperialism, both in its formal and informal manifestations. A key strength of this volume is its interdisciplinary approach to the topic, challenging readers to synthesize multiple analytical lenses to better understand the multivalent connections binding Russia and Asia together.

Jane F. Hacking is Professor of Russian at the University of Utah. She is the author of *Coding the Hypothetical* (1998). She publishes in the areas of L2 Russian phonology and the development of second language proficiency. In 2017 she was recognized for Outstanding Contribution to the Profession by the American Association of Slavic and East European Languages.

Jeffrey S. Hardy is Associate Professor of History at Brigham Young University. He is the author of *The Gulag After Stalin: Redefining Punishment in Khrushchev's Soviet Union* (2016), which was awarded honorable mention for the W. Bruce Lincoln Prize by the Association for Slavic, East European, and Eurasian Studies.

Matthew P. Romaniello is Associate Professor of History at Weber State University and editor of *The Journal of World History*. He is author of *Enterprising Empires: Russia and Britain in Eighteenth-Century Eurasia* (2019) and *The Elusive Empire: Kazan and the Creation of Russia, 1552–1671* (2012).

Routledge Studies in Modern History

For a full list of titles, please visit: https://www.routledge.com/history/series/
MODHIST

Russia in Asia

Imaginations, Interactions, and Realities

Edited by
Jane F. Hacking, Jeffrey S. Hardy and
Matthew P. Romaniello

Routledge
Taylor & Francis Group

LONDON AND NEW YORK

First published 2020
by Routledge
2 Park Square, Milton Park, Abingdon, Oxon OX14 4RN

and by Routledge
52 Vanderbilt Avenue, New York, NY 10017

Routledge is an imprint of the Taylor & Francis Group, an informa business

British Library Cataloguing-in-Publication Data
A catalogue record for this book is available from the British Library

Library of Congress Cataloging-in-Publication Data
Names: Hacking, Jane F., editor. | Hardy, Jeffrey S., 1978- editor. |
Romaniello, Matthew P., editor.
Title: Russia in Asia : imaginations, interactions, and realities / edited by
Jane F. Hacking, Jeffrey S. Hardy, and Matthew P. Romaniello.
Description: London ; New York, NY : Routledge/Taylor &
Francis Group, 2020. |
Series: Routledge studies in modern history |
Includes bibliographical references and index.
Identifiers: LCCN 2020011022 (print) | LCCN 2020011023 (ebook) |
ISBN 9780367357115 (hbk) | ISBN 9780429341298 (ebk)
Subjects: LCSH: Russia--Relations--Asia, Central. |
Asia, Central--Relations--Russia. | Soviet Union--Relations--Asia, Central. |
Asia, Central--Relations--Soviet Union. | Russia--Colonies--Asia. | Asia,
Central--Colonization. | Russians--Intellectual life--19th century. |
Russians--Intellectual life--20th century. | Russia--Civilization. |
Asia, Central--Civilization.
Classification: LCC DK857.75.R8 R87 2020 (print) |
LCC DK857.75.R8 (ebook) | DDC 303.48/24705--dc23
LC record available at https://lccn.loc.gov/2020011022
LC ebook record available at https://lccn.loc.gov/2020011023

ISBN: 978-0-367-35711-5 (hbk)
ISBN: 978-0-429-34129-8 (ebk)

Typeset in Times New Roman
by Taylor & Francis Books

Contents

PART II
Interactions 77

PART III
Realities 163

Illustrations

Figures

Tables

Contributors

Naomi Caffee is Assistant Professor of Russian at Reed College. She is the author of several articles on literature in the Russian Imperial context, focusing on the use of Russian by non-Russian writers in the Caucasus, Central Asia, and Siberia. Her current book project is a transnational investigation of Russian-language literature across and beyond the Russian cultural sphere.

Michael J. Corsi is a Ph.D. candidate in history at Ohio State University. With prior degrees in biology and history, he is a historian of science who investigates healthcare and medicine in the Russian Empire and Soviet Union. Of particular interest to Corsi are the Asian borderland regions of the Far East and Central Asia.

Yuan Gao is a Ph.D. candidate in history at Georgetown University, with prior educational experience at Fudan University, Moscow Pedagogical State University, and Nazarbayev University. Her research focuses on the nineteenth-century Russian and Chinese Central Asia, with particular interests in Russian and Qing imperialism, transnational connections along Russian and Qing borders, and the environment in Central Asia.

Lenore A. Grenoble is the John Matthews Manly Distinguished Service Professor in the Department of Linguistics at the University of Chicago. She is the author or editor of dozens of articles and books, including *Saving Languages* (2006) and *Language Policy in the Former Soviet Union* (2003), as well as the recipient of several prestigious grants and awards. Her research is wide-ranging, with emphasis on language contact, endangerment, and revitalization; language documentation; and discourse and conversation analysis.

Jane F. Hacking is Professor of Russian at the University of Utah. Her primary areas of research are Second Language Phonology and Second Language Proficiency. She is the author of *Coding the Hypothetical* (1998) and publishes in both Slavic journals (*Slavic and East European Journal, Canadian Slavonic Papers*) and mainstream linguistics journals (e.g., *Foreign Language Annals,*

Journal of Phonetics). She co-founded and co-directed the Second Language Teaching and Research Center at the University of Utah.

Jeffrey S. Hardy is Associate Professor of History at Brigham Young University. His primary research focus is prison systems and the Soviet Gulag in particular. He has published a series of articles and book chapters on this topic in recent years and his first book, *The Gulag After Stalin: Redefining Punishment in Khrushchev's Soviet Union* (2016), was awarded honorable mention for the W. Bruce Lincoln Prize by the Association for Slavic, East European, and Eurasian Studies.

Xenia Srebrianski Harwell is Assistant Professor of German at the United States Military Academy at West Point. She is the author of *The Female Adolescent in Exile in Works by Irina Odoevtseva, Nina Berberova, Irmgard Keum, and Ilsa Tielsch* (2000) along with several book chapters and articles on a range of topics in both German and Russian literature and culture. Particular interests include gender, youth, memory, and the cultural productions of Russian émigré communities.

Ryan Tucker Jones is Associate Professor of History and the Ann Swindells Chair at the University of Oregon. His research centers on the environmental history of Russia and the Pacific Ocean. He has published one book—*Empire of Extinction* (2014)—and several articles on these subjects. His current book project is an environmental history of Russian and Soviet whaling and is under contract with the University of Chicago Press.

Jessica Kantarovich is a Ph.D. candidate in linguistics at the University of Chicago. Her studies focus on sociolinguistic variation, language identity, and language documentation in the former Russian Empire. Particular areas of interest include indigenous languages in Siberia, Russian in Alaska and Ukraine, and heritage Lithuanian spoken in Chicago.

Chechesh Kudachinova is currently a secondary school teacher in the Altai Republic, with prior experience as a translator and NGO coordinator. She received her Candidate of Philosophy degree from the State Lomonosov University in Moscow and is *doctor designatus* in Russian history at Humboldt University in Berlin. Her research interests include the intersections of power and natural resources across the Russian Imperial space.

Alina Novik is a Ph.D. candidate in cultural history at the European University at St. Petersburg. Her work is interdisciplinary, combing artistic analysis with social history, and explores the production and reception of magic lantern shows, panoramic spectacles, and visual media in nineteenth-century Russia.

Matthew P. Romaniello is Associate Professor of History at Weber State University, editor of *The Journal of World History,* and former editor of *Sibirica: Interdisciplinary Journal of Siberian Studies.* He was previously Professor of History at the University of Hawai'i. He is the author of *Enterprising*

Empires: Russia and Britain in Eighteenth-Century Eurasia (2019) and *The Elusive Empire: Kazan and the Creation of Russia, 1552–1671* (2012).

Ilya Vinkovetsky is Associate Professor of History at Simon Fraser University. He has published a range of articles and a book, *Russian America: An Overseas Colony of a Continental Empire, 1804–1867* (2011), on the Russian Empire in North America, particularly its relationship with indigenous peoples. His research interests also include the flow of goods and people along Russian trade routes in East Asia and colonialism in a comparative context.

Zhen Zhang is Postdoctoral Fellow in the School of Arts at Peking University, having completed his Ph.D. in comparative literature at the University of California, Davis. His work explores the intersection of Soviet and Chinese socialist culture, particularly in the reception of translated Soviet texts in Communist China.

Acknowledgments

This edited volume presents selected papers from the *Asia in the Russian Imagination* conference, which was held at the University of Utah in March 2018. The conference was the culmination of a series of programmatic and curricular efforts launched in 2014 by the University of Utah's Russian Program. Conceived of as the *Siberia Initiative,* this four-year project by the Russian Program sought to introduce greater curricular focus on Asian Russia and to offer a series of lectures and extra-curricular activities in support of this aim. With generous funding from the Department of Education through the University of Utah's Asia Center (a Title VI National Resource Center), guest speakers delivered lectures in the areas of anthropology, environmental studies, history, film studies, and linguistics. A new course, titled *Russia and Asia*, was also developed and will be taught for the third time in the fall of 2020.

The *Asia in the Russian Imagination* conference was held in the fourth and final year of this initiative and invited proposals that explored political, economic, and socio-cultural interactions from a variety of disciplines, perspectives, and historical periods. The conference opened with a keynote presented by Evgenii Golovko, Director of the Institute for Linguistic Studies at the Russian Academy of Sciences, and over the next two days some thirty-five scholars from North America, Europe, and Russia delivered papers that addressed the conference theme. The eleven papers selected for this volume capture the conference's interdisciplinary spirit, and the authors and editors have worked to develop a volume of complementary and cohesive textual explorations of Russia's engagement with and contemplation of Asia. An additional four papers from the conference appeared in a special issue of *Sibirica: Interdisciplinary Journal of Siberian Studies*, volume 19, number 1 (2020).

As editors of this volume, we would like to thank all who have made it possible. Members of the conference advisory committee who helped us by lending their expertise to the conceptualization of the conference and who reviewed abstracts are Eric R. Laursen (University of Utah), Robert Thomas Argenbright (University of Utah), Marisa Karyl Franz (New York University), Jessica Graybill (Colgate University), Lenore Grenoble (University of Chicago), and John Ziker (Boise State University). The conference enjoyed

Figure 0.1 "A map of the route to Mosco & Pekin," from John Bell, *Travels from St. Petersburg in Russia to Diverse Parts of Asia* (1763), reproduced by Special Collections, University of Hawai'i Libraries.

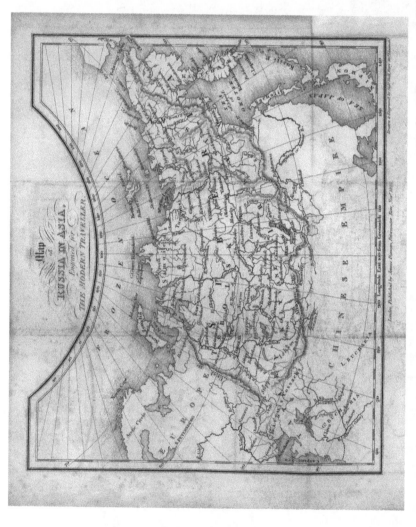

Figure 0.2 "Map of Russia in Asia," from *The Modern Traveller* 10 (1825), reproduced by Special Collections, University of Arkansas Libraries

generous support from the University of Utah's Asia Center, whose funding made it possible for us to support travel costs for attendees joining us from Russia and modest stipends for graduate student attendees. We were grateful as well for support from Berghahn Publishing, the University of Utah's Center for Second Language Teaching and Research, and the Departments of History and World Languages and Cultures.

We also thank the University of Arkansas's Porter-Pathfinder Library's Special Collections for providing us permission to reproduce the "Map of Russia in Asia" from 1825, and the University of Hawai'i at Manoā's Special Collections for permission to reproduce "A map of the route to Mosco & Pekin." Hamilton College's Special Collections, along with Shoshana Keller and Marianita Peaslee, provided us permission for "Vue Générale De Constantinople" in Alina Novik's chapter. Carmen Caswell of the University of Chicago prepared the maps featured in Lenore Grenoble's chapter, and Nicole Simmons assisted us in preparing the manuscript for submission to the publisher. Finally, our thanks to Robert Langham and his team at Routledge for their assistance throughout the process.

Imaginations, interactions, and realities

Jane F. Hacking, Jeffrey S. Hardy and Matthew P. Romaniello

During Russia's Great Northern War with Sweden, numerous Swedish prisoners of war were sent into internal exile to Siberia. These men took up residence across the region during their captivity, with several becoming key informants about Siberia's peoples, geography, and resources for Russia's newfound Academy of Sciences. Philip Johan von Strahlenberg (d. 1747), for example, acted as Daniel Gottlieb Messerschmidt's (1685–1735) local informant during Messerschmidt's expedition for the Academy in the 1720s. After leaving Russia to return to Sweden, Strahlenberg published his own geographic description of the region, *Das Nord-under Ostliche Theil von Europa und Asia*, first published in Stockholm in 1730, which was translated into English, French, and Spanish in the following decade. The work of Messerschmidt and Strahlenberg was discussed across Europe, even cited by Voltaire in his biography of Peter the Great as the source of his knowledge about Siberia.[1] Whether working for the Russian government or held by it in captivity, foreign specialists strongly influenced how Europeans conceived of Russia's Asian possessions.

This is not to imply there was a singular vision of the Russian Empire imposed by foreigners. Jan Frederick Bernard (d. 1752), for example, was another Swedish captive, but Bernard wrote about "Grand Tatary," an enormous region from the Volga River in the west to China in the east. Bernard was impressed with this territory, noting that "This vast Country is under the finest Climate of the Universe, & of extraordinary goodness & Fertility," but he also recognized some of its challenges, "as it is also one of the higher of the habitable World, it wants Water in Several Places."[2] Bernard's idea of an expansive Tatary, with "Asia" beginning at the Don River, had historic roots, existing since the classical era.[3] In fact, it was naturalists such as Strahlenberg and Messerschmidt who were working against this older vision through their fieldwork and travels across the region.

In order to understand the size and scale of the region, the Russian government dispatched cartographic expeditions at the same time the Academy of Sciences was commissioning its naturalists. Ivan Kirilov and V. N. Tatishchev's mission in the 1730s produced the material to claim the Ural Mountains divided Europe from Asia. The government endorsed these conclusions to fix the line between the continents further to the east than "Grand Tatary" supporters such as Bernard described.[4] Even the official cartographic expedition, and the endorsement of the Russian government, failed to persuade everyone within the empire that its Asian portion began at the Ural range. Writing to Voltaire in 1767, Catherine the Great announced "Here I am in Asia; I wanted to see it for myself. There are in this city twenty different peoples, who bear absolutely no resemblance to one another."[5] But Catherine did not write from Tobol'sk or Irkutsk, much less from Kiakhta on the border with China. She wrote from Kazan' on the Volga River, 500 miles west of the Ural Mountains, as close to Moscow as it was to Russia's cartographic division with Asia on the eastern side of the mountain range. Nor were the obstacles to moving Asia to the east limited to the tsars, as the indigenous communities of Eurasia were largely excluded from any part of this process. It would not be until men like Chokan Valikhanov (1835–1865), a Kazakh trained at the Russian Geographical Society, joined the academic discussions in the nineteenth century that an indigenous understanding of geography, even filtered through European science as Valikhanov's work was, became incorporated into this complex process.[6]

With multiple versions of Russia's Asia circulating within the empire and across Europe, its physical reality may not have been the dominant idea of the region. Asia in the academic, and primarily Western, imagination became a foil for the idea of Russia as a European space. Conceptually dividing the empire into European and Asian territory was as much, or more, about moving Moscow and St. Petersburg into Europe as it was about recognizing the diverse populations, languages, and faiths that existed across the enormous Eurasian expanse. Postcolonial theorist Homi Bhabha suggested that "the study of world literature might be the study of the way in which cultures recognize themselves through their projections of 'otherness'."[7] There is no doubt that Russian officials, educated elites, and artists and authors projected "otherness" onto Siberia and other parts of Asia. For Russia, this process dates back to the Muscovite era, as historian Valerie Kivelson has demonstrated through her work in cartography. Siberia was a divine kingdom, a true paradise on Earth.[8]

Recent scholars have built upon Bhabha's work to understand the ways in which this "othering" process influences the formation of modern identities. Literary scholar Roberto M. Dainotto, for example, interrogated the idea of "Eurocentrism," arguing that it was impossible for Europeans "to form a sense of European identity by making recourse to Asia or anything outside of Europe."[9] Russia, by comparison, by working between its European and Asian aspects, formed a unique imperial identity for its possessions and for the neighboring territories with which it engaged diplomatically, economically, and at times militarily. Dainotto was also critiquing the idea that an abstracted understanding of an "Orient" might have been essential to the formation of a European identity. And indeed, while Russian scholars initially experimented with an "Orientalist" understanding of the empire and the broader Eurasian landmass following the ideas of Edward Said, recent works have argued that Russia had an independent conception of various Russian "Orients," rooted in its particular geography.[10]

Russia's Asian possessions were thus never stable in the academic or popular imagination or in geographic definitions. The border shifted time and again throughout the seventeenth and eighteenth century as outpost foundations and new settlers moved further east toward the Pacific and south toward the Muslim khanates. In the nineteenth century, Russia's military conquest of Central Asia and the creation of Russian Turkestan expanded the Russian presence in Eurasia. These new territories stretched the limits of Russian imperial authority, rebelling in the era of World War I, and not pacified by the new Soviet government until the end of the 1930s, if then. The parallel revolt in the Russian Far Eastern province, and its declaration of independence that lasted for nearly a decade, only demonstrated how weak the connection between the Russian Empire and its Asian possessions had been. Attempts to impose administrative order over the region fluctuated, with different waves of settlers and exiles, each forced to migrate to the region for different reasons.[11] The emancipation of the serfs in the nineteenth century rapidly increased the pace of Russian settlement in the region, dramatically changing Siberia and Central Asia. This process only continued in the twentieth century with the Soviet government's investment in exploiting the region's natural resources, often with the labor of exiles and prisoners.[12]

Before the mass migrations into Russian Asia that began in the final decades of the nineteenth century and continued into the late Soviet era, few could have predicted that in the twenty-first century there would be three Siberian cities among Russia's largest (Novosibirsk, Omsk, and Krasnoiarsk each have more than one million residents). Novosibirsk, Russia's third largest city according to the 2010 census, was only established in 1893! While Russia's separation from Asia was defined by its distance from Europe, real or imagined, in its early history, whatever distance might have existed has long since been eradicated by modern improvements in mobility and transportation. The Trans-Siberian Railroad of the early twentieth century and subsequent rail, road, sea, and air connections have fundamentally altered the spatial connection between Russia and Asia.

Any volume that considers the legacy of Russia existing between Europe and Asia necessarily addresses the spatial dimensions of the empire. This "spatial turn" owes a great debt to the pioneering work of Henri Lefebvre, who suggested there was a "conceptual triad" of space: spatial practice, in which spaces are defined through physical production; representations of space, linked to the idea of producing order through knowledge and signs; and representational spaces, in which the symbols and significance of spaces may become detached from the physical reality.[13] For much of the empire's history, the idea of Russia in Asia did threaten to overwhelm the physical reality of the geographic expanse. Therefore, Lefebvre's admonition to avoid "detaching" the idea of space from physical reality is a key to thinking about Russian Asia. Geographer Edward Soja, furthering Lefebvre's work, reiterated the importance of social geography, "which recognizes spatiality as simultaneously a social product (or outcome) and shaping force (or medium) in social life."[14] Russian studies has responded to the challenge of social geography by demonstrating the continuing importance of settlement, and human mobility more broadly, throughout Russia's history.[15] One of the dangers of focusing on settlement is to envision an Asian empire where settlers lived in isolated pockets rather than grappling with the overall interaction of multiple ethnolinguistic groups in integrated communities.

Both visions of Russian Asian communities are true, if not necessarily historically stable. In the early years of Russian settlement, Siberian outposts attempted to keep indigenous communities separate from the new settlers, but this action became less practical as the centuries passed. The challenge for scholars is not to privilege the experiences of the settler communities, even as available sources, and the challenge of understanding multiple languages, might reinforce this bias. Indeed, Russia and the Soviet Union did not only project their authority in the region but also responded to their ongoing encounters with the numerous, and multi-confessional, populations of Siberia and Central Asia. These colonial interactions ultimately resulted in the creation of the modern Central Asian republics and Siberia's autonomous republics and regions.

While space may be the unifying theme of all of the essays contained herein, the volume is no less indebted to "the imperial turn" that has dominated the field since the early 1990s. Historian Larry Wolff argued that the dissolution of the Warsaw Pact "largely invalidated the perspective of half a century, compelling the reconsideration of Europe as a whole."[16] The emergence of independent nations following the collapse of the Soviet Union revealed the paramount importance of identity across the region. In 1982, anthropologist Eric Wolf challenged scholars to restore "the people without history" to our historical narratives, to be wary of accepting "oppositions between those who 'belong' and those who do not, and engenders distinctions of gender, rank, and privilege favoring some kin over others."[17] Following the disruption of the collapse of the Soviet state, James Forsyth and Yuri Slezkine each published a monograph relating the importance of the diversity of peoples of Siberia, answering Wolf's challenge to restore these "people without history" to history of Russian Asia.[18]

Since the 1990s, there has been considerable effort to understand the demographic pluralities of Russian Asia, and the contemporary challenges of small ethnolinguistic groups maintaining their identity throughout the Soviet and post-Soviet era. The United Nations identified nearly 3,000 languages that were in danger of dying out by the end of the century, and not a small number of them are currently being spoken in Siberia.[19] More historical studies have focused on the interaction of diverse populations throughout Russian Asia in order to enrich our understanding of the diversity of imperial experiences. Recent scholars have highlighted individual biographies in order to humanize the "progress of history."[20] This is not a trend isolated to the historiography of the Russian Empire, as imperial studies have benefitted generally from the new interest in transnational, "entangled" lives that force a reassessment of the multiple identities, loyalties, and interests of men and women in an increasingly connected world. This conclusion supports recent scholarship that challenges the arbitrary separation of "formal" entanglements (diplomatic and military engagements) and "informal" ones (the activities of merchants, consumers, and other private individuals).[21]

The themes identified in this introduction will be found woven throughout the eleven chapters of this volume. These individual contributions represent a variety of disciplinary approaches and time periods, but taken together they further our broader conceptual understanding of how Russians thought of, interacted with, and administered different parts of Asia, and how indigenous peoples received, responded to, and altered the Russian imperial project. The chapters are loosely organized into three chronological and topical sections, titled "Imaginations," "Interactions," and "Realities," that ultimately challenge readers to synthesize multiple analytical lenses to better understand the multivalent connections binding Russia and Asia together

The first section, "Imaginations," explores how Russians conceptualized the physical and human geography of Siberia, Altai, Constantinople, and China, from the eighteenth to the late nineteenth centuries. It starts with a chapter by Ryan Jones, who explores one of the most influential eighteenth-century works on the geohistory of Siberia: Peter Simon Pallas's 1778 *Betrachtungen über die Beschaffenheit der Gebürge*. This Enlightenment-era text, based on the German scientist's travels through the Russian Empire, formulated a new theory on the creation of the earth that was debated by famed naturalists such as Linnaeus and Buffon. As an adviser to Catherine II, Pallas also included in his work justification for the expansion of the Russian Empire into Asia and for the autocratic nature of its governing structure. Ultimately, although Pallas's scientific theories would ultimately be disproven, his arguments concerning the links between science, geohistory, and empire proved more durable.

Chechesh Kudachinova's chapter continues the investigation into how Asia was imagined by exploring the varying ways that the Altai region has been described in the Russian cultural sphere and the historical resilience of one of its most well-known monikers: the Golden Mountains. Drawing on the theoretical lens of New Spatial History, it draws close links between mineral resources, empire, and cultural imagination in arguing that the idea of "golden mountains" obscured the reality of a more complex geographical space. Notably, this popular vision of the Altai as the "golden mountains" was not an ancient one. Rather, it was a byproduct of European scientific knowledge situated in the midst of imperial expansion in the 1700s. The knowledge-making claims by three generations of German naturalists in the imperial service forged this myth, which proved instrumental for imagining and incorporating the remote place into the imperial space. In the end, this conception proved durable, lasting into the Soviet era and beyond.

The third chapter, by Alina Novik, shifts focus to southwestern Asia by investigating the public display of panorama paintings in both Europe and European Russia in the early nineteenth century. As a case study of this phenomenon, Novik studies in detail public reception of two panoramas of

Constantinople in Russia and the United Kingdom in the late 1820s. Constantinople—technically in Europe but widely thought of as Asian due to its position as the capital of a Muslim empire—was a popular subject throughout the continent at this time and for Russia its significance was linked with the Russo-Turkish wars. Analyzing different accounts of the panoramas in widely read periodicals reveals the political and cultural meanings invested in the image and explains both the historical roots of these ideas and their cultural meaning to the contemporary public. It also demonstrates that the exhibition in St. Petersburg in particular became an occasion for the mass media to impose on its audience an "official" memory politics that involved gazing at Constantinople as if it was part of a restored Byzantium.

In the final chapter in the first section, Ilya Vinkovetsky explores the history of direct Russian geographical knowledge of China. Though Russia shared a long history of diplomatic interaction and trade with China, it was not until the second half of the nineteenth century that it began to gain reliable first-hand knowledge of China's interior, including its extensive transportation network. Prior to the 1870s, Russian experience in China was limited almost exclusively to Beijing, a few seaports, and the overland direct routes between the Russian border and Beijing. But the 1870s saw Russians undertake a number of exploratory trips along China's roads and waterways, and the Imperial Russian Geographic Society soon published the descriptions of these routes. These published travel accounts represent an important benchmark in the advance of Russian imagination about China.

The second section in this volume, "Interactions," continues the theme of imagination, but does so in the context of multifaceted interpersonal relations between Russians and various "Asian" peoples in the late Imperial and Soviet eras. The first chapter in this section, by Yuan Gao, explores captivity narratives that were published, reprinted and read in nineteenth-century Russia, and examines their significance for understanding Russia's presence in Central Asia and, more importantly, the representations of Central Asia in Russian culture. Captivity narratives not only tell of the vulnerability and uncertainty of the empire during its expansion, but also reveal the rapid shift of power in Central Asia in the nineteenth century. They witness Russian captives' growing awareness of Central Asia as Russia's future colonization and the captives' self-awareness of their Russian and imperial identity. And they demonstrate how Russian readers, based on the coercive interaction of military captivity, were taught to think about Central Asia and its inhabitants as wild and brutal, ripe for imperial conquest and Russian civilization.

Chapter 6, by Xenia Srebianski Harwell, furthers the theme of interactions by investigating the writings of Mitrofan Srebrianski (1870–1948), a military chaplain with the 51st Chernigov Regiment in the Russo-Japanese War. During his two-year absence from home, he kept a regular diary recording his experiences and sent letters home to his family. These sources provide an intimate portrait of his encounter with the East—first in Russian Siberia and then in China. This chapter focuses on the ways in which Srebrianski's narrative constructs and explains war in Asia, depicts military life and the Chinese milieu, and portrays the physical, spatial, and spiritual limits of his experience. As letter-writer, observer, and representative of the clergy, Srebrianski offers a unique perspective on the war in China and the Asian "Other," as well as the revolutionary events taking place in Russia. But he also places himself and his fellow Russians in the category of "Other," providing a self-conscious view of how the Russian Empire was experienced by its practitioners and its subjects.

Naomi Caffee's chapter then brings the volume into the Soviet era by investigating two writers whose works, as well as their tragic fate under Joseph Stalin, formed the genesis of the Sakha national literary tradition. Petr Chernykh-Yakutskii (1882–1933) and Platon Oiunskii (1893–1939) were Russian-educated members of the Sakha intelligentsia and early members of the Soviet Writers' Union who gave voice to indigenous peoples' struggles under the Soviet system. Oiunskii's seminal work of revolutionary mysticism, "The Red Shaman" (1925), re-casts Sakha shamanic rituals and cosmology within a Soviet teleological framework. Chernykh-Yakutskii's 1934 short story "Bad Medicine" explores the same dynamic but attachment to Sakha rituals ultimately ends in tragedy for the protagonist and his family. The themes of ritual and violent sacrifice in these works—which reflect the authors' own experiences of revolution and life under totalitarianism—elucidate the complexities of the ideological transition to Stalinism, as well as its lasting consequences for indigenous peoples of the Soviet Union. This dynamic lies at the heart of the Sakha national identity building process in the early Soviet era and, as shown by recent scholarship and contemporary stage adaptations of "The Red Shaman," it still resonates with audiences today.

The last chapter in the second section, by Zhen Zhang, investigates the Chinese translation and reception of the historical novel *Port Arthur* (1942), written by Aleksandr Nikolaevich Stepanov (1892–1965), which won the Stalin Prize for literature in 1946 for its treatment of the Russo-Japanese War (1904–1905). In a highly patriotic tone, it laments the defeat of the imperial Russian navy to the Japanese, embracing wholeheartedly the heroism of Russian soldiers and navy commanders and demonizing the Chinese. In the post-World War II political landscape, the official sanction and recognition of the novel in the Soviet Union generated controversy and criticism among the Chinese readership even during the honeymoon period of Sino-Soviet relations in the 1950s. Premier Zhou Enlai criticized the novel harshly on several different occasions because it envisaged Russian dominance in Manchuria at the end of World War II and portrayed the Chinese as evil. This critique foreshadowed and then accompanied the Sino-Soviet split in the early 1960s and China's alliances with postcolonial states in Southeast Asia and Africa.

The final section of this volume, "Realities," brings the narrative of imaginations and interactions into the late Soviet and post-Soviet eras, with more focus on the lived experience of Central Asian and Siberian peoples under Russian rule. It starts with Michael Corsi's chapter on the interaction of

Soviet officials and wounded Kyrgyz veterans after the conclusion of the World War II. The Soviet government collectively referred to this displaced group of former soldiers as "invalids," a comprehensive category that included both individuals who had suffered physical and psychological damage as well as their families. The Soviet government took as its responsibility the provision of services necessary to reintegrate these people back into society, including money, food, clothing, temporary housing, and other articles for their material well-being; reeducation and the creation of programs dedicated to improving their "social level"; and the consultation of committees whose responsibility it was to push these people back into the workforce. As official documents show, the decisions made by various organs of the government, particularly the Ministry of Public Welfare, served a dual purpose. While these decisions may have immediately provided temporary relief to ex-soldiers and their family members, their real purpose was to integrate these individuals into the Soviet world on terms dictated by Soviet officials themselves.

Chapter 10, by Lenore Grenoble, then extends the discussion of "realities" into the post-Soviet era, exploring language and socio-cultural shifts in the Sakha Republic. A major factor driving language shift in this region is urbanization, which is bringing major lifestyle changes and introducing cultural tension. While young people often prefer an urban lifestyle and adopt Russian as their everyday language, many other indigenous peoples reject it, seeing cultural and linguistic identity as connected to engagement with traditional activities on the land. Immigration to Yakutsk from other parts of Eurasia, in particular from Central Asia and the Caucasus, has also radically changed the local language ecologies, presenting new pressures to minority indigenous communities. The legacies of imperialism and the pressures of urbanization have also caused non-linguistic harm to indigenous communities in the Sakha Republic, including high rates of poverty, disease, and alcoholism. Ultimately, one of the best defenses against such social ills, Grenoble finds, is the preservation of indigenous language vitality.

The final chapter of the volume, by Jessica Kantarovich, continues this discussion of language and identity in northeast Siberia by exploring indigenous languages and cultures in Sakha and Chukotka. She finds that most minority indigenous language speakers in these areas (the Evenki or Yupik, for example) were traditionally bilingual in Sakha or Chukchi, depending on where they lived, and, in the twentieth century, Russian became increasingly spoken as well. In the post-Soviet era, however, Russian has replaced Sakha and Chukchi as the regional *lingua franca*, but this process has not been even. The Chukchi, who held out longer against Russian imperialism, have actually been losing language primacy faster due to their nomadic lifestyle and lack of centralized leadership. This process was accelerated under the Soviet system when Chukchi children were sent to boarding schools where they spoke only Russian. Yet even among the more sedentary Sakha, whose language enjoys special administrative status that Chukchi does not, a language shift toward Russian is slowly occurring.

Notes

1 Originally published as *Histoire de l'empire de Russie sous Pierre le Grand*, 2 vols. (Paris, 1759 and 1763). This translation is from Voltaire, *The History of the Russian Empire under Peter the Great*, in *The Works of M. de Voltaire*, vol. 20, trans. T. Smollett, et al. (London: J. Newberry, 1763), 29.

2 Wellcome Library, Rare Materials, MS.1143, f. 6, Jan Frederick Bernard, "A Relation of Grand Tartary, drawn up from the Original Memoirs of the Suedes, who were Prisoners in Siberia, during the War between Sueden and Russia. Translated from the French, printed at Amsterdam 1737," trans. William Farrington.

3 The history of the Europe-Asia divide has been discussed by Erika Monahan, "Moving Pictures: Tobol'sk 'Traveling' in Early Modern Texts," *Canadian-American Slavic Studies* 52 (2018): 1–29, esp. 3–13.

4 Monahan, "Moving Pictures," 7.

5 A. Lentin, ed. and trans., *Voltaire and Catherine the Great: Selected Correspondence* (Cambridge: Oriental Research Partners, 1974), #14, 29 May/9 June 1767, 48.

6 Scott C. Matsushita Bailey, "A Biography in Motion: Chokan Valikhanov and His Travels in Central Asia," *Ab Imperio* 1 (2009): 165–90.

7 Homi K. Bhabha, *The Location of Culture* (New York: Routledge, 1994), 17. Bhabha and other postcolonial theorists have influenced scholarship on Russia. For example, Alexander Etkind, *Internal Colonization: Russia's Imperial Experience* (Cambridge: Polity Press, 2011).

8 Valerie Kivelson, *Cartographies of Tsardom: The Land and its Meanings in Seventeenth-Century Russia* (Ithaca: Cornell University Press, 2006), esp. chap. 5. The metaphor of Siberia as Heaven on Earth is one of the themes explored in Galya Diment and Yuri Slezkine, eds., *Between Heaven and Hell: The Myth of Siberia in Russian Culture* (New York: St. Martin's Press, 1993).

9 Roberto M. Dainotto, *Europe (In Theory)* (Durham: Duke University Press, 2007), 7.

10 For example, Daniel R. Brower and Edward J. Lazzerini, eds. *Russia's Orient: Imperial Borderlands and Peoples, 1700–1917* (Bloomington: Indiana University Press, 1997); David Schimmelpennick van der Oye, *Russian Orientalism: Asia in the Russian Mind from Peter the Great to the Emigration* (New Haven: Yale University Press, 2010); Vera Tolz, *Russia's Own Orient: The Politics of Identity and Oriental Studies in the Late Imperial and Early Soviet Periods* (Oxford: Oxford University Press, 2011).

11 For example, see Alison K. Smith, "Movement and the Transformation of Siberia in the Eighteenth Century," *Sibirica* 16: 2 (2017): 44–67.

12 Fiona Hill and Clifford Gaddy, *The Siberian Curse: How Communist Planners Left Russia Out in the Cold* (Washington, D.C.: The Brookings Institution, 2003).

13 Henri Lefebvre, *The Production of Space*, trans. Donald Nicholson-Smith (Malden, MA: Blackwell, 1991), 33.

14 Edward W. Soja, *Postmodern Geographies: The Reassertion of Space in Critical Social Theory*, (London: Verso, 1989), 7.

15 For example, Nicholas B. Breyfogle, Abby Schrader, and Willard Sunderland, eds., *Peopling the Russian Periphery: Borderland Colonization in Eurasian History* (New York: Routledge, 2007); and John Randolph and Eugene M. Avrutin, *Russia in Motion: Cultures of Mobility, 1850 to the Present* (Urbana: University of Illinois Press, 2012).

16 Larry Wolff, *Inventing Eastern Europe: The Map of Civilization on the Mind of the Enlightenment* (Stanford: Stanford University Press, 1994).

17 Eric R. Wolf, *Europe and the People without History* (Berkeley: University of California Press, 1982, 1997), 386.

18 James Forsyth, *A History of the Peoples of Siberia: Russia's North Asian Colony 1581–1990* (Cambridge: Cambridge University Press, 1992); and Yuri Slezkine, *Arctic Mirrors: Russia and the Small Peoples of the North* (Ithaca: Cornell University Press, 1994).

19 UN News, "Protection of minority languages is a human rights obligation, UN expert says," 12 March 2013; https://news.un.org/en/story/2013/03/434112-protection-minority-languages-human-rights-obligation-un-expert-says, accessed 9 August 2019.

20 For example, Stephen M. Norris and Willard Sunderland, eds., *Russia's People of Empire: Life Stories from Eurasia, 1500 to the Present* (Bloomington: Indiana University Press, 2012); Willard Sunderland, *The Baron's Cloak: A History of the Russian Empire in War and Revolution* (Ithaca: Cornell University Press, 2014).

21 See, for example, April Lee Hatfield, "Reluctant Petitioners: English Officials and the Spanish Caribbean," in *Entangled Empires: The Anglo-Iberian Atlantic, 1500–1830*, ed. Jorge Cañizares-Esguerra (Philadelphia: University of Pennsylvania Press, 2018), 197–216, esp. 198–9.

Part I
Imaginations

1 "These plains of Great Russia were once the bottom of the sea"

Peter Simon Pallas, Siberian geohistory, and empire

Ryan Tucker Jones

This essay examines one influential work on geohistory (an eighteenth-century science that was in some senses a precursor to modern geohistory) to come out of the eighteenth-century Russian Empire, Peter Simon Pallas's 1778 *Betrachtungen über die Beschaffenheit der Gebürge* (translated as *On the Nature of Mountains and on Changes which have occurred on the Globe particularly in the Russian Empire*). It demonstrates the important role Siberia played in Russian and European imaginations of deep history at the time. Pallas, a German who was educated at universities in Halle, Göttingen, and Leiden, was perhaps the brightest star in the firmament of the St. Petersburg Academy of Sciences. Pallas won his fame by publishing an account of his extensive travels through the Russian Empire (especially Siberia) in the 1760s, an expedition he followed up with decades of botanical, zoological, geographical, and geological work.[1] He was also a trusted advisor to Empress Catherine the Great (r. 1762–1796), a position which brought him many rewards. The *Betrachtungen* built upon the observations Pallas had made during his travels in Siberia and the Ural Mountains and presented a new theory of geohistory. Its impact at the time was significant, especially in the challenge it presented to Georges-Louis Leclerc le Comte de Buffon and other respected geological systematizers.

Filled with fantastic and now discarded notions of cataclysmic prehistoric floods and volcanoes, the *Betrachtungen* has not entered the canon as one of the key texts of Enlightenment natural history. However justified this neglect may be in terms of the development of modern geohistory, the *Betrachtungen* helps illuminate Enlightenment juxtapositions of political and natural historical conceptions as well the intellectual history of the Russian Empire. The *Betrachtungen*, in fact, was nearly as much an imperial as a scientific text, composed and read in the context of great power rivalry. Additionally, Pallas's practice of imperial geohistory can be seen as homologous to later, influential Russian notions of Eurasianism, which postulated close links between the development of human culture and the natural world and helped justify the Soviet Empire in an era of decolonization.[2] In a similar manner, Pallas claimed a geological logic behind the Russian Empire, especially its Asian portion. He also claimed that the size and power of the Russian Empire offered unique working conditions for the naturalist interested in understanding the entire world. Because Russia was so big, the world and the empire, in fact, were nearly indistinguishable. No place in the empire demonstrated these insights to Pallas quite as well as the vast spaces of Siberia.

Empire and the production of the *Betrachtungen*

Imperial circumstances surrounded Pallas's composition and presentation of the *Betrachtungen*. While ideas about the formation of geological strata had been building in his mind since his Siberian travels in the early 1760s, it was the visit of two emperors to St. Petersburg that provoked the grand scope of the *Betrachtungen*. First, the future emperor Joseph II of Austria visited the St. Petersburg Academy of Sciences, where he heard Pallas present some of his theories. Then, on June 23, 1777, Gustav III of Sweden came to St. Petersburg searching for support in his imperial ambitions in Denmark and Norway. It was on this occasion that the Academy announced that "The Academy Director will hold a welcoming speech and Professor Pallas will give a treatise on the formation of mountains, in French."[3] Only Pallas's work, it appeared, was worthy of the prestigious imperial visit. Though his ideas on earth formation were then still vague, Pallas decided to hurriedly throw together a much grander theory worthy of his audience. The *Betrachtungen* was the result. It was an 80-page description of Russian geohistory, an attack on other geologists, and a presentation of Pallas's own general theory on earth formation. Enjoying some measure of fame, the *Betrachtungen* would later be published and translated into several European languages.[4]

Connections between empire and geohistory were not merely academic for Pallas. In Russia, powerful people had a deep interest in Enlightenment science. Four years later, in March, 1781, Catherine the Great unexpectedly approached Pallas and spoke to him for "a half an hour ... about learned things, particularly about Buffon's *Epochs of Nature*, and then about some Siberian objects ..."[5] The renowned French naturalist's *Epochs* were the focus of much of Pallas's wrath, built as they were upon theoretical musings rather than direct observation. Buffon and perhaps the best-known naturalist of the eighteenth century, Karl Linnaeus, feuded over everything from literary style to schemes for systematizing nature (with the Linnaean system of binomial nomenclature eventually prevailing), and often the arguments carried tones of imperial rivalry.[6] Pallas presumably disabused Catherine of her infatuation for foreign natural history in favor of homegrown science. Certainly, the attentions of the empress were flattering for an ambitious scientist like Pallas, and he was careful to mention Catherine's largesse in his works of natural history.

However, Pallas experienced moments of dissatisfaction with the Russian Empire as well. His conversation with Catherine about the *Epochs* did not, at least temporarily, shake his growing determination to leave Russia. "Still," he wrote fellow academician and friend Gerhard Friedrich Müller, "I hope not to remain in Russia any longer, and this circumstance will have no influence on me."[7] Pallas did not achieve this hoped-for departure, and the reasons were a complex mixture of loyalty to the Russian imperial project, opportunities for further scientific work, and money. On the last score, he complained frequently, noting that "I cannot feed myself only with hopes for much longer!"[8] Accordingly, in the early 1780s, Pallas again made plans to leave Russia: "I would like to return to my fatherland this year. The outlook and hopes here do not look very good for me, and also the promises which they have tried to hold me here seem to be in the courtly style, and thus will not help much."[9] However, imperial attachments proved stronger than he had anticipated. While claiming not to be interested in the perquisites of imperial status, in the 1790s Pallas accepted elevation into the nobility and received a tidy sinecure in the newly conquered Crimea. Prosaic concerns also played a role; Pallas wrote to English naturalist Joseph Banks in 1782 that "There was indeed some possibility of my quitting this Country last year. But since the Empress has almost doubled my Salary, & bestowed emoluments & honours on me more than I expected, I believe I shall remain ever fixed in Russia."[10] The flatteries and briberies of empresses were a powerful factor in the natural historian's career choices, especially in the status-obsessed eighteenth century. Thus, did Russian imperial expansion redound directly to Pallas's material and social benefit.[11]

Whatever the state of his sometimes-fragile imperial loyalties, though, Pallas explicitly credited the Russian Empire with providing the crucial framework for his geohistory. Imperial context, in fact, is what he claimed gave the *Betrachtungen* the advantage over other works. When surveying the contemporary geological literature, including writings by such luminaries as Buffon and Austria's Christoph Delius, he noted that "all have made the mistake ... of basing their findings on just one special observation and cause ... which makes them fall into the confusion of arbitrary suppositions." The reason for such a narrow point of view was that these Europeans had formed ideas "with national bias focused on their own region and have created ideas of the formation of the entire earth based on the mountains of their own homelands."[12] These were the unfortunate strictures under which Buffon and others worked, yoked to the patronage of relatively diminutive states.

Pallas, on the other hand, enjoyed the support and unique intellectual opportunities provided by an expansive polity. "Under the protection of our great and sublime empress," wrote Pallas, "I have traveled through nearly the entire breadth of Asia as well as a good part of both great mountain ranges which support the inhabited earth." His travels had taken him across the Ural Mountains (hardly great, but still significant in Europe's geographical imagination), to the Caucasus, the northern limits of the Himalayas (in Russia's Altai), and all the way to Kiakhta south of Lake Baikal, all without leaving the confines of the Russian Empire. This experience of the "great expanse of the Russian Empire" as well as Pallas's reading had given rise to some new thoughts on the formation of the earth.[13] The experience of being a subject of the Russian Empire allowed Pallas the opportunity to construct a philosophy of earth history that was both comprehensive and based on first-hand observation. This set Pallas's geohistory on much firmer ground than the great and wild systematizers such as Buffon, who rarely left Paris (despite the fact that he once grandly recommended others "going from the burning sands of the Torrid regions to the glaciers of the Poles, ... descending from the summits of mountains to the bottom of the oceans, ... comparing wastelands with wastelands").[14]

Pallas referred on several occasions to the importance of the "wide Russian rule"[15] and this formulation was more than just a statement of geographical fact. Instead, the phrase directly referenced some of the most important ideas that Russians held about their empire. For Empress Catherine II, vastness was a key argument in defense of Russian autocracy. Borrowing from the legal and climatic theories of philosophes Montesquieu, Christian Wolff, and others as interpreted by the Russian historian Vasilii Tatishchev, she explained that "the Extent of the Dominion requires an absolute Power to be vested in the Person who rules over it."[16] More liberal and dispersed forms of government were fine for England or Holland, but the vast Russian territory demanded a concentration of authority. A second, and more optimistic, interpretation of the empire's growing bulk was that it placed Russia on par with other European empires, both past and present. The Moscow jurist S. E. Desnitskii, writing in the 1760s, proclaimed Russia's conquests greater even than those of Greece and Rome, the two classical imperial archetypes.[17] If, as many admitted, the Russian Empire lacked the mercantile success of the British Empire and the intellectual clout of the French Empire's philosophes, then it did at least impress based on its sheer size. And, as Russia multiplied its conquests and advanced in the arts and sciences, these vast spaces meant that the empire could embark on a civilizing mission as grand as that of any of its predecessors or competitors. "Our great empress has still more to hope for," wrote Pallas's friend and fellow academician Gerhard Friedrich Müller, "She can give an entire quarter of the globe a new appearance."[18]

Years later, the St. Petersburg naturalist Karl Ernst von Baer agreed with Pallas about the benefits of a Russian imperial point of view for science. Von Baer contrasted Russian scientific research there to the unfocused, peripatetic labors of Linnaeus's students, often cited as the standard for empirical research in natural history. That famous group of "twelve disciples" (including Johann Falck, a companion of Pallas who committed suicide during the Siberian travels) had undertaken their researches in "unconnected and widely separated regions," whereas Pallas and others had researched an "immense, unbroken stretch of land." Sharpening the scientific results of these travels was the fact that "because this stretch of land ... was essentially a part of the sufficiently known central and northern Europe, for the first time scientists could survey the distribution of a huge number of organic bodies."[19] This posthumous analysis of Pallas's labors captured two essential points that Russians often made about their own empire—that it was uniquely positioned vis-à-vis Europe so as to be a part of it, but much larger, and also that its contiguity rendered it more natural than overseas empires. This was the same argument nineteenth-century climatologists and Soviet Eurasianists would later employ, claiming that the entirety of an immense region stretching from the Urals to Transbaikalia "shared similar physiographical characteristics ... and thus cohered to create a single integral space."[20]

Pallas's *Betrachtungen*, then, relied on and reinforced popular imperial propaganda that stressed Russia's unique vastness. He hinted at political ideas about ruling the empire and added a new association—that the Russian Empire, particularly given its large Asian territory, was the best place in the world for doing theoretical science. Pallas's work in and for the Russian Empire had not only resulted in a more broadly-based geohistory, but also contributed to the prestige and self-definition of that empire, then and in subsequent centuries. This was evident, too, in the conclusions Pallas came to about the history of the earth.

Geohistory and empire

Pallas's claim that the breadth of the Russian Empire allowed him special insight produced some expansive thinking. In a breathtaking passage (a single sentence whose two-page length nearly matched its geographical purview), he described Russia's Ural Mountains as a single unbroken range stretching from their southern terminus in Central Asia through the middle of Russia, up to the island Novaya Zemlya, connecting via a "horseshoe shape" with the "granite cliffs" of Finland and Scandinavia, up to Nordkapp, over to Spitsbergen, and through the North Pole to North America.[21] Thus were Canada and Kazakhstan essentially joined as part of the same geographical entity whose center point lay in Russia. If the geohistory was perhaps faulty, the geopolitical implications were potentially powerful.

Assuming that sea ice would be thicker over shallower water, Pallas thought that such a continuation of mountains through the unknown North Pole would "render useless all attempts by the commercial peoples of Europe to find a Polar passage to China and Japan."[22] He returned to the same theme when discussing the Northwest Coast of America, again dismissing the arguments in favor of a northern passage.[23] The impossibility of a northern sea route was one of Pallas's favorite concerns, and it expressed his Russian patriotism at its fiercest. An open polar lane would bypass the Russian Empire's strategic location between Europe and Asia and fulfill the hopes of the mercantile British, then main rivals of Catherine. If such speculation about undersea mountain formations exceeded Pallas's insistence on first-hand observation, at least the *Betrachtungen* here might help dissuade the British from looking too closely into those same regions. In the twenty-first century, notions of geological contiguity between Siberia and the North Pole play a rather different role, now seen by some Russians as indicators that Russian lands extend to the potentially resource-rich undersea Lomonosov Ridge.

Imperial concerns, and the imperial lens Russia offered, also informed Pallas's contributions to three principal debates then current in geohistory—plutonism versus neptunism, biblical versus geological timescales, and gradualist versus catastrophist explanations of geological changes. In each case, Pallas used the vastness of his research field to find consilience between the extreme positions. But in the last debate, he managed with the help of his Siberian experience to form an unusually precise and revolutionary vision of catastrophic geological change that had powerful connections with Russians' conceptions of their own protean history.

One of Enlightenment geohistory's principal disagreements concerned the relative importance of volcanic activity (a stance known as plutonism) against that of water (neptunism) for explaining the development of the mineral world. This debate erupted in 1787 with the German geologist Abraham Gottlob Werner's publication of *Kurze Klassifikation und Beschreibung der verschiedenen Gebirgsarten* (*Short Classification and Description of the Various Species of Rock Masses*), which hotly denied the plutonist position.[24] However, disagreement had been simmering for decades on the issue, with water loyalists such as Nicolas Desmarest presenting theories opposed by those such as the influential Scottish naturalist James Hutton and other devotees of fire.[25] A parallel debate centered on the relative merits of a uniform or catastrophic history of geological change. In 1788 Hutton laid out a comprehensive argument in favor of the gradual and regular uplift of the land through volcanic processes, balanced out over the long run by erosion. Strongly influenced by the Scottish Enlightenment, which stressed orderly change in the natural world, Hutton still conceived of the universe as a "perpetual-motion machine built by the perfect workmanship of God."[26]

Pallas addressed this burning geological question with caution and a willingness to accept some truth in all sides of the disagreements. In fact, the *Betrachtungen* provided one of the most balanced and reasoned explanations for the potential of neptunists and plutonists to find agreement. "The work of fire-spitting mountains," Pallas wrote about volcanoes, "can still be seen bringing islands out of the depths of sea," clear testament to the creative power of lava.[27] The Aleutian Islands, then being explored by Russian fur-traders, provided numerous examples of such explosive potential, as new islands were even then emerging out of the sea. The plutonist powers visible in the modern world were every bit powerful enough—if extended through a very long time period—to explain most of the present shape of the earth. Pallas's main argument with plutonists was their refuge in a "completely arbitrary" central fire that burned forever in the earth's bowels.[28] At the same time, there was evidence of water's transformative effects all around Siberia. Nearly everywhere he had gone in that landlocked region, Pallas had observed hundreds of fossilized marine creatures. He found the banks of the river Ufa "very thick with sea animals, and as if sewn together from broken mussels, etc." With the help of such evidence, Pallas was convinced that "one finds at every step the old traces of an ocean … either from a former flood or from the powerful retreat of a huge mass of water ..."[29] Whereas Werner would later be accused of deriving his uncompromising neptunism from personal experience that was too parochial, Pallas suffered no such limitations.[30] As the wide research field of the Russian Empire had revealed, neither an exclusively fire- or water-derived geohistory would do.

Pallas's *Betrachtungen* concerned itself not only with geological strata and their origins but also inevitably with the questions of fossils. Older ideas about fossils as nature's whimsical creations that—despite all appearances—had nothing to do with real organisms, had mostly receded. Some geologists, such as John Woodward, now argued that fossils might hold the clue to the riddle of geological time. Woodward, though, did still insist on a diluvial explanation for their presence high up in mountains.[31] Here Pallas's Russian imperial experience again played a role, for his travels had taken him to the world's richest fund of fossilized animal life, and in particular the home of many spectacularly intact, large, unfamiliar, well-preserved mammals. From the seventeenth century, Siberian explorers had continuously unearthed huge elephant-like animals from the permafrost, and had given them their name, mammoth.[32] In the mid-eighteenth century, the mammoth had emerged for some as a new proof of the biblical flood.[33] Located so far from the habitat of modern elephants, the mammoth's presence in Siberia was usually put down to some massive deluge. As such it was used primarily to support a catastrophist—and often a determinedly biblical catastrophist—interpretation of geohistory.

Pallas had found that, if anything, Siberia's mysterious animal remains were more numerous than reported. There he discovered the remains of "Indian animals, bones from elephants, rhinoceroses, and gigantic buffalos, which are uncovered in our land in such massive numbers and attract such curiosity. In Siberia ... one finds remains of strange animals along almost every river."[34] In Russia, too, the fossil question was vexed. At some point Pallas fielded the question of the relationship between mammoth carcasses and the biblical flood from the Archbishop of Novgorod, who was well versed on the subject. Unfortunately, no record of a reply exists, so we do not know how Pallas handled this delicate bit of interpolation.[35] What we do know is that Pallas was convinced his personal experience of travel in the Russian Empire had helped shape his views on the subject:

> the issue remained problematic for me until I traveled through the regions in which these monuments [*Denkmäler*] were found, and saw with my own eyes the proof of such a remarkable event that had taken place, and became convinced of the probability of the truth that our earth had been overtaken by a catastrophic flood ...[36]

The proof of a catastrophic flood lay, in his mind, in the way that these animals' bones were scattered about in the ground and were mixed together with fossilized wood. For intact specimens he offered the explanation that the flood must have been so sudden and massive enough to "bring these dead bodies to these cold regions before despoliation began to destroy their soft tissues."[37] Such statements indicate that Pallas was not ready to countenance what scientists today assert—the idea that the mammoth had once inhabited Siberia, but was now extinct. Few naturalists in Pallas's time accepted the idea of extinction.[38]

Pallas, though a deeply religious man, was ready to put aside traditional belief on many occasions. He had undergone in the past decade something of a transformation in his attitude towards the biblical flood. During his Siberian travels, Pallas had pointed towards Noah's flood as the force likely to have carried the animal there from its southern habitat. However, in the *Betrachtungen* he criticized others, including Woodward, who used this as the only explanation for the clear evidence of formerly higher sea levels. Instead, Pallas now noted, there were several potential causes of large-scale flooding, including a Noahic flood, a tsunami caused by a comet, or instead a much more gradual lowering of a formerly world-spanning ocean.[39] Any possible flood may have been that described in the bible, but it might also have been one or several floods present in other East Asian and near-eastern myths. On the subject of deep time, Pallas was again prepared to make concessions. Some geological strata, he admitted, "appear to be older than the organized Creation"[40] Later, he waxed eloquent:

> These mountains present us the oldest chronicle of our earth ... The archive of nature, already present before the oldest sagas and the invention of writing. It has been given to our generation to explore, to elucidate, and to bring them to light; however, several centuries will not exhaust their mysteries.[41]

Pallas had achieved something of the enlightened balance that made him one of the most respected natural philosophers of the age. His theory of earth formation avoided dogmatic declarations throughout, and, buttressed by immense learning and travel, offered probably the most comprehensive view of geohistory then available (at least in such short form). To integrate the various mechanisms—water, fire, gradual change, and catastrophism—as well as his various methodologies—observation and theory—Pallas proposed a three-part history of the earth correlated with three basic layers of earth. Underlying the Urals and all mountains was an ancient core of granite devoid of fossils. Volcanic uplift may have played a part in their formation. Above the granite lay a limestone layer with fossils created by a gradually retreating world ocean. A third element, however, chock full of fossils and other animal remains, showed the signs, Pallas thought, of an entirely different phenomenon—here was evidence of the global catastrophe or catastrophes.

It was this last, most recent and dynamic layer, which provoked Pallas's most ambitious—and most revolutionary—speculations. It was also here where the harmonics between geohistory and empire rang most clearly in his work. Catastrophism was hardly unique to Pallas, but in the *Betrachtungen* he offered an exceptionally concrete and expansive history of fire and flooding unprecedented in other, highly abstract accounts. Based on his observations throughout Siberia, Pallas reasoned that a world-spanning flood must have come from somewhere in Southeast Asia, both because of the orientation of Siberian mountains and because most of the fossils and preserved animal carcasses had their closest analogs around the Indo-Pacific. Additionally, the Pacific and Indian coasts offered many present-day examples of geological activity: "The volcanoes in these regions still rage and are the largest in the entire world." Therefore, uniting both neptunist and plutonist explanations, Pallas surmised that at some point the Philippines, Sunda, and the Moluccas had broken out of the sea with a volcanic explosion. Such plutonist force would have displaced a huge mass of water, sending some northwards towards the Asian and European mountains, where this flood would have been constantly reinforced with new tsunamis. The results would have been written clearly in the Siberian landscape, and accorded exactly with what Pallas had observed:

> ... it would have devastated the low areas of these countries and created great gaps ... ripping away the top soft layers of the ground, and after assaulting the lower areas of mountains which make up parts of Asia, it would have entered the flatlands of this region of the world and filled them with materials ... including the mud ripped up by the flood, which would be deposited in layers and would have included the remains of trees and animals which had been caught up in this disruption and buried chaotically, then exposed with the slow erosion of the mountains ... which created the entire Siberian plain ...[42]

Finally, all of this excess water would have eventually disappeared down immense subterranean caverns near the North Pole.

Pallas's Russian experience had a direct influence on this geohistorical account. In the fall of 1777, one of St. Petersburg's frequent floods arrived with special furor. Pallas witnessed the rising waters first-hand and appended a description of the event to the *Betrachtungen*'s disquisition on the world flood:

> during the entire night of 9/10 September (three days before the full moon) a storm full of fury arrived, first from the Southwest and then West ... Around five o'clock in the morning the storm broke the banks and with unbelievable speed covered trees, bridges, and harbors under two ells of water, especially on Vasily Island [where Pallas lived] and the Petersburg side. Those places most exposed to the sea saw trees torn up and heavily laden carts carried far inland and destroyed. Things would have been even worse had the storm not turned to the North around eight o'clock in the morning, after it had already raised the water level ten feet higher than normal.[43]

Though it may seem exaggerated, Pallas claimed such experiences were key to his conception of the potentially devastating impact of flooding. St. Petersburg's tragic experience was just one of many examples of how strong tides could interact with storm surges to produce massive floods. Recent events in Peru, possibly the devastating earthquake of 1746, although Pallas does not specify, and Kamchatka added to Pallas's sense that the earth was prone to both gradual transformation and devastatingly quick changes, whether springing from fire, water, or both.[44]

In contemplating the stunning transformations the earth must have experienced in the past, Pallas returned to the image of the empire and remarked on the strangely interlocked histories of prehistoric catastrophes and historic triumphs:

> From the consideration of the lime and clay-beds, it follows, that all these plains which became the fatherland of the mighty Russian nation; a seed-bed of heroes, the last refuge of science and art; a stage for the miracle of the vast and creative spirit of Peter the Great, and a field for his great successor [Catherine the Great] to bring happiness to a million subjects, to make an example to the kings of the Earth and to amaze its people, I say all these plains of Great Russia—were once the bottom of the sea.[45]

Several messages are contained in this remarkable passage. First of all, Pallas offered a standard evocation of his patron, Catherine's, magnanimity and support of science. This was not the first time he praised the empress like this, nor would it be the last. Secondly, however, his reference to Peter the Great reflected a more precise connotation of empire's ability to transform itself and the natural world upon which it acted. Peter's "vast and creative spirit" was considered in Catherine's time the beginnings of Russian civilization; a protean force that had yanked its people out of formlessness. This, of course, was the metaphor Pallas sought to invoke to help readers understand the magnitude of past changes, but also to hint at a longer, linked story of unfolding geological and imperial change. By conflating and extending the ideas of imperial and geological change to Siberia, Pallas again claimed the naturalness of the Russian Empire, and marked it as one capable of producing changes as dramatic as those he depicted here for his readers (and originally to his imperial audience).

This essay has already discussed how Pallas aligned himself with Russia's geopolitical interests and felt the attraction of the empire's monetary and social benefits. There was another, deeper sense, in which Pallas identified with the empire. Its projects of enlightened improvement accorded well with naturalists' own inclinations. In 1793 in his *Neue Nordische Beyträge*, Pallas published accounts of the growth of towns and mining in the eastern colonies. Besides satisfying his readers' curiosity, Pallas "had another reason for making known" these developments:

> I want to root out the harmful prejudices that many, especially those abroad, have of Siberia. Siberia is as splendid (*vortrefflich*) a country as any other in the world at a similar latitude. Here, in an almost unbelievable manner, huge, impenetrable woods and wildernesses have been turned into inhabited

boulevards, while desert steppe has been turned into fruitful fields, all through the tireless care and the matchlessly wise governance of our most glorious monarch Catherine II.[46]

In private Pallas may have referred to Siberia as wild "in fact and name," [47] but in his public contributions to the European Republic of Letters he stressed the Siberia that was becoming something else. For his work with St. Petersburg's Free Economic Society, established to promote agriculture throughout the empire, Pallas wrote an influential article supporting Siberian grain cultivation, especially of *kraipivo* (Siberian stinging nettles), along with flax.[48] If Pallas was relatively silent about the great destruction of animals then taking place in the Siberian fur trade, he remained perhaps Russia's greatest champion of improvement in its colonies.

The strongest point of confluence, then, between Pallas's imperial concerns and his geohistory occurred precisely at the point of transformation. A cautious and deliberate naturalist, he had produced a thorough and diplomatic history of geological formation. However, an imperial motif can be discerned running throughout Pallas's description of Eurasian geohistory. The Russian Empire had given him both a uniquely global viewpoint (or at least continental—Russian theorists were fond of talking of the "continent-ocean") as well as a model of transformative power. Russia, perhaps to a unique extent during this era, conceived of itself as embarked upon a task of change.[49] It, like contemporary European empires, would transform the "wilderness" found in their overseas colonies. Russia had been entrusted with an even greater expanse of land and peoples in need of cultivation and was thus tasked with an even grander mission. Furthermore, the empire itself was embarked on a process of transforming itself from the barbarous days of Muscovy into an enlightened empire worthy of comparison with its rivals (a process Alexander Etkind has termed "internal colonization").[50] Pallas, then, had produced a geohistory that both reflected the apex of Russian imperial power and an account of the earth's breathtaking historical changes worthy of the more contemporary feats of Peter and Catherine.

In a process that mirrored the work of Russian historians of the same time period, Pallas added geohistorical evidence to claims that Russia possessed a uniquely progressive autocracy.[51] His claims for the earth's revolutionary history might seem to support a revolutionary agenda, as similar claims would during the French Revolution, but in fact the essence of the Russian autocracy was thought to be dynamism, not stasis. Later Eurasianists would discuss how "a particular geographical milieu ... places the stamp of its own characteristics on the human communities which develop in it."[52] Pallas conceived of the relationship between geohistory and human history in a different manner, however. He stressed not the fixed character that it might impart on a polity but claimed instead that it was the very process of radical change which characterized Siberia both in the prehistoric past and in the current century of enlightened imperial expansion. Everywhere in Enlightened Europe, the natural world was used as a template to guide social and political behavior.[53] In

Russia, the emerging practice of geohistory, with its expansive view across space and centuries, found a way to both validate the empire and encourage it to do revolutionary work upon the earth.

The *Betrachtungen* gained only a moderate number of European converts, but its reviewers were often attentive to the imperial context and message conveyed. One French author noted that "In June 1777, this illustrious scholar read at a meeting of the academy of St. Petersburg, at which the King of Sweden was present, a dissertation on the formation of mountains, and the changes, which our globe has undergone, especially in Russia."[54] London's *The Monthly Review* noted that Pallas had gained his knowledge "by the order and peculiar encouragement of the Empress of Russia ... to examine the state of Nature in these vast regions." Besides examining the imperial origins of the *Betrachtungen*, the English author could not resist flights of poetic fancy that hinted at the relationship between Russian nature and grand systematic conclusions:

> Having lived for ten years in the midst of these mountains, and studied their majestic beauties, which are as much adapted to suggest systems to the Naturalist, as numbers to the Poet, he [Pallas] comes after the *Burnets*, the *Whistons*, the *Woodwards*, the *Mallets*, the *Scheuchzers*, and the *Buffons*, and says,—Gentlemen,—with your leave—*I also am a system-maker.*[55]

Other reviewers were less ready to accept Pallas's claim of the near universality of Russian space. "M. Pallas," wrote an Englishman in 1806, "very justly observes that many geologists have formed their opinions ... from what they have observed of those in their own country ..." However, "The author has himself inclined a little to the same practice, in a detailed account of the structure of the mountains of the Russian Empire ..."[56] Irish naturalist Richard Kirwan, a later defender of the biblical flood, cited Pallas approvingly.[57]

The reaction of H. B. de Saussure, Pallas's contemporary, provides perhaps the best sense of how the latter's geohistory had been productively intertwined with empire. Saussure rejected many of Pallas's conclusions, including the idea that fossilized plants and animals had been swept northwards from India as well as the notion of a global flood originating in the Indian Ocean. However, Saussure was prompted by Pallas's gigantic geographical imagination to consider global causes of Alpine geohistory. In addition, Saussure adopted a modified catastrophist view of geohistory, which he intended to publish, though an early death ended those plans.[58]

It is no coincidence that naturalists in the British American colonies (and early American Republic) envisioned geological changes most similar to Pallas's in their scale and transformative ability. Their nascent empire, too, was wringing stunning changes out of the landscape, making pre-historical precedents imaginable and useful. As historian Richard Judd has written, "National pride and available evidence disposed most early American geologists to favor catastrophe as the primary agent of geological change."[59] Some American geologists' visions ran nearly to the extraordinary lengths that Pallas's had. In 1776, Lewis Evans published speculations about huge inland seas contained behind the Appalachian Mountains that suddenly burst through, depositing fossils everywhere. A few decades later, Henry Hayden imagined a massive tidal wave originating in Norway sweeping across the Atlantic and renewing America with an awesome baptism. And yet, subtle differences remained between the two geological traditions, which were also redolent of imperial divergences. American geologists assumed the deep earth was undergoing constant improvement befitting the progressive trajectory of cultivation. Pallas, though, ended his *Betrachtungen* with a pessimistic coda:

> The small activity of volcanoes in certain parts of the oceans, of which we have many examples in history, and whose sad results we have seen in our time, must give rise to the fear that the entire world may again experience their destructive results. Happy, then, are those who live in the mountains, whose choice to live in the Alps would seem to have brought them a sad fate. They will be the plantings of a new human generation; bloodless conquerors reclaiming the plains destroyed by flood.[60]

This was an ambiguous final statement on imperial futures that few American geologists would have shared.

Pallas's *Betrachtungen*, ostensibly a straightforward work of geohistory, coded an imperial story influenced by the context of its creation. It expressed a Russian vision of the transformation of vast lands—Siberia most prominently—that was shaded by Pallas's own enthusiasm for empire. As Pallas's travels through Siberia showed, empire facilitated the study of geohistory. At the same time, knowledge of the earth could be harnessed to naturalize imperial structures, as it was in both Russia and the early American Empire. Peter Simon Pallas, a man buoyed, buffeted, and polished by the behemoth of early-modern empire, could only envision an earth history as transformative and overwhelming as the realm he served and the lands he traversed.

Notes

1 For abundant detail on Pallas's professional life, see Folkwart Wendland, *Peter Simon Pallas: Materialien einer Biographie* (Berlin: De Gruyter, 1992).

2 For more on Eurasianism, see Mark Bassin, "Nationhood, Natural Regions, *Mestorazvitie*: Environmentalist Discourse in Classical Eurasianism," in Mark Bassin, Christopher Ely, and Melissa K. Stockdale, eds., *Space, Place, and Power in Modern Russia* (DeKalb: Northern Illinois University Press, 2010); Mark Bassin, Sergey Glebov, and Marlene Laruelle, eds., *Between Europe and Asia: The Origin, Theories, and Legacies of Russian Eurasianism* (Pittsburgh: University of Pittsburgh Press, 2015); Sergey Glebov, *From Empire to Eurasia: Politics, Scholarship, and Ideology in Russian Eurasianism, 1920s – 1930s* (DeKalb: Southern Illinois University Press, 2017).

3 Quoted in Wendland, *Peter Simon Pallas*, 592.

4 Peter Simon Pallas, *Betrachtungen über die Beschaffenheit der Gebürge* (Frankfurt and Leipzig, 1778); Albert v. Carozzi and Marguerite Carozzi, *Pallas' Theory of the Earth*

26 *Ryan Tucker Jones*

in German (1778). Translation and Reevaluation. Reaction by a Contemporary: H.-B. de Saussure (Geneva: Société de Physique et d'Historie Naturelle, 1991).

5 Pallas, "Letter to Muller, March 24, 1781," *Archive of the St. Petersburg Branch of the Academy of Sciences*, f. 21, op. 3, no. 22a.

6 Lisbet Koerner, *Linnaeus: Nature and Nation* (Cambridge: Harvard University Press), 28–9.

7 Pallas, "Letter to Muller, March 24, 1781." *Archive of the St. Petersburg Branch of the Academy of Sciences*, f. 21, op. 3, no. 22a.

8 Pallas, "Letter to Muller, April 15, 1781." *Archive of the St. Petersburg Branch of the Academy of Sciences*, f. 21, op. 3, no. 22a.

9 Pallas, "Letter to Muller, Jan 9, 1781." *Archive of the St. Petersburg Branch of the Academy of Sciences*, f. 21, op. 3, no. 22a.

10 Peter Simon Pallas, "Letter to Joseph Banks, March 26/April 6th, 1782," in the British Library Manuscript Department, Add MS 8095, pp. 105, 105 op.

11 Pallas, "Letter to Muller, April 15, 1781"; "Letter to Muller, Jan 17, 1782." *Archive of the St. Petersburg Branch of the Academy of Sciences*, f. 21, op. 3, no. 22a.

12 Pallas, *Betrachtungen*, 4.

13 Pallas, *Betrachtungen*, 9.

14 Jacques Roger, *Buffon: A Life in Natural History* (Ithaca: Cornell University Press, 1997), 239.

15 e.g. Pallas, *Betrachtungen*, 4.

16 L. Jay Oliva, ed., *Catherine the Great* (Englewood Cliffs, NJ: Prentice-Hall, 1968), 53, 54; Cynthia Hyla Whittaker, "The Idea of Autocracy among Eighteenth-Century Russian Historians," *Russian Review* 55: 2 (1996): 149–71.

17 Hans Rogger, *National Consciousness in Eighteenth-Century Russia* (Cambridge: Harvard University Press, 1960), 258; see also Richard Wortman, *Scenarios of Power: Myth and Ceremony in Russian Monarchy from Peter the Great to the Abdication of Nicholas II* (Princeton: Princeton University Press, 2006).

18 Gerhard Friedrich Müller, *Bering's Voyages: The Reports from Russia*, trans. Lydia Black (Fairbanks: University of Alaska Press, 1986), 139.

19 Karl Ernst von Baer, *Berichte über die Zoographia Rosso-Asiatica von Pallas, abgestattet an die K. Akademie der Wissenschaften zu St. Petersburg von Dr. K.E. von Baer* (Königsberg, 1831).

20 Deborah Coen, "Imperial Climatographies from Tyrol to Turkestan," *Osiris* 26 (2011): 45–65; Bassin, "Nationhood, Natural Regions, *Mestorazvitie*," 56.

21 Pallas, *Betrachtungen*, 17.

22 Pallas, *Betrachtungen*, 17–21.

23 Pallas, *Betrachtungen*, 44.

24 A. G. Werner, *Kurze Klassifikation und Beschreibung der verschiedenen Gebirgsarten* (Dresden, 1787).

25 Kenneth Taylor, *The Earth Sciences in the Enlightenment* (Aldershot: Ashgate, Variorum, 2008); Mott T. Greene, *Geology in the Nineteenth Century: Changing Views of a Changing World* (Ithaca: Cornell University Press, 1982), 19–38.

26 Peter Bowler, *The Earth Encompassed: A History of the Environmental Sciences* (New York: Norton, 1992), 133.

27 Pallas, *Betrachtungen*, 67, 68.

28 Pallas, *Betrachtungen*, 7.

29 Pallas, *Betrachtungen*, 53.

30 Greene, *Geology in the Nineteenth Century*, 27.

31 Martin Rudwick, *The Meaning of Fossils: Episodes in the History of Palaeontology* (Chicago: University of Chicago Press, 1972), 90.

32 Claudine Cohen, *The Fate of the Mammoth: Fossils, Myth, and History* (Chicago: University of Chicago Press, 2004).

33 See for example Johann Phillip Breyne, "A Letter from John Phil. Breyne, M.D. F. R.S. to Sir Hans Sloane," *Philosophical Transactions of the Royal Society* 40 (1737), 129.
34 Pallas, *Betrachtungen*, 63.
35 "Narratio incolarum de animali Mamont dicto," n.d. in Staatsbibliothek zu Berlin, MS. germ. fol. 788.
36 Pallas, *Betrachtungen*, 64.
37 Pallas, *Betrachtungen*, 65.
38 Ryan Tucker Jones, *Empire of Extinction: Russians and the North Pacific's Strange Beasts of the Sea* (Oxford: Oxford University Press, 2014), Chapter 5.
39 Pallas, *Betrachtungen*, 7.
40 Pallas, *Betrachtungen*, 48.
41 Pallas, *Betrachtungen*, 49.
42 Pallas, *Betrachtungen*, 80.
43 Pallas, *Betrachtungen*, 72.
44 Pallas, *Betrachtungen*, 76.
45 Pallas, *Betrachtungen*, 58.
46 Peter Simon Pallas, *Neue Nordische Beyträge*, volume VII (St. Petersburg, 1793), 147.
47 "Pallas to Müller, September 13, 1773," in RAN, f. 21, op. 3, no. 222, 185.
48 Peter Simon Pallas, "Izvestiia o Vvedennom skotovodstve i zemlepashestve v Kamchatke i okolo Okhotska, pri Udskom ostroge lezhashchem podle Okhotskago moray," *Trudy Volnago Ekonomicheskogo Obshchestva* XXXIII (1783).
49 Cynthia Hyla Whittaker, "The Reforming Tsar: The Redefinition of Autocratic Duty in Eighteenth-Century Russia," *Slavic Review* 51: 1 (1992): 77–98.
50 Alexander Etkind, *Internal Colonization: Russia's Imperial Experience* (Cambridge: Polity Press, 2011). Etkind borrows the concept from imperial Russian historians of the nineteenth-century.
51 Whittaker, "The Idea of Autocracy."
52 Bassin, "Nationhood, Natural Regions, *Mestorazvitie*," 56.
53 Lorraine Daston and Fernardo Vidal, eds., *The Moral Authority of Nature* (Chicago: University of Chicago Press, 2004).
54 Pierre Nicolas Chantreau, *Philosophical, Political, and Literary Travels in Russia During the Years 1788 and 1789*, v. I (Perth: R. Morison, 1794), 284.
55 *The Monthly Review or Literary Journal* 61 (1780), 591.
56 *The Critical Review, or Annals of Literature* 7 (1806), 533.
57 Richard Kirwan, "An Essay on the Declivities on Mountains," *The Transactions of the Royal Irish Academy* 8 (1802): 50.
58 Carozzi and Carozzi, *Pallas' Theory of the Earth*, 63.
59 Richard Judd, *The Untilled Garden: Natural History and the Spirit of Conservation in America, 1740–1840* (Cambridge: Cambridge University Press, 2009), 143.
60 Pallas, *Betrachtungen*, 87.

2 The view of the golden mountains

The Altai and the historical resilience of the imagination

Chechesh Kudachinova

The Altai, the range of mountains in Central Asia extending from East Kazakhstan into Northwest China and Mongolia, passes through Russia, and it is here that this geographical landmark acquired multiple mental representations, enjoying a near mythological presence across Russian culture. The terrain invokes the standard "Tibet" imaginary: snow-capped peaks, verdant valleys, and crystal-clear lakes, lacking only lamas in crimson robes. Post-Soviet development has transformed the Altai Mountains into an alluring commercial asset causing the once pristine environment, where the sources of the Ob River originate, to suffer significantly. The tourist industry promotes the region as an unspoiled natural world, though since Soviet times it has become a fallout zone for second stages of rockets launched from the Bai-konur Cosmodrome in Kazakhstan; space launches regularly litter "Siberian Switzerland" with debris and toxic fuel.

Despite its peripheral location, the Altai Mountains receive a great deal of popular attention. A proposed railroad connecting West Europe with China has recently replaced the previous plan of constructing a Northwest Siberian gas pipeline across the Altai to Russia's largest neighbor to the East. The 2003 earthquake, presumably caused by contested excavations of Scythian mummies from the Ukok Plateau burial mounds, along with regular helicopter poaching by central and local officials produce wide media coverage for this otherwise event-less and sparsely populated region far off the Trans-Siberian Railroad. In the two most recent decades, fascination with the Altai has soared, as evidenced by over one million visitors per year and the construction of the Russian political leader's mountain retreat: a luxurious complex with roof ridges in the Oriental style, the so-called "Putin's dacha" appeared in the midst of the Altai Republic, one of Russia's most economically depressed regions with a high unemployment rate.

The Altai is known for its magnificent vistas, but for scholars it is distinguished by its diverse historical representations. As a native of the region, I am puzzled by the multiple contrasts between its indigenous meanings, the extravagant exterior images, and the harshness of local existence. A variety of agents have created and exploited its symbolic capital, turning the geographical landmark from a blank spot into a powerful site of imagination. The external gaze entangled early modern Siberian mapmakers and imperial officials,

German naturalists and Orthodox missionaries, travelers, painters, and peasants alike in a series of shifting relationships in different periods of time. Their efforts turned the Altai into a culturally significant landscape defined by a number of spatial metaphors: "Siberian Switzerland," the "golden mountains," "Northern Shambala," and the "pearl of Siberia," to name just a few. Many of them continue to predominate in the minds of most people outside of the region. To communities of Old Believers (*raskol'niki*), the Altai came to embody "the White Waterland" (*Belovod'e*), a fabled place free from government persecution.[1] Attracted to the mysticism with which the painter Nicholas Roerich associated this place, adherents of his cult and spiritual seekers of all sorts revere the place as the substitute of the mythical Shambala.[2] In search of identity, Turkic-speaking people from the post-Soviet space and beyond consider the Altai to be the home of their ancestors.

A comprehensive overview of how the Altai appeared on Russian mental maps has not been a matter of extensive scholarly examination. I hope to fill this obvious gap by exploring the entrenched vision of the "golden mountains" that has practically overshadowed the present social and economic realities in the region. The vision needs to be examined for its continuities in different forms, and the ways in which the past infuses the present. To accomplish this I will explore the production and circulation of the image in a larger historical context, seeking to frame the circumstances and settings through which it persisted in the Russian popular perceptions. How did the "golden mountains" come into being? What actors were involved in its dynamics? What formed the major constituting forces in its crystallization? What cultural instruments transformed the Altai into an imperial fantasy?

The most pervasive narrative explains the Altai Mountains as "golden," referring to late nineteenth-century linguistic claims.[3] However, the "Altai" concept has a broad range of cultural and spatial connotations in the Mongol and Turkic knowledge system, none of which relates to the precious metal. Its meanings incorporate the name of the mountainous terrain and a type of highland landscape; geographical space generally; a homeland; and any other location upon the earth.[4] "Altai" is used as a female Mongol and a male Turkic name, yet it is also the label of the mountain spirit, the creator and master of the Altai domain.[5]

By using the analytical lens of resource imaginations, I will call the traditional interpretation into question in order to demonstrate that the "golden mountains" appeared under different knowledge-making circumstances a century earlier. More precisely, my goal is to historicize the myth as a spatial phenomenon by discussing the dynamics of cultural production, circulation, and consumption of the vision in the period between the 1740s and the 1940s. The chapter argues, first, that the framing had no historic existence prior to the works of the German naturalists in Russian imperial service. Second, I suggest that the "golden mountains" came into view through Enlightenment modes of imagining imperial expansion and efforts at a reasonable explanation of the Eurasian frontier. Finally, the chapter maintains that social and cultural support turned the vision into an essential empire-building tool and the major interpretative strategy by which the Altai had been integrated into imperial space.

What complicates my narration is that throughout the eighteenth century the production of this vision unfolded in the midst of two overlapping processes: (1) the unfocused cartographical mapping of the Altai Mountains; (2) the spatial making of the "Altai" region that included four elements: the mountain range, the nearby flatlands, the metallurgical plants, and mineral resources. On the one hand, this natural feature frequently figured in imperial military reports and travel depictions. On the other, it "drifted" across the Western and Russian maps, taking different locations across Central Asia. In other words, the geographical landmark and the surrounding territory were themselves in the process of becoming, with the "golden mountains" emerging in the midst of the interactions between mental and geographical maps.

Theoretical framework

This chapter contributes to "new spatial history," an emerging body of recent scholarship seeking to highlight the centrality of geographical space and spatial thinking in Russian history.[6] An appreciation of mineral endowment as a spatial phenomenon, for example, brings together diverse research on the creation, imagination, and transformation of mineral wealth in new ways. Seeking to create a coherent research framework, I also draw from theoretical principles of human geography, the discipline that traditionally explores imagination as a tool of non-empirical knowledge making. Two interrelated concepts in particular inform my framework: *imaginary geographies* and *resource imaginations*.

The notion of *imaginary geographies* emphasizes the instrumentality of "geographies of the mind" in shaping our perceptions of distant places.[7] This idea has stimulated different approaches across historical scholarship. The notion provides some important vistas concerning acts of conceptualizing distant spaces, yet it closes others, no less important; for example, divergent imaginings of mineral resources of the remote areas. The possible insights that we might gain by directly applying imaginary geographies to the production of the "golden mountains" are still limited.

However, this serves as a good entry point to a more complex and still unsettled framework of *resource imaginations*, borrowed from anthropologists Elizabeth Ferry and Mandana Limber's work on expressions of interactions between nature and society that creates resources.[8] I further integrate my approach with the insights of geographer and political ecologist Michael Watts.[9] Although he did not use the concept explicitly in his studies on oil's symbolical order, Watts singled out the role of the social imaginary, a realm in which natural resources operate, and its ability to create a world of illusions. Two broad themes are discernible here. First, mineral endowment has a symbolic significance, taking on a mythic life of its own. Resources come to mean different things to different people; their shifting meanings are contested.

Second, resource imaginations form an imaginary space, where the symbolical meanings of material objects can be constructed. This highlights the instrumentality of resource imaginations in the making of spatial knowledge.

I engage this concept for its explanatory potential in historical analysis. As a complex and elusive concept, it enables us to map multiple and shifting connections between the imagination and material substance that go unnoticed otherwise. One advantage of using it is that it forms a convenient label to summarize non-empirical but enduring cultural responses to resources and the representations of those resources. For the purposes of this chapter, I narrow its meanings to Russian perceptions of mineral wealth, a series of historically constrained attitudes and anxieties towards the significance of mineral assets. This notion highlights the dynamic processes by which historical actors and networks constructed, validated, and consumed mineral wealth in the form of symbols and myths. In this case, resource imaginations also allow us to explore patterns of Russian historical perceptions of the Altai Mountains.

I argue that the intersection of imaginary geographies and resource imaginations enables a more accurate understanding of how the vision emerged in the course of expansion. Although my framework cannot explain every single detail, it provides novel insights into the making of the extractive periphery, exposing the entangled links between the imperial perceptions, the place, and its mineral content.

My main argument is that the emerging resource imaginations constructed the frontier Altai landscape, infusing it with enduring cultural meanings. The rise of the "golden mountains" illustrates how resource concerns regarding the remote setting were produced and became mainstream. In order to advance this perspective, I argue that the production and dissemination of the vision allows us to observe how certain spatial modalities of resource imaginations have taken shape in a variety of historical contexts. My focus serves to address the following broader questions. How can we connect imagination, space, and minerals analytically in the ways that power relations connected them historically? What patterns of resource imaginations came into existence in this case? What cultural forces shape the perception of mineral visions? How do visions become elements of mainstream resource imaginations?

The Altai Mountains in early Eurasian geographies

The *Secret History of the Mongols*, dating from the 1240s, forms one of the earliest texts referring to the Altai Mountains, whose northern part was inhabited by the Turkic-speaking Naimans and Merkits defeated by Chinggis Khan's armies.[10] The writing of the Italian traveler Marco Polo featured the Altai Mountains as the mythical burial place of the powerful Mongol rulers.[11] Popular among the European mapmakers, this became one of the most frequently depicted locations of "Great Tartary" in the form of *alchai mons sepultura imperial*. [12]

The idea of "Altai" may have appeared in the Muscovite records as early as the mid-1650s, when the diplomatic mission headed by the merchant Fedor Isakovich Baikov traversed the Irtysh River and across West Mongolia to Beijing, a route that few contemporaries chose to travel. However, what could have been the earliest Russian reference to the Central Asian landscape was marked by its absence. The passage exhausted the travelers physically and emotionally; most likely, Baikov did not care to register the name of the terrain he crossed: "one has to go between rocky mountains; they are very tall, great snow does not melt; there is neither water nor food for cattle, these are barren places."[13]

In the closing decades of the seventeenth century, we come across several "Altai" references in Muscovite accounts.[14] Though located beyond Russian control, the West Mongol terrain held an important place in Siberian cartography, forming one of the most frequently represented Asian highlands in the works of the mapmaker Semen Ulianovich Remezov.[15] Blending actual knowledge and imaginary geographies, he rendered *Kamen' Velikii Altai* (the Great Rock Altai) as a transcontinental chain stretching from the Central Asian heartland to the Pacific coast and a source of the Ganges, the Selenga, and the great Siberian rivers.[16] His expansive imagining of the frontier landscape that he had never experienced firsthand suggests the impact of Mongol-Turkic geographies on early modern Russian thinking.[17]

In the same decade that Remezov labored on mapping the Altai, it became the setting of the chain of important geopolitical events. Galdan Boshoktu (Blessed) Khan (r. 1671–1697), the powerful leader of the West Mongol Zunghars (Oirats), gradually consolidated his hold over neighboring people and augmented military strength. Seeking hegemony over Central Asia brought him into long conflicts with the Qing Empire. The pacification of the northwestern frontier became a pivotal concern in Chinese strategy. After a series of battles, he was defeated and escaped in 1696. The spring of the following year, when Qing troops were about to invade West Mongolia, Galdan Khan suddenly died near Khovd in the Altai Mountains.[18]

From "Demidovia" to "Romanovia" (1700s–1750s)

The demise of the rebellious khan marked a period of relative peace in the Qing dynasty's northwestern frontier. Meanwhile, inspired by European scientific achievement, the Kangxi emperor (r. 1661–1722) embarked on the large endeavor of mapping his expanding domain through the help of Jesuit missionaries.[19] While other ministers in the imperial service charted more prominent locations such as the Great Wall, Fathers Jourtoux, Fridelli, and Bonjour fulfilled a less spectacular task, traveling across the Mongolian frontier in 1711 and 1712. Their maps indicated the mountain range *Altai alin-i dube* (the Manchu notions for a mountain *alin* and *dube*), providing its longitude and latitude. The northernmost Altai figured as the "summit" and the southernmost extreme as the "end."[20]

A chain of hills named as *A-eul-t'ai shan* appeared in another contemporary map, a rough sketch of Central Asia attached to a report by the Manchu ambassador Tulisen, who traveled to Kalmyk Khan Aiuka on the Volga River (1712–1715). The Beijing deputation took the traditional Russian route across East Siberia, via Irkutsk and Tobolsk. The map indicated the Altai Mountains were politically under the rule of Galdan's successor Tsewang Rabdan and geographically as the source of the Irtysh, the Yenisei, and the Selenga River.[21] I suggest that these two cartographical depictions of the Altai terrains demonstrate nascent Qing territorial claims on the Zunghar domain; the Manchus considered the Altai a potential continuation of their expanding realm.

Unlike the Jesuit fathers, Russian cartographers were less successful in mapping the Altai. First, Remezov's mapping legacy was thoroughly neglected. Second, the territory was not an area of primary political focus. The landmark "roamed" across the Siberian borderland maps until the 1770s when it finally gained a fixed position in the imperial cartography.

Despite lacking cartographical work, Russian power slowly encroached on the foothills of the mountainous terrain populated by the Turkic-speaking Teleuts, the Zunghar vassals. The northwesternmost part of the Altai Mountains along with the nearby flatlands formed a contested geopolitical zone between Russia and the Zunghar confederation. Russian colonization intensified in the 1720s with Akinfii Demidov (1678–1745), one of the top Petrine metal producers, hearing of rich copper deposits in the upper Ob River basin. By launching the Kolyvano-Voskresenkie factories, the developer created a personal power base in the foothills of what would be soon called the Altai Mountains.

The rest of the story is well covered by the historical narrative. Rumors that Demidov secretly mined auriferous silver reached St. Petersburg. Despite his privileged position at the court and past services, Akinfii Nikitich failed to retain possession of the manufacturing plants. In 1747, two years after Demidov's sudden death, the plants were confiscated from his heirs without indemnity payments, and the cabinet of Empress Elizabeth (*Kabinet Eio Imperatorskogo Velichestva*), the executive body in charge of the Russian monarch's personal finances, assumed control of silver production.[22] Easily extractable ore, charcoal, waterpower, and cheap labor were plentiful, and a defense line of forts was rapidly built to protect the plants from the Zunghars. Thus, the nomadic lands became a strategically vital area, with the Crown's metallurgical works appearing on the eastern edge of the empire.

A flood of precious metals from the Kolyvanskie plants poured into the St. Petersburg mint; heavily protected caravans loaded with precious metals crossed Russia on the way to the capital several times a year. The "Age of Silver," the rising domestic species production, established Russia as Europe's primary producer of precious metals.[23] In the decade from 1748 through 1759, the output of gold reached 1,430 kg, an equivalent of 962,372 rubles, but silver production equaled 45,184 kg, worth 2,231,087 rubles.[24]

Available evidence suggests that the earliest conceptualization of the territory of the plants as the "golden mountains" appeared in the works of the Second Kamchatka Expedition (1733–1743), organized by the Imperial Academy of Sciences. The German naturalist Johann Georg Gmelin visited Demidov's plants with his colleague Gerhard Friedrich Müller in summer of 1734. Gmelin's logbook mentions copper mines, topographical details, and an excursion to a Teleut settlement.[25] As is evident from his notes, the territory around the plants had not been considered "Altai." However, as early as 1747, giving an overview of Siberian geography in the preface to his monumental work *Flora Sibirica*, Gmelin pointed to the mountain range between the Irtysh and the Ob River as the "golden mountains," explaining its incredible mineral wealth (*ibi fub nomine Altaiensis, i.e. aurei célèbre est*). Russian naturalist Stepan Krasheninnikov translated this knowledge-making claim as "Altanskye, which is golden" (*Altanskie, to est' zolotye*). [26]

Gmelin's remark formed only a tenuous start to the conception of Altai as golden, unheeded as it was by many contemporaries. Meanwhile, tragic events on the other side of the empire resulted in a cardinal change of power balance in Central Asia. Zunghar internal divisions led to an aggressive Qing campaign across West Mongolia and the subsequent Zunghar genocide in the mid-1750s.[27] Their extermination and the disastrous condition of the Teleut shifted the balance of power in Russia's favor. The north of the Altai Mountains fell firmly within the Russian sphere of control, while the southern segment remained in Outer Mongolia under Chinese rule. Unlike other areas, Russia accomplished the conquest of a large swathe of Central Asian territory without military force. On the one hand, the new power balance created stability on the border; on the other, Russia faced a rising eastern rival as close as in the Altai Mountains that had from then on a clear geographical connection with the Middle Kingdom.

Factually, the former Zungharia was a geopolitical backwater for both empires. Russia's concerns mostly focused on the area southeast of Lake Baikal, where the Kiakhta section formed a vibrant point of interactions, being the most convenient transit route and the main trade center, as Ilya Vinkovetsky observes in his contribution to this volume.[28] The opposite was the case on the west. The nineteenth-century military geographer Mikhail Veniukov depicted the Altai Mountains as the safest segment along the imperial borderlines.[29] Here, the boundary with the Qing was negotiated only in 1864, with commercial exchange following afterwards.[30]

Between two empires (1760s–1810s)

The rivers of auriferous silver from the Kolyvanskie plants along with irreversible geopolitical changes in Central Asia prompted new ways of thinking about the frontier region. The early 1760s saw modest attempts at mapping it through resource concerns. However, this emerging lens stood in stark contrast to the suggestions made before the discovery of precious metals, namely in the decade from the mid-1730s through the early 1740s. Fond of analyzing the names of the newly subjugated places as well as areas of potential conquest, Vasilii Nikitich Tatishchev, an imperial administrator with extensive metallurgical experience, proposed two meanings of the "Altai," the mountain range between Siberian and Zunghar lands. Using basic Tatar linguistic skills, the geographer and historian claimed that it meant either the "Six Mountains" (*Shestigorie*) from *alty* (six) + *tau* (mountain) or the "Six Months" (*shestimesiachnye*) from *alty* (six) + *ai* (month), explaining that nomads roamed across first the northern, then southern side of the mountain range for six months each.[31]

However, more remarkable suggestions would now occasionally circulate within the corridors of government. In a 1761 report to Empress Elizabeth, the cabinet secretary Count Alsuf'ev, concerned about further exploration of the mountain range surrounding her silver plants, referred to it as the "Altanskie mountains" (*Altanskie*), using Stepan Krasheninnikov's earlier translation.[32] Russian culture could have offered a more convenient way of mapping the place as "golden." The coin *altyn,* a piece of the Tatar material legacy, had been an integral part of everyday life since the early time.[33] In fact, *altyn* stems from *alty* (six), whereas *altyn* indeed means gold. Although not coined in gold, the idea of *altyn* may have bridged the material and imaginary realm, increasing the cultural meanings of the place. Still influential in the mid-century, the historical legacy of the *altyn* might have worked as a link associating the location with precious metals it produced.

Another mapping opportunity appeared when golden work from the ancient graves of Siberia and the recently conquered areas in South Russia was presented to the young Empress Catherine in 1763. She ordered Gerhard Friedrich Müller to provide a historical overview that appeared in the following year. The Enlightenment scholar created wide imaginary connections between empire, archeology, and geology, associating ancient metal works with the corresponding metals hidden in the surrounding mountains. In his opinion, copper items uncovered in the burial mounds near the Sayan Mountains in South Siberia indicated that this ridge could accommodate copper.[34] The same applied to the Kolyvanskie plants that Müller visited along with Gmelin and where he purchased golden items dug from ancient barrows. According to Müller, he presumed that this also applied to the local mountain range: "Alta means gold in the Mongol and Kalmyk language, and from it I had assumed that those mountains should contain gold. My assumption turned out right for the Kolyvano-Voskresenskie factories."[35]

The speculation emerged from the context of his earlier participation in the Second Kamchatka Expedition. However, a clear time lag lies between the 1734 visit and the 1764 knowledge-making claim supporting Gmelin's presumption. I suggest that neither to him nor to Gmelin did the place resonate with gold until the plants began to produce precious metals. Müller derived cultural meanings through the lens of resource imaginations in a subtle way, referring neither to metal exploitation nor to indigenous knowledge but by producing a tenuous link to archeological findings, linguistic markings, and a superficial understanding of the terrain.

Not supported by detailed travel reports, the above references remained isolated knowledge-making efforts. The member of the Imperial Academy of Sciences Peter Simon Pallas visited the Kolyvanskie silver plants and the "Altai Ore Mountains" in the following decade, rendering the location as the "wealthiest mining site" of imperial Russia.[36] In his new theory of geohistory as analyzed in the contribution by Ryan Jones in this volume, Pallas broadly defined the Altai as the greatest mountain chain in Siberia and one of the key knots connected to the Ural Mountains, going far beyond the Russian Empire, southwards to Tibet.[37]

However, things dramatically changed in 1781, when a new learned periodical by Pallas *Neue Nordische Beyträge zur physikalischen und geographischen Erd- und Völkerbeschreibung, Naturgeschichte und Oekonomie* (*New Northern Contributions to Earth Sciences, Geography, Anthropology, Natural History, and Economy*) offered a new explanatory framework for the abundance of precious metals at the Kolyvanskie plants. One of the early issues of this series in natural sciences contained an account with the lengthy title "The Description of the Altai Mountains from the Chinese book Daizyn-itun-Dshi translated by Rossokhin, the translator of the Academy, deceased in 1759 in Saint Petersburg and born in Nerchinsk."[38] The original account is now stored in G. F. Müller's archival portfolios.[39] We know neither when Müller obtained it, nor why he hesitated from publishing it in his periodicals. It is difficult to exactly date when the record was translated from Manchu into Russian and then to German, but the frequent references to the Manchu *alin* (mountain) suggest that it did not present ancient Chinese knowledge of Central Asia. It could be dated from the mid-seventeenth century, when the Manchu seized power in China, to 1740, when the interpreter Illarion Rossokhin returned from China to Russia.[40] In any case, the source adds an important link in the knowledge-making network, highlighting the contribution of early German scientists into the making of the myth.

Despite the title, the account reported little about the Altai, covering a larger area of Mongolia and its important geographical features, rivers, and lakes. However, the introductory line provided a strong support for the special meaning of the landscape: "'Altai-alin' is a compound word, the first half of which is Mongolian, and means gold, and the other is Manchu, meaning mountain. Thus, the meaning of the word is a golden mountain. Since ancient times", the report continued, "this mountain was called in Chinese *Gin Shall*, which means the same." This depiction thus stated that the Altai Mountains meant "golden" in the double way, referring to both Mongol and Chinese, while the Manchu *alin* (a mountain) served as a bridge between both channels. Despite the obvious misreading of *shan'* (*gin* – golden; *shan'* – a mountain in Chinese), *Gin Shall* sounded as ultimate truth, generating clear linguistic evidence from the opposite side of the border. The cultural hierarchy of the Russian Empire considered Mongol people as economically and culturally backward subjects. Although the Mongol language formed a primary linguistic channel of knowledge making, it seems that the link seemed intellectually insufficient; in other words, the Chinese reference strengthened the meanings of the Mongol place name. The ultimate authority of the Qing cultural source eliminated any possible doubts concerning the credibility of the "golden mountains."

The description of the buffer area between the Russian and Qing empires seems reliable in terms of local geography. The iconography of *Altai Alin*, however, trigger doubts concerning its cogency, as it employed a set of details that would match any highland terrain: "its height reaches the clouds and the Milky Way," "a mother of all mountain ranges going northwest and east," and "eternal snow that lasts over summer." It seems likely that another Asian mountain range was, in fact, at play in the Manchu depiction. Separating the eastern Tarim Basin from Tibetan Plateau, *Altyn Tagh* (*A-er-shan*) can be effortlessly translated from the Turkic languages as the "golden mountain." Its maximal height reaches over 6,000 meters, whereas the highest Altai peak is only 4,506 meters. Gold had been mined in Altyn Tagh since ancient times.[41] In a sense, the snow-capped Altyn Tagh, located in present-day northwest China, would be the perfect "Gin-Shan" by matching the linguistic and iconographical terms: gold mining, eternal snow, and extreme heights.

Another point against the credibility of "The Description of the Altai Mountains from the Chinese book Daizyn-itun-Dshi" is a discrete object with a similar name, *Altan Alin* (the Altan Mountains) in southeastern Mongolia, which featured on the Qing Jesuit maps.[42] The subtle difference between *altan* and *altai*, as well as between *Altai Alin, Altan Alin* and *Altyn-Tag* would hardly pose a big question for Chinese geographers given the immense spaces of Gobi Desert and Mongolia that lay between the Great Wall and the Altai Mountains. Blending facts and fantasies about the frontier landscape, the account combined concrete geographical data along with slippery imaginary geographies.

This case illustrates Enlightenment modes of thinking and imagining new imperial areas, exposing efforts at reasonable explanation and systematic ordering of the Eurasian frontier.[43] The rising lens of resource imaginations gave the knowledge-makers a pragmatic perspective, validating suggestions developed in the context of expansion. However, although eighteenth-century Russia developed its own history of the cultural interactions with the enigmatic eastern power, the production of the vision occurred in the context of German Enlightenment.[44] Derived neither from contacts with native informants nor from firsthand observation of the unexplored environment, but rather inspired by the intellectual engagement with imaginary Asia, this piece of knowledge appeared at the intersection of European thought and two Eurasian empires, "imported" from afar and made locally in St. Petersburg.

Qing geographers mapped the location as the "golden mountains," making no references to local mineral resources but misinterpreting the language of the subjected people. The "enlightened" approach of Pallas and others was more capacious; their determination to give a reasonable explanation weaved all elements into the picture: auriferous silver, the Mongol language, the Manchu-Chinese record, and the geographical location at the intersection of two expanding empires. The information from the eastern source was filtered through the imperial framework to create a new perspective on a faraway landscape. German thinkers thus performed the role of cultural inter-mediaries, offering the Russian public not only a rational clarification of mineral abundance but also a new set of attitudes toward the region of the Crown. Here, the Enlightenment view on the Altai Mountains concurred with the Russian imperial perspective.

The representation of the Altai as the "golden mountains" this time did not go unnoticed, as it appeared in a period when the Kolyvanskie factories were gain-ing increasing visibility on the imperial stage, shaping what was known about the remote but important location. The following decades saw several geo-graphers and mining experts make use of the "golden mountains."[45] Russian poetry, seizing on the newly coined image, provides another glimpse into how elites constructed imperial space. The official and poet Gavrila Romanovich Derzhavin incorporated the catchy metaphor in the ode *The Depiction of Felitsa* (*Izobrazhenie Felitsy*, 1789) dedicated to Empress Catherine. The poem advanced a new spatial framework, expanding Eurasian geographies:

> Her throne is on the Scandinavian,
> the Kamtchatkian and the golden mountains
> [Prestol eio na Skandinavskikh,
> Kamchatskikh i zlatykh gorakh.][46]

Engaging the geographical landscapes from the Baltic to the Pacific, Derzhavin encouraged readers to reimagine the empire through a triangle, drawing a line from the northern Khibiny Mountains eastwards to the peninsula of Kamchatka, and southwards to the Altai Mountains, highlighting it as one of the major links in the chain, which the poet visualized. A brief look at recently produced maps of the empire enabled the readership easily to envision the frame.[47]

Still, while the "golden mountains" gained some foothold in the Russian imagination at the close of the eighteenth century, there is not enough evi-dence to claim that it exerted a strong, continuous influence upon con-temporaries. The German-speaking scientific periodical was not an easy document to access and other references remained relatively sparse. Thus, the "golden mountains" were unable to enter mainstream Russian consciousness. Sooner or later, the imperial fantasy that came into view in upper circles of Russian science and literature could have fallen into obscurity, constrained by the limits of elite knowledge spaces.

The revival of the myth (1820s–1910s)

With the production and consumption of the vision of the "golden moun-tains" far from widespread by the end of the eighteenth century, how did it ultimately become entrenched in the Russian consciousness? I argue that this framing stayed "alive" and matured through a phenomenon that geographer

Tuan Yi-Fu has called "social support."[48] The "golden mountains" continued to float in Russian imaginary geographies due to continuingly elaborated stories that had been generated about the spatial illusion. Two watershed moments were particularly instrumental in the advancement of the legend in the nineteenth century.

The first point came with Alexander von Humboldt's journey to the Russian Empire in 1829.[49] While visiting the Ural region, the explorer made a spontaneous decision to extend the original itinerary, venturing deeper into the Asian heartland. After observing the imperial metallurgical production plants, he journeyed to the Altai border to pay a visit to a Qing border station inhabited by two Chinese officers and dozens of Mongol soldiers. It seems that the short excursion formed the culmination of his entire voyage: "the real pleasure of the Asian journey was only brought about by the Altai."[50] Humboldt was well aware of the efforts at explaining the meaning of the region that had preceded him in the region. However, he took them a step further, suggesting that the landmark on the edge of the Russian Empire played a global role in the continental topographical framework, forming one of Asia's four major geologies along with the Celestial Mountains (the Tian Shan), the Kunlun, and the Himalaya.[51]

The wide reception of Humboldt's journey and ensuing works by the imperial readership placed the "golden mountains" on a new trajectory, transferring the myth from elite knowledge to the public domain. Humboldt's claims began to gain wide acceptance in Russian scientific and popular circles, fostering special thinking about the intercontinental role of the peripheral landmark. The 1834 Senate order renaming the Kolyvanskie factories into the Altai factories can be considered one of its pivotal implications.[52] The Altai mining region (*Altaiskii gornyi okrug*) formed a larger part of the West Siberian Tomskaia province (*guberniia*); the separate governing body (*gornoe nachal'stvo*) regulated all regional issues. The region took a special position in the imperial spatial order, supplying financial resources for the Russian monarch's personal wealth.[53]

This iteration of imaginary geographies was powerful and compelling precisely because it mobilized the neighboring empire, the frontier landscape, and mineral wealth, setting the general tone for the cultural rediscovery of the mountain range. Within a few years of Humboldt's trip, geologists discovered substantial reserves of alluvial gold in the Altai Mountain range. For a century, gold had been recovered from auriferous silver through a complex mining procedure; now it could be extracted with less effort, taking the gold production in the Altai mining region to 14,400 kg annually from the 1830s through the 1860s.[54] The increasing gold output further shaped Russian perceptions of the place.

However, Humboldt's legacy should be considered in a twofold way. On the one hand, the 1830s saw the immediate enthusiastic reception of his voyage by the Russian public.[55] On the other hand, the sudden burst of active use of the image of the "golden mountains" would soon decline.[56] I suggest that the long-lasting impact of another authoritative source, the translation of the German geographer Carl Ritter's work *Geography of Asia* (*Zemlevedenie Azii*) initiated by Petr Semenov-Tian-Shanskii, the chairman of the Imperial Russian Geographical Society (IRGO), would firmly embed the "golden mountains" in Russian perceptions. Three massive volumes of *Geography of Asia* that appeared between 1859 and 1877 supplied a wide array of geographical and historical information about the Altai area, while the "golden mountains" formed the core prism through which the place was viewed by the public.[57]

The framing of Altai by Ritter and Semenov visualized the Altai for various layers of Russian society that had neither physical access to the region nor control over its extensive natural wealth but utilized it through fictional means. The convincing explanatory model combined three important attributes that resonated with the public: China, the expanding Russian empire, and gold. By playing a key role in raising public awareness about the region, it became an important linking vision between what the reading public knew about the area they would never visit and what they wanted to know about it.

As a guide to the farthest end of the empire, the symbolic landscape traveled various imperial routes and crossed cultural boundaries. With the growth of the number of printed materials in the second half of the century, the myth took on a life of its own in different social spaces. The circulation of the vision moved from imperial centers to enlightened provincial public in the Siberian cities of Tomsk and Barnaul. Larger and more diverse mainstream audiences participated in its textual "consumption," generating multiple imaginary links to the distant territory. The "golden mountains" frequently appeared in geological and mining literature, as well as in statistics.[58] It became commonplace in magazine articles, travel guides and reports, teaching materials, etc.[59] Pamphlets for illiterate Russian peasants resettling to Siberia were no exception either. Abundant natural endowment, favorable agricultural conditions, and a milder climate unlike the rest of Siberia made the region the most sought-after target for hundreds of thousands of peasants.[60]

Meanwhile, throughout its expansion, Russia incorporated wide territories stretching from the Volga River to Far East, which were inhabited by Turkic and Mongol (Kalmyk and Buriat) peoples. These areas accommodated a number of place names that could be translated as the "golden mountains" as well: *Altyngana, Altyn-tau, Altyn-imel', and Altyn-tiube.* [61] While they may sound golden, however, none of these locations acquired a special spatial myth of its own. Like the Altai Mountains themselves, there is not much evidence confirming that they derive their meanings from the yellow metal. The Turkic prefix *alt/ald* (below, in front of) complicates the interpretations already discussed even further.[62]

The "golden mountains" finally reached iconic status toward the closing decades of the nineteenth century, despite the decline of metal reserves that brought an end to the region's long mining era. Yet the standstill of industrial exploitation and the rising peasant migration were unable to erase the landscape in imagination. With resource imaginations penetrating everyday life, it had become deeply fixed in mainstream perceptions. A discovery of ancient stone walls in Mongolia made this particularly evident. Influenced by what was already known, the "Altun-Iish Mountains" appeared as the "golden mountains," giving rise to another powerful narrative.[63]

The "golden mountains" dominated the iconography of the geographical landmark, capturing the imaginations of both real and armchair travelers, reflecting a hope for prosperity and a sense of optimism for the future. "Social support" provided the cultural coherence of the vision, which was received as a symbol of imperial expansion and the embodiment of Russia's abundant natural wealth. Mainstream resource imaginations bridged the otherwise unbridgeable gaps between the plants and eastern etymology, turning the Altai into the equivalent of the land of undreamed riches.

Communist alchemy and Scythian riches (1920s–1940s)

The final section of this chapter focuses on the points that maintained the Altai as the "golden mountains" in popular Soviet perceptions. The collapse of tsarist Russia along with the change in political and social order did not significantly affect the imperial fantasy. The 1920s saw the "renaissance" of the vision of the territory that stood in stark contrast to the historical reality. Although the civil war in the newly established Oirotskaia Autonomous region (*Oirotskaia avtonomnaia oblast'*) spanned through the mid-1920s, real and imaginary geographies would be rigorously at work transforming the "tsarist fringe" into an organic part of the socialist state.

As Emma Widdis pointed out in her study, increasing mobility and the urge to explore the peripheries empowered people to travel over previously inaccessible areas.[64] The Soviet Union urgently required minerals for industrialization projects; a host of geological expeditions traversed the Altai in search of wealth within the subsoil. These decades witnessed another gold rush taking shape in the region. The Romanov dynasty had gone, but the yellow metal was still there in sufficient quantity. Armed with wash pans, thousands of prospectors searched for alluvial gold in the Altai riverbeds.[65] Unlike previous gold discoveries, this one occurred in the cinematic age, giving it a special visual expression. One of the earliest Soviet sound films *The Golden Lake* (*Zolotoe ozero*, 1935) was shot on the coast of the Teletskoye (*Altyn*) Lake in the Altai terrains.[66]

Finally, cultural exploration of the Asian periphery framed the "golden mountains" in a new perspective. When early Muscovites entered Siberia's flatlands, they came across man-made hills, ancient burial mounds (*bugry*) covered by soil and stone. Throughout the seventeenth century, Russian tomb hunters dug up multiple graves looting and smelting items of precious metals once used to adorn the dead.[67] Despite native attempts to protect the sites they considered to be the tombs of their ancestors, vandals literally emptied the golden and silver "hills" by the dawn of the eighteenth century. When Tsar Peter ordered the Siberian governor Matvei Gagarin to bring ancient treasures for his newly established collection, there was plainly not much left to gather.[68]

However, ancient people also buried their rulers and members of the princely families deep within inaccessible mountainous terrains. Although pillaged in antiquity, some tombs escaped the later attentions of grave robbers. Briefly investigated by the imperial Orientalist Vasilii Radloff, the undisturbed sites in the Altai became a Mecca for generations of Soviet archeologists. Excavations by Mikhail Gryaznov and Sergei Rudenko in the 1920s and 1940s made important discoveries of Scythian culture.[69] The frozen ground of Pazyryk and Shiba tumuli preserved fascinating artifacts dating from the eighth to the second century BC: well-preserved mummified bodies, a wealth of items fashioned in gold and bronze, wood, leather, and even felt. The exceptionally rich Altai collection of the State Hermitage Museum contains over six thousand archeological articles, including gold adornments and luxury objects of amazing artistry depicting powerful animal imagery, Indian silk, Persian carpets, etc. These numerous items made of precious metals further reinforced the idea of the Altai as the figurative "golden mountains." Thus, Soviet archeology reinforced G. F. Müller's suggestion linking its place name with its mineral content.

In the same era as archeological discoveries and gold rush, a novel set in the Altai was published in Leningrad. *The Golden Mountain* is a lesser known work by Alexander Beliaev, a highly regarded science fiction writer.[70] Though crammed with ideological clichés, the work makes an important contribution to our understanding of the "golden mountains" in the early Soviet imagination. One of its characters, Clayton, is an American adventurer-turned-journalist assigned with the task of finding a Russian physicist, Vasilii Nikolaevich Mikulin, a member of the Russian Academy of Sciences and the Royal Society of London who had mysteriously vanished from Leningrad at the zenith of glory. Pursuing the goal of the alchemist, the enigmatic genius is about to succeed with the transmutation of lead into gold. Getting closer to a breakthrough, his work may empower Soviets to flood the world with cheap gold, destroying Western capitalism and turning history in a radically different direction. Where would Mikulin relocate his research if not to the Altai Mountains? Rumors about "the fire falling down from the sky" indicate his whereabouts, and Clayton stays to observe the busy life of the settlement centered on the intellectual firepower of Mikulin.

The scientist claims that "Altai" means *Kinshan,* a "golden mountain" in Chinese. It hides enormous gold reserves, but these may now safely remain beneath the soil: his methods of generating cheap laboratory gold would produce vast amounts of the precious metal. However, artificial gold was not the only goal of revolutionary Russia in Mikulin's imagination. Soon, sugar and silk would be manufactured from wood, oil from coal, diamonds from glass, and so forth. The chemical transmutation unfolds along with the transformation of the Westerner into an active member of Soviet society. When ordered to destroy the lab, Clayton quickly switches sides. Bandits attack the scientific citadel, but Mikulin deploys an invisible weapon: a security system transmitting electrical rays.

Alexander Beliaev's work developed in the zeitgeist of contemporary science fiction. A somewhat similar novel, *Engineer Garin and His Death Ray* (*Giperboloid inzhenera Garina*, 1927) by Aleksei Tolstoy, featured a Russian physicist Garin, a selfish genius obsessed with the idea of creating a utopian society and controlling the world. Unlike Garin, the Soviet scientist Mikulin refuses to seek mastery over the planet. Unlike Tolstoy, who invented an imaginary Golden Island in the Pacific Ocean, Beliaev had no need to create a fictitious golden mountain, as it already loomed large on mental maps. Like a palimpsest, Beliaev's novel added new layers of significance to the Altai Mountains but did not erase the earlier ones. Presenting the remote Asian landscape as a sci-fi laboratory wherein a bright communist future is about to be produced, Beliaev pushed the boundaries of the locally situated imagery to the global scale, allowing the whole world to share in the consumption of the "Soviet golden mountain."

Conclusion

By linking histories of imperial expansion, knowledge production, and imagination, this chapter has attempted to propose an alternative explanation for the rise of the powerful myth of the "golden mountains," an image generated and shaped by resource concerns. This reference still dominates the iconography of the Altai, subsuming existing indigenous spatial understandings. Making mountains of cash from the "golden mountains," the modern tourist industry recycles imperial resource imaginations and attests to the observation of geographer Charles Withers that in several ways, the Enlightenment is still with us.[71]

Two points must be stressed in this connection. First, the "golden mountains" form a striking example of spatial knowledge borne out of imperial exploration. As the product of German Enlightenment incorporated into empire building, the vision forms a trans-imperial phenomenon, bringing together Russian expansion and the presence of diverse people and cultures on the Eurasian frontiers. This tiny facet in the larger picture of Euro-Sino-Russian interactions was constructed and mediated by a group of foreign intellectuals. Rooted neither in indigenous knowledge system nor in local histories, it emerged from the contact between Western thought and Chinese spatial knowledge.

Second, the historical existence of the vision was implicated in the larger production of imperial space. A hybrid cultural phenomenon combining German intellectual interests, quasi-Mongol linguistic forms, and the Manchu source; the image stamped the peripheral landmark and the surrounding region within the imperial aesthetic landscape. The "golden mountains" offered fertile opportunities to those who sought to make sense of the expanding frontier. The vision provided diverse audiences with a convincing cultural framework by which to appreciate the symbolical fruits of expansion. Historical resource imaginations, whose defining force I have attempted to map, generated multiple spaces for the production and consumption of the "golden mountains." These spaces proved effective precisely because they were flexible and adaptable, enabling the fantasy to escape the context of the original production and enter into circuits of mainstream culture.

Notes

1   *I would like to extend my sincere gratitude to the organizers of the conference, Asia in the Russian Imagination, and the University of Utah for providing me with travel funds. I thank the editors for their extremely helpful suggestions regarding this chapter, as well as Svetlana Tiukhteneva. I would like to acknowledge the support of the Gerda Henkel Foundation for the gathering of the material for this article and the Paulsen Foundation for its completion. This article draws upon work from my Ph.D. thesis, *Mapping the Altai in the Russian Geographical Imagination, 1650s – 1900s* (Humboldt University, Berlin, 2015). All remaining mistakes and deficiencies are entirely my own.

    K. V. Chistov, *Russkie narodnye sotsialno-utopicheskie legendy* (Moscow: Nauka, 1967), 239–90.

2   John McCannon, "By the shores of white water: The Altai and its Place in the Spiritual Geopolitics of Nikolas Roerich," *Sibirica* 2: 2 (2002): 166–89.

3   Vilhelm Thomsen, *Inscription de l'Orkhon. Memoires de la Societe Finno-Ougrienne V* (Helsingfors, 1896), 110, 158; B. I. Vladimirtsov, "Geograficheskie imena orkhonskikh nadpisei, sokhranivshiesia v mongol'skom," *Doklady Akademii Nauk S.S.S.R. 1929 goda*, 10 (Leningrad, 1930): 169–74.

4   V. A. Kazakevich, *Sovremennaia mongol'skaia toponimika* (Trudy Mongol'skoi Komissii, 13), (Leningrad: AN SSSR, 1934), 8; Gustaf Ramstedt, *Kalmückisches Wörterbuch. Lexica Societatis Fenno-Ugricae*, vol. 3 (Helsinki: Suomalais-Ugrilainen Seura, 1935), 8.

5   Grigorii Potanin, *Ocherki Severo-Zapadnoi Mongolii. Rezultaty puteshestviia, vypolnennogo v 1879 godu po porucheniiu IRGO. Materialy etnograficheskie*, vol. 5 (St. Petersburg, 1883), 262; Andrey Anokhin, *Materialy po shamanstvu u altaitsev, sobrannye vo vremia puteshestviia po Altaiu po porucheniiu Russkogo komiteta dlia izucheniia Srednei i Vostochnoi Azii. Sbornik Muzeia Antropologii i Etnografii*, vol. 4 (Leningrad, 1924), 15.

6   Nick Baron, "New Spatial Histories of Twentieth Century Russia and the Soviet Union: Surveying the Landscape," *Jahrbücher für die Geschichte Osteuropas* 55 (2007): 375–400. Key works: Mark Bassin, *Imperial Visions: Nationalist Imagination and Geographical Expansion in the Russian Far East. 1840–1865* (Cambridge: Cambridge University Press, 1999); Mark Bassin, Christopher Ely, and Melissa Stockdale, eds., *Space, Place and Power in Modern Russia: Essays in the New Spatial History* (DeKalb: Northern Illinois University Press, 2010).

7   John Wright, "Terrae Incognitae: The Place of the Imagination in Geography," *Annals of the Association of American Geographers* 37: 1 (1947): 1–15. On the philosophical approach to space see the classic work, Henri Lefebvre, *The Production of Space*, trans. Donald Nicholson-Smith (Oxford: Blackwell, 1991).

8   Elizabeth Ferry and Mandana Limbert, "Introduction," in *Timely Assets: The Politics of Resources and Their Temporalities*, eds. Elizabeth Ferry and Mandana Limbert (Santa Fe: School of Advanced Research Press, 2008), 3–24.

9   Michael Watts, "Petro-Violence: Community, Extraction, and Political Ecology of a Mythic Commodity," in *Violent Environments*, eds. Nancy Peluso and Michael Watts (Ithaca: Cornell University Press, 2001), 189–212; idem, "Natural Resources," in *Patterned Grounds: Entanglements of Nature and Culture*, eds., Steven Harrison and Nigel Thrift (London: Reaktion, 2004), 177–9.

10 *Die Geheime Geschichte der Mongolen. Aus einer mongolischen Niederschrift des Jahres 1240 von der Insel Kode'e im Keluren Fluß*, trans. and ed. Erich Haenisch (Leipzig: Otto Harrasowitz, 1941), 144, 158, 177, 194, 196, 198, 205, 207.

11 *The Book of Sir Marco Polo: The Venetian Concerning the Kingdoms and Marvels of the East*, trans. and ed. Henry Yule, 3rd edn (London: John Murray, 1903), 269.

12 Piero Falchetta, *Fra Mauro's World Map. With a Commentary and Translations of the Inscriptions* (Venezia: Brepols, 2006), 679.

13 "Stateinyi spisok F. I. Baikova," Variant 2, in *Pervye russkie diplomaty v Kitae*, eds. N. F. Demidova and V. S. Miasnikov (Moscow: Nauka, 1966), 121.

14 John F. Baddeley, *Russia, Mongolia, China. Being Some Record of the relations between them from the beginning of the XVIIth Century to the Death of Tsar Alexey Mikhailovich A.D. 1602–1676*, vol. I (London: Macmillan, 1919), CXXXIII; "Dopolnenia Tobolskoi Redaktsii," *Kniga Bol'shomu Chertezhu*, ed. K. N. Serbina (Leningrad: AN SSSR, 1950), 187.

15 See Valerie Kivelson's fruitful discussion of Remezov's works in *Cartographies of Tsardom: The Land and its Meaning in Seventeenth Century Russia* (Ithaca: Cornell University Press, 2006).

16 "Chertezh zemli vsei bezvodnoi i maloprokhodnoi kamennoi stepi," "Chertezh vsekh sibirskikh gorodov i zemel," in *Chertiozhnaia kniga Sibiri, sostavlennaia tobol'skim synom Semenom Remezovym v 1701 godu*. Faksimil'noe izdanie, vol. 1 (Moscow: PKO Kartografiia, 2003), nos. 20–21.

17 See the analogies: S. V. Bakhrushin, "Tuzemnye legendy v 'Sibirskoi istorii Remezova,'" *Istoricheskie izvestiia, izdavaemye IOIMU*, nos. 3–4 (1916): 3–28.

18 Peter Perdue, *China Marches West: The Qing Conquest of Central Eurasia* (Cambridge: Belknap Press of Harvard University Press, 2005), 174–208.

19 There is an extensive literature, see Cordell D. K. Yee, "Traditional Chinese Cartography and the Myth of Westernization," in *The History of Cartography: Cartography in the Traditional East and Southeast Asian Societies*, vol. 2, bk. 2, eds. John Brian Harley and David Woodward (Chicago: University of Chicago Press, 1994): 170–202.

20 Walther Fuchs, *Der Jesuiten-Atlas der Kanghsi-Zeit. Seine Entstehungsgeschichte nebst Namensindices für die Karten der Manjurei, Mongolei, Ostturkestan und Tibet* (Monumenta Serica. Monograph Series, IV) (Peking: Fu-Jen-Universität, 1943), 136; Henri Bernard, "Note complementaire sur l'Atlas de K'ang-hi," *Monumenta Serica. Journal of Oriental Studies of the Catholic University of Peking* XI (1946): 196.

21 The original report appeared in 1723. The Russian translation "Opisanie puteshestviia, koim ezdili kitaiskie poslanniki v Rossiu," *Ezhemesiachnye sochinenia i izvestiia o uchenykh delakh* (July–November 1764). For the detailed analysis of the map, see Gaston Cahen, *Les Cartes de la Sibirie au XVIIIe siècle. Essai de bibliographie critique* (Paris: Impremie Nationale, 1911), 136–45.

22 G. I. Spasskii, *Zhizneopisanie Akinfiia Nikiticha Demidova, osnovatelia mnogikh gornykh zavodov, sostavlennoe iz aktov sokhranivshikhsia u ego naslednikiv i iz drugikh svedenii* (St. Petersburg, 1833); *Polnoe sobranie zakonov Rossiiskoi imperii: Sobranie pervoe*. 45 vols. (St. Petersburg, 1830), vol. 12, no. 9403, 700–701 (Hereafter *PSZ*).

23 Ian Blanchard, *Russia's Age of Silver: Precious-metal Production and Economic Growth in the Eighteenth Century* (London: Routledge, 1989), 90–152.

24 *PSZ*, vol. 15, no. 11185, 616–17.

25 *Johann Georg Gmelins Reise durch Sibirien, von dem Jahr 1733 bis 1743*. New edition published as *Expedition ins unbekannte Sibirien*, ed. Dittmar Dahlmann (Deutsch-russische Literaturbeziehungen; X) (Sigmaringen: Thorbecke, 1999), 136–41.

26 Johann Georg Gmelin, *Flora Sibirica Sive Historia Plantarum Sibiriae*, vol. 1 (St. Petersburg, 1747), xv. The Russian translation: *Perevod s predisloviia, sochinennogo professorom Gmelinym k Pervomu tomu Flory Sibirskoi* (St. Petersburg, 1749), 19.

27 Perdue, *China Marches West,* 256–89; Mark Elliot, *Emperor Qianlong: Son of Heaven, Man of the World* (New York: Longman, 2009), 90–95.

28 Clifford Foust, *Muscovite and Mandarin: Russia's Trade with China and Its Setting, 1727–1805* (Chapel Hill: University of North Carolina Press, 1969).

29 M. I. Veniukov, *Opyt voennogo obozreniia russkikh granits v Azii* (St. Petersburg, 1873), 227.

30 The Treaty of Chuguchak, in *Sbornik pogranichnykh dogovorov, zakluchennykh Rossiei s sosednimi gosudarstvami* (St. Petersburg, 1881), no. 52, art. 1–3.

31 *Leksikon Rossiiskoi, Istoricheskoi, Geograficheskoi, Politicheskoi i Grazhdanskoi. Sochinennyi gospodinom Tainym Sovetnikom i Astrakhanskim Gubernatorom Vasil'em Nikitichem Tatishchevym,* pt. 1 (St. Petersburg, 1793), 35–6, idem, "Obshchee geograficheskoe opisanie vsei Sibiri" (1736), in *Izbrannye trudy po geografii Rossii,* ed. A. I. Andreev (Moscow: IGL, 1950), 49. Similarly, Tatishchev decoded the Caucasian Beshtau Mountain as the "Five Mountains," "besh" means "five," Ibid., 189.

32 "Doklad deistvitelnogo statskogo sovetnika Alsuf'eva," *PSZ,* I, vol. 15, no. 11185, 622.

33 *Altyn* became part of the Russian financial system in the fourteenth century circulating widely from the 1650s. I. G. Spasskii, "Altyn v russkoi monetnoi sisteme," *Kratkie soobshcheniia o dokladakh i polevykh issledovaniiakh Istituta istorii material'noi kul'tury,* vol. 66 (Moscow, 1956): 12–20.

34 The naming of new areas basing on local resources was typical in the period. One of the Komandorski Islands off the Kamchatka Peninsula was called "Mednyi" (Copper) due to copper pieces discovered on its coast. *Novyi i polnyi geograficheskii slovar' Rossiiskogo gosudarstva, ili Leksikon,* ed. F. A. Polunin, vol. 3 (Moscow, 1788), 265.

35 Gerhard Friedrich Müller, "Iz'iasnenia o nekotorykh drevnostiakh v mogilakh naidenykh," idem, *Istoriia Sibiri. Opisanie Sibirskogo tsarstva,* ed. A. I. Andreev, vol. 1 (Moscow: AN SSSR, 1937), 520–22.

36 Peter Simon Pallas, *Reise durch verschiedene Provinzen des Russischen Reiches,* pt. 2 (Graz: Akademische Druck- und Verlaganstalt, 1967), 205–8.

37 Peter Simon Pallas, *Über die Beschaffenheit der Gebirge und die Veränderungen der Erdkugel,* ed. Folkwart Wendland (Leipzig: Akademische Verlagsgesellschaft, 1986), 32–3.

38 "Beschreibung des altaischen Gebürges aus dem chinesischen Buche Daizyn-itun Dschi. Übersetzt durch den 1759 zu Petersburg bei der Akademie verstorbenen, aus Nertschinsk gebürtigen Translateur Rossichin," *Neue Nordische Beyträge zur physikalischen und geographischen Erd- und Völkerbeschreibung, Naturgeschichte und Oekonomie,* vol. 1, no. 2 (St. Petersburg, Leipzig, 1781): 223–7.

39 Rossiiskii gosudarstvennyi archiv drevnikh aktov, f. 199, op. 1, portf. 349, ch. 1, d. 28.

40 Illarion Rossokhin (1717–1761) learnt Manchu and Chinese at the Russian Ecclesiastical Mission in Beijing. After his return in 1740, he served as the translator at the Academy of Sciences. For his activities see Gregory Afinogenov, *The Eye of the Tsar: Intelligence Gathering and Geopolitics in Eighteenth-Century Russia* (Ph.D. diss., Harvard University, 2016), 137–57.

41 E. M. Murzaev, *Priroda Sintsiana i formirovanie pustyn' Tsentralnoi Azii* (Moscow: Nauka, 1966), 337.

42 "Carte Generale de la Chine", "Onzieme Feuille particuliere de la Tartarie Chinoise", in *Nouvelle Atlas de la Chine, de la Tartarie Chinoise, et du Thibet: Redigee Par mr. D'Anville, Géographe Ordinaire de sa Majesté Très-Chrétienne* (La Haye, 1737), nos. 2, 18.

43 See the discussion in David Livingstone and Charles Withers, "Introduction," in *Geography and Enlightenment,* ed. by idem (Chicago: University of Chicago Press, 1999), 1–28.

44 I am grateful to Matthew Romaniello for sharing his observations on this issue. On Russia and China in the Enlightenment age: Maggs Widenor, *Russia and 'le reve chinois'* (Studies on Voltaire) (Oxford: Voltaire Foundation, 1994). On China's impact in the German thought: *Discovering China. European Interpretations in the Enlightenment*, eds. Julia Ching and Willard Oxtoby (New York: Rochester University Press, 1992) (Library of the History of Ideas, VII).

45 Ivan Renovants, *Mineralogicheskie, geologicheskie i drugie smeshannye izvestiia o Altaiskikh gorakh, prinadelzhashchich k Rossiiskim vladeniiam* (St. Petersburg, 1792); Ivan German, *Sochinenia o Sibirskikh rudnikakh i zavodakh*, III (St. Petersburg, 1797), 233; L. Maksimovich, A. Shchekatov, *Geograficheskii slovar' Rossiiskogo gosudarstva*, vol. 1 (Moscow, 1801–1804), 138–9; Evdokim Ziablovskii, *Noveishee zempleopisanie Rossiiskoi imperii*, pt. 1 (St. Petersburg, 1807), 39.

46 *Sochineniia Derzhavina Stikhotvoreniia*, ed. Iakov Grot, vol. 1, pt. 1 (St. Petersburg, 1864), 274.

47 "Novaia Karta Rossiiskoi Imperii, razdelionnaia na Namestnichestva" (St. Petersburg, 1786).

48 Yi-Fu Tuan, "Language and the Making of Place: A Narrative Descriptive Approach," *Annals of the Association of American Geographers* 81 (1991): 689.

49 Gustav Rose, *Mineralogisch-geognostische Reise nach dem Ural, dem Altai und dem Kaspischen Meer*, vol. 1 (Berlin, 1837), 503–613.

50 The letter to Count von Cancrin, the Russian Minister of Finances, dated with 29 (15) August 1829, in *Perepiska Aleksandra von Gumboldta s uchionymi i gosudarstvennymi deiateliami Rossii*, no. 28 (Moscow: AN SSSR, 1962), 80.

51 Aleksandr Gumboldt fon, "O gornykh kriazhakh i vulkanakh vnutrennei Azii, i o novom vulkanicheskom izverzhenii v Andakh," *Gornyi Zhurnal* 3, no. 9 (1830): 308–22; "O gornykh sistemakh Srednei Azii. Iz noveishego sochinenia barona Gumboldta," *Moskovskie Vedomosti*, nos. 102–3 (1831); nos. 1–2 (1832).

52 *Polnoe sobranie zakonov Rossiiskoi imperii: Sobranie vtoroe.* 129 vols. (St. Petersburg, 1834), vol. 9, pt. 1, no. 6915, 221–2.

53 M. I. Strukov, *Kratkii ocherk Altaiskogo gornogo vedomstva Kabineta Ego Imperatorskogo Velichestva* (St. Petersburg, 1896).

54 P. P. Semenov, *Geografo-statisticheskii slovar' Rossiiskoi Imperii*, vol. 1 (St. Petersburg, 1863), 77–80.

55 Typical is *Puteshestvie barona Aleksandra Gumboldta, Erenberga i Rose v 1829 godu po Sibiri i k Kaspiiskomu moriu*, trans. I. Neronov (St. Petersburg, 1837).

56 There is a considerable time lag between his works and their reception in Russia. Only the Altai chapter of his *L'Asie Centrale* (1843) appeared in Russian in 1915. *Tsentral'naia Aziia. Issledovaniia o tsepiakh gor i po sravnitel'noi klimatologii*, trans. and ed. D. N. Anuchin (Moscow, 1915), 142–85.

57 *Zemlevedenie Azii Karla Rittera. Gornaia strana Nebesnogo khrebta (Tian-Shan'), prostranstvo mezhdu Tian-Shanem i Altaem (Kitaiskaia i Russkaia Dzhungaria), Altaiskaia sistema s Kitaiskoi storony. Istoriia otkrytiia i zaselennia iuzhnoi Sibiri*, ed. and trans. P. P. Semenov, vol. 2 (St. Petersburg, 1859); *Zemlevedenie Azii Karla Rittera. Altaisko-Saianskaia gornaia sistema v predelakh Rossiiskoi imperii po kitaskoi granitse*, ed and transl. P. P. Semenov, vol. 3 (St. Petersburg, 1860); *Zemlevedenie Azii Karla Rittera. Dopolneniia k tomu III. Altaisko-Saianskaia gornaia sistema po noveishim svedeniiam 1832–1876 gg.* ed. P. P. Semenov and G. N. Potanin, vol. 4 (St. Petersburg, 1877).

58 A. I. Kulibin, "Opisanie Kolyvano-Voskresenskikh zavodov v 1833 godu," *Gornyi Zhurnal*, 1, no. 1 (1836): 162; Semenov, *Geografo-statisticheskii slovar'* St. Petersburg, 1863), 73; *Tomskaia guberniia. Spisok naselennykh mest po svedeniam 1859 goda.* Izdan Tsentralnym statisticheskim Komitetom Ministerstva vnutrennikh del (St. Petersburg, 1868), 4; I. V. Mushketov, "Mineral'nye bogatstva Altaia," in *Zhivopisnaia Rossia*, ed. P. P. Semenov, vol. 11 (Moscow, 1884), 225; A. M.

Loranskii, *Gornaia statistika. Kurs lekzii, chitannykh studentam Gornogo Instituta v 1894/95 uchebnom godu* (St. Petersburg, n.d), 47.

59 *Karmannaia knizhka liubitelei zemlevedeniia*, 2nd ed. (St. Petersburg, 1849), 244; V. Mamyshev, "Altai," *Biblioteka dlia chteniia* 129 (1855), 35–62; *Altai i ego mineralnye bogatstva.* Narodnoe chtenie Kievskogo obshchestva gramotnosti (Kiev, 1885), 1; V. P. Shchepetov, *Altai. Proshloe i nastoiashchee gornoi strany* (Tomsk, 1890), 1; V. V. Sapozhnikov, "Zolotoe ozero i zolotaia gora. Iz puteshestvii po Altaui letom 1895 goda," *Estestvoznanie i geografiia* 2 (1897): 113–21; V. A. Dolgorukov, *Putevoditel' po vsei Sibiri i sredneaziatskim vladeniiam Rossii* (Tomsk, 1900–1901), 305.

60 Over 650 000 peasants settled from 1860 through 1903. A. A. Kaufman, "Zemelnyi vopros i pereselenie," in *Sibir, ee sovremennoe sostoianie i nuzhdy*, ed. I. S. Melnik (St. Petersburg, 1908), 78–140; Donald Treadgold, *The Great Siberian Migration: Government and Peasant in Resettlement from Emancipation to the First World War* (Princeton: Princeton University Press, 1957), 71–2. *Rasskazy o Zapadnoi Sibiri, ili o guberniiakh Tobol'skoi i Tomskoi, i kak tam zhivut luidi*, 2nd edn (Moscow, 1898), 49.

61 Semenov, *Geografo-statisticheskii slovar'*, 80–82.

62 E. M. Murzaev, *Slovar narodnykh geograficheskikh terminov* (Moscow: Mysl', 1984), 47–8.

63 Dated 6–7 B.C., it read, "This year I went to fight Tiurgesh, I passed through the Altun taiga area and the river of Irtysh." S. E. Malov, *Pamiatniki drevnetiurkskoi pis'mennosti Mongolii i Kirgizii. Texty i perevody*, ed. E. I. Ubriatova (Leningrad: AN SSSR, 1959), 27.

64 Emma Widdis, *Visions of a New Land: Soviet Film from the Revolution to the Second World War* (New Haven: Yale University Press, 2003), 100–111.

65 M. K. Rastsvetaev, *Nedra Oirotii* (Novosibirsk: ZSKI, 1937), 41–4.

66 The film featured geologists, a gang of outlaw gold prospectors, the natives, and a shaman. V. A. Shneiderov, *Vosem' kinoputeshestvii* (Moscow: Iskusstvo, 1937), 141–66.

67 N. Kondakov and I. Tolstoi, *Russkie drevnosti v pamiatnikakh isskustva*, vol. 3 (St. Petersburg, 1890), 33–68.

68 S. I. Rudenko, *Sibirskaia kollektsiia Petra* (Moscow: AN SSSR 1962), 11.

69 M. P. Griaznov, *Pazyrykskii kurgan* (Moscow: AN SSSR, 1937); S.I. and N.M. Rudenko, *Iskusstvo skifov Altaia* (Moscow: GMII, 1949)

70 Alexander Beliaev (1884–1942) is known by his *Chelovek-amfibia* (*The Amphibian*, 1929) and the cult Soviet film *The Amphibian Man* (1962), the echo of which can be heard in the recent motion picture *The Shape of Water* (2018). The novel appeared in "Bor'ba mirov" ("The Worlds' Struggle," no. 2) in 1929.

71 Charles Withers, *Placing the Enlightenment: Thinking Geographically About the Age of Reason* (Chicago: University of Chicago Press, 2007), 240.

3 Imaginary travel to imaginary Constantinople

A painted panorama, the periodical press, and the Russo-Turkish War (1828–1829)

Alina Novik

In the fall of 1828, a new visual attraction appeared in St. Petersburg. It was a *circular panorama* of Constantinople, a 200-foot-long canvas (about 61 meters) painted by the artist Manzoni (whose first name is unknown) and exhibited in a specially constructed wooden rotunda on *Bol'shaia Morskaia* street. The panorama of Constantinople, just like most other nineteenth-century paintings of this kind, has not survived, but it is possible to get a general idea of what it looked like from iconographical sources that its creator might have used (above all, Antoine Ignace Melling's engraved views of Constantinople, see Figure 3.1) and its written descriptions, primarily in the periodical press.

The effect the panorama had on the viewer was described by V. N. Basnin, a member of a well-known Siberian merchant family, in a letter to his relatives:

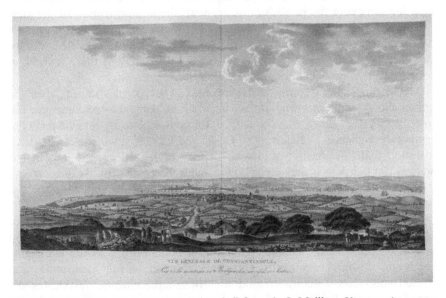

Figure 3.1 "Vue générale de Constantinople," from A. I. Melling, *Voyage pittoresque de Constantinople et des rives du Bosphore* (1819); reproduced courtesy of Special Collections, Burke Library, Hamilton College

I visited the panorama of Constantinople and the Imperial Public Library yesterday. The first is extremely complimented in *Otechestvennye zapiski* (*Notes of the Fatherland*) and indeed, even if it does not depict the perfection of nature then at least its fine imitation is worth approving. ... The best thing in it is the air. The sun has not yet appeared, but it is close and hides right behind the buildings of Seraglio. Its shine spread out over the visible parts of the sky, distant mountains, and the sea is expressed excellently. Mount Olympus with its snow top majestically ascends to heaven; [it is situated] behind a number of other mountains stretching towards the Marmara Sea and finally forming a scarcely remarkable but very sacramental cape. This is on the left while on the right side,—the water adjoins Seraglio, and I must admit that sultans knew how to choose the most adorable place ...[1]

Basnin who had come to St. Petersburg mostly for cultural and educational reasons, was probably seeing a panorama for the first time in his life, and as he described it for those who had never seen one,[2] he was interested in the art form itself rather than in its content. At the same time, authors of leading St. Petersburg periodicals were thrilled by the subject of the panorama—Constantinople. This city was of great interest to the audience of the Russian capital due to the on-going Russo-Turkish War, which had begun in April of the same year.[3] *Otechestvennye zapiski* (mentioned by Basnin) placed the review of the panorama directly after a report on armed hostilities and wrote: "it was, perhaps, impossible to choose a better time than now for satisfying the public's curiosity with the demonstration of the view of the Ottoman capital."[4] Meanwhile, the review of the *Severnaia pchela* newspaper (*Northern Bee*) appealed to historical memory and the idea of Russia's Byzantine legacy.[5] In this chapter, I will analyze these reviews in relation to the historical context in which they appeared.

Methodologically, I ascribe to Denise Blake Oleksijczuk's stance, when she writes about panoramas and British imperialism that "the meanings are not inscribed in the image but constituted through its use by individual, contemporary audiences."[6] Referring to Guglielmo Cavallo's and Roger Chartier's assertion that "the meanings of texts depend of the forms and the circumstances through which they are received and appropriated by the readers and listeners,"[7] she suggested that this approach may be equally applied to the history of the perception of not only verbal, but also visual texts.

The chapter consists of two parts, examining respectively "imaginary travel" and "imaginary Constantinople." The first part describes the invention and distribution of the circular panorama around Europe in the late eighteenth and the early nineteenth centuries, comments on how panoramas and related spectacles were understood as "travel-replacements," explicates the specificity of the Russian market for such visual entertainments, and finally, comments on the demand for panoramic views of Constantinople in both Russia and Western Europe thus providing historical context for the exhibition. The second part analyzes the reviews of the panorama of Constantinople in the press and indicates the ideas it appealed to and comments on their re-actualization in the course of the Russo-Turkish War (1828–1829).

Throughout its history, Russia fought with the Ottoman Empire more frequently than with any other country. In particular, from the end of the eighteenth century, the Russo-Turkish wars occurred every 15 to 30 years. During these times, the Turkish army suffered one defeat after another and therefore was pictured by Russians as the opposite of Russia itself, which took the paths of conscious westernization and significantly improved its style of warfare. The situation reversed after the Crimean War (1853–1856) when Russia experienced a crushing defeat because the Ottoman Empire had successfully applied Western knowledge and military technologies.[8] At the same time, Russian-Turkish conflicts were a peculiar form of indirect relations between Russia and Europe, since Russia's actions in the Middle East could upset the established balance of forces in Europe.[9]

By historicizing the "correct" reception of the panorama suggested by *Severnaia pchela* and *Otechestvennye zapiski*, this chapter aims to reveal the political and cultural meanings invested in the panorama by Russian journalists and to explain both their historical roots and cultural meaning to the contemporary public. Additionally, I argue that these meanings were determined by the political position these media maintained. Since the painting provided a very detailed, topographically accurate, and almost "photographic" image of Constantinople (as the genealogy of panoramic painting is rooted in the military topography), it seemingly did not give rise to the interpretations brought to the panorama by the mass media. I claim that the panorama of Constantinople was interpreted by the periodicals of St. Petersburg as a majestic illustration of the on-going war and used as a tool to justify Russia's claims to the depicted city.

Imaginary travel: a panorama among other "travel-replacements"

A circular panorama was a giant and extremely realistic painting that completely surrounded its spectators; it was invented by the Irish artist Robert Barker (1739–1806), based in Edinburgh, in 1787. It was meant to be seen in a specially constructed rotunda that presupposed a number of structural elements meant to increase the "proper effect" of the exhibited view. These elements were an elevated viewing platform that prevented visitors from getting too close to the picture, a roof construction that obscured the painting's top edge, and a circular glazed opening in the rotunda's ceiling that illuminated the painting (Figure 3.2.).[10] The only way to the viewing platform was through a dark tunnel where the visitors' eyes became used to the darkness, so when they finally saw the panorama they were primed to mistake it for reality. Such realistic paintings, improved by optical illusion, mostly portrayed remarkable distant sights and were to help spectators "travel" there, at least in their imagination.[11]

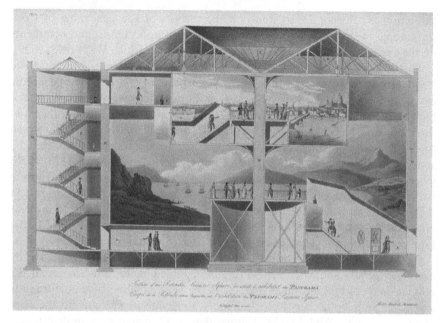

Figure 3.2 "Section of Robert Barker's *Rotunda*, Leicester Square, in which is Exhibited the Panorama;" from Robert Mitchell, *Plans, and Views in Perspective, with Descriptions, of Buildings Erected in England and Scotland* (1801).

The growing popularity of the panorama on the one hand and its high costs, immobility, and limitations as an artistic form on the other, stimulated the appearance of many other *panoramic spectacles* including diorama, diaphanorama, cosmorama, padorama, georama, europorama, and many other "oramas." Though "imaginary travel" was still the most popular subject of all the panorama-related spectacles, the fluctuations in it were partially determined by differences in the technology they used.

While a circular panorama created an illusion of total immersion into the picture and was suitable for the depiction of a particular sight, a cosmorama, an exhibition of "perspective views" demonstrated through glazed openings often used the motif of "imaginary travel" around the world (or through a particular region), a ribbon-shaped "moving panorama" reeled from one coil to another thus sequentially showing all parts of the view was best suited for the image of long extensive travels, etc. Quite often, such exhibitions were the only opportunity for the average citizen to witness other geographical destinations.

Robert Barker, however, is remarkable not only as the inventor of the medium but also as the creator of the first two panoramas of Constantinople. During the first years of running his panorama rotunda in London, the first ever enterprise of this kind, Barker created and demonstrated panoramas of British cities and naval battles won by Great Britain. In 1801, he exhibited two panoramic views of Constantinople taken from the Tower of Galata and the Tower of Leander, retrospectively, from the "European" and "Asiatic" sides. The shift in subjects may be explained by the increased competition among panoramists as Barker's patent for his invention expired the same year. Simultaneously, Barker's paintings of Constantinople were a logical continuation of his early British panoramas since in the views of the Ottoman capital, as Oleksijczuk claims, "British supremacy is masqueraded as objectivity."[12]

The panoramas were also attractive to British audiences as the historical context of their first exhibition involved the alliance between the British and Ottoman Empires against Napoleonic France (Great Britain joined forces with Turkey in 1798) as well as the fashion for Ottoman products and goods. Additionally, Oleksijczuk noted that the exhibition of the panoramas coincided with the birth of European Imperialism, as suggested in Edward Said's *Orientalism* and Johannes Fabian's "Culture and Imperialism," which partially explains the interest of Europeans towards the East in general and the city of Constantinople in particular.[13] Therefore, the panorama and related spectacles grew out of European imperial expansion and colonialism and emerged together with tourism and the public's curiosity about distant parts of the world.

The Russian market for panoramic spectacles, however, was different from that of Great Britain. While Barker knew his audience and could take into account its expectations while creating the exhibits, the Russian public saw only those that had previously been exhibited abroad and brought to Russia by foreigners who could hardly have accounted for Russian tastes. Although the fashion for panorama-related exhibitions reached St. Petersburg in 1804, only five years later than it came to Paris (which had immediately become one of the main European centers of the transnational market for panoramic entertainments), Russian artists did not produce circular panoramas until at least the 1860s. Nevertheless, in the first half of the nineteenth century, it was possible for the public of St. Petersburg and Moscow to see approximately two dozen large-scale circular and semi-circular panoramas, including those of Vienna, Prague, Riga, Moscow, Rome, Palermo, London, Paris, St. Petersburg, and, of course, Constantinople.

Interestingly, half of them portrayed the last three cities: there were three panoramas of Paris, three of Constantinople, and at least the same number of St. Petersburg. Since Russia did not produce circular panoramas itself, the only way to obtain the rare panoramas of St. Petersburg was to actually draw them "from nature," and although the paintings were meant to be exported, quite often their creators first exhibited them in the city that the panoramas depicted. At the same time, a large number of panoramas of Paris and Constantinople exhibited in the Russian capitals of St. Petersburg and Moscow had nothing to do with local specificity as it was no more than a consequence of the popularity of and demand for these subjects in Western Europe from where panoramas were mostly imported to Russia.[14]

Russians, however, frequently interpreted the content within some of the European circular paintings quite differently than their European creators and audience may have understood them. This was particularly the case for the panoramas of Constantinople and Paris, cities that in the first half of the nineteenth century were associated with Russia's two enemies in the West and in the East: (post-)Napoleonic France and the Ottoman Empire. For instance, the reviews of the panoramas of Paris exhibited in St. Petersburg (excluding the one exhibited in 1804) published in *Severnaia pchela* and *Otechestvennye zapiski* referred to the French Invasion of Moscow (1812) and the Battle of Paris (1814).[15] Although the earlier panorama exhibited in the early 1820s was brought from Austria, another of France's enemies, and portrayed Paris right at the moment when the allied forces of Russia, Austria, and Prussia were occupying it in 1814, a later circular painting that came to Russian lands directly from France in the mid-1840s portrayed Paris quite neutrally and did not give rise to dredging up the past.

The reception of a number of panoramas of Constantinople exhibited in Russia between the mid-1820s and the mid-1830s is no less remarkable. Although, during this period, the audience of St. Petersburg and Moscow could see three panoramas of the Ottoman capital (1825, 1828–1829, 1834–1836), most attention was drawn to the one exhibited in St. Petersburg in the midst of the Russo-Turkish War of 1828–1829, while the two other paintings were almost overlooked. For example, the only review of the earliest of the three exhibits, which took place in Moscow in 1825, is limited to a few lines in the *Moskovskii telegraf* (*Moscow Telegraph*). This assessment (1825) is more sarcastic than informative or complimentary as the newspaper wrote (quoting the advertisement of the panorama in the "Greco-Russian" language):

> The owner of the Panorama [of Constantinople] announces that the artist who drew it *used everything to decorate his art*. Then it's strange that the Panorama is pretty bad, poorly arranged and does not produce any charm. The colours are rough and the figures are unnatural; only the explanations given to the visitors by the Panorama's owner himself, in the Greco-Russian language, are very *sweet.* [16]

The last of three exhibitions, namely the one of the mid-1830s, did not attract much attention either. The only review (1834) of the St. Petersburg exhibition of a marvelous circular panorama of Constantinople painted by Antonio Sacchetti (1790–1870), a Venetian artist who worked as a decorator and managed his own "topographic cabinet" (*gabinet topograficzny*) for panoramas and dioramas in Warsaw,[17] was published in *Severnaia pchela* and attested that the painting

> is a masterful work in terms of art, but outdated and incorrect as contemporary Constantinople has nothing in common with the panorama of the Sultan's capital that is now exhibited: in the panorama, you see Constantinople as it was ten years ago, but since then it was burned down and rebuilt many times![18]

When the panorama was transported to Moscow, the reviews appeared in the Moscow press, too. They were warmer that those by the St. Petersburg newspapers, but still very brief. For example, a review in *Moskovskie vedomosti* (1834) commented, "those who have been in the sumptuous and picturesque [Ottoman] capital assure that nothing in the artistic world contains more accuracy and perfection!"[19] The famous journalist and publisher P. I. Shalikov's article (1835) noted, "Who hasn't heard of the glory and the fall of old Tsar'grad and who did not tremble daily about the fate of new Constantinople five years ago! How is it possible not to visit it, at least passing through, and not to look at least on its tiled roofs?"[20] Thus, a reference to the Russo-Turkish War of 1828–1829 appeared in the assessments of Sacchetti's panorama exhibited in Russia in the mid-1830s. Nevertheless, the brief mention in *Moskovskie vedomosti* (*Moscow News*) is in no way comparable to the complex conceptual models that the periodical press of St. Petersburg built around Manzoni's panorama that had been exhibited in the city beginning in October of 1828.

Imaginary Constantinople: the panorama and the war

The history of Manzoni's panorama of Constantinople before and after it was exhibited in St. Petersburg is unknown and very little is known about the artist himself. According to the reviews, the panorama was created by the artist Manzoni, who was "known for many works of this kind."[21] In particular, *Otechestvennye zapiski* attests that Manzoni created a moving panorama of Moscow of more than four meters long, which Nicholas I gave his mother the Empress Maria Feodorovna.[22] Additionally, the review points out that in the summer of 1828, the artist created the panoramic view of St. Petersburg taken from the observatory tower of the Kunstkamera;[23] this fact was proof of Manzoni's competence as a panoramist since the tower was the point from which most of the panoramic images of St. Petersburg had been taken beginning in the eighteenth century.[24] Manzoni's panorama of Constantinople was taken from the Tower of Leander, which also was a very special point as one of Barker's panoramas was taken from there, too.

The announcement about the panorama exhibition published in the advertising section of the main newspaper of the Russian capital, *Sankt-Peterburgskie vedomosti* (*St. Petersburg News*), pointed out:

> The view is taken from the Tower of Leander; on the one side, you can see a seraglio with its gardens; the city of Constantinople located on seven hills, the harbour, the main buildings, a part of the city inhabited by the Franks, the Turkish and Greek cemetery and so on. On the left of Constantinople, you see the village of Beşiktaş, where the Sultan's summer seraglio, the residence of one of his wives, is situated; a chain of hills disappearing at the mouth of the Bosphorus, consisting ... the end of Europe. On the opposite bank, Asia begins and the magnificent city of Skutari appears in the

foreground of the picture. The third seraglio, the beautiful mosque Ayazma-Jami, the Cape of Chalcedon, the Prince Islands, Bruzi mountains, Mount Olympus, the islands Pita, Olens, and Marmara complete the charm of this wonderful picture. ...

Among many ships of all sizes [that came] from all the lands, you may see the Sultan on a barge donated by the Venetians and preserved with the greatest diligence; the whole of his court follows him; he heads to his summer seraglio. A number of rowers, their clothes and so on are depicted with the greatest accuracy.[25]

The advertisement also noted that "the architectural details of houses and public buildings ... and ... everything that is part of this beautiful image were awarded the approval of the excellent artists of this capital" and that "the people who lived in Constantinople recognized the smallest details."[26] In addition to this, the panorama was described in two reviews published in two media, *Otechestvennye zapiski* and *Severnaia pchela*, which require particular discussion.

The *Otechestvennye zapiski* magazine, the first periodical to mention the panorama, was founded in 1818 by a representative of the Ministry of Foreign Affairs, P. P. Svin'in. In 1818, he began issuing an annual collection of articles entitled "Otechestvennye zapiski," which in a couple of years was transformed into a monthly magazine that ran for the next ten years. The magazine, therefore, was established during the rise of Russian patriotism provoked by the French Invasion (1812) and the publication of N. M. Karamzin's "History of the Russian State" (1818). *Otechestvennye zapiski* satisfied the tastes of the majority of readers both in the Russian capitals and provinces and therefore obtained wide readership: the magazine published nearly 1,400 copies, which at that time was a quite significant number.

The magazine's main focuses were the history and ethnography of Russia, which were quite often covered by professional historians.[27] In addition, it published historical sources, descriptions of archaeological finds, reports on military campaigns (as mentioned above, one of them was followed by the review of the panorama), contemporary chronicles of St. Petersburg, literary criticism, and travel notes about Russia and other countries written primarily by the publisher himself.

Besides this, Svin'in constantly looked for Russian (mainly provincial) inventors, craftsmen, and self-taught artists and eloquently described their talents. In his passionate desire to prove that Russian lands were full of naturally gifted people, the publisher often tried to pass off mediocre amateurs as outstanding geniuses. At the same time, he often made mistakes, embellished the truth, manipulated facts, and eventually earned himself the reputation of a pathological liar. In particular, A. Ye. Izmailov, a popular writer, a publisher of the *Blagonamerennyi* magazine (*Well-Intentioned*), and therefore one of Svin'in's main competitors, wrote a fable "Liar" (1824) that ridiculed Svin'in's propensity for exaggerating. A similar image that clearly referred to Svin'in appeared in a short story "Little Liar" (1830) written by A.

S. Pushkin. It is plausible, however, that Svin'in's contemporaries were critical of his reluctance to cover the more serious problems of contemporary Russia and his desire to curry favor with the current government rather than for his rich imagination.[28]

The *Severnaia pchela* newspaper was the first Russian private literary and political newspaper, founded by F. V. Bulgarin in cooperation with N. I. Grech in 1825 (in the 1830s, these two publishers became monopolists in the mass media market of St. Petersburg). The newspaper was designed for the widest possible readership and gained popularity during the first year of its existence. Although at first *Severnaia pchela* adhered to liberal views, it turned to conservative ones after the Decembrist Uprising (December 14/26, 1825). The newspaper was subsidized by the government and, by the late 1820s, it became an implied voice of the Third Section of the Emperor's Chancellery,[29] the secret police created by Tsar Nicholas I after his accession to the throne (1825). Additionally, the newspaper had a monopoly on publishing of political news.

The reviews published in these periodicals emphasized that Manzoni had spent three years in Constantinople working on the giant portrait of this city,[30] which was probably true as work on panoramas usually took years to complete. In this case, Manzoni began working on the painting no later than in 1825, when nothing could clearly predict the forthcoming war. However, it is possible that the Russo-Turkish War that began in April 1828 had encouraged Manzoni to finish work as soon as possible as it suddenly became extremely topical for both audiences, Russian and European. The last mention of the panorama's exhibition in St. Petersburg press and playbills appeared in January 1829. [31] Afterwards Manzoni could transport his panorama to Western Europe, where Constantinople still aroused interest, in large part due to the on-going war between Russia and Turkey. For example, in 1829, a new panorama of Constantinople appeared in London. The view taken, just as in cases of Manzoni's and Barker's panoramas, from the Tower of Leander by Barker's pupil Robert Burford (1791–1861) was displayed in Barker's panoramic rotunda bought from his son Henri Aston Barker (1774–1856) who had inherited the father's business after his death in 1806.[32]

The British and Russian periodical press of these times interpreted Manzoni's and Burford's panoramas, which were taken from the same point and appeared on the scene one after the other, very differently. The review of Burford's panoramas, dated August 21, 1829, published in *The Gentleman's Magazine*, is a particularly eloquent example as it mentions Russian claims to Constantinople and expresses Great Britain's identification with "all Europe": "At this time, when the capital of Islamism is threatened by a semi-barbarous and hostile army, and when all Europe is anxiously awaiting the select of the struggle, the subject chosen is one of the peculiar interest, and cannot fail to be an object of public attraction."[33]

Unlike *The Gentleman's Magazine*, which referred to the Russians as "semi-barbarous and hostile," the review of Manzoni's panorama published in *Severnaia pchela* (24 November 1829) described them as enlightened Europeans opposed to backward aborigines. In addition, unlike the British reviewer who calls Constantinople the capital of Islamic faith, the Russian author described the city as the cradle of Orthodoxy and appealed to the idea of Russia's Byzantine legacy:

> The view of seraglios, minarets, and mosques makes a sad impression at the thought of splendour and glory of Constantinople in the times of the first Eastern Emperors. Looking at the dome of St. Sophia, [you] remember that this is the cradle of Orthodoxy, where the Great Duchess Olga took Holy Baptism! Pious shepherds came to Russia from here, to enlighten Great Duke Vladimir ... In this temple, the daughters of the Greek Emperors prayed, leaving their fatherland, and going to Russia to their bridegrooms, the Great Dukes of Russia. At this place, the guard of Varangian-Russes and Slavs retained the throne of the Emperors.[34] Isn't it the place where the wise monks were deliberating the compilation of the Slavic letters? From this place, they brought us, to Kiev, Arts and Science on the ramps of Trade. *Is it not on these gates Oleg nailed his shield?* [35] And *our Russian eagle*, whose victorious wings fluttered over the Alps and Ararat, over the banks of the Seine and Euphrates, over ice Lapland and blessed Armenia, our Russian eagle is a monument to *the blood union of Russia and Byzantium*. The *double-headed black eagle was the emblem of the Eastern Empire*, and would have been lost in oblivion if it had not been hidden under the Russian gonfalons. How many memories glorious for the Russian [occur] at the sight of the minarets and the piles of houses where ignorance and fanaticism nest now, where Science and Art have no place, and where the educated European is reputed to be a despicable creature, the Giaour! Of course, [there is] no city [that] would be as interesting to us as Constantinople. *This is our Rome!*[36]

It might be suggested that the description of Constantinople as "our" Rome, the center of "our" Orthodox religion, refers to the idea of *translatio imperii* and the concept of "Moscow, the third Rome." The doctrine was formulated by the Pskov monk Filofei in the early sixteenth century, but it was almost completely forgotten until the 1860s (even though a patriarchate charter that contained the idea was published in a popular series of historical documents in 1819, it gained the attention of historians, but not of the general public.)[37] In either event, the review strongly emphasizes the idea of the "blood union" between Russia and Byzantium ostensibly proved by the double-headed eagle that, as suggested by the newspaper, moved from the Byzantine coat of arms to that of Russia. Though according to a long-held belief, Zoe Palaiologina who married Ivan III in 1472 brought a double-headed eagle to Moscow as her dowry to Ivan III. The symbol first appeared on the tsar's seals only in 1497 while the idea of the Russian tsars' rights towards a Byzantine legacy was suggested by Venetians looking for allies in their struggle against the Ottomans and this, at first, did not attract much attention.[38]

The description of Constantinople as an Orthodox shrine and "our" Rome might allude to the Greek Plan of Catherine II. According to the ideology of this project, Russia received the Orthodox faith from Greece and thus was supposed to return the favor by reclaiming Greek lands from Turkey and reviving the Byzantine Empire with the capital of Constantinople. As the restored Byzantium was supposed to be ruled by the empress's grandson Konstantin Pavlovich while the role of the Russian emperor was assigned to his elder brother Alexander, it was assumed that relations between the Russian and Byzantine empires would be fraternal and Russia would be assigned the role of an elder brother.[39]

Additionally, Catherine II introduced the motif of Oleg's shield (*Olegov shchit*) used in the review of *Severnaia pchela* to the literary tradition.[40] This motif refers to the legend (*letopisnoe predanie*) of the Varangian duke Oleg's Byzantine campaign of 907. The legend describes Oleg's successful raid on Byzantium where he took a ransom and nailed his shield to the gates of Constantinople thus denoting the victory. The idea of a new Constantinople campaign that fully corresponded to the Greek plan appeared in the historical drama "The Beginning Rule of Oleg" (1786) written by the empress on the eve of the Russo-Turkish War of 1787–1791.

Expansionist connotations of the literary motif were forgotten in the early nineteenth century, but then reappeared during the Russo-Turkish War of the late 1820s, namely in the summer of 1829. When the Russian army had taken Adrianople and thus opened its way to Constantinople the image of Oleg's shield became a symbol of the anticipated victory.[41] The other commonplace of these literary works was the image of the double-headed eagle that also appeared in the review of *Severnaia pchela*.[42] It is noteworthy that both images were used in the newspaper article several months before the Russian army made significant progress in fighting against the Ottomans, which stimulated a wave of ideologically engaged poetry actively appealing to the same concepts.

The review of *Severnaia pchela*, therefore, described not an actual city portrayed by Manzoni, but rather an imaginary space associated with the ideas and the symbols that the newspaper referred to. The article suggested looking at Constantinople not as a contemporary Ottoman city, but as the capital of "ancient Byzantium" where Russian religion, writing, and culture in general originated. Such description was inspired by "historical memories that naturally arise at the sight of ancient Byzantium" as the newspaper later commented.[43] A similar trope was used in the review in *Otechestvennye zapiski* that entreated the spectator to transfer himself mentally into Byzantium; the detailed description of the panorama was ended with the exclamation: "in a word, nothing is missed to fascinate the eyes of the viewer and to transfer his imagination into glorious Byzantium."[44] Both reviews in a sense suggested that the spectators transfer themselves not only in space, but also in time, either to the Byzantine past or into an imaginary future when Constantinople would be the capital of Byzantium restored with the active participation of Russians.[45]

Nevertheless, it turned out that the idea of capturing Constantinople had in fact quite little in common with Nicholas I's actual plans concerning the military campaign in Turkey. In a letter to the commander-in-chief of the Russian army I. I. Diebitsch, written immediately after the occupation of Adrianople, the Russian tsar called the capture of Constantinople an accident that he "prayed the God not to allow" and demanded that the peace treaty be signed as soon as possible.[46] In September 1829, the warring parties signed the Treaty of Adrianople that concluded the war. The courageous dreams about entering the Ottoman capital were not destined to come true. Since then, Constantinople might have been captured by Russians only in the Russian imagination.

In summary, the war that had broken out between Russia and Turkey in the late 1820s gave Manzoni's panorama political significance. The painting became an occasion to express the attitude towards the enemy, to declare Russia's superiority over the Ottoman Empire, and even to imagine this city a part of a restored Byzantium. The ideas of the Byzantine legacy of Russia expressed in *Otechestvennye zapiski* and *Severnaia pchela* sought to legitimize Russia's rights concerning the city of Constantinople, although the panorama itself pictured Constantinople with "photographic" accuracy and did not give rise to any such ideas. As argued above, the mass media sought to impose on its audience an "official" memory politics, as they understood it in the end of 1828.

Notes

1 *This article was prepared within the framework of the Young Russian Scholars Helsinki Fellowship Program (YRUSH) implemented by the Aleksanteri Institute (University of Helsinki) with the support of the Kone Foundation. V. N. Basnin, "Peterburgskie vpechatleniia molodogo sibiriaka v 1828 g." in *Kupecheskie dnevniki i memuary kontsa XVIII – pervoi poloviny XIX veka*, comp. A. V. Semënova et al. (Moscow: ROSSPEN, 2007), 198–9. Here and below the translation from Russian is mine — A. N.

2 Basnin's letter says that a person who accompanied him on a trip to St. Petersburg, one Nikolai Fedorovich, "will tell you how cosmoramas and panoramas are controlled", see, ibid., 199.

3 On the Russo-Turkish war of 1828–29 and its outcomes, see, V. I. Sheremet, *Turtsiia i Adrianopol'skii mir 1829 g.: Iz istorii vostochnogo voprosa* (Moscow: Nauka, 1975).

4 "Panorama Konstantinopolia," *Otechestvennye zapiski* 36, 102 (1828): 172.

5 "Panorama Konstantinopolia (V Bol'shoi Morskoi, vozle doma Kosikovskogo)," *Severnaia pchela*, no 141 (1828), [4].

6 Denise Blake Oleksijczuk, *The First Panoramas: Visions of British Imperialism* (Minneapolis: University of Minnesota Press, 2011), 26.

7 Gugliemo Cavallo and Roger Chartier, eds. *A History of Reading in the West* (Amherst: University of Massachusetts Press, 1999), 4; as quoted in Oleksijczuk, *The First Panoramas*, 24.

8 Viktor Taki, *Tsar' i sultan: Osmanskaia imperiia glazami rossiian* (Moscow, Novoe literaturnoe obozrenie, 2017), 7. It is worth noting however, that Western military technologies had been adopted from Westernized Russia by the Ottoman Empire (see, ibid., 115).

9 Taki, *Tsar' i sultan*, 9.

10 Oleksijczuk, *The First Panoramas*, 1–2. On panorama, also see, Stephan Oettermann, *The Panorama: History of a Mass Medium*, trans. Deborah Lucas Schneider (New York: Zone Books, 1997); Bernard Comment, *The Painted Panorama*, trans. Anne-Marie Glasheen (New York: H. N. Abrams, 2000); Ralph Hyde, *Panoramania! The Art and Entertainment of the "All-Embracing" View* (London: Trefoil in association with Barbican Art Gallery, 1988).

11 Another common means of imaginary travel, travel writing, has attracted a number of scholars. One of the key problems of such research is the representation of non-western people and lands in European travel literature of modern times. On this topic, see, e.g. Stephen Greenblatt. *Marvelous Possessions: The Wonder of the New World* (Chicago: The University of Chicago Press, 2017); Peter Hulme, *Colonial Encounters: Europe and the Native Caribbean, 1492–1797* (London; New York: Routledge, 1992); Mary Louise Pratt, *Imperial Eyes: Travel Writing and Transculturation* (London; New York: Routledge, 2008). On Russian orientalism and Russian representations of Turkey in particular, see, Taki, *Tsar' i sultan*.

12 Oleksijczuk, *The First Panoramas*, 93.

13 Oleksijczuk, *The First Panoramas*, 91–3.

14 Dietrich Neumann, for example, listed Paris and Constantinople among "the cities that travellers visited on their Grand Tour" thus explaining common interest in the panoramic spectacles showing these destinations, see, Dietrich Neumann, "Instead of the Grand Tour: Travel Replacements in the Nineteenth Century," *Perspecta* 41 (2008): 49.

15 Although panoramas were usually presented to the public as a substitute for real travel to the depicted place, the panoramic painting of Paris demonstrated in St. Petersburg in the early 1820s was described by *Otechestvennye zapiski* as a change, as "It would be strange now if any of the Russians were proud (as before) even that his cousin was going to Paris!" Additionally, the review claimed that the panorama would be especially interesting to the Russian soldiers who had participated in the French Campaign as the circular painting was nothing but a reminder of their generosity, see, "Uveselenija publiki v proshedshem velikom postu," *Otechestvennye zapiski* 1, 1 (1820): 145.

16 "Moskovskie zapiski," *Pribavlenie k Moskovskomu telegrafu* 1, 1 (1825): 6.

17 Laurence Senelick, Peter Bilton et al., eds, *National Theatre in Northern and Eastern Europe, 1746–1900* (Cambridge: Cambridge University Press, 1991), 229.

18 R. M. "Narodnye uveseleniia na Svetloi nedele, v 1834, v Peterburge," *Severnaia pchela*, no. 109 (1834), 434.

19 "Sem' chudes," *Moskovskie vedomosti*, no. 100 (1834), 4744.

20 Zritel' [P. I. Shalikov], "Moskovskie zrelishcha 1835 goda. Stat'ia dlia inogorodnykh," *Moskovskie vedomosti*, no. 11 (1835), 504.

21 "Panorama Konstantinopolia," *Otechestvennye zapiski*: 173.

22 Interestingly, Alexander I's wife, the empress Elizabeth Alexeievna, also had a moving panorama, which was a copy Karl Hampeln's (1794–1880s) 10-meter-long aquatint depicted "The Festival of Ekaterinhof" (Ekateringofskoe gulian'e) she received a gift from the artist who in his turn was granted a gold watch by the empress (S. I. Velikanova, "Novye fakty tvorcheskoi biografii K. K. Gampel'na" in *Russkaia grafika XVIII – pervoi poloviny XIX veka: Novye materialy*, ed. E. I. Gavrilova (Leningrad: Iskusstvo, 1984), 134). Paper panoramas such as these gained popularity in the 1820–30s. They were meant to be demonstrated by means of small oblong wooden boxes with a couple of coils inside. One of the most famous examples of the moving panorama was the 15-meter-long paper ribbon depicting *Nevskii prospekt* engraved after V. S. Sadovnikov's watercolor drawings and released in the first half of the 1830s.

23 "Panorama Konstantinopolia," *Otechestvennye zapiski*: 173–4.

24 A number of panoramic views taken from the observatory tower includes Ottomar Elliger's three views of St. Petersburg (c. 1729), a series of engravings (commonly known as a "panorama") by John Augustus Atkinson (1804, 1806–07), Angelo Toselli's watercolour panorama (1817–20) that was later cut into separate pieces, and the circular panoramas of St. Petersburg by Johann Friedrich Tielker (1805) and Joseph Stöger (1820). Additionally, in 1825, Tielker took a panoramic view of the devastating flood in St. Petersburg (1824) described in A. S. Pushkin's poem "The Bronze Horseman." The last view could have been demonstrated in one of cosmoramas in Moscow in the same year as *Otechestvennye Zapiski* wrote: "one nimble and inventive speculator shows in Moscow a cosmorama of the flood of St. Petersburg — and although this terrible event is depicted very poorly ... it still arouses the curiosity of the Muscovites, etc.," see, "Vypiska iz pis'ma Izdatelja Ot. Zapisok k Redaktoru," *Otechestvennye zapiski* 22, 62 (1825): 443.

25 *Sankt-Peterburgskie vedomosti*, no. 96 (1828), 1352. Also, see, Rossiiskii gosudarstvennyi istoricheskii arkhiv (RGIA) f. 497 (Direktsiia imperatorskikh teatrov MIDv), op. 4, d. 3019, l. 14 (playbill of the Panorama of Constantinople, [January] 1829).

26 *Sankt-Peterburgskie vedomosti*, no. 96 (1828), 1352.

27 On *Otechestvennye zapiski*'s coverage of historical and archeological subjects, see, A. A. Formozov, "Pervyi russkii istoriko-arkheologicheskii zhurnal," *Voprosy istorii*, 4 (1967): 208–12.

28 Irina Kulakova, "Otechestvennyi mechtatel," *Otechestvennye zapiski*, no. 3 (2002): 361–73. Retrieved from http://magazines.russ.ru/oz/2002/3/2002_03_31.html; Oleg Proskurin, "Pervye 'Otechestvennye zapiski', ili O lzhi i patriotizme," *Otechestvennye zapiski*, no. 1 (2001): 270–77. Retrieved from http://magazines.russ.ru/oz/2001/1/pr.html. Also, see, D. P. Lyshchinskaia, "Zhurnal 'Otechestvennye zapiski' P. P. Svin'ina v politicheskom kontekste 1820-kh gg.," *Vestnik RGGU. Seriia "Istoriia. Filologiia. Kul'turologiia. Vostokovedenie"*, 13, 93 (2012); 66–72.

29 On the cooperation between the Third Section and the editor-in-chief of *Severnaia pchela* F. V. Bulgarin, see, A. I. Reitblat, *Faddei Venediktovich Bulgarin: ideolog, zhurnalist, konsul'tant sekretnoi politsii: stat'i i materialy* (Moscow: Novoe literaturnoe obozrenie, 2016), 87–113.

30 Reitblat, *Faddei Venediktovich Bulgarin*, 87–113. Also, see, "Panorama Konstantinopolia," *Otechestvennye zapiski*: 174.

31 "Smes'," *Severnaia pchela*, no. 1 (1829), [3]; RGIA f. 497, op. 4, d. 3019, l. 14.

32 On Burford and his panoramic enterprise, see, Oetterman, *The Panorama*, 113–14, and Richard D. Altick, *The Shows of London: A Panoramic History of Exhibitions, 1600–1862* (Cambridge, Mass., London: Belknap Press of Harvard University Press, 1978), 137–40.

33 "Panorama of Constantinople," *The Gentleman's Magazine* 99 (part 2), 8 (1829): 156. The review in *The Gentleman's Magazine* became one among many anti-Russian articles in the London periodical press of this time. In many respects it was promoted by Klemens Metternich, the Austrian Minister of Foreign Affairs who encouraged Turkish resistance and advocated the creation of the coalition of Austria, Great Britain, Prussia, and France that was to demand that Russia conclude a peace treaty with Turkey. Metternich's anti-Russian articles had been published in many London periodicals including "The Morning Post". Metternich was trying to convince English society that the Russo-Turkish war might lead to serious political turmoil in Europe if the British Empire did not intervene. Metternich's anti-Russian intrigues were met with sympathy in London. See, Sheremet, *Turtsiia i Adrianopol'skii mir*, 72, 79.

34 "Panorama Konstantinopolia," *Severnaia pchela*, [4].

35 "Panorama Konstantinopolia," *Severnaia pchela*, [4]. Emphasis here and below is mine—A. N.

36 "Panorama Konstantinopolia," *Severnaia pchela*, [4],

37 Marshall Poe, "Izobretenie kontseptsii 'Moskva–Tretii Rim'," *Ab Imperio*, 2 (2000): 62, 71; Sergey A. Ivanov, "The Second Rome as Seen by the Third" in *The Reception of Byzantium in European Culture since 1500*, eds. Przemysław Marciniak and Dion C. Smythe (Farnham, Surrey; Burlington, VT: Ashgate, 2015), 58.

38 Ivanov, "The Second Rome," 56–7. Also, see, G. Alef, "The Adoption of the Muscovite Two-headed Eagle: A Discordant View," *Speculum* 41 (1996): 1–20.

39 Andrei Zorin. *Kormia dvuglavogo orla ... Russkaia literatura i gosudarstvennaia ideologiia v poslednei treti XVIII – pervoi treti XIX veka* (Moscow: Novoe literaturnoe obozrenie, 2001), 36.

40 Roman Leibov and Aleksandr Ospovat, "Siuzhet i zhanr stikhotvoreniia Pushkina 'Olegov shchit'," in *Pushkinskie chteniia v Tartu*, vol. 4 (Tartu: Ülikooli Kirjastus, 2007): 72.

41 Leibov and Ospovat, "Siuzhet i zhanr stikhotvoreniia Pushkina," 73–4; see also, A. L. Ospovat, "'Olegov shchit' u Pushkina i Tiutcheva (1829)," in *Tynianovskii sbornik. Tret'i Tynianovskie chteniia*, eds. M. O. Chudakova et al. (Riga: Zinatne, 1988): 61–9.

42 Leibov and Ospovat, "Siuzhet i zhanr stikhotvoreniia Pushkina," 62–3.

43 "Opticheskoe puteshestvie," [1].

44 "Panorama Konstantinopolia," *Otechestvennye zapiski*, 172–3. Nevertheless, just in three weeks after the cited review was published in *Severnaia pchela*, the same newspaper noted that Manzoni's panorama "is at a very low level in terms of art" ("Opticheskoe puteshestvie," *Severnaia pchela*, no. 151 (1828), [1]), Although, in November, *Severnaia pchela* wrote: "The fog covering the mountains is painted masterly and the perspective is represented with the greatest accuracy. Especially the Thracian Bosporus is depicted so naturally that the eyes are deceived," ("Panorama Konstantinopolia," *Severnaia pchela*, [4]) the assessment changed dramatically in mid-December when the newspaper pointed out: "The houses are painted badly, the water at the forefront is neither good, and the figures are not worth a picayune. Shadows are arranged in a wrong way and that is why there is no optical illusion at all. In the panorama of Paris that was exhibited here before it seemed that you saw a city itself while in the panorama of Constantinople you see a poor picture. The only good thing [in it] is the view of the Bosphorus and the mountains on the Asiatic side, so we praised it" ("Opticheskoe puteshestvie," *Severnaia pchela*, no. 151 (1828), [1]).

　　Such a shift in the estimates can be explained by the circumstance that Manzoni's panorama was competing with Joseph Lexa's cosmorama commonly known as "optical journey." The publisher of *Severnaia pchela* was trying to promote Lexa's numerous public exhibitions, so invariably praised his establishment. In particular, the quoted article told about Lexa's new exhibition that consisted of 12 "perspective views" including those of "Seraglio with its surroundings in Constantinople" and "Burning of the Turkish Navy at Navarino" (See, the advertisement of Lexa's cosmorama, *Sankt-Peterburgskie vedomosti*, no. 96 (1828), 1352; no. 97 (1828), 832; no. 98 (1828), 884). Comparison of Manzoni's panorama and Lexa's cosmorama was made, of course, in favor of the latest, although Siberian traveller Basnin preferred the panorama as evidenced by his letter to Irkutsk: "The natural light gives advantage [rather] to the painting, than to the optical travel, but the latter is no less curious due to its depiction of the light of fire and night" (Basnin, "Peterburgskie vpechatleniia," 198).

45 Ostensibly inspired by the Greek Plan, ideas of capturing Constantinople might have another source from the same period, i.e. Muslim legend about the forthcoming defeat of the Ottoman capital that was promoted, in particular, by one of Catherine II's envoys. This text was first published in Russian in 1789 and remained popular in the early nineteenth century as proved by the publication of a number of later editions (Taki. *Tsar' i sultan*, 111). The newly resurrected

Byzantium-related myths were part of the context in which P. Ia. Chaadaev composed an early philosophical letter that contained the following passage: "Driven by a baneful fate, we turned to Byzantium, wretched and despised by nations for a moral code that was to become the basis of our education" (see, P. Ia. Chaadaev, Philosophical Letters and Apology of a Madman, trans. and introduced by Mary-Barbara Zeldin (Knoxville: Univ. of Tennessee Press, 1969), 42; quoted after Ivanov, "The Second Rome," 59.) Although the letter was published only in 1836, it is known that it was written between 1828–30.

46 Sheremet, *Turtsiia i Adrianopol'skii mir*, 60.

4 Chinese roads in the Russian imagination and in reality

The 1870s as a decade of discovery

Ilya Vinkovetsky

Chinese tea bound for Kiakhta is not sewn into hides, but simply wrapped in felts made of camel or sheep fur. Packed in this fashion, the tea chest is loaded onto the humped back of a camel and makes its way to the town of Maimachin [Maimaicheng]—travelling from southern China to Mongolia, then across all of Mongolia through its endless Gobi Desert, and finally arriving at Maimachin on the Russian border. Shipping tea on camels involves a good deal of fuss for the Chinese. Each camel can only carry between two and four chests. Consequently, around 500 or even 1000 camels are required for a reasonable shipment.[1]

This is a quotation from Dmitrii Ivanovich Stakheev's 1870 work entitled *From China to Moscow: The Story of a Tea Chest*. Stakheev was a well-known St. Petersburg journalist and his readers in the Russian Empire of the third quarter of the nineteenth century—at least many of them, including his editors—did not question the suggestion of thousands of camels descending on China's tea growing regions. The section of Stakheev's popular short book dealing with the transport of tea across China immediately followed the chapter in which he discussed how the tea is grown, gathered, and prepared. In this manner, a clear impression was created that all the way from the tea estate to the Russian border the tea was transported exclusively on camels. Never mind the fact that, as the account proceeded, with one notable exception, Stakheev's examples of the problems associated with camel travel came almost exclusively from the Gobi Desert of Mongolia.[2] Thus, Stakheev's book, which claimed to present an accurate account of the way that tea was shipped from its point of origin in China to the consumer market in European Russia, painted a picture of a robust camel transportation network spanning across all of Mongolia and much of China—literally from the edge of Siberia across the Gobi Desert and China's varied topography and climatic regions from the north to the south.

This picture is incorrect. For today's historian of Eurasian mobility, the suggestion of thousands of camels descending on the tea regions of southern China raises red flags.[3] But, perhaps more productively, it also raises questions about the depth of knowledge that even educated Russians had of the interior of China at the time of the publication of Stakheev's book—in 1870, a good decade after the signing of the Treaties of Tianjin (1858) and Beijing (1860) that allowed the Russians entry into China.[4]

Accurate knowledge about the interior of China remained hard to come by for Russians in the years prior to the 1870s. With that absence of specificity in mind, we can see why scholarly literature on mid-nineteenth century Russian views of China deals mainly with general cultural perceptions.[5] Russian intellectuals viewed through a fog of cultural difference and abstraction much of the part of "the East" that was outside of their imperial realm, the closed interior of China very much included. In other words, as was the case with other Europeans, in viewing the unfamiliar zones of China and other East Asian lands, the Russians were prone to Orientalist biases and misconceptions.[6] Yet even as they remained largely in the grip of Orientalist frameworks, Russia's scholars, inspired by both imperial ambitions and scientific curiosity, introduced and elaborated an increasingly sophisticated apparatus for exploring this unfamiliar East, resulting eventually in a new branch of knowledge (*Vostokovedenie*—"Orientology" or "Oriental Studies").[7] Still, as the 1870s began, the Russians had little practical knowledge of China's vast transportation network, which until the 1860s had been entirely closed to them.

Stakheev's China

Dmitrii Stakheev (1840–1918) had never been inside China proper, but he had seen it. That is because his account was based on his personal experience of working for a few years in the late 1850s as a clerk for his father's tea trading company in Kiakhta, where, as part of his responsibilities, he negotiated and socialized with Chinese merchants and their agents living in the adjacent settlement of Maimaicheng, located just across the border from Kiakhta.[8] A small, purpose-built merchant town, Kiakhta had been the primary, and at times the only, point of trade interaction between China and Russia for more than a century.[9] The lucrative China-Russia trade conducted there attracted some of Russia's most prominent merchants. Hailing from the town of Elabuga, Stakheev was a son of one of the wealthiest merchants of the Volga-Kama region, who had sent him to Kiakhta to learn the family trade.[10]

However, just at the time when Stakheev was working there, the Kiakhta trade was about to go into permanent decline. So, as a young man, he had an opportunity to witness a disappearing world. While interacting with the Chinese, who invited him to a specially designated area to negotiate trade deals, Stakheev saw the camel caravans arrive in Maimaicheng.[11]

The stories of how they got there, however, came from his Chinese interlocutors. We do not know how much these interlocutors, usually communicating with the Russians by means of the so-called Kiakhta pidgin, embellished their stories, or whether they tried to mislead their inquisitive Russian questioner, perhaps to conceal trade secrets.[12] Much could have been lost simply as a matter of routine miscommunication. In any event, it would *seem* that Chinese merchants in Maimaicheng, who invariably belonged to the Shanxi commercial league, would have had greater incentive to conceal the details of their trade from the Russians in Kiakhta—with whom they were constantly negotiating the price of tea—than to disclose them.[13] Stakheev included some of the tales his interlocutors conveyed about the transportation of tea across China in his story. This technique is in contrast to Stakheev's account of how tea was cultivated—that text he simply lifted almost word-for-word from a well-known book by Father Iakinf (Nikita Iakovlevich Bichurin).[14] Justifying this inclusion, Stakheev claimed that the veracity of Iakinf's account was confirmed by a "Chinese acquaintance" of his at Maimaicheng/Kiakhta.[15] But we should bear in mind that Iakinf was confined during his time in China (1807–1820) to Beijing, and had not visited the tea growing regions: his information came strictly from books.[16] Thus, despite centuries of trade relations and diplomatic exchanges, as well as the presence of the Russian Orthodox Spiritual Mission in Beijing, the information about basic facts of daily life in Qing China that even the most curious and knowledgeable Russians possessed by 1870 was predominantly second-hand and often misleading—or downright wrong.[17] Stakheev, writing his book from memory and from the distance of St. Petersburg, had limited material to work with.

Boots on the ground

Keeping this dearth of basic knowledge in mind allows us to appreciate the significance of published geographical accounts by Russian travelers through China in the 1870s. These travelers, after all, provided first-hand information. One of them, the merchant N. F. Veselkov, simply described a route through Mongolia.[18] The Imperial Russian Geographical Society (RGS) found even Veselkov's brief, technical, and dry report worthy of publication.[19]

Archimandrite Palladii, a well-known ecclesiastic official with Russia's Beijing Spiritual Mission, published his 1870 observations on the route from Beijing to Blagoveshchensk, across Manchuria.[20] In comparison to Veselkov's sparse account, Palladii's report, which was apparently explicitly solicited by the Geographical Society, was relatively detailed and gossipy. The scholarly Palladii, whose secular name was Petr Ivanovich Kafarov, mentioned the special permission he had to obtain from the Chinese government to make the travels.[21] He also noted that Chinese authorities seemed visibly suspicious of his motives for making the journey.[22] He discussed, among other details, the receptions he was treated to along the way.

P. F. Unterberg's and Z. L. Matusovskii's travel accounts—both based on travels in the same year of 1875—are distinguishable from Palladii's and Veselkov's by the authors' penetration deeper south into China proper.[23] Unterberg's account covered the route from Tianjin to Zhenjiang, and included a detailed discussion of travel along (and beside) the Imperial Canal. Unterberg was traveling a well-trodden trade and provisioning route between northern and central China.[24] This was the same route that carried some of the Russia-bound tea, albeit in the opposite direction. Of course, that Russia-bound tea was but a miniscule fraction of the intra-Chinese trade that was facilitated by this route, which connected China's major population centers and agricultural areas of the north and south.

An accomplished military cartographer and topographer, Matusovskii[25] took as his point of departure the Yangtze River port city of Hankou, a pivotal location for China's tea trade with Russia.[26] His account traced a section of a route northward up the Han River (as far as Hanzhong, a town in the Shaanxi province) and thus described a crucial leg of a route by way of which a large proportion of Russia-bound tea had traveled on the way from Hankou to Kiakhta.[27] The irony was that, even within the category of tea that was still shipped continentally in the mid-1870s, this route for transporting tea had been largely abandoned and replaced by a new route less than ten years earlier.[28] Thus the Russian reading public did not see a description of this, previously essential, route for transporting Chinese tea to Kiakhta until after its commercial relevance had passed.

First-hand observations

What stands out from the travel accounts of these Russians, all published in the periodical publications of the RGS, is their emphasis on the practical and the particular. They read like spy accounts—which, in a real sense, they were. These were essentially intelligence reports of commercial and military importance, Unterberg's and Matusovskii's work more explicitly so than Veselkov's and Palladii's.[29] To illustrate the point, Unterberg surreptitiously (and later openly) measured distances throughout the route, while also making important side notes.[30] He was working toward, in short, producing an annotated map. A map of this sort could potentially facilitate future imperial activity.[31]

The timing of the opening of China's interior to Russian travelers coincided with another development: It was during the decade of the 1870s, as the historian Claudia Weiss has shown in her study of the role of the RGS in Russia's imperial appropriation of Siberia, that academic geography made significant strides in the Russian Empire as a discipline.[32] From this perspective, the attention to the links between Siberia and China took on a more scholarly as well as practical veneer. All four accounts showed a specific concern with transportation connections to the Russian Empire: Veselkov and Palladii documented roads that provided gateways from Russia to China, whereas Unterberg and Matusovskii demystified China's vital internal commercial routes. As he carried out that task, Matusovskii also documented the path from Hankou all the way to Russian-controlled Central Asia.[33] They paid particular attention to the material conditions of the roads and waterways and the surrounding terrain. They documented, more or less systematically, the modes and networks of China's transportation infrastructure—the variety of people, animals, carts, and vessels in use—as well as the lodgings and the amenities along the routes.

The local cultural attitudes that they highlighted were those concerned with Chinese views of Europeans in general and Russians in particular. These accounts convey a strong sense of the stark separateness of European and Chinese spheres. For example, we learn from Palladii that "all Europeans" customarily stopped in the same location [*Davan miao*] on the way between Tianjin and Beijing, because it is "the most comfortable and best edifice."[34] Unterberg's observation was more jarring: The Chinese, Unterberg related, consider the European "a foreign devil" [*zamorskii chërt*] [35] and "the European is despised everywhere in China, and even if the outward relations of the Chinese to us assume not only a polite, but even a friendly character, that is in most cases only for the sake of some common interests. In his soul the Chinese hates the European, fully realizing that, under the guise of bringing civilization, the latter aims only to exploit the country.... With this in mind, in the cities and the settlements we were not allowed, for example, into the best hotels, so that their reputations are not compromised."[36] "The further inside the country we moved," Unterberg continued, "the harder it was for us to find lodging."[37] Thus, we can see that, in Unterberg's perception at least, the Chinese people he encountered in his travels viewed the Russians as they did Europeans in general.[38] The lumping of the Russians with the other Europeans by the Chinese indicated by Unterberg's observations contradicted the notion, articulated by some Russians, that their relationship with the Chinese was fundamentally different from that of other Europeans.[39]

After Unterberg's party boarded an American steamship that sailed on the Yangtze between Hankou and Shanghai, he contrasted its comfort to the discomfort of the Chinese vessel they had left and the filth of the Chinese hotels where they had stayed.[40] (Here it should be remembered that they were not let into the more reputable Chinese hotels, according to Unterberg's own account.) These kinds of comments involving hygiene, cleanliness, and comfort, and highlighting the cultural distance between the European Russians and the Chinese, echo numerous other similar comments made by various European travelers seeped in the same cultural milieu and are thus hardly original.[41]

Qing transportation networks through Russian eyes

The Russian authors' specific observations on transportation infrastructure and networks, although they may appear on first sight dry, technical, or mundane, are actually more interesting and revealing. These early travel accounts provide varied data and corresponding cultural observations. For example, Unterberg related how, when his party switched from a land-based to a waterborne mode of transportation (from mule-driven carts to a Chinese vessel on the Imperial Canal), transferring the freight from the carts to the boat required hiring a different set of workers. "Our carters, even though we offered to pay them a special bonus, did not agree [to make the transfer of goods] because they feared reprisals from the specialized loaders [*arteli nosil'shchikov*]." Making note of this, Unterberg observed that "the differentiation of labor constitutes an important characteristic of Chinese social life."[42]

Unterberg and Matusovskii both documented the presence of human boat haulers—on the Imperial Canal, in Unterberg's case; on the Han River, in Matusovkii's.[43] The description that Unterberg provided is strikingly emotional in tone. On the Imperial Canal, Unterberg noted, "[t]he most depressing and difficult impression was always made by the boats or junks pulled by rope, sometimes by 10 to 20 people. Bending and straining exhaustively, these Chinese boat haulers [*burlaki*] walk at a measured pace along the shore, singing a sad boat hauler song ... another company [*artel'*] of sailors helps them with oars."[44] Such a sight, of course, would not have been out of place on Russia's Volga River; the Chinese boat haulers made an evident impression on Russian observers but they did not compare the Chinese haulers to the Russian ones.[45]

Matusovskii made particular note of his travel along land routes on which animals were not to be seen (or were seen very rarely)—and human haulers took their place. In one instance, for seventeen days, he wrote, "we were compelled to travel here by a native method [*po tuzemnomu sposobu*], that is, with the use of haulers [*nosil'shchikov*] and on foot. The absence of pack animals [*v'iuchnykh zhivotnykh*] in this area is explained first of all by the absence of feed grasses... the surplus of human population naturally causes great availability of labor, and in that way people, for the sake of their survival, become competitors of animal labor. That is the reason that a traveler in many Chinese locales does not see roads suitable for wheeled traffic even in places where... they could theoretically exist."[46] Like Unterberg, Matusovskii repeatedly commented on the varieties of labor involved in travel and transport.

Numerous other observations on both technical and cultural matters mark these travel accounts. Road conditions were a common preoccupation: "Improvement of Chinese roads is almost never undertaken, and as the majority of them are dirt roads, it is not difficult to imagine their condition after several days of rain," Unterberg complained and equated riding on these roads in a cart to "torture" [*pytka*].[47] In contrast, he had high praise for the animal pulling the cart: Unterberg praised the mule as the essential, indeed "invaluable," animal for traveling China's roads and transporting freight, noting that animal's phenomenal endurance, strength, and flexibility.[48] Mules he found much better suited to the conditions of the route he described than horses, which he also saw used.[49] Unterberg also paid attention to the people: "Our drivers [of the carts pulled by mules] were Chinese Tatars [*kitaiskie tatary*], who dominate the carting trade [*izvoznyi promysel*] in northern China."[50] Matusovskii saw China's actual tea plantations and described their layout.[51] As we have already seen, he and the other travelers paid attention to the infrastructure of tea transport.[52] These are just a sample of the observations on travel networks and modes of transportation in the accounts. Taken together, they provided the Russian reading public with a much more detailed and sophisticated picture of transportation within China.[53] This resulting picture hints at the motives of the RGS for publishing these travel accounts.

Geographical imperialism

To be sure, details of tea manufacture and transport were not the RGS's main concern. But the transportation infrastructure of China as a whole was of considerable interest. And this interest was shared by Russia's military planners: as the historian David Schimmelpenninck van der Oye reminds us, the RGS had many military and naval officers among its senior members, and "much like the geographical societies that had been founded in the West somewhat earlier, its curiosity was more than purely academic."[54] Like these other geographical societies, the RGS lent a veneer of scientific legitimacy to projects of military surveillance. This motive was demonstrated most clearly in the case of its sponsorship of an 1870s traveler who has not been covered in this essay—namely Nikolai Mikhailovich Przheval'skii.[55] Przheval'skii's four lengthy expeditions through the Chinese Empire, beginning in 1870 and ending in the mid-1880s, have attracted considerably more popular and scholarly attention than the travel notes of Matusovskii and Unterberg. Then again, besides being a particularly energetic explorer, Przheval'skii was a prolific writer, an ardent self-promoter, and an outspoken imperialist.[56] Scholars may debate the implications of Przheval'skii's aspirations (he advocated an aggressive program of expansion that was perhaps beyond Russia's reach—a posture that, in the view of some, encouraged posturing that eventually led to the debacle of the Russo-Japanese War) but what is important here is that, like that of Russia's other explorers of the Qing Empire in the 1870s, Przheval'skii's case demonstrated just how little the Russians really knew of China's interior.[57]

Conclusion

Had Dmitrii Stakheev, himself a collaborator of the RGS, published his *Story of a Tea Chest* just a few years later, he would have had to revise and upgrade his account of how tea made its way through China to the Russian border.[58] Tea was transported across China in a myriad of ways, with human haulers, boats, horses, oxen, vessels of various kinds, boat haulers, sailors, packers, loaders, carters, and other human and animal actors playing roles along the routes before the tea arrived in northern China where the camel caravans took their turn. But in 1870, the Russians knew precious little about the manufacture and transport of a drink that was already so integral to their culture.[59] The colonial origins of the ever familiar and popular Russian *chai* were, as a well-worn Orientalist phrase would have it, shrouded in mystery.

Similar ignorance had long prevailed among the British: indeed, until Robert Fortune's spying forays into China's interior in the 1840s, educated Europeans of all nationalities assumed that green and black tea came from different plants.[60] While large parts of China remained off limits to foreigners, Chinese merchants were able to keep such knowledge from them. Even after the Qing Empire was forced to open its ports and provide maps to outsiders, it took the Russians some time to get oriented, especially outside the port cities and the capital. The 1870s became a time when they began to fill in some of the sizable blanks in their knowledge. The Imperial Russian Geographical Society eagerly publicized the discoveries and made it possible for ordinary Russians to acquire a more accurate picture about how a drink many of them imbibed on a daily basis wound up in their samovars and cups. But even after these publications, the Russians' knowledge of interior China remained sparse and superficial. Writing in the late 1880s, Matusovskii noted that the Russian state still had no adequate [*udovletvoritel'nye*] maps of the southern half of China.[61] Russian imagination was still catching up to Chinese reality.

Notes

1 *I am grateful to Jeremy Brown, Yuexin Rachel Lin, and the editors of this volume for useful suggestions and advice and to Irina Lukka of the Finnish National Library for bibliographic help.

    D. S. Stakheev, *Ot Kitaia do Moskvy: Istoriia iashchika chaiu* (St. Petersburg: Izdanie knigoprodavtsa M. O. Vol'fa, 1870), 14–15.

2 Stakheev, *Ot Kitaia do Moskvy*, 15–18.

3 As a general rule, camel caravans operated in the area north of Beijing, although they ventured farther south as well. See Martha Avery, *The Tea Road: China and Russia meet across the Steppe* (Beijing: China Intercontinental Press, 2003), 69. Camels were particularly well adapted to crossing the Gobi, although oxcarts were also used there; see Robert Gardella, *Harvesting Mountains: Fujian and the China Tea Trade, 1757–1937* (Berkeley: University of California Press, 1994), 38–9.

4 On the treaties and the world they created, see Robert Nield, *China's Foreign Places: The Foreign Presence in China in the Treaty Port Era, 1840–1943* (Hong Kong: Hong Kong University Press, 2015).

5 On Russian views of China, see Susanna Soojung Lim, *China and Japan in the Russian Imagination, 1685–1922: To the Ends of the Orient* (New York: Routledge, 2013).

6 On Russian Orientalism, see David Schimmelpenninck van der Oye, *Russian Orientalism: Asia in the Russian Mind from Peter the Great to the Emigration* (New Haven: Yale University Press, 2010).

7 On this development, see Schimmelpenninck, *Russian Orientalism*, 153–98, and Vera Tolz, *Russia's Own Orient: The Politics of Identity and Oriental Studies in the Late Imperial and Early Soviet Periods* (New York: Oxford University Press, 2011).

8 For a brief description of Maimaicheng (literally, "buy-sell city" or "city of commerce") in the late eighteenth/early nineteenth century, see Clifford M. Foust, *Muscovite and Mandarin: Russia's Trade with China and Its Setting, 1727–1805* (Chapel Hill: University of North Carolina Press, 1969), 92–5. Using the Wade-Giles transliteration system, Foust renders this settlement's name as "Mai-mai-ch'eng."

9 Following the termination of Russian caravan traffic after the Kiakhta treaty of 1727, legal trade between the Chinese and Russian empires was restricted to this one border crossing, where both Qing and Russian government officials regulated it. On the so-called Kiakhta system that developed there, see Mark Mancall, "The Kiakhta Trade," in *The Economic Development of China and Japan: Studies in Economic History and Political Economy*, ed. C. D. Rowan (New York: Praeger, 1964), 20.

10 For more on the Stakheev family, see I. V. Maslova, *Kupecheskaia dinastiia Stakheevykh* (Elabuga: Izdatel'stvo EGPU, 2017).

11 The Chinese merchants were forbidden (by the Chinese government) to enter Russia: the Russian merchants negotiating with them crossed the border from

Kiakhta to Maimaicheng: M. I. Sladkovskii, *Istoriia torgovo-ekonomicheskikh otnoshenii narodov Rossii s Kitaem (do 1917 g.)* (Moscow: Nauka, 1974), 168–9.

12 In a different work, Stakheev wrote that the Chinese merchants at Maimaicheng often deliberately coordinated misinformation with the intent of gaining advantage over the Russians: Stakheev, "Kiakhta," in *Zhivopisnaia Rossiia: Otechestvo nashe v ego zemel'nom, istoricheskom, plemennom, ekonomicheskom i bytovom zhnachenii*, ed. P. P. Semenov (St. Petersburg: Izdatel'stvo M. O. Vol'f, 1895), vol. 12, part 1, 176.

13 On the Shanxi commercial league, see Cho-yun Hsu, *China: A Cultural History*, trans. Timothy D. Baker and Michael S. Duke (New York: Columbia University Press, 2012), 473–74; Avery, *Tea Road*, 53, 64–5; A. P. Subbotin, ed., *Chai i chainaia torgovlia v Rossii i drugikh gosudarstvakh. Proizvodstvo, potreblenie i raspredelenie chaia* (St. Petersburg: Tipografiia Severnago Telegrafnago Agentstva, 1892), 343. The Shanxi league insisted that in their dealings with the Russians in Kiakhta all the Chinese merchants adhere to a set of specific rules: Sladkovskii, *Istoriia torgovo-ekonomicheskikh otnoshenii*, 196.

14 Iakinf Bichurin, *Statisticheskoe opisanie Kitaiskoi imperii*, vol. 2 (St. Petersburg: Tipografiia Eduarda Pratsa, 1842).

15 Stakheev, *Ot Kitaia do Moskvy*, 7.

16 For more on Bichurin, see Susanna Soojung Lim, *China and Japan in the Russian Imagination, 1685–1922: To the Ends of the Orient* (New York: Routledge, 2013), 64–6; and Nikolay Samoylov, "Russian-Chinese Cultural Exchanges in the Early Modern Period: Missionaries, Sinologists, and Artists," in *Reshaping the Boundaries: The Christian Intersection of China and the West in the Modern Era*, ed. Gang Song (Hong Kong: Hong Kong University Press, 2016), 35–47, esp. 40–43.

17 One small group of Russians knew more about China's interior than the others: the handful of Russian tea merchants who had just recently—in the 1860s—established tea factories in Hankou with smaller branches in Fuzhou and Jiujiang; Chinyun Lee, "From Kiachta to Vladivostok: Russian Merchants and the Tea Trade," *Region* 3: 2 (2014), 195–218, see 199. But, mindful of the commercial advantage of their firms, they apparently preferred to keep their knowledge discreet.

18 "Zametki minusinskago kuptsa N. F. Veselkova na puti iz Dzinzilika v Irkutsk," *Izvestiia Imperatarskago Russkago Geograficheskago Obshchestva*, 9: 5 (1873), 157–62. Dzindzilik was a military station.

19 On the establishment and activity of the Imperial Russian Geographical Society, see Nathaniel Knight, "Science, Empire and Nationality: Ethnography in the Russian Geographical Society, 1845–1855," in Jane Burbank and David Ransel, eds., *Imperial Russia: New Histories for the Empire* (Bloomington: Indiana University Press, 1998), 108–41 and Mark Bassin, "The Russian Geographical Society, the 'Amur Epoch,' and the Great Siberian Expedition, 1855–1863," *Annals of the Association of American Geographers*, 73: 2 (1983), 240–56.

20 "Dorozhnyia zametki na puti ot Pekina do Blagoveshchenska, chrez Man'chzhuriiu, v 1870 godu, Arkhimandrita Palladiia," *Zapiski Imperatarskago Russkago Geograficheskago Obshchestva, po obshchei geografii*, vol. 4 (St. Petersburg: Tip. V. Bezobrazova i Kom., 1871), 329–463.

21 A native of the Chistopol' *uezd* in Kazan' province, Petr Ivanovich Kafarov, aka Palladii (1817–1878), was trained at the Kazan' seminary before he transferred to the Moscow Religious Academy. After receiving training in Chinese language from Bichurin and another teacher, he first made his way to Beijing in 1840 and lived there intermittently for over thirty years. Building on his training and experience, he became one of Russia's most prominent Sinologists. An author of several publications dealing with China, he also compiled a Russian-Chinese dictionary, which was finished by another expert after Palladii's death.

22 Many Chinese officials and scholars perceived foreigners who came to study China's geography as facilitators of potential imperial aggression; see Yen-P'ing

Hao and Erh-min Wang. "Changing Chinese Views of Western Relations, 1840–95," in *The Cambridge History of China*, eds., John K. Fairbank and Kwang-Ching Liu, 11: 142–201 (Cambridge: Cambridge University Press, 1980), 176.

23 P. F. Unterberg, "Ocherk puti ot g. T'ian'-Tszina do g. Chzhen'-Tzian" v Kitae," *Zapiski Imperatarskago Russkago Geograficheskago Obshchestva, po obshchei geografii,* vol. 11 (St. Petersburg: 1886), 1–58; Z. Matusovskii, "Kratkii topograficheskii ocherk puti, proidennogo russkoi ekspeditsiei po Kitiau v 1875 godu ot g. Khan'-kou do Zaisanskogo posta," *Zapiski Imperatarskago Russkago Geograficheskago Obshchestva, po obshchei geografii,* vol. 8 (St. Petersburg: Tipografiia Imperatorskoi Akademii Nauk, 1879), 249–74. At the time, Zaisan (Zaysan) was a border post settlement of the Russian Empire; its present location is in eastern Kazakhstan.

24 Unterberg spent almost a year in 1875–1876 travelling in a loop: from Irkutsk to Kiakhta, then across the Gobi to Kalgan (Zhangjiakou), Tianjin, Shanghai, and Hong Kong—and back again through the ports of China and Beijing, before travelling to Japan and from there back to Russia (Unterberg, "Ocherk puti," 1). The published account of the route in *Notes of the Imperial Russian Geographical Society* cited here covers only a fraction of these travels.

25 Zinovii Lavrovich Matusovskii (1842–1904) would become a more prominent figure in later years as one of Russia's leading experts on China's geography. His magnum opus would be Z. L. Matusovskii, *Geograficheskoe obozrenie Kitaiskoi imperii* (St. Petersburg: Imperatorskaia Akademiia nauk, 1888), a work of compilation that combined the geographical knowledge of Russian and European observers.

26 Hankou was an important gathering place for Russia-bound tea via the continental route to Kiakhta and became even more pivotal as the key port for the then-emerging maritime route. On this maritime route, the tea would be shipped directly from Hankou to Odessa, via the Suez Canal (Subbotin, *Chai i chainaia torgovlia,* 346). On Hankou's commercial significance, see William T. Rowe, *Hankow: Commerce and Society in a Chinese City, 1796–1889* (Stanford: Stanford University Press, 1984).

27 The Han River, as Matusovskii noted, in places had a rather strong current (Matusovskii, "Kratkii topograficheskii ocherk," 257).

28 Lee, "From Kiachta to Vladivostok," 204.

29 On Russian intelligence on the Qing at an earlier time, see Gregory Afinogenov, *The Eye of the Tsar: Intelligence-Gathering and Geopolitics in Eighteenth-Century Eurasia* (Ph.D. diss., Harvard University, 2016).

30 Unterberg, "Ocherk puti," 17–18.

31 On the connection between cartography produced by post-Beijing Treaty Russian scientific and military expeditions into China and imperial expansion, see Victor Zatsepine, *Beyond the Amur: Frontier Encounters between China and Russia, 1850–1930* (Vancouver: UBC Press, 2017), 74–80.

32 Claudia Weiss, *Wie Sibirien 'unser' wurde: Die Russische Geographische Gesellschaft und ihr Einfluss auf die Bilder und Vorstellungen von Sibirien im 19. Jahrhundert* (Göttingen: V & R unipress, 2007), 147–87.

33 Matusovskii conducted his work as part of a larger Russian expedition that was tasked with studying eastern and central China as well as western Mongolia. The participants were instructed to research the commercial and geographical aspects of these regions, with an eye to military relevance: E. V. Boikova, *Rossiiskie voennye issledovateli Mongolii (vtoraia polovina XIX – nachalo XX veka)* (Moscow: Institut vostokovedeniia RAN, 2014), 116–17.

34 "Dorozhnyia zametki," 334.

35 Unterberg, "Ocherk puti," 27.

36 Unterberg, "Ocherk puti," 30–31.

37 Unterberg, "Ocherk puti," 31.

38 Some Chinese prejudices about Europeans are presented in Yen-P'ing Hao and Erh-min Wang, "Changing Chinese Views of Western Relations," 178–9.

39 On Russian nationalist visions of Asia and the Asians, see Mark Bassin, *Imperial Visions: Nationalist Imagination and Geographical Expansion in the Russian Far East, 1840–1865* (Cambridge: Cambridge University Press, 1999), 45–57.
40 Unterberg, "Ocherk puti," 52.
41 On attitudes of European travelers in the colonial world, see Mary Louise Pratt, *Imperial Eyes: Travel Writing and Transculturation*, 2nd edn (New York: Routledge, 2007).
42 Unterberg, "Ocherk puti," 43–4.
43 Unterberg, "Ocherk puti," 46; Matusovskii, "Kratkii topograficheskii ocherk," 256–7.
44 Unterberg, "Ocherk puti," 46.
45 On the boat haulers in Russia, see F. N. Rodin, *Burlachestvo v Rossii* (Moscow: Mysl', 1975).
46 Matusovskii, "Kratkii topograficheskii ocherk," 252–3.
47 Unterberg, "Ocherk puti," 16.
48 Unterberg, "Ocherk puti," 15.
49 Unterberg, "Ocherk puti," 15.
50 Unterberg, "Ocherk puti," 16.
51 Matusovskii, "Kratkii topograficheskii ocherk," 254.
52 Palladii, for example, made specific notes on tea transportation in "Dorozhnyia zametki," 334.
53 Looking at a very different situation, the historian Eileen Kane has discussed how a similar effect of creating a comprehensive geography of another foreign region—in that case, the Arabian Peninsula—was produced by a compilation of published travel narratives composed by Muslim hajj travelers of the Russian Empire: see Eileen Kane, *Russian Hajj: Empire and the Pilgrimage to Mecca* (Ithaca, NY: Cornell University Press, 2015), 47–85.
54 Schimmelpenninck, "Reforming Military Intelligence," in *Reforming the Tsar's Army: Military Innovation in Imperial Russia from Peter the Great to the Revolution*, eds., David Schimmelpenninck van der Oye and Bruce W. Menning (New York: Cambridge University Press, 2004), 143–4.
55 Richard Wortman, "Russian Noble Officers and the Ethos of Exploration," in Wortman, *Visual Texts, Ceremonial Texts, Texts of Exploration: Collected Articles on the Representation of Russian Monarchy* (Brighton, Mass.: Academic Studies Press, 2013), 290.
56 On Przheval'skii and his aspirations, see Daniel Brower, "Imperial Russia and Its Orient: The Renown of Nikolai Przhevalsky," *The Russian Review* 53: 3 (1994), 367–81; and Karl E. Meyer and Shareen Blair Brysac, *Tournament of Shadows: The Great Game and the Race for Empire in Central Asia* (New York: Basic Books, 1999), 224–40, and Wortman, "Russian Noble Officers," 292.
57 On the implications of Przheval'skii's reckless ambition, see David Schimmelpenninck van der Oye, *Toward the Rising Sun: Russian Ideologies of Empire and the Path to War with Japan* (DeKalb: Northern Illinois University Press, 2006), 40–1.
58 Stakheev became a member of the RGS in 1869, apparently largely on the merits of his amateur ethnographic works on eastern Siberia: M. N. Nikol'skii, "Biografiia D. I. Stakheeva," in *Sobranie sochninenii D. I. Stakheeva* (St. Petersburg: Tovarishchestvo M. O. Vol'f, 1902), vol. 1, p. ix.
59 For a cultural history of tea in the Russian Empire, see Audra Yoder, "Tea Time in Romanov Russia: A Cultural History, 1616–1917," (Ph.D. diss., University of North Carolina, Chapel Hill, 2016).
60 See Sarah Rose, *For All the Tea in China: How England Stole the World's Favorite Drink and Changed History* (London: Penguin, 2010), 88–9 and Alistair Watt, *Robert Fortune: A Plant Hunter in the Orient* (London: Kew Publishing, 2017), 254–5. Fortune was not the discoverer that these biographers claim, based on his 1843 observations publicized in Robert Fortune, *Three Years' Wanderings in the*

Northern Provinces of China (London: John Murray, 1847), 198–200, 218. There were apparently British specialists who had knowledge that green and black tea could be produced from the same plants for some years prior to Fortune's publication but that knowledge was not widely circulated; on that knowledge, which dated from perhaps the 1810s, see Samuel Ball, *An Account of the Cultivation and Manufacture of Tea in China* (London: Longmans, Brown, Green and Longmans, 1848), 147. And yet, even if we accept the 1810s as the decade when this knowledge was revealed to the Europeans, this was still more than a century and a half after tea appeared in Europe; all this time eminent European botanists remained in the dark. That said, by the 1870s, the British, with their tea plantations in India, were well ahead of the Russians in terms of overall knowledge about tea production. See Jayeeta Sharma, *Empire's Garden: Assam and the Making of India* (Durham: Duke University Press, 2011) and Erika Rappaport, *A Thirst for Empire: How Tea Shaped the Modern World* (Princeton: Princeton University Press, 2017), 85–119.

61 Matusovskii, *Geograficheskoe obozrenie*, p. II.

Part II

Interactions

5 Captivity and empire

Central Asia in nineteenth-century Russian captivity narratives

Yuan Gao

In 1876, *Russkii invalid*, the official newspaper of the Ministry of War of the Russian Empire, published an article about Foma Danilov, a Russian soldier from the Turkestan Infantry Battalion. As this article recorded, Danilov was captured in the Fergana valley in 1875 by the Qipchaq leader Pulat-Khan during General Mikhail Skobelev's conquest of the Kokand Khanate. Pulat-Khan was so savage that "slaughtering people, like slaughtering sheep, gave him great pleasure." He threatened Danilov and promised wealth to him if he would be willing to convert to Islam, while the Russian solider answered: "I was born with this faith, and I will die with it; I swore an oath to my tsar and I will never betray him." He was then seriously wounded by shooting and suffered torture until he died. The "natives" (*tuzemtsy*) then commented on his heroic death: "This Russian soldier died like a *bogatyr* (an epic hero)."[1]

Fyodor Dostoyevsky read this newspaper article and was deeply impressed by this episode from Russia's military campaigns in Central Asia. In the 1877 issue of *A Writer's Diary*, he enthusiastically discussed the significance of Danilov's heroic martyrdom. As Dostoyevsky elaborated, this Russian soldier represented "the genuine image of the whole of our People's Russia," where there was "no falsity, no compromise with the conscience," but "only an astounding, primitive, elemental honesty." He further asserted that "the people have Foma Danilovs by the thousands." He saw in Danilov "one of the most ordinary and unremarkable representatives of the Russian People," the universal greatness of Russian spirit.[2] Later, Dostoyevsky incorporated this incident into his novel *The Brothers Karamazov*: Smerdiakov and Fedor Karamazov's religious servant Grigory discuss how a Russian soldier was captured by "Asians" and "flayed alive." They then debate for a long time about how a Russian is supposed to behave among Asian captors. This disputation reflects one of the central themes that Dostoyevsky intended to represent in his last novel—as Joseph Frank notes, it is faith as "the irrational core of the Christian commitment" that was "posed centrally in Russian culture."[3]

In both cases, captivity appeared to be an important theme in the imagining of Asian civilizations and Russian identity in nineteenth-century Russian culture. In the newspaper article, by attributing the collection of materials about Foma Danilov to the military commander Skobelev, who had already completed the annexation of Kokand and captured Pulat-Khan when the article was published, Russia's accomplished conquest of Kokand was justified and celebrated. The Khan's brutality exaggerated the threat of Skobelev's adversary in this expedition, while the indigenous people's appreciation of Danilov as a *bogatyr* implied a certain acceptance of Russia's presence. In Dostoyevsky's incorporation of Danilov's captivity, in order to highlight the universal and unshakable faith that is deeply embedded in the Russian people, the brutality of the "Asian" captors was exaggerated (Danilov was executed by shooting; Dostoyevsky's Russian soldier is "flayed alive" by the "Asians"), while the historical context is blurred (the captive and the captors are nameless in Dostoyevsky's story). By contrasting the captors' atrocities and the captive's heroic martyrdom, Dostoyevsky turned the captivity story into a symbol of the fundamental dichotomy between reason and faith, Christianity and Islam, and eventually, Russians and Asians.

While captivity narratives have developed as a popular genre in Europe and in America since the sixteenth century—for instance, Barbary captivity in British culture and Indian captivity in American culture—the genre seems underdeveloped in Russian culture.[4] It gained prominence only in the nineteenth century. The twelfth-century epic poem *The Tale of Igor's Campaign*, which records the Rus' prince Igor's captivity by the Polovtsians of the Don region, was discovered in 1800 and was adapted by the composer Alexander Borodin into a popular opera in 1890. In the 1820s, during Russia's penetration into the Caucasus, Pushkin created the most prominent image of a Russian captive among the Circassian mountaineers in *Kavkazskii plennik*. Apart from these two works, other captivity stories, both fictional and non-fictional, remain obscure. It is the aim of this chapter to explore some of the captivity narratives that were published, reprinted, and read in nineteenth-century Russia, and to examine their significance for understanding Russia's imagination of and presence in Central Asia.

Focusing on the captivity theme, this chapter explores diverse individual captivity stories written within this grand context of imperial expansion. It aims to show that captivity narratives not only show the vulnerability and uncertainty of the empire during its expansion but also reveal the rapid shift of power in Central Asia in the nineteenth century. They witness Russian captives' growing awareness of Central Asia as Russia's future zone of colonization and the captives' self-awareness of their Russian and imperial identity. By retelling their captivity stories, captive-narrators attempted to show that their experiences as captives were also useful and valuable. They managed to turn trauma into personal, even national triumph. They were both victims and vanguards of Russia's colonialism of Central Asia.

Context, authorship, and publication

Nineteenth-century captivity narratives about Central Asia were produced within the grand context of Russia's contact with steppe nomads and Russia's advance into the region. As Michael Khodarkovsky puts it, if the steppe was akin to the sea, the nomads were seamen, many of whom were "pirates" living off looting the passing ship.[5] Steppe nomads' high speed and mobility appeared to be great advantages in guerrilla warfare and raiding activities. Captives, who could be kept as labor or for ransom, or sold to slave markets for income, had been an important revenue source and item of trade for steppe captors since the sixteenth century.[6] The logistical problems in the vast territories of the Kazakh steppe, and the "porous and indefensible nature of the steppe frontier" made Central Asia "the worst possible place to try to build a frontier" since it was both difficult and expensive to maintain.[7] Yet, driven by the yearning for prestige to compete with the other European empires, the quest for a secure frontier and trade routes, Russia kept advancing into Central Asia, and transformed the entire region from a volatile borderland into a part of a colonial empire towards the end of the nineteenth century.[8] Towards the middle of the century, the imperial army established lines of fortresses and took control of the Kazakh steppe. In the 1860s, Russian conquered Tashkent, turned the Khanate of Kokand and the Emirate of Bukhara into protectorates, and established the governor-generalship of Russian Turkestan in 1867. The Khivan Khanate was conquered in 1873 and Russia fully annexed the Transcaspian Region in the beginning of the 1880s.[9] Russia's construction of fortification lines in the steppe region succeeded in reducing the number of Russians falling into captivity, but sporadic raiding activities still threatened Russian travelers to the steppe. By the time Central Asia was fully conquered by the Russian Empire, as Jeff Eden notes, "the region's social landscape had been shaped by a millennium of slavery."[10]

This chapter focuses on published captivity narratives by various Russian soldiers and specialists captured and enslaved in the Central Asian region, including narratives of Vasilii Mikhailov, Filipp Efremov, Savva Bol'shoi, and Nikolai Severtsov.[11] The authors of Russian captivity narratives were usually imperial soldiers or experts in natural sciences. Among the four selected narratives, Filipp Efremov and Vasilii Mikhailov were captured during their military service in the army. In 1774, as a non-commissioned officer in the Nizhnii Novgorod infantry regiment, Efremov was sent to an outpost in the Kazakh steppe during the climax of the Pugachev rebellion to protect the vulnerable borderland from the uprising. The outpost was later attacked by the rebels, and Efremov was captured by Kazakh tribesmen. Two months later, Efremov was sold to the Bukharan *ataliq Daniyal-biy,* the second Manghit ruler of Bukhara, and served in the Bukharan army for at least two years before he managed to escape.[12] Subsequently he visited Khiva, Persia, and India, and from India he took a boat to London and finally returned to St. Petersburg in 1782. Another captive-narrator, Vasilii Mikhailov, served in the Astrakhan Cossack Host. In 1770, he was captured by the Kalmyks during a military mission against the Kalmyk Khan Ubashi.[13] Subsequently he was sold to Kazakhs and then to Khivans, and after numerous failed escape attempts he managed to return to Russia by himself.

Savva Bol'shoi was a prominent doctor, and Nikolai Severtsov was a well-known zoologist.[14] In 1803, Bol'shoi was commissioned to join Iakov Gaverdovskii's diplomatic mission to Bukhara.[15] A group of Kazakh raiders attacked the mission for the goods on their way to cross the Syr Darya. Bol'shoi was captured by the raiders, and he then spent nine months in the Kazakh steppe as a slave laborer, being transferred from one host to another. As for Severtsov, he was commissioned by the Imperial Academy of Sciences to join a two-year scientific mission in the Lower Syr Darya to conduct geographical and zoological surveys of the steppe in 1856. In 1858, Severtsov was captured by the Kokandis during his survey near Fort Perovsky (now Kyzylorda). He spent a month as a hostage and was then released owing to negotiations between Kokandi tribesmen and the Russian commanding general of the Syr Darya line, Alexander Danzas.

Three of these four narratives were written by the captives themselves in Russian. Mikhailov's experience in captivity, however, was recorded by Benjamin Bergmann, a Lutheran pastor who was sent to the Kalmyk steppe for a scientific mission by the Imperial Academy of Sciences. Bergmann met Mikhailov during this mission; he wrote down the story of Mikhailov's captivity by Kalmyks, Kirgiz, and Khivans. This account was first published in German in Riga in 1804, then was translated into English and published in London in 1822, thus Bergmann's intended readership was probably Western European.[16]

In terms of publication, some captivity narratives were published in journals, but most of them were issued as individual accounts. Efremov's narrative was published and reprinted multiple times in 1786, 1794, and 1811. Efremov edited and revised some of the editions. A map of Efremov's itinerary, a glossary of Bukharan words, and an ethnographic section were added to different editions. The history journal *Russkaia starina* reprinted his account in 1893. Bol'shoi's notes were published in several issues of *Syn otechestva* in 1822. Severtsov published his account in 1856. Based on narrators' actual encounters with captors, the observations recorded in captivity narratives were believed to be authentic first-hand accounts of an alien land and its peoples. These narratives were being written and read as a unique type of travelogue and ethnographic record.[17]

At the same time, it should be noted that only a small number of captives who managed to return had an intention to write about their captivity experiences. Most captives were either unable to return or did not leave any written accounts. There are many unpublished archival documents about ordinary peasants or fishermen from the Astrakhan, Ural'sk, or Orenburg regions, carried off during Central Asian steppe nomads' raids on Russian settlements. In selecting published narratives, I focus on those writings that attempt not only to record, but also to narrate and construct first-hand experiences of capture, enslavement, and escape/release, which means they were written consciously for a broad readership, rather than simply for the purpose of reportage.[18]

Imagining force, benevolence, and resistance

How should a "real" Russian and Christian captive act in their encounters with captors from an alien culture? This central aspect to Russian captivity narratives in the nineteenth century was often represented through an omnipresent point of tension—captors' attempts to tame the captives, and the captives' effort to resist. Using force or benevolence, the Central Asian captors in these narratives try to transform their captives into submissive servants or subjects of their societies. The Russian captive heroes, on the other hand, passively or actively resist the possibility of conversion, accommodation, or transculturation to show their religious faith and loyalty to the empire. As the example of Foma Danilov shows, by writing about their endurance and resistance, the narrators portrayed the Russian captives as heroes who are able to demarcate themselves from the tyrannical and backward captive-taking cultures and show their true "Russianness" and religiosity.

Violence and torture were dominant themes in the genre of captivity narrative used to emphasis the tyrannical "otherness" of the captive-taking culture. The narrators were keen to record not only the torture inflicted on them, but also the native violence they had witnessed. As many Russian captives of this period were captured during raids and military operations, force was applied by the captors to intimidate and tame the captives, so that they would give up struggling and be obedient. The depiction of violence was a vital element. It explained why it was impossible for the captives to escape, and it set the scene for the heroic resistance that the narrator depicted in the text that followed.

For instance, Efremov provided a vivid torture scene that took place during his captivity in Bukhara in the 1770s. He described how the Bukharan *Daniyal-biy* attempted to convert him to Islam by torturing him for three days, while he withstood and showed his complete adherence to Orthodoxy. As he recorded:

> The torture of me went in this way: They put a *pood* of salt in a large wooden tub, then poured hot water into it. After the salt dissolved and the water cooled down, they tied me up, stuck a wooden stick into my mouth, and started to flush the salty water down my throat. People usually die from this torture after one day, but they intended to keep me alive, thus after each hour's torture they let me drink three cups of melted sheep fat, which would absorb all the salt and clear the stomach from top to bottom ... I was tortured like this for three days. Seeing that the torture done to me was futile, the *Atalyk* tried to persuade me to at least swear allegiance to serve [him], which I had to do outwardly.[19]

Through this paragraph Efremov intended to convey two messages about his captivity to his readers. The first is that the *atalyk*'s attempt to convert Efremov to Islam failed, because the protagonist withstood the torture heroically. His heroism even convinced the *atalyk* to make a concession so that Efremov could keep his faith. The second is that his service in the Bukharan army was just an outward compromise. As he explained, under the captor's threats, he had to swear allegiance to *Daniyal-biy*, but he said, "I made the oath only by my tongue, but not by my soul, for my soul can only feel the zeal to serve the Empress of All Russia."[20] This outward compromise created the setting for his subsequent heroic feats in the *atalyk*'s army and his tactical escape from Bukhara. By justifying his physical service to the *atalyk* and emphasizing his psychological loyalty to the Empress and Orthodoxy, Efremov depicted himself as a multi-faced captive-protagonist, who was capable of serving his Central Asian captors as a military professional, while keeping his Russian identity. He portrayed himself as the kind of resourceful captive-hero who would wait for years among his captors for the chance of escape. Being aware of the significance of loyalty to one's faith and sovereign, Efremov incorporated the self-fashioning of his heroism into his writing of a vivid ethnographic account of a Central Asian torture.

At the same time, the dynamics of imperial expansion were also reflected in the writing of violence in captivity experiences. The increasing security and Russia's extension of colonial rule over Central Asia slightly changed the tone of captivity narratives. Not only did the number of these narratives decrease in the second half of the century but also the captors' application of violence and force also became restrained.

The different experiences of Savva Bol'shoi and Nikolai Severtsov can best illustrate the dynamics of power on the steppe in the nineteenth century. When Bol'shoi was captured, he was dragged to the Kazakh tribe and humiliated by the tribesmen. As he records in his *Zapiski*, in the tribe, some Kazakhs, "cursed monsters," humiliated him with "all malicious gibes and abuses," and some spat on his face and "make different grimaces." Other tribesmen threatened him by showing their weapons—some "whipped him on his naked body" and some "poked his throat, teeth and eyes with knives."[21] He was forced to work as a slave among the Kazakh tribesmen for a year. By contrast, in 1858, during a scientific expedition on the Lower Syr Darya, Nikolai Severtsov, a well-known Russian zoologist, was also captured by the Kokandis in the same region. At that time the Russian army had already taken the Kokandi fortress of Ak-Mechet', but sporadic conflicts and raids by the armies of Kokand still threatened Russian control in this steppe region. The Kokandi captors were well aware of the empire's military moves. Severtsov barely encountered any violence. The tribesmen kept him for ransom and bargained with the Russian armies, and they also tried to obtain information from Severtsov about Russia's military operations. He did not engage in forced labor and was well-treated by the tribal leaders. While Bol'shoi was only shabbily dressed during his captivity, Severtsov was permitted to ask for a softer cushion on his saddle.[22] Severtsov also noticed this himself, as he writes: "... they still treated me humanely. In 1852 the Kokand Kirgiz captured three Siberian Cossacks, who were injured as badly as I was. Before riding, they were dragged for three *verst* on lassos, but I was dragged just for ten steps."[23] Severtsov spent only a month in captivity and then was released owing to the negotiation between Kokandis and the Russian commanding general of the Syr Darya line, Alexander Danzas. Bol'shoi and Severtsov were captured almost in the same region. Their different fates provide a reflection of Russia's growing presence in the Kazakh steppe.[24]

Although the conventional images of barbarous captors and resisting captives are deeply embedded in the notion of captivity, actual experiences were in fact diverse and complex. For instance, for the captors, force was not the only way to coerce captives into compliance. In the narratives, there are also many descriptions about how captors tried to entice their slaves by various means so that they might relinquish thoughts of escape. This process usually involved the masters' benevolence and the prospect of marriage. The protagonists depicted in the captivity narratives, however, always took these adaptations to their circumstances of slavery as threatening factors. No matter how well the captive-protagonists lived among the Central Asians, they repeatedly stressed their longing for Russia and eagerness to escape. Efremov, for instance, mentioned that *Daniyal-biy* awarded him land and money and promoted him for his heroic feats in the Bukharan army, but he did not show appreciation for *Daniyal-biy*'s awards. The real threat was not that of living in captivity, but of losing one's "Russianness" by succumbing to these temptations.

Some slave owners treated their slaves very humanely, as seen in Mikhailov's slavery in Khiva.[25] Mikhailov suffered mostly from the treatment from his Kazakh captors. While he could still eat properly among the Kalmyks, he suffered from hunger all the time with the Kazakhs, and his feet were always put in shackles and hands fastened with ropes. In Khiva he enjoyed a most comfortable life as a slave. He happened to be purchased by a kind master from an ordinary Khivan family, who treated him like a brother. Mikhailov was assigned only some trifling domestic work. He dressed decently and ate properly.[26] His master's family was very tolerant of his rebellion. After one failed attempt at escape, when the owner was about to flog Mikhailov, the owner's wife threw the whip away and persuaded him to forgive Mikhailov: "Everybody prefers his own country to any other; how can you find fault with him for wishing to return home? Abuse him no longer, but rather endeavor, in future, to *gain his affections* by kindness." The master then treated Mikhailov as usual, or even better. After this incident, Mikhailov recalled that once on the street he tried a home-made beverage from berries and he really liked it. When he told his master, the master was very pleased to show his kindness, so he himself went to the market immediately to shop for berries and made the beverage for Mikhailov.[27] This episode shows the master's genuine endeavor to please the slave, which is a completely different picture from the torture and violent scenes examined above.

As portrayals of captors were always intended to highlight the character of the captive-narrators, the master's unusual kindness was described as a test and an obstacle that Mikhailov needed to pass. Mikhailov was very alert to the benevolence shown to him. The master once proposed Mikhailov's marriage with a

Khivan woman, and he promised to provide gold and sixty sheep for this marriage, as long as Mikhailov remained in his family. Mikhailov, however, was very alarmed at the possibility of staying in Khiva permanently, so instead of securing him, his master's proposal led directly to his first attempt to escape.[28] Unlike violence, which the captives could resist by their physical strength, resisting the master's benevolence required the captives' inner strength and an extremely strong attachment to their homeland. Benevolence represented undesirable, if comfortable, confinement, and resistance to it was the captives' last but the most important pursuit – the pursuit of freedom. This asserted longing for liberty was the captives' most frequently used arguments against their captors in their written accounts of experiences.

For nineteenth-century Russian captives, Orthodoxy was a key element to identify Self and Other. Efremov's episode of torture presents an example of resistance to forcible conversion. Yet most narratives do not depict episodes of attempted violent conversion. Adherence to Christianity was mainly shown in the captives' everyday life. The captive-narrators tended to demonstrate their religiosity despite the hardship of life among the infidel captors. For example, Bol'shoi resisted the local culture in a passive way. In 1803, Gaverdovskii's diplomatic mission to Bukhara was attacked by Kazakh raiders and Bol'shoi was captured by Kazakh tribesmen. After he was captured, Bol'shoi refused to have any further contact with his captors. As a slave laborer, his main job was collecting wood, lifting water, and cooking, and he suffered from hunger all the time. But even when "a day is as long as a year in hunger," he still refused to talk with his captors. He used silence to demarcate himself from them. In this process, religion provided him with the most crucial spiritual prop. He described how the belief in Orthodoxy supported him in captivity: "I spent most of the time there in silence. What did I do, then? My first task is doing morning and evening prayers, which I did mostly in secret … . When I was away from the *aul* for woods and water, I first recited some poems and cried (the first of which was always *Molitvu proliyu ko Gospodu* (Payer to the Lord), which percolates through my soul and always makes me burst into plentiful of tears)."[29]

Therefore, the captors' violence and their torturing of the captives were consciously highlighted to follow the conventions of the genre, and to foreground the threat of captive-taking cultures that Russia was facing in the nineteenth century. The captors' benevolence was portrayed as undesirable confinement for the captives, who saw the captors' cultures as inherently inhospitable and degrading. Apart from the heroic martyrdom that Dostoyevsky portrayed, a close examination of the narratives of the survivors shows that captives intended to demonstrate their sustained and tenacious efforts to preserve their "Russianness." Orthodoxy provided the captives with their primary spiritual support, and Empire served as the place that the captives longed for, and where they could return after captivity. By writing about their endurance and resistance, the narrators depicted Russian captive heroes who were able to demarcate themselves from the captive-taking cultures while keeping their Russian spirit intact.[30] The demarcation from Central Asian captors and unshakable "Russianness" are the prominent features that Dostoyevsky saw in Foma Danilov, and the captive-narrators highlighted in themselves.

Imagining a Central Asian hero

In early captivity narratives, the central hero tended to be the captive himself; thus, little space was left for highlighting individuals from the captive-taking cultures. Native people were generally pictured as an undifferentiated group, with the exception of a few figures who played a part in the protagonists' captivity sequences of capture, enslavement, and escape, such as *Daniyal-biy* in Efremov's narrative, and Mikhailov's Khivan slave-owner. The captors were more frequently portrayed as people who were predominantly violent, yet impotent in love and civility. For instance, Bol'shoi recorded his physical vulnerability before his Kazakh captors' humiliation and threats; at the same time, he laughed at their "folly" of fighting among themselves for plunder and their ignorance in medicine.

Yet among the narratives, a prominent Central Asian male figure can be found in Severtsov's writing. Severtsov provided a detailed description about a Kirgiz (Kazakh) in Kokandi service called Dashchan, whom he encountered among his captors. As Severtsov noted, Dashchan was the leader of the group of Kokandi raiders who had captured him. Severtsov's first impression of Dashchan was quite favorable—Dashchan spoke "pure Russian with a soft and ingratiating tone," and he treated this Russian captive very well: he brought Severtsov food and *airan*, and at night, when Dashchan noticed that Severtsov was resting his head on his elbow, he shared his pillow with Severtsov. The further description of Dashchan is worth examining as it is almost the only well-portrayed native individual from all the narratives. Severtsov's representation of Dashchan challenges some earlier stereotypes of the Kirgiz people and provides an impressive image of a Central Asian version of Bestuzhev-Marlinsky's Ammalat-Bek and Tolstoy's Hadji Murat.

Severtsov used an English phrase to express his appreciation of Dashchan's appearance and manner: "a gentleman robber." As he described, Dashchan looked different from most Kokandi Kirgiz. While most Kirgiz people were "stumpy, with high cheekbones, flat noses and wide faces" and look like "sluggish bumpkins dressing in robes," Dashchan's face was "European ... more soft and pleasant ... No cunning and greediness is shown on this face, but only carefree daring, the desire to live and making fun, sensitivity, and even some happy and unfeigned kindness."[31] During his captivity, Severtsov observed Dashchan's riding moves and manners. Dashchan was pictured as a "handsome horseman" in a way that echoes Alexander Pushkin's portrayal of the swift Circassian mountaineers in *Kavkazkii plennik*. Dashchan's beloved horse, a brisk *karabair*, easily went for two days without forage, and Dashchan also kept his joy and vitality along the way. After two days of riding, his "neat silk belt and brown robe made from fine broadcloth were not greasy, but only a bit dusty …; it was clean even inside his shirt!" Severtsov, in contrast, was exhausted and grimy. Dashchan's manner reversed Severtsov's understanding of the Kirgiz people. He wrote: "How could a Kirgiz have such neatness?!"[32]

Severtsov was impressed not only by Dashchan's appearance, but also by his way of living. As "a gentleman robber," Dashchan had begun raids and robbery from his early youth, but Severtsov explained that steppe raiding was not the threatening and dangerous business that people usually imagined it to be. It was rather a way of living, a kind of art and enjoyment for the natives, and it had certain rules that needed to be followed. For instance, it was not allowed to raid tribesmen's guests or friends.[33] Before Russian military forces started to gain control in this region, *baranta*, the native word for raiding, was an established custom of Kirgiz people. As Virginia Martin points out, etymologically the Kazakh word *barimta* (*baranta*) means "that which is due to me."[34] It was not a crime, nor *grabezh* (robbery) nor *nabeg* (raid), the Russian words that were used to refer to *baranta*. Rather, it was "a legitimate judicial custom embedded in the Kazakh culture understanding of wrongdoing, honor and revenge" and a sanctioned custom that created *batyrs*, a Kazakh term for "hero" or "valiant warrior."[35] Raiders who were courageous, tactful, and composed were admired and honored, and Dashchan happened to be a virtuoso of *baranta*. He was quite familiar with the steppe and the nomads, and he dared to go raiding even by himself. At the same time, Dashchan did not rob out of greed—he generously shared his plunder with other tribesmen. As Severtsov noted, having taken the Kokandi fortress of Ak-Mechet', the Russians tried many times to capture Dashchan, but all without success.[36] There were rumors that Dashchan had been killed, but he scotched the rumors by launching and taking part in new raiding activities. For his prowess and generosity Dashchan was considered by his tribesmen to be a *batyr*. This image of valiant raiders and slave captors can be seen as one of the usual pictures of the Kazakhs in Russian imagination in the nineteenth century. Yet where most imperial Russians tended to show a lack of understanding in *baranta*, Severtsov, as a captive, gained extraordinary insight into this Kazakh custom during his captivity.[37]

Moreover, what might connect Ammalat-Bek and Hadji Murat with Severtsov's Dashchan is his further discussion of the tension between steppe raiding activities and Russia's growing presence in Central Asia, and this was brought about by Russia's direct confrontation with Central Asian tribesmen in the 1850s. As Severtsov observed, raiding was a usual way of life for steppe tribesmen. Yet when Russia started to pursue not just nominal, but actual control of the steppe region, raiding activities were criminalized. "Raiders became rebels," and what the tribesmen thought of as prowess, the Russians considered a crime; thus these "last *batyr*-riders, who are practicing their daring within the steppe which are now possessed by Russians, gradually lost the land beneath their feet for their heroic feats."[38] Severtsov expresses sympathy towards Dashchan, a representative of the "last *batyr*-riders" on the steppe. As he noticed, Dashchan was a true heroic figure, but he was born in the wrong age, in which he would only be considered as a "rebel" and a "criminal." "Is it his fault that he was born too late, that the clash with superior, yet alien Russian norms brought him to penal servitude?"[39] Dashchan's clash with the empire in Central Asia recalls the fate of Ammalat-Bek and Hadji Murat in the Caucasus. The empire's expansion was already irresistible; a native individual could only be a subject or a victim of this process.

What is also striking in Severtsov's narrative is that he not only portrayed his masculine captor but also presented Dashchan's "Oriental" wife, presenting a vivid native couple of a kind that rarely appears in written narratives. As he described, Dashchan's wife was as good-looking as Dashchan: her skin was white, her cheek was rosy, and her face also had "European" features. She did not cover her hair, which was "black, thick, silky and carefully brushed," and she was able to ride a horse like a man. Severstov referred to her as a "decent coquette" (*koketka poryadochnaya*). He recalled how she told him, with a playful smile, that "it is joyful to be with them [the tribesmen]; they have many women here, especially in Turkestan, and women here are fine."[40] This coquettish Oriental beauty and the "gentleman robber" present a rare Oriental match that fills the gap of sexual imagination of the Central Asian Orient. As a captive-observer, Severtsov encountered not only the masculinity of the Orient, but also its femininity. While Dashchan's presence was shaken by the empire's expansion, his wife's words seem to have opened a romantic and sexual fantasy that could be cultivated and developed.

Imagining Central Asian land and medicine

Captivity narratives in nineteenth-century Russia were being written and read as a unique type of travelogue and ethnographic record. For the narrators, their experiences in captivity provided them with opportunities to engage with captive-taking cultures. The main focus of this section is the accounts about Central Asian land, nature, and cultures that the nineteenth-century Russian captives chose to record in their narratives. With land and medicine as two specific examples, this section aims to reveal that the captives' gaze is inherently unequal—during captivity, the captive-narrators were confined and restrained; nevertheless, under the surface of passive suffering, the imperial captives were actually the ones who were ultimately free to construct their captors' society. For captives who were not ethnographers or scientists, such as Efremov and Mikhailov, captivity provided unique possibilities for observation that could compete with the studies of their scholarly contemporaries. For Dr. Bol'shoi and the zoologist Severtsov, captivity was both an adventure and a space to demonstrate their superior European knowledge. By recounting their captivity stories, narrators responded to early travelogues about the region, attempting to show that their experiences as captives were also valuable. They managed to turn trauma into personal, even national triumph, showing that they were both victims and vanguards of Russia's colonialism of Central Asia.

Some captive-narrators not only retold their captivity stories but also devoted special sections to ethnographic accounts. By doing so, they responded to early travelogues or ethnographic records about Central Asia. In Russia's encounters with Central Asia, early missions focused more on the establishment of diplomatic relations with Central Asian rulers and the natural obstacles in their journeys to reach these cultures.[41] At the same time, the development of natural science was also an influential factor in Russia's exploration in Central Asia, especially after the establishment of the Russian Academy of Sciences in 1725 and the publication of the first official atlas of the Russian Empire, *Atlas rossiiskoi*, in 1745.[42]

The need to define the boundary of the empire and the interest in exploring its potential colonies yielded numerous missions and geographical expeditions to Central Asia in the eighteenth and nineteenth centuries. Imperial travelers attempted to seek both justification for and benefits of Russia's expansion into Central Asia. For instance, in his mission to Khiva in 1793, Major E. I. Blankennagel' recorded his encounters with Russian captives in Khiva and a legend that he heard from a Russian slave that Khiva abounded with gold and silver.[43] As a supporter of Russian expansionism, Blankennagel' called Khiva a "New Peru," and proposed to conquer Khiva in order to free Russian slaves and explore its economic promise.[44] As Chechesh Kudachinova has explored in her chapter in this volume, Alexander von Humboldt was also invited by Nicholas I to explore the nature of "Asiatic Russia." He made the trip in the summer of 1829, when he traveled along the frontiers of Chinese Dzungaria, the fortification line of the Kirgiz steppe and the shores of the Caspian Sea, and discovered numerous natural resources such as gold, diamonds, and platinum in the Urals and gold on the Kirgiz steppe.[45]

In their descriptions of lands, captive-narrators also attempted to contribute to the construction of Central Asia as a site of economic promise. The most obvious example is Efremov's record of two mines, a gold mine and silver mine, in Khiva in his 1811 edition of *Stranstvovanie*. A comparison of the 1784 manuscript and 1811 edition of *Stranstvovanie* shows that this episode was consciously added by Efremov or by Petr Kondyrev, the editor of 1811 edition and a lecturer in history and geography at Kazan University. As in Efremov's manuscript, he mentioned that gold and silver from India, Persia, and China were traded by merchants (mainly Tatars) in Bukharan markets.[46] In his subsequent travels in India, he described Bengal as the place where a large amount of gold, silver, diamonds, pearls, and silk could be found. Eighteenth-century Bengal in Efremov's accounts is a rich and exotic land. He described people there riding elephants with boxes and cushions made with gold, silver, and silk. The rich Bengali men wore "gold necklaces, earrings and rings" and women "gold earrings, nose rings and finger rings."[47]

In the 1811 edition, keeping the exotic picture of India, Efremov deliberately added the description about the potential of mines in Central Asia. It stressed that there was no mine in Bukhara, but a Russian there told Efremov that a Russian slave in Khiva had once found "two mountains with gold and silver." According to the narrative, this Russian slave was a member of Alexander Bekovich-Cherkassky's fatal expedition to Khiva in 1716. After its defeat by the Khivans and Bekovich's death, soldiers and experts of this expedition were enslaved and forced to serve the Khivan Khan. One of the Russian slaves found these two mines and reported to the Khan that with them the Khan could "build all houses in Khiva with pure silver and cover all of them with pure gold."[48] Intending to hide this information to avoid military invasion, the Khivan Khan executed this Russian slave, and ordered others not to exploit these two mines.

This legend about hidden treasures in Khiva was so widespread in the Russian imagination in the eighteenth and nineteenth centuries that almost all Russian travelers to Khiva mentioned it in their travel writings. Overall, based on the travel accounts, the fervor for exploring Khiva's hidden gold and conquering the land still existed, even intensified, after Bekovich's disastrous campaign. Together with the appeal to free Russian prisoners of war from Khiva, the gold delusion was both a justification for and benefit of Russia's expansion into Central Asia. The picture was not quite reciprocal; it was rather a part of the general expansionist rhetoric within the Empire. By weaving this legend into his narrative, Efremov intended to turn his captivity experience into a valuable account.

On the other hand, apart from verifying other travelogues, captive-narrators also attempted to challenge the popular imagination by writing down their actual experiences. Severtsov's account about his month-long captivity among Kokandi Kirgiz is one example of this. Severtsov was commissioned to join a two-year scientific mission in the Lower Syr-Darya to conduct geographical and zoological surveys of the steppe. Before describing his trip, Severtsov noted how an officer who had just returned from Central Asia "enthusiastically" described the rich fauna and flora in the Lower Syr-Darya. In the officer's description, Syr-Darya is "powerful, full-flowing and torrential." The river is surrounded by "strong and fresh vegetation" of "vast reeds, willows with flexible withes, poplars with dark green leaves, oleasters with small silvery foliage" and saxaul trees "in fanciful shape." These plants develop a "graceful grid on the transparent blue of the sky." Various and abundant animals can also be seen on the steppe. Pheasants appear "at every step;" iridescent Persian beeeaters are shining under the sun in the "warm and refreshing air;" fish hawks are hovering above Syr-Darya, and tigers, boars, deer and wild goats are hiding in the thickets … Spring on the steppe is like an "Italian winter."[49] The Russian officer's picture of the lower Syr-Darya is manifestly touristic. This kind of enjoyment and excitement about the nature in Central Asia became possible in the late 1850s when the Kazakh steppe was brought into Russia's control. It indeed heightened the zoologist Severtsov's expectations for this expedition.

But when Severstov arrived in this region, he was deeply disappointed by his actual experience. In his narrative, he described how he felt himself "being deceived" by the officer. He arrived in a "stormy and freezing winter" between 1857 and 1858, and when spring came, it was absolutely not an "Italian winter."

Snow and bitter cold lasted until April, and vegetation was "deathly pale." The land was "unattractive" with "friable, racked and dry sand," dust "floated in the air" covering all greenery and flowers, and even the blue sky was dirtied by sand and dust. When Severtsov went hunting, wild animals hid themselves immediately. The fauna and flora were rather "poor" and "monotonous," which Severtsov described as "zoological poverty."[50] Severtsov's actual experience was neither enjoyable nor exciting; it was rather accompanied by coldness, dust, and the feeling of nausea.

Both richness and emptiness in the imagination of the Central Asian land served as reminders of possible rewards and disappointment in Russia's colonization of Central Asia. Efremov's account of the treasures in Khiva was an appeal for expansion when actual conquest had not yet begun, while Severtsov's personal experience was written after Russia's conquest of the Kazakh steppe and during the military clashes with Kokandi tribesmen. They both showed attempts to characterize Central Asian land and nature based on their European knowledge. As captives, they depicted themselves as vanguards of Russia's exploration and exploitation of Central Asia.

Apart from land and nature, Russian captivity narratives also provide intriguing sources on Central Asian medical practices. Captives, as observers, documented how their captors cured them of their injuries caused by violent capture and local diseases they had observed. Besides that, Russian captives mentioned their experiences of being considered by captors as doctors and healers, no matter whether they had medical knowledge or not. An examination of these accounts not only show the tension between Russian and Central Asian medical practices, but also provides an aspect to see how Central Asian peoples situated European medicine in their culture.

Some noticed that many native treatments were very effective. For instance, Severtsov recorded that the Kokandi Kirgizs treated him with "raw and fresh mutton" to heal the wounds he suffered during capture. During the day they covered Severtsov's wound with raw meat for absorbing ichor, and at night they applied powders made from herbs and turtle eggs. This "pure Kokandi treatment" proved to be very practical. His wound healed within several days.[51] Yet in these writings about Central Asian medicine, inequality in knowledge is quite evident. As representatives from the European civilization, Russians and Russian captives felt themselves more qualified in defining the effectiveness or ignorance of Central Asian cultures.

Most captives focused more on constructing the backwardness of Central Asian ethnomedicine. For example, as a Russian doctor captured by Kazakh tribesmen, Bol'shoi paid special attention to record Kazakh medicine in his *Zapiski*. With mockery he described the tension between him and the tribesmen in their different perception of medicine. When Bol'shoi encountered Kazakh ethnomedicine, he felt it completely in contrast to European medicine, which is based on theory, knowledge, and empirical practices. As Bol'shoi records, Kazakh tribesmen had a peculiar understanding about the doctor's role. They believed that a doctor was able to not only make a diagnosis, but also tell fortunes. When Bol'shoi told them that he could not make a diagnosis based merely on taking a pulse, the Kazakhs complained: "What sort of doctor are you?"[52] Not only were doctors supposed to possess mystical power in the ideas of the Kazakhs, Russians were also unusual in the tribesmen's imagination: they believed that "every Russian is able to produce supernatural acts such as predicting frost, making weather warmer, raising horrible storms, making rainfall, bringing or driving away thunder cloud, etc."[53]

Further evidence of the tribesmen's medical absurdity is portrayed in their way of viewing and applying medicament. Bol'shoi records a case when he asked a tribesman for some medicines for treatment, but the next day the man came back with pieces of wax, a cork, and half of a coffee bean that Kazakhs obtained from raiding a Russian caravan, asking whether these were drugs or not. For these "drugs" this Kazakh had paid a sheep.[54] Besides this, most of the time tribesmen just carried these "medicines" with them as "talisman" in the hope of warding off disease. The drugs that they obtained by plundering Bol'shoi's mission were similarly wasted by tribesmen as they distributed them as amulets.[55] These superstitious ideas and practices from Kazakh tradition were seen by Bol'shoi as ignorance of tribesmen's medical knowledge. Bol'-shoi's mission to the steppe was initially to assist his compatriots in their travel; while being captured, he was forced to treat his captors and to confront the "Otherness" of Kazakh culture, thus his record mainly focuses on the conflict, tension, and alien nature of the captors' culture.

On the other hand, for other captives such as Mikhailov, Kazakh tribesmen's superficial understanding of medical knowledge was something that they could take advantage of. Mikhailov's account of captivity contains an intriguing episode about his experience of working as a healer for a Kazakh boy. After escaping from his Kalmyk captors, he was then captured by Kazakh tribesmen, among whom he always suffered from hunger. When his Kazakh owner's grandson had asthma, Mikhailov, a former Russian Cossack, was asked to heal this boy together with "a Kalmyk sorceress" (most likely a Shaman). The Kazakhs believed that since Mikhailov "hast lived among the Russians and Kalmucs and they have skillful physicians," he "must know a remedy for the disease."[56] Thus Mikhailov pretended to be a physician for a while, during which he enjoyed special authority and freedom. Though not possessing any prior medical skills, he suggested a treatment that the boy should not drink milk, but only mutton-broth. This advice not only miraculously helped the boy to recover, but also procured Mikhailov a good meal (mutton-broth) that he had not had for a long time.

Backwardness was easily constructed in the sphere of medicine. Any Russian could be a master, at least in medicine, of the captive-taking cultures. Not only because some natives already acknowledged the fact that Russians were superior in this field, but also the natives were easily manipulated due to ignorance and superstition regarding European knowledge.[57] As Mary Louise Pratt argues, imperial expansion generated "contact zones", where "disparate cultures meet, clash, and grapple with each other, often in highly asymmetrical relations of domination and subordination."[58] Russian captivity narratives present a form of such "contact zone," where Oriental captors confine imperial captives, while captives define and construct captors. By constructing a picture of backwardness and ignorance in captive-taking cultures, the captive-narrators succeeding in showing their sense of superiority despite their abject positions. They demonstrated their capacity for knowing and mastering their captors' cultures. Thus, writing of captivity is not merely the retelling of experiences; it also shapes ideas, creates discourse, and constructs identities of both captives and captors, usually in a highly asymmetrical way.

Conclusion

In her comprehensive study of British captivity narratives about the Mediterranean, America, and India from the seventeenth to the nineteenth century, Linda Colley reveals the dynamics of power of the British Empire in its overseas expansion. As she notes, captivity narratives are "imperfect, idiosyncratic, and sometimes violently slanted texts," but they are also "astonishingly rich and revealing, both about the British themselves, and about the mixed fortunes and complexities of their dealings with other peoples."[59] They not only tell of the opposition and antagonism between the British captives and their captors but also reveal the interdependence between British Empire and its colonization.

The nineteenth-century Russian captivity narratives are similarly imperfect yet revealing. They are a recollection of the vulnerabilities and uncertainties of early travels, and they also remind us of the miscommunication and misunderstanding that could occur when different cultures meet. Russian captives relied on the imagination of alien or brutal captive-taking Asian cultures to express their own imperial identities. Despite their confinement, Russian captives confidently felt themselves as representatives of European powers in relation to Central Asian cultures. Overall, captivity was a prominent theme in describing imperial Russia's frontier experiences.

This chapter has shown that written accounts of captivity experiences was a conscious process, with certain themes appearing consistently in different narratives. Captors' unsuccessful attempts to tame their captives, including both force and benevolence, were accentuated to highlight Russian captives' willpower, their ability to deal with different adversities, and their persistent longing for their homeland – Russia. Captivity was also a platform for captives to demonstrate their superior knowledge over Central Asian civilizations. Russian captives showed their capacity to master Central Asian lands and civilize Central Asian peoples, which implied further possibilities for expansion and colonization.

The writing of captivity experiences had certain paradigms to follow, yet it also changed and evolved over time according to the shift of power between the captors' and captives' societies. Specifically, in Russia's relations to Central Asian societies, the rapid expansion into Central Asia witnesses Russian captives' growing awareness of their captors as Russian subjects. This shows that Asia in imperial Russia's imagination was certainly not static; it changed over time along with Russia's increasing contact with and control of the region.

Notes

1 *I would like to thank Alexander Morrison, Katya Hokanson, and Victoria Thorstensson for their guidance and assistance throughout the research and writing of this chapter, and also Gregory Afinogenov for his comments on an earlier draft.

In 1875, Pulat-Khan led a rebellion against the ruler of the Kokand Khanate Nasruddin Khan. The imperial Russian army, led by Mikhail Skobelev with the authorization of Konstantin von Kaufman, attacked Kokand at the same time. The Fergana valley was incorporated into Russian Turkestan right after the campaign in 1876. The records about Foma Danilov can be seen in "O geroicheskoi smerti unter-ofitsera Danilova," *Russkii ivalid*, 1876, April 27, No. 90, 2 and in *Turkestanskii sbornik*, vol. 424, 78–80.

2 Fyodor Dostoevsky, "Foma Danilov, a Russian Hero Tortured to Death," in *A Writer's Diary, Volume 2: 1877–1881*, trans. Kenneth Lantz (Evanston: Northwestern University Press, 1997), 820–25.

3 Joseph Frank, *Dostoevsky: The Mantle of the Prophet, 1871–1881* (Princeton: Princeton University Press, 2003), 570.

4 For the popularity of captivity narratives in British and American cultures, see for instance: Roy Harvey Pearce, "The Significances of the Captivity Narrative," *American Literature* 19: 1 (Mar. 1947), 1–20; G. A. Starr, "Escape from Barbary: A Seventeenth-Century Genre," *Huntington Library Quarterly* 29: 1 (1965), 35–52.

5 Michael Khodarkovsky, *Russia's Steppe Frontier: The Making of a Colonial Empire, 1500–1800* (Bloomington: Indiana University Press, 2004), 29.

6 Khodarkovsky summarizes steppe nomads' slave raiding activities from the sixteenth to the eighteenth century. See: Khodarkovsky, *Russia's Steppe Frontier*, 21–6. Since the sixteenth century the biggest threat for Russia had been the Crimean Tatars. Before the annexation of Crimea in 1783, Crimean Tatars, sometimes allied with Nogays, conducted almost annual raids in the Pontic steppe. For the slave trade by Crimean Tatars see: Alan Fisher, "Muscovy and the Black Sea Slave Trade," *Canadian-American Slavic Studies* 6: 4 (1972), 575–94. For the captives and slaves in Central Asia see: Alessandro Stanziani, *Bondage: Labor and Rights in Eurasia from the Sixteenth to the Early Twentieth Centuries* (New York: Berghahn Books, 2004), 63–100; B. D. Hopkins, "Race, Sex and Slavery: Forced Labour in Central Asia and Afghanistan in the Early 19th Century," *Modern Asian Studies* 42: 4 (2008), 629–71.

7 Khodarkovsky, *Russia's Steppe Frontier*, 7; Alexander Morrison, "'Nechto eroticheskoe', 'courir après l'ombre'? – logistical imperatives and the fall of Tashkent, 1859–1865," *Central Asian Survey* 33: 2 (2014), 165.

8 The motivation of Russia's conquest of Central Asia is examined in Morrison's articles. See: Alexander Morrison, "Introduction: Killing the Cotton Canard and getting rid of the Great Game: rewriting the Russian conquest of Central Asia, 1814–1895," *Central Asian Survey* 33: 2 (2014): 137 and Morrison, "'Nechto eroticheskoe'," 165.

9 For a brief chronology of Russian conquest of Central Asia after 1865 see Hélène Carrère d'Encausse, "Systematic Conquest, 1865 to 1884," in *Central Asia: 130 Years of Russian Dominance, A Historical Overview*, ed. Edward Allworth (Durham: Duke University Press, 1994), 131–50.

10 Jeff Eden, *Slavery and Empire in Central Asia* (Cambridge: Cambridge University Press, 2018), 1.

11 *Adventures of Michailow, a Russian captive, among the Kalmucs, Kirghiz, and Kiwenses. Written by Himself* (London: Sir Richard Phillips & Co., 1822); Filipp Efremov, "Rossiiskogo unter-ofitsera geviatletnee stranstvovanie i prikliucheniia v Bukharii, Khive, Persii i indii i vozvrashchenie v Rossiiu, napisannoe im samim v sanktpeterburge v 1784 g.", *Russkaia starina*, 1893, No.7, 125–49; Fillip Efremov, "Stranstvovanie Filippa

Efremova v Kirgizskoi stepi, Bukharii, Khive, Persii, Tibete i Indii i vozvreshenie ego ottuda cherez angliiu v rossiiu" in *Puteshestviia po vostoku v epokhu Ekateriny II* (Moscow: Vostochnaia literatura, 1995); Savva Bol'shoi, "Zapiski Savvy Bol'shogo o prikliucheniiakh ego v plenu u kirgiz-kaisakov v 1803 g. i 1804 g.," *Syn otechestva*, 1822, No. 11, 168–76; No. 12, 214–20; No. 14, 289–303; No. 15, 24–34; No. 35, 49–68; Nikolai Severtsov, *Mesiats plena u kokantsev* (St. Petersburg, 1860).

12 For more information about Daniyal-*biy* and the changing role of the rank *ataliq* in Bukhara in the eighteenth century, see: Wolfgang Holzwarth, "The Uzbek State as Reflected in Eighteenth Century Bukharan Sources," in *Nomaden und Sesshafte: Fragen, Methoden, Ergebnisse*, Vol. 2, eds. Thomas Herzog and Wolfgang Holzworth (Halle: Orientwissenschaftliche Hefte 15; Mitteilungen des SFB "Differenz und Integration," 2004), 107–9.

13 This military mission took place when the Kalmyks in Russia started to depart for Jungaria. Michael Khodarkovsky has a thorough study about the tension between Russian authorities and Kalmyks in 1770–1771. See in Michael Khodarkovsky, *Where Two Worlds Met: The Russian State and the Kalmyk Nomads, 1600–1771* (Cornell: Cornell University Press, 2006), 230–32.

14 In 1802 Savva Bol'shoi went through the first thesis defense in the Academy of Medicine and Surgery in St. Petersburg. See in L. F. Zmeev, *Istoriia imperskoi voenno-meditsinskoi akademii* (St. Petersburg, 1898),148. As for Severtsov, in 1856 he won the Demidov Prize, an annual national scientific prize of the Russian Empire, for his zoological study of Voronezh Governorate.

15 The background of this mission is that in 1802 Nikolai Rumyantsev, the Russian minister of commerce, obtained a report about a Bashkir counterfeit money maker hiding in Bukhara. The Russian government asked the Bukharans to turn over the criminal to them, but the Bukharan amir refused, so Rumyantsev proposed a diplomatic mission to Bukhara, and this proposal was sanctioned by tsar Alexander I. Lieutenant Iakov Gaverdovskii was then appointed by Rumyantsev as the leader of this diplomatic mission. Besides diplomatic tasks, the aim of the mission also included a geographical survey of the Kazakh steppe and the Bukhara khanate. See in N. A. Khalfin, *Rossiia i khanstva srednei azii* (Moscow: Nauka, 1974), 63–4.

16 Benjamin Bergmann, trans., *Schicksale des Persers Wassilij Michailow unter den Kalmüken, Kirgisen und Chiwensern* [Written from notes furnished by Mikhailow] (Riga: Bartmannschen Buchhandlung, 1804); *New Voyages and Travels; consisting of originals and translations*. Vol. 7 (London: Sir Richard Phillips & Co., 1822).

17 Alexander Morrison has kindly shared his unpublished article, which includes a valuable record about one contemporary reading of Severtsov's captivity narrative as a travelogue. It is a record from the diary of F. S. Dobrovol'skii, a member of the garrison at Fort Vernoe, who in June 1864 wrote that as it was 42 degrees outside, "I am occupying myself reading the book by N. Ia. (sic) Severtsev *Mesiats plena u kokantsev*, in reading which it is possible to acquaint oneself a little with the *Kokandtsy*, their way of life, fortresses, troops, commanders, and with the town of Turkestan in all its filthiness, as an example of all Central Asian fortresses, and to know that the editor was a zoologist, as even though he was slightly wounded in hand to hand combat, he does not cease to pay attention to the plants and birds he sees by the road." from *Rossiiskii Gosudarstvennyi Voenno-Istoricheskii Arkhiv* (RGVIA), f.66 'Dobrovol'skii F. S.' op. 1, g. 84, "Chernoviki i otryvki dnevnika F. Dobrovol'skogo vo vremia ego voennoi sluzhby v Turkestane", l.1ob.

18 One example of the reportage about Russian captives in Central Asia is: "Nevol'niki v Khive," *Vestnik efropy*, 1815, No. 7, Part 80. Another example of official report on captivity is Mikhail Galkin's records on Russian captives who were released by the Bukharan Khanate in 1858 after Ignat'ev's diplomatic mission in *Etnograficheskie i istoricheskie materialy po rednei azii i orenburgskomu kraiu* (1868).

19 Fillip Efremov, "Stranstvovanie Filippa Efremova v Kirgizskoi stepi, Bukharii, Khive, Persii, Tibete i Indii i vozvreshenie ego ottuda cherez angliiu v rossiiu," *Puteshestviia po vostoku v epokhu Ekateriny II* (Moscow: Vostochnaia Literatura, 1995), 185.
20 Efremov, "Stranstvovanie Filippa Efremova," 150.
21 S. Bol'shoi, "Zapiski Savvy Bol'shogo o prikliucheniiakh ego v plenu u kirgiz-kaisakov v 1803 g. i 1804 g.," *Syn otechestva*, No. 12, 1822, 217.
22 Severtsov, *Mesiats plena*, 51.
23 Severtsov, *Mesiats plena*, 23.
24 One example is A. Tatarinov's *Semimesiachnyi plen v Bukharii* (1867). In 1865 Tatarinov came to Bukhara as a traveler with a Russian diplomatic mission, but their mission was imprisoned by the Emir for seven months. Although Tatarinov records the hostility towards Russians during his stay in Bukhara, the mission did not meet any violence or torture. They were overall under house arrest until the Emir released them. See A. A. Tatarinov, *Semimesiachnyi plen v Bukharii* (Moscow and St. Petersburg: Tip. M. O. Vol'fa, 1867). Katya Hokanson kindly provided another valuable reference about a similar "captivity" incident that happened to the Swiss traveler Henri Moser in Bukhara in 1883. He records that when he traveled to Bukhara in the company of a Russian envoy, they were kept by the Emir as a "virtual prisoner" for three weeks. They were probably kept as hostages as part of Bukhara's diplomatic policy in their relations with Russia. See, Seymour Becker, *Russia's Protectorates in Central Asia: Bukhara and Khiva, 1865–1924* (London: Taylor & Francis, 2004), 168.
25 Alan Fisher points out that the Koran orders Muslim slave owners to treat the slaves humanely and encourages them to free slaves, as it is recognized as a kind of pious act. Fisher, "Muscovy and the Black Sea Slave Trade," 576.
26 *Adventures of Michailow*, 27.
27 *Adventures of Michailow*, 35.
28 *Adventures of Michailow*, 31.
29 Bol'shoi, No. 14, 302.
30 This image of suffering Russian captives echoes some captivity stories about the Caucasus. For instance, while examining the issue of captivity, theft and gift in the Caucasus on historical, literary and anthropological levels, Bruce Grant suggests that the image of the Russian captives constructed in these captivity stories, for instance, in Pushkin's *Kavkazskii plennik*, can be termed as "the good Russian prisoner," a Promethean figure who suffers from his generosity, and the Russian captives are a "Promethean gift to the Caucasus of the Russian empire." The myth about the good Russian prisoner naturalizes Russia's violent military actions in the Caucasian mountains and justifies this violence. See: Bruce Grant, *The Captive and the Gift: Cultural Histories of Sovereignty in Russia and the Caucasus* (Ithaca: Cornell University Press, 2009).
31 Severtsov, *Mesiats plena*, 31.
32 Severtsov, *Mesiats plena*, 44.
33 Severtsov, *Mesiats plena*, 32–3.
34 Virginia Martin, "Barïmta: Nomadic Custom, Imperial Crime," in *Russia's Orient: Imperial Borderlands and Peoples, 1700–1917*, eds. Daniel R. Brower and Edward Lazzerini (Bloomington: Indiana University Press, 1997), 251, 264.
35 Martin, "Barïmta," 250.
36 Severtsov, *Mesiats plena*, 35.
37 As Virginia Martin points out, evidence demonstrates a lack of understanding on the part of Russian observers of barimta as nomadic custom. "The 1822 Regulations [*Ustav o Sibirskikh Kirgizakh*, Regulations on the Siberian Kirgiz] defined it as *grabezh*; Levshin used it to mean 'the holding of criminals or their relatives' and 'the stealing of cattle'. An article in *Sibirskaia gazeta* in 1886 used the term

barimta to describe repeated incidents of horse theft by Kazakhs. The steppe governor-general [Maksim Antonovich Taube], in his 1898 annual report, discussed *barimta* as 'cattle' theft." See Martin, "Barïmta," 258.

38 Severtsov, *Mesiats plena*, 33–4.

39 Severtsov, *Mesiats plena*, 37.

40 Severtsov, *Mesiats plena*, 49.

41 See, for instance, Ron Sela "Prescribing the Boundaries of Knowledge: Seventeenth-Century Russian Diplomatic Missions to Central Asia," in *Writing Travel in Central Asian History*, ed. Nile Green (Bloomington: Indiana University Press, 2013), 69–88.

42 *Atlas rossiiskoi, sostoiashchei iz deviatnadtsati spetsial'nykh kart predstavliaiushchikh vserossiiskuiu imperiiu s pogranichnymi zemliami, sochinonnoy po pravilam geograficheskim i noveishim observatsiiam, s prilozhennoiu pritom general'noiu kartoiu velikiia seia Imperii* (St. Petersburg, 1745).

43 E. I. Blankennagel', *Zamechaniia maiora Blankennagelia, vposledstviie poezdki ego iz Orenburga v Khivu v 1793–94 godakh* (St. Petersburg, 1858), 15.

44 Blankennagel', *Zamechaniia maiora Blankennagelia*, 16, 21.

45 A. von Humboldt, *Central-Asien. Historischer Bericht uber Herm A. v. Humboldt's Reise nach Siberien.* 1844; William MacGillivray, *The Travels and Researches of Alexander von Humboldt: Being a Condensed Narrative of his Journeys in the Equinoctial Regions of America, and in Asiatic Russia; Together with Analyses of his More Important Investigations* (Cambridge: Cambridge University Press, 2009; first published in Edinburgh,1832), 408, 412–13.

46 Efremov, "Stranstvovanie," 1794, 158.

47 Efremov, "Stranstvovanie,"168.

48 Efremov, "Stranstvovanie," 208.

49 Severtsov, *Mesiats plena*, 8–9.

50 Severtsov, *Mesiats plena*, 10–11.

51 Severtsov, *Mesiats plena*, 68. An early short story *Kirgizskii plennik* (1826), written by an ethnographer Petr Kudriashev, contains a description about a similar treatment. In this story, after a Cossack, Fedor, is taken back to the Kazakh aul, the tribesmen apply their cure in order to make Fedor recover from the serious injury he gets from the battle so that he can start working as a slave. The treatment—covering the wound with a fresh and warm sheepskin – proves to be very simple but effective. "The method of treatment was the easiest: everyday Fedor was covered by a hot sheepskin, which was just taken from a sheep. This simple treatment was very helpful for our sergeant. He, after five weeks, completely recovered." Petr Kudriashev, "Kirgizskii plennik (byl' Orenburgskoi linii)", *Otechestvennye zapiski*, Vol. 28, No. 79 (Oct., 1826), 280.

52 Bol'shoi, No. 14, 297.

53 Bol'shoi, No. 14, 297. A reference can be made to John Castle's account, in which he writes about his trip to Abulkhair Khan in 1734 and that Kazakhs considered Castle's "European objects," such as wigs and watches, as something "magical". See in John Castle, "Journal von der AO 1736 aus Orenburg zu dem Abul Geier Chan der Kirgis-Kaysak Tartarischen Horda," *Materialen zu der Russischen Geschichte* (Riga, 1784) trans. Sarah Tolley and ed. Beatrice Teissier, *Into the Kazakh Steppe: John Castle's Mission to Khan Abu'lkhayir* (1736) (Oxford: Signal Books, 2014), 9–10.

54 Bol'shoi, No. 14, 296.

55 Bol'shoi, No. 14, 299. Paula Michaels explains the use of amulets in Kazakh ethomedicine: "Men and women alike adorned themselves and their homes with amulets meant to defend against the evil eye and keep dangerous spirits at bay. Shamans and mullahs both prepared and sold amulets to protect their wearers from illness. Shamans made them from sacred or endowed with special strength to resist or cure disease ... Mullahs typically prepared amulets that consisted of a

small vessel containing a tiny scroll with a Quranic verse or prayer." Paula Michaels, *Curative Powers: Medicine and Empire in Stalin's Central Asia* (Ithaca: Cornell University Press, 2003), 31.

56 *Adventures of Michailow*, 18.

57 Further study on the constructed backwardness of Central Asian medicine during late imperial Russia in Cassandra Cavanaugh, "Backwardness and Biology: Medicine and Power in Russian and Soviet Central Asia, 1868–1934," (Unpublished Ph.D. diss., Columbia University, 2001), 18–94.

58 Mary Louise Pratt, *Imperial Eyes: Travel Writing and Transculturation*, 2nd edn (New York: Routledge, 2008), 7.

59 Linda Colley, *Captives: Britain, Empire and the World, 1600–1850* (London: Jonathan Cape, 2002), 15.

6 Imperial dreams and the Russo-Japanese War

The diary of Field Chaplain Mitrofan Srebrianski

Xenia Srebrianski Harwell

When the Russo-Japanese War broke out, Mitrofan Srebrianski (1870–1948)[1] was a military chaplain with the 51st Chernigov Dragoon Regiment, head-quartered in Orel, Russia.[2] He accompanied the troops to Manchuria, and during his two-year absence, from June 1904 to May 1906, sent letters back to his family.[3] These letters were serialized in the *Vestnik Voyennogo Svyashchennika (Journal of the Military Priesthood)*, and later collected and published as *Dnevnik' polkovogo svyashchennika (iz' vremen' Russko-Yaponskoy voyny)* (*Diary of a Regimental Priest [from the period of the Russo-Japanese War]*), with the second edition appearing in 1912.[4] Later, Mitrofan Srebrianski became the Father-Confessor at the Martha-Mary Convent in Moscow, which had been founded and was run by Grand Duchess Elizaveta Fedorovna, sister of Empress Alexandra. During the Soviet period, Srebrianski spent many years in the Gulag and in exile.

The Russo-Japanese War, eclipsed by later events of the twentieth century, was still remarkable in military history for several reasons: the large number of casualties, the cost of the war, and the length of the periods of fighting.[5] Likewise, due to subsequent events in Russia, diaries such as Srebrianski's were suppressed, and religious figures largely disappeared from history.[6] Nataliya Anatol'yevna Srebrianskaya argues that one of the values of Sreb-rianski's diary is that it presents an account that differs from the typical Soviet interpretation of the war.[7] David Wells and Sandra Wilson point out that "grand narratives" are not the only representations of war and that "interpretive and reflective discourse" by individuals rounds out the historical picture and may lead to a broader understanding of an event.[8] As letter-writer, observer, and representative of the educated clergy, Srebrianski offers a unique perspective on Asia through his descriptions of interactions with the local population and culture of Manchuria on the one hand, and through the attitudes toward Asia and Asians manifested in his diary, on the other. We have no record outside Srebrianski's diary as to how and when he became aware of Asia, or who might have influenced his thought. We can draw con-clusions about his attitudes only from what he writes, and since he is writing to family and friends, i.e. people he would view as like-minded individuals, we may assume that he is not concealing or dissembling in his letters. In comparing his words to the wide range of opinions about Asia coexisting in Russia at that time, as discussed in great detail by historian David Schimmelpenninck van der Oye, we can discern where Srebrianski might fit along the continuum of attitudes towards China and Japan.[9] There is no indication in Srebrianski's diary that he had a predetermined view of Asia, although, as we shall see in this chapter, at times his views did coincide to some degree with disparate currents of thought running through Russian society. Related to this, is the question of what our own expectations of an individual such as Srebrianski—a cleric and a patriot—might be in terms of his view of Asia, and how his diary confirms or challenges these expectations.

Srebrianski's diary is also of interest in its description of the war and its aftermath. Although Srebrianski makes clear that his diary is solely a narrative of personal experiences and an eyewitness account of what he saw within a narrow frame, and that it will not provide an extensive military account of battles, he nevertheless was present at key land battles of the war, such as Mukden and Liaoyang, and his diary is structured according to date and geographical location of battles and skirmishes. This makes it possible to follow his movements in the course of the war and to compare his account to the accounts and conclusions of others.[10] Of particular note, and a subject that Srebrianski himself highlights, is his description of the demeanor and behavior of the soldiers in his care. His positive depiction of his soldiers' battle-readiness and devotion to duty may be examined and compared to other accounts of the Russian troops fighting in the Russo-Japanese War.

While providing an intimate portrait of his encounter with the East—both in Russian Siberia and then in Manchuria, Srebrianski's diary also illustrates the extent to which the war was a pivotal moment for him personally, in that it forced him to consider, articulate, and reconsider ideas in a way he might not have done otherwise. My discussion will focus on Srebrianski's narrative construction of the encounter with war, depiction of life in the Chinese milieu, and portrayal of the physical, spatial, and spiritual limits of his experience. The earnest tone of his diary belies the fact that he was only 33 when his journey to Manchuria began.

The journey east

Mitrofan Srebrianski was an individual firmly and seamlessly embedded within the cultural and religious practices of the Russian nation. Born on 1 August 1870 in the village of Tresvyatskoye near Voronezh to Vasiliy Vasil'yevich Srebrianski, Srebrianski came from a long line of priests and priests' daughters reaching as far back as the 1700s. After attending the Voronezh Theological Seminary, but not then wishing to become a priest, Srebrianski received permission from his father to study veterinary science in Warsaw. After marrying Ol'ga Vladimirovna Ispolatovskaya in 1893, Srebrianski decided to enter the priesthood. In 1894, he served the 47th Dragoon Tatar Regiment as deacon and then as priest. In 1896, he was assigned to the

Dvinsk Military Cathedral, and in 1897, upon the invitation of a general in the regiment, he was appointed priest at the Pokrovskii Church of the 1st Dragoon Chernigov Regiment in Orel. Srebrianski gained a reputation as an energetic worker for the social good, a helper of the poor, an empathetic listener with a comforting presence, and a superb orator.[11] Beloved by his parishioners, he was instrumental in building churches, establishing a school and a library in Orel, and in community building, to which he contributed his own resources and personal effort.[12] Srebrianski also had a proclivity for the written word as well as previous experience with diary writing.[13] For example, honored by being selected to participate in the religious ceremonies involving the 1903 canonization of St. Seraphim of Sarov, Srebrianski recorded the events in detail.[14]

Srebrianski's war diary begins on the day of his departure for Manchuria, situating him immediately within the context of the war. Regimental music plays at the railroad station. Though anguished at the imminent separation from his family and parishioners, Srebrianski nonetheless immediately indicates his willingness to make the personal sacrifice for the triumvirate of Russian patriotism—faith, tsar, and fatherland. He says:

> Oh, dear Lord, how difficult this is! The call to abandon everything and everyone and to start upon a distant path, to war, reverberates with pain in my heart. Yes, if not for the holy principles—Faith, Tsar, and the cherished Homeland, and for my firm belief in them, it would be difficult to control myself. Only the knowledge that we are going to defend the *soul of Russian life,* and for the sake of this specifically, we sacrifice everything, are inspired, and take courage.[15]

Srebrianski tells his parishioners that he is thankful for the opportunity to serve, and grateful that his Christian faith will support him: "How wonderful it is that we are Christians!"[16] As the train sets off, however, Srebrianski thinks of home and friends, and becomes emotional when he sees his church through the train window. Sitting on the inside of the window frame, looking out, and feeling the train move further and further from its starting point, Srebrianski has a momentary sensation of confinement both in the physical sense and in understanding the lack of control over a fate of his own choosing. He imagines the train taking him farther away from his home and writes to his family, "However, the steel machine does not slumber, but keeps pulling us forward, not to you, but away from you, further and further forward."[17] Later, in Manchuria, Srebrianski feels most secure when he and the troops are positioned close to the railway line, which, in his mind, continues to be his connection to Russia while he is in the theater of war.

Srebrianski's journey across Russia and through Siberia is part of his eastern experience and a prelude to Manchuria. As he travels further and further away from home, he moves along a path that conveys him from the familiar to the increasingly unfamiliar.[18] Initially, he remains within his own contextual space by meeting priests and visiting the churches and monasteries that are situated along the route. He scours the countryside for chapels, judging the presence of the religious structure within the landscape as markers of civilization. At the same time, as a traveler along the recently constructed Trans-Siberian Railroad, on his way to war with Russian troops, and looking for these architectural signs of nationhood, he too is inscribing himself in the track of Russian imperialism, outward expansion, and colonialization.[19] When he sees Innokentskii Monastery, for example, he recalls that the first missionaries to the region are buried here.[20] In Omsk, he remembers Ermak as the hero who brought lands to the Russian empire, while overlooking the leader's self-interest and lawlessness.[21] Listening to a group of his regiment's soldiers singing as they float down the river in a boat, Srebrianski visualizes Ermak as a hero similarly floating down the river with his band of men, their voices raised in song and fellowship. This romantic image in Srebrianski's imagination results in a contemplative nationalistic and patriotic reverie on song, which segues into that on the Russian soldier:

Oh, the song of the folk, it is genuinely Russian! It, like music, gives expression to the soul of the people. Do you hear with what a broad wave the song of our warriors pours forth? What expansiveness, strength, and energy there is in their song. Only Russian warriors can sing in this way. In their song is clearly heard genuineness, simplicity, faith and strength, a powerful strength ... that is not lost in the face of attack, but moves forward again and again until it reaches its goal. When the goal is reached, the enemy is forgiven—Rus' kisses him. Yes, there is a uniqueness to the song of Russian troops.[22]

On this eastward journey, Srebrianski also notices and is impressed by various signs of Siberian development. He notes the cities that are expanding in size near railroad stations, and comments on how the dense taiga of just a decade ago has been transformed into the settlement of Novonikolayevsk, with a population of 40,000 settlers and numerous schools and businesses.[23] He appears to be familiar with certain resettlement policies, recalling that settlers may not cut down trees, but may cut grasses anywhere in the open lands. He remarks on several of the indicators of Russia's commerce, including the bustling traffic on the rivers, and he salutes achievements of Russian technology such as a blast furnace and large-span railroad bridge construction.[24] He also describes the Baikal Railroad itself in great detail.

As he moves farther east, the familiarity of Siberia as a Russian space lessens. Srebrianski observes the gradual intrusion into the "Russian" landscape of mosques and Muslim cemeteries, chauvinistically comparing them to the greater beauty of Russian Orthodox churches. In contemplating the mosques, Srebrianski thinks to himself that people say the Russians are not patient. He does not elaborate on this idea, but I would suggest that he is perhaps alluding to the government's policy towards Islam in Russia at this time. According to historian Robert Geraci, during this period, Russians tended to believe that if left to interact with Russian culture, Muslims would soon recognize its superiority, convert to Christianity, and assimilate.[25] Beyond these remarks, Srebrianski offers only superficial commentary on the peoples of Siberia. He mentions some of the customs and traditions of the Buriats and the dress of the Kirghiz, and he registers surprise that there is a large Jewish population in Mariinsk.[26]

Crossing Siberia, Srebrianski is particularly aware of the demarcation points that herald transitional spaces—the Volga, the Russia-Asia border, and the place where "not too far" from Russia turns into "distant" from Russia. These caesuras along the landscape again remind Srebrianski of the distance from home, but now with the added realization of the nearness of war. Each demarcation point is sufficiently significant to him to be marked by prayer and ritual, particularly that between Europe and Asia. He writes:

> We traveled past Urzhumka Station, the last in Europe, and Mikhail and I began to serve the moleben.[27] Slowly, singing the hymn to St. Mitrofan, we arrived at the sacred stone post, on one side of which is written "Asia," and on the other—"Europe." While singing "Dear Jesus, save us," and "Holy Mother of God, save us," we crossed the border. Standing on the platform and stairs of the rail car, I blessed Europe, and then, turning, I blessed Asia. This moment will remain in my memory forever. While we sang "Save us, O Lord," everyone kissed the cross, and I went through all the train cars.[28]

Finally, the most spatially crucial border is the last, that between Russia and Manchuria. And symbolically, as the train arrives, Srebrianski sees hillsides of crosses from past battles. This marker on the landscape brings him face to face with the reality of war.

The religious geography of wartime Manchuria

Tim Cresswell points out that space does not have a meaning that is natural and obvious, but one that it is encompassed within a process created by people.[29] As a traveler through Siberia, Srebrianski is primarily observing and reacting to the spaces he traverses. With the exception of decorating his railroad compartment with icons, he can do little to change his environment. Along the railroad route, he is a borrower of pre-existing spaces (churches or chapels) that have a predetermined role as sacred places. Once across the border, this primarily passive negotiation of space necessarily comes to a halt. Since no legitimate sacred spaces in the form of churches or chapels exist to meet his needs, Srebrianski faces the task of shaping a space initially void of meaning into one that will enable him to continue his sacred traditions in service to the troops. This space may be a part of the open natural environment of Manchuria, or a structure with Chinese owners, which must be acquired through cultural negotiation.

Overcoming this spatial challenge defines Srebrianski's experience in Manchuria. As he engages in this process, he is working within two distinct but converging spatial spheres. The first is the ever-shifting war space, a space of movement and uncertainty. The second is dependent on the first and must constantly be sought out and built anew as the theater of war shifts to alternate locations. The first sphere needs and demands the spiritual component and places value on it. The second sphere, the physical location borrowed from the alien culture, is indifferent to the spiritual component but is forced to accommodate it. The result is an interplay of Russian and Chinese structures and spaces, with the former characterized by their temporary nature, not only because of the shifting locations of war but also because they are being superficially superimposed upon the long-standing traditional structures belonging to the Chinese. Further, the temporary ownership of the Chinese space for the Russian spiritual ritual can also be seen as symbolic for the temporary nature of the sojourn of Russian troops on Manchurian soil.

As Srebrianski moves with his troops or to the different locations where his troops are spread out, he is required to construct and deconstruct the sacred space anew. Occasionally, the spiritual space he enters is unpredictable, as for example, when he gives communion to a soldier crushed by a cart. He comments, "Did I ever think that I would administer sacraments to the sick right on the ground, almost on a pile of manure, among horses?"[30] Sometimes, events necessitate the performance of the religious ceremony in an outdoor location. Usually, however, and preferable to that, is the *fanza*, or a Chinese home with a courtyard, that is requisitioned for his use when it is available. The *fanza*, as a structure belonging to a Chinese family, already has its own pre-established spatial and social function. On one occasion, when Srebrianski appropriates this space, he replaces Buddhist religious artifacts with Russian Orthodox sacred objects. Pulling down Buddhist images, he builds an iconostasis with Russian icons in their stead. In doing so, he appears to be creating a kind of equivalency of religious imagery, although he himself does not note the signification of this act. Under extreme circumstances, however, as when a *fanza* is particularly filthy, Srebrianski will not display his sacred objects. In demonstrating his reverence for them, he highlights their difference and the fact that they do not actually belong in that space. In a similar vein, when conducting a service in a *fanza*, Srebrianski sees himself and his soldiers as out of place: "Oh, what a picture. In faraway Manchuria, instead of a church, Christian warriors gathered in the courtyard of a Chinese *fanza* to remember in prayer and eternal memory a comrade who fell while fulfilling his duty and oath."[31]

The difficulties involved in finding a suitable *fanza* and pressing it into service for the religious ceremony resolve themselves when Srebrianski receives a "portable" church—a tent-like structure and some collapsible furniture—from Grand Duchess Elizaveta Feodorvna, the royal head and sponsor of his regiment.[32] The tent church immediately becomes Srebrianski's most valued possession, simplifies the appropriation of space for the religious ritual, and even more clearly suggests that no long-term foothold will be established in the Manchurian space. It does not, however, alleviate Srebrianski's occasional sense of otherness, which he experiences in both the *fanza* church and the portable Orthodox church. On one occasion, in the process of preparing a

space for the religious ceremony, Srebrianski experiences a double and competing view of the Self. On the one hand, he naturally sees the Chinese, whose
space he is occupying, as the Other. More unexpectedly, he simultaneously
has the experience of observing himself—his own movements and actions
within the Chinese space—from the perspective of the Chinese:

> We took all the Chinese gods off the walls first. Then we separated out a
> portion of the fanza, hung up the icons and the gates. I set up the por-
> table altar. It turned out to be a very nice church. Everyone gathered
> again around 9, ... and I conducted the holy liturgy. From the street we
> could hear the noise of many voices. In the windows we could see the
> heads of curious Chinese.[33]

Following the gaze of the local people back to himself, he sees his own
Otherness. His thoughts turn to ancient times, when the early Christians were
considered to be the Other, and he sees similarities with his own situation:

> Unwillingly I began to think about the ancient Christians, as in the first
> centuries of Christianity in populous pagan Rome; those few who
> acknowledged the true God met at the homes of true believers ... Their
> entire appearance bore the imprint of concentration and veneration while
> around them in the streets of Rome swarmed crowds of thousands of
> their brothers who were still 'sitting in the darkness' ... And now, stand-
> ing before the holy altar, it occurred to me that we today are like the
> ancients. In populous pagan Mukden, a 'small cohort' of Christians
> gather to celebrate the risen Christ ... And look at how heartfelt their
> prayer, how inspired their singing! And around them many thousands of
> brothers who do not yet know Christ are wrangling and bustling about.[34]

At another point, Srebrianski draws a parallel between himself and early Christians, recalling that they have weathered the storms of persecution in the past. In
Suyutunyu, he sets up a church with difficulty due to the wind and cold. He
thinks symbolically that the Church has faced challenging winds before, and that
it stands as a port among storms, strengthening spirits and bodies:

> We started setting up the church. It was extremely difficult: the ground was
> frozen ... The wind was tearing the tent and the icons. Our hands were stiff
> with cold. At last with great effort we set up the church ... The wind beat
> it furiously, clumps of snow and dirt flew. The ropes creaked, our church
> bent. ... But the Lord continued to bless us with his icon and the cross
> above remained steadfast. ... Unwillingly, a comparison entered my mind.
> For a long, long time now the holy church of Christ has stood in the uni-
> verse. And during its long life what kinds of winds of unbelief attempted to
> destroy it! We had the persecution of the faith, when the blood of martyrs
> was shed for entire centuries ... Then came the time of heresies ...[35]

Once the tent church is set up, it underscores the contrast between inside and outside. Inside the church, it is festive and green at Pentecost, for example, whereas outside, Srebrianski faces travel through a harsh barren landscape scattered with bloated dead animals. Now again, outside is the Other, whereas inside, the portable church elicits a sense of camaraderie and group cohesion. Outside is war; inside the troops can briefly forget it is wartime.

According to Anne Buttimer, a loss of space often means a loss of identity.[36] At one point during the war, the troops and Srebrianski are in an encampment for a longer period of time. They engage in a ritual of naming—the swamp near the encampment becomes the Neva, and the dirt road nearby—Nevsky Prospekt. While they perform this action in jest, it can also be interpreted as a gesture in which the soldiers inscribe their identity into the available spatial sphere:

> The village in which we lived was located right near the permanent way of the railroad ... Parallel to this strip was a long, turbid puddle. This was unanimously designated as our "Neva," and the road itself as "Nevsky Prospekt." Each evening ... people took walks along the road. Everyone came out from their "jails", starting with the generals and ending with us mere mortals.[37]

The tent church too performs this identity-inscribing function. Even though it is an incomplete re-creation of the original Russian Orthodox structure, in its association with it, the tent church maintains its referentiality and reflects the national space, thereby restoring identity. This is true on a personal level for Srebrianski and for others as well. After setting up the tent church for the first time, Srebrianski writes:

> It turned out so cozy that not only I, but everyone who came to us to pray was absolutely delighted. You enter the little church, and you forget about China, Mukden, the war—it is as if in an instant you have been transported to dear Russia.[38]

To the soldiers, Srebrianski himself, as a priest in the tent church, is a comforting and familiar symbol of home, and soldiers participate enthusiastically in preparing for church festivals in an attempt to recreate the mood of festivities as it was at home. The temporary church, whether tent or fanza, also upholds the spiritual and military order simultaneously. It recreates the military hierarchy in that during services, the leadership stands in front, followed by officers, and with regular soldiers farther back or outside. Likewise, in his sermons, Srebrianski combines the spiritual and the military as well. He admonishes soldiers to pray, confess, and accept, but also to maintain discipline in war, to follow orders, to support one another, and to perform honestly the tasks assigned by tsar and God. He calls soldiers who have fallen in battle heroes in that they fulfilled their earthly duties as both warriors and Christians, and he promises that they will be given the final victory, i.e. eternal life. He preaches that in eternity we will learn why God has allowed this war to occur, and that it was certainly because he loves the Russian people and wants them to return to him. In all of these various ways, unchanged cultural practices from Russia operate within a closed system to sustain cultural identity and replay the social order of home.

The presence of the temporary church within the Manchurian space in wartime also has significance from the point of view of the morality narrative for both the Russian soldiers and the Chinese residents. If we assume that social spaces are configured according to the moral beliefs of a society, as Rosalyn Deutsche theorizes,[39] and that in encoded landscapes, "individuals tell morally charged stories about themselves and the social structure of the society in which they live, "[40] then the presence of the church, both visually and in its ritual practices, invites a narrative that Russian soldiers can tell each other and the outside world, about themselves as moral individuals, necessarily engaged in war. The narrative may also convey the message that the war itself is moral. This speaks to Betsy Perabo's notion of the Christian soldier in the Russo-Japanese War.[41] As she points out, during this period the troops were routinely referred to as a valorous Christ-loving military who would earn their spot in Heaven through their actions in war.[42] This was the belief of the Bishop of the Russian Orthodox Church in Japan, Nicolai, and Srebrianski's own theology is also consistent with this idea in that he "reminded soldiers" that war and faith are compatible.[43] Srebrianski saw no conflict, for example, between the idea of a soldier and of a Christian hoping to be accepted into the Kingdom of Heaven. Perabo points out that a prevalent idea of the time was that the war experience of soldiers "should be structured by Christian rituals and ideas."[44] Srebrianski, too, acted on the assumption that all Russian soldiers were actively Russian Orthodox and would expect the church to accompany them to war. Finally, Perabo writes that many people saw the defeats of war as "divine punishment" for a lack of faith.[45] This idea as an explanation for military losses gradually emerges in Srebrianski's diary as well, as military losses accumulate.

Srebrianski's depictions of local inhabitants and religions

When Srebrianski turns his attention to the Chinese, he views them through the prism of his humanity and religious sensibilities. Although initially taken aback by their poverty and large numbers, and by the chaos of their cities, his assessment of them gradually becomes more nuanced.[46] He particularly acknowledges those who initiate positive interactions with him. He notes the respect he himself receives from some Chinese in regard to his position as a religious leader, and the Chinese individuals who show an interest in the religious aspects of his work are described more fully in his diary. For example, he singles out a Chinese man who is attracted to the liturgy and another who is entranced by Russian liturgical music. He describes fully a Chinese aristocrat and colonel in the Chinese army, who befriends him and finds him a large fanza for his religious services, and then does him the honor of attending, dressed in magnificent regalia.

Srebrianski's interaction with the local people characterizes him further as empathetic to the plight of the local population:

> Here is another example. Feeling sorry for one family, which had been torn in two, I gave the old man a ruble. Out of joy, he got on his knees. Touched, I raised him up, almost with tears in my eyes. And guess what? About 20 minutes pass, and the old man brings in a small chicken and gives it to me as a gift, firmly refusing to take any money for it.[47]

Srebrianski shows kindness to the poor and contributes money to a Chinese woman whose *fanza* burned down. On numerous occasions, he expresses his sympathy for innocent Chinese displaced by the war and fleeing their homes, and then scrounging for whatever they can find when the Russians break camp. In this regard, Srebrianski finds it hard to accept the "normalcies" of war:

> We are traveling through the countryside. The heathen temple had evidently been a nice one, but now it was a complete ruin—the gods were smashed into pieces, and are lying around on the ground like trash. The doors have been stripped and broken. The bell is smashed. Who is responsible? Some blame the Cossacks, others the chunchuzy, and others reason that, "after all, there is a war going on here," so it is normal ... Perhaps it is *normal* in war, but my heart tightens from this *normalcy,* if one can express oneself thus. Then this means that Napoleon had the right to turn Uspenskii Cathedral into a stable? After all, there was war then too![48]

Srebrianski also expresses discomfort at having to requisition *fanzas,* and he does attempt to reimburse the owners in some way. At one point, he even states that he is grateful there is a better life after death because of how much the Chinese suffer in this life. From the theological perspective, this may sound unusual, since Srebrianski is implying that non-Christians may also be rewarded in the afterlife. However, it is in keeping with the Russian Orthodox understanding that we as humans do not know God's plan. Srebrianski's open-mindedness engenders relationships of trust with the Chinese. As one sign of this, he is invited by his hosts to visit a women's *fanza*:

> I entered. The presence of women was palpable ... There was a bench with red pillows, several mirrors, dried flowers, a book with embroidery designs ... The older wife ... was smoking opium. ... The husband offered me the pipe and was very surprised when I refused. ... The wife poured me a cup of tea. Sugar was not customary. We started a lively conversation. I speak no Chinese, and he speaks not a word of Russian.

For this reason, our conversation was accompanied by such mimicry and gesticulation that it became funny.[49]

Srebrianski also describes a merry evening in which Russians and Chinese are housed together and try to learn each other's language. On several occasions, Srebrianski looks to the Chinese for the normal human interaction that he is deprived of in a war setting. During one stop, his regimental staff is housed on the property of a rich Chinese man. One *fanza* is unused and the Chinese women of the family are housed there. Srebrianski describes what happens:

> I went out into the yard. Some little children ran out into the yard ... I missed children so much that I immediately got into their crowd, showed them some affection, and began to play with them. Happy, carefree children's laughter could be heard in the entire large yard. The "madams" (this was how the Chinese referred to their wives) heard that the Russian captains were not bad, and their women's curiosity got the better of them. ... First their heads appeared, and then out they came ... One Chinese woman held a baby. I approached and gestured for the baby to come to me. And what happened? He began to laugh and held his hands out to me. Of course, I took him ... The baby was very happy and continued to laugh, to the delight of his mother.[50]

Ultimately, though eager to return home, Srebrianski expresses regret at leaving some of the Chinese people with whom he has become more closely acquainted.

When Srebrianski has something critical to say about the Chinese who do not support the Russians, it is measured in tone. Srebrianski mentions the Chinese criminal bands, the *chunchuzy*, as the enemy, but is emotional in thinking about the fate of a group of them captured by the Russians. He recalls a *fanza* intentionally littered with manure to prevent the Russians from billeting there but understands why it was done. He remembers being shot at by Chinese and Japanese while crossing a river, but at the same time recalls that a Chinese man once rescued a drowning Russian soldier, and that a group of Chinese men hid and protected an escaped (from the Japanese) Russian soldier for an entire month at their own peril. Srebrianski also does not hesitate to condemn incidents initiated by Russian soldiers to take advantage of Chinese citizens. He disapproves of a Russian officer who will not allow a rickshaw driver to rest, for example, and he is critical of a Russian soldier who steals a pipe from a Chinese man and participates in reclaiming it from the soldier to return it to its rightful owner.

Srebrianski does not speak extensively or in depth about Buddhism or other Eastern religions.[51] He does take an interest in the depiction of Buddhist deities, especially in that they are both male and female, and in that some wear military outfits. On a visit to a Buddhist monastery he is particularly intrigued by the figure of a goddess:

On the left was a figure ... with nine heads, with eight large hands and 26 small ones. On the palm of each hand was an eye, and she had wings on her back ... two hands were clasped in prayer, as among Catholics, four were in the act of making a blessing, in the seventh hand was a luk, and in the eighth—a mirror.[52]

He attempts to interpret the symbolism of this figure:

It seems to me that the heads signify the wisdom of the godhead, the multiple hands—omnipotence, the multiple eyes—omniscience, wings—omnipresence; hands folded in prayer signifies that the godhead hears the prayers of the people; hands in the form of blessing signify mercy and thanksgiving, the luk—justice, and the mirror—moral purity.[53]

Srebrianski is also drawn to examine examples of Buddhist architecture, including cemeteries. Impressed by the careful and uniform construction of towns, he sincerely regrets the war damage and destruction to which they are subject.[54] In particular, Srebrianski is fascinated by the wall of the city of Mukden, near his encampment. To him, the wall symbolizes the contrast between ancient and contemporary Chinese civilization:

Yes, the ancient Chinese were capable of creating a religion, art, all of their sacred architecture, palaces, walls. Today's Chinese have not created anything new and do not maintain the old. Walls are crumbling, palaces are covered in rot and dust ... No one would think of making repairs—no one cares.[55]

Srebrianski reflects that by not taking care of their unique architecture and by allowing bureaucratic greed to sacrifice ancient buildings and art to ruin, the Chinese people demonstrate that they do not value their past. Srebrianski's musings on the state of Chinese architecture leads him to ponder the Chinese attitude towards religion. He expresses the conviction that the Chinese religion has ossified into a cult of the ancestors and is no longer a living religion. The Chinese still have the talent to create beauty, he feels, because they produce beautiful flowers in terrible soil through sheer hard work, but do not devote the same hard work to seeking out the spiritual. Srebrianski readily admits that his ideas may be superficial but pushes forward modestly to consider the Japanese and their spiritual state. In one of the rare instances in which Srebrianski mentions the Japanese, he theorizes that they are in a similar spiritual state as the Chinese:

It is said that the Japanese have lost even more of their religion. They fill the *inner emptiness* of their lives in pursuit of a foreign civilization, which they hurry to incorporate into their own lives. But they are unwilling to also incorporate the spirit of European civilization, *the spirit of life*, i.e. a true religion capable of filling their inner emptiness.[56]

Srebrianski predicts that in the future, the Japanese will become exhausted from the cultural appropriation of foreign cultures and will then experience a spiritual renewal.[57]

Personal struggles and the end of the war

Srebrianski applies the same standard of duty and bravery to himself as he does to his soldiers. During his first religious service in China, Srebrianski almost passes out at the sound of cannon fire in the background. Gradually, though, he becomes accustomed to war and, unlike some chaplains, bravely remains with his men under dangerous conditions, knowing that they value his presence. He often states that the Russian soldiers in his spiritual charge do not spare themselves, and that he has to work for them as a son of the fatherland and because of his duty as a citizen. With time, the pressures of military life and the constant danger accumulate. He sees Japanese corpses being eaten by dogs. He finds an amputated leg and Chinese remains that he reburies, and he is sickened by dead animals. But most importantly, Srebrianski is pained to bury soldiers in their bloodied and torn uniforms, thereby denying them that last gesture of respect, and to bless soldiers he knows are going to their death. He struggles with the extent of the sacrifice the troops make, and wonders at the resiliency of the human spirit. Additionally, he must constantly respond to the rebukes of his family and friends, who repeatedly insist in their letters that he remain with the supply wagons instead of venturing into areas of battle. He explains the vital role he feels he plays amongst the troops:

> Forgive me that I write letters and diary so sparingly. There is no time for anything. We have no supplies, ... just our horses... I am somehow very tired. We reach our destination and I am happy with my spot—I lie down and stay there, resting. I don't want to do anything. Some people continue to ask me why I am not in the supply train. But, dear ones, I am a field chaplain, not service personnel. I am needed here; my place is with my spiritual children. Had I not been here, the soldier wounded on 25 April would have died without communion, and the soldier killed on the 28th would have been buried without a memorial service. And do you realize how much priests are valued here? In one regiment the priest always stays back with the supply wagons. So there the field doctor has taken up some of the duties of the priest ...[58]

Though exhausted, Srebrianski forges on, even volunteering with the Red Cross in order to comfort the wounded. His living conditions (cockroaches, rats, temperature extremes), and especially the constant changes in location day and night, take their toll on him. He begins to lose his hair, and the stress of the situation is manifested in homesickness and in a physical and spiritual exhaustion that appears to border on depression. However, Srebrianski continues to fight against his limitations, drawing on his faith to give him strength to remain true to his vows. This personal crisis comes at a time when troop losses are growing, and victory appears to be doomed. In his weakened condition, Srebrianski even allows doubt to seep into his mind about the leadership qualities of the Russian military leaders, whom he generally otherwise respects. He writes:

> I feel fatigue, ... apathy ... Sometimes tears rise in my throat and I am ready to weep ... In my soul I feel like I have died ... Some kind of indifference has overcome me ... For 11 months now we have been riding, walking, have been heartsick at the appearance of the surrounding destruction ... and at the constant dangers, we suffer physically from the constant filth, stink ... and experience no joy, not a single victory. ... I am not losing heart. I am true to my duty and vows ... I can passionately attest to the fact that most of our troops continue to be strong and firm in their resolve to fulfill their duty. Yet unwillingly a thought enters my mind—perhaps, after all, our leadership is actually poor?[59]

The stress of war losses are compounded by Srebrianski's growing awareness of the events taking place in Russia, including Bloody Sunday, and the uprisings and strikes in various cities and along the railroad.[60] He tries to explain away the riots in Vladivostok and Chita as having to do with a local population that is the Other, i.e. consisting of Sakhalin residents, exiles, and Poles, all of whom, he notes, have nothing to do with the army. However, Srebrianski is extremely upset with the Russians in European Russia for what he feels is their lack of patriotism and a betrayal of the Russian soldier, which he believes is having a negative effect on troop morale. Moreover, Srebrianski sees this as a transgression in Russia's hour of need. "Sinful Russia, when will you repent and become holy again?"[61] he laments.[62] Srebrianski's thinking does gradually evolve, however, as he begins to view strikes in Russia as a superficial issue when compared to the life and death stakes of war. For himself, he finds refuge in religion, concluding that it is a comfort to be a Christian, and in making an even greater commitment to his soldiers—to minister to every single soldier in his spiritual care by serving liturgies and giving communion every day for the three weeks prior to their departure from China.

The stressor that Srebrianski seems unable to put into perspective, and that rouses the irritation and passion of this normally sanguine diary writer, is the press reports concerning the war. It seems to Srebrianski that the press is fomenting the uprisings by feeding false or inaccurate information to the public about the war and the behavior of the soldiers. He goes further, condemning the press for publishing actual lies, or what we today might refer to as "fake news."[63] He writes:

> We read newspapers out loud, and I must admit that often we become indignant at the insolent lies of some scribblers about the order in and life of our army. Even people who have never been here write about us. For

example, they say that the troops have nothing to eat, that it is cold and their clothes are of poor quality. In reality, the contrary is true. They eat very good meats no fewer than twice a day, receive bread, tea, and sugar, live in dug-outs that are much warmer than our fanzas, and everyone has a sheepskin jacket, felt boots, cloth foot bindings, and a fur hat.[64]

Srebrianski accuses journalists writing about the war of levying unfair criticism at the military, without themselves having been present at the front,[65] and pointedly shares his opinion that the Germans are reporting events more accurately than the Russians:[66] "It is true that the Germans write more truthfully about us. For example, they say that our army has everything it needs for the time of year and for the soldier's stomach."[67] Time and time again, Srebrianski defends his soldiers for their loyalty, heroism, and willingness to sacrifice everything for their country against the smears of the press. He goes so far as to accuse the press of being traitors for undermining military efforts while the war is still in progress.[68] In speaking of the valor of the Russian soldiers facing multiple hardships, Srebrianski elevates them by comparing them to knights of old.[69] He emphasizes that a soldier is willing to spill his blood for the homeland and the tsar and contrasts the behavior of soldiers to what is being reported in the press, asserting that it is the journalists who are dishonorable. As if to underscore his opinion of the press, Srebrianski throws his newspapers into the filthiest corners of the *fanza*. Realizing that his vehement outbursts against the press in support of the troops are exceedingly emotional, Srebrianski then apologizes to his readers.

Another aspect of Srebrianski's defense of the troops and of his anger is that he believes that Russia gave up the war prematurely.[70] He writes that he and the troops do not consider themselves defeated, or losers, even if the Russian people do. It should be noted that when Srebrianski praises the Russian soldier, he does not make comparisons with the Japanese soldier through the prism of a Russo-centric sense of superiority, but simply focuses his attention on the positive attributes of the Russian. It is probably the case that Srebrianski did not know very much about the Japanese military in general terms, just as he probably had scant knowledge of Japan in general. For example, on one occasion, Srebrianski suggested that one area in which the Russian military was superior, and the Japanese military was at a great disadvantage, was in dealing with war in winter. What Srebrianski did not know was that Japan had "drilled regiments of troops in subzero weather on Mount Hakkoda in northern Japan for a Siberian campaign."[71] Srebrianski also once expressed an erroneous belief regarding the ancestry of the Japanese people. During the battle of Shakhe-Inkou, Srebrianski decided to pray to Saint Sergius, noting that this saint had blessed Dmitry Donskoy for victory over Mamai of the Qipchaq Khanate, and claiming that the Russians were now in similar circumstances, fighting the Japanese, who, according to him, were related to the Tatars.

The issue of identity and the Other becomes more complex towards the end of Srebrianski's diary. While we might expect Srebrianski to perceive the Japanese enemy as the Other, we also see his attitude towards European nations that do not support Russia, the anti-war journalists, and especially the revolutionaries and strikers evolve in such a way that he begins to view them as the Other as well. He comments on the strikers:

> Oh, I am too Russian. I feel bitterness and pain for our failures, our humiliation. But my soul absolutely fills with shame when I think about the internal Russian scandals, and the absence of patriotism among many ... I never thought that now, when we have to put everything else aside and think only about saving the honor of our dear homeland, we have found so many traitors, false Russians who organize strikes ...[72]

Thus, segments of the Russian population participating in uprisings against the government are so unrecognizable to Srebrianski in terms of being a Russian phenomenon that they appear alien to him. In the course of his diary, Srebrianski offers various readings as to why the Russians are fighting the war and why they are losing it. At this particular juncture, he offers as an explanation for the Japanese victories the fact that the Japanese are a patriotic people. In doing so, Srebrianski is actually speaking directly to the Russians who are involved in uprisings and in slanted journalism, chastising them for what he sees as their own lack of patriotism.

In displaying anger at events in Russia and at Russian journalists, and in defending the Russian soldier from criticism, Srebrianski is, whether consciously or not, fighting to shape the collective memory of the Russo-Japanese War by the nation. To Srebrianski, the version of the war being offered by journalists is far removed from his lived experience with Russian soldiers, and does not coincide with the collective experience of the war by soldiers at the front. In part, then, his diary is a means of presenting his narrative as a corrective to that being cast by the press.

The diary does not describe the train trip back to Orel since Srebrianski is no longer writing letters home. We know that he is returning to a Russia that is different from the one he left. During Srebrianski's time away, Nicholas II had reaffirmed his rule (March 1905) and formed a parliament (August 1905). By October 1905 soviets had been formed and were multiplying. In that same month, Nicholas II granted broad constitutional rights to citizens and established the Duma, before dissolving it in early 1906.[73]

After the war, Srebrianski received several honors, including the highest honor a military chaplain could be awarded – a gold pectoral cross on a St. George ribbon. His regiment received many distinctions for its service and was the only regiment to be so honored.[74] The journey east to Asia was beneficial for Srebrianski, expanding his worldview and bringing him an experience that allowed him to confront more deeply questions of existence, citizenship, and media. It allowed him to look at his homeland from a distance and to reformulate his basic values in a way that he might not have been able to do had he remained at home, especially if he had had to rely solely on the press reports he disliked so much for his information.

The history of the tent church also does not end with the conclusion of the Russo-Japanese War. According to Srebrianskaya, in June 1906 Grand Duchess Elizaveta Feodorovna came to Orel to greet the returned Chernigov Regiment.[75] The troops stood before the regimental church as she arrived. Located next to the regimental church was the tent church that the Grand Duchess had donated to the regiment and that had traveled with it throughout the war. Later, when the Martha-Mary Convent was being built by the Grand Duchess, the first iconostasis at the cloister was made from parts of the portable tent church.[76]

In 1906 Srebrianski was elevated to archpriest,[77] and two years later he left Orel for Moscow at the invitation of Grand Duchess Elizaveta Fedorovna to take the position of Father-Confessor of the Martha-Maria Convent.[78] During World War I, the convent cared for wounded soldiers. After the revolution, Srebrianski continued his work there even after the arrest of Grand Duchess Elizaveta Fedorovna on 23 April (6 May) 1918, and the convent remained partially functional until 1925.[79] Srebrianski's work and his participation in the Russo-Japanese War had serious repercussions for him during the Soviet period. In early 1923, he was arrested as a member of the organization "Russian Orthodox Church." He was viewed as particularly dangerous by the Bolsheviks because he was well-known among the clergy and the "former people," was the spiritual father of Grand Duchess Elizaveta Fedorovna, had had direct access to Tsar Nicholas II, and was in General Kuropatkin's army during the Russo-Japanese War. He was sent into exile in the Tobol'sk area, returning to Moscow and the convent in February 1925.[80] In April 1925, he was arrested and imprisoned again, and released in July 1925, after the convent had already been closed.[81] In February 1930, Srebrianski, now living in exile in Vladychnya, was arrested for the third time for membership of a cult, expressing monarchist views, and anti-Soviet agitation. He was sent to prison in Tver'. Between April 1930 and early 1933 Srebrianski spent time on Kego Island in the Arkhangel'sk region (on the northern Dvina), in camps in Kandalaksha (Murmansk region on White Sea) and Pechora (Komi Republic), where he worked outdoors in the timber industry, and in Vorkuta (Komi Republic).[82] After the fall of the Soviet Union, the humanitarian and charitable work of the Martha-Mary Convent was once again recognized, and interest in the life and work of Mitrofan Srebrianski grew. Srebrianski was canonized in the Russian Orthodox Church in 2000 and his remains now rest in a cathedral in Tver'.

Conclusions

Around the time of the Russo-Japanese War, Russia did not have a monolithic view of the East, and the spectrum of attitudes towards Asia among its citizens was wide-ranging. Asia scholars tended to be relatively nonjudgmental about the subjects of their research. Most Russians did not consider Asia a "yellow peril" prior to the war, and most did not think or worry about Japan and China at all. Some people felt a kinship to Asia, did not see it as Other, and believed that all people were basically the same. Others felt that China was a great ancient civilization, neither unchanging or immobile, and a peaceful neighbor.[83]

Negative views of Asia were also represented among the Russians. According to Wells and Wilson, it was the religious philosophers Konstantin Leont'yev and Vladimir Solov'yev who first developed the idea of the "yellow peril" as being a threat to Russia and Christianity.[84] In addition, it was Solov'yev who claimed that Chinese culture had ossified. Some journalists and military leaders took the view that Russia must defend itself against the "yellow wave."[85]

Some thinkers looked at Asia while referencing Europe. For example, some were critical of the West and felt that the West was trying to impose its decadent culture on Asia. Others were less extreme, did not see the West as having a superior culture to that of Asia, and believed that Russia should get closer to its Asian roots. On the other extreme, some people believed that Western civilization, as superior, would be a gift to China.[86]

Srebrianski's position along this continuum of attitudes towards Asia may be inferred from his diary. He did appear to share the idea that China and Japan were spiritually and artistically stagnant nations. We do not know the origins of his thinking, but might posit a line from the religious philosophers mentioned above. While deeply embedded in his faith, Srebrianski was not an ideologue—there is no evidence that he imagined a "yellow peril" prior to the war, and he generally refrains from racially-charged stereotyping. However, in the midst of war and in the face of Japanese victory, he did feel the need to sound an alarm:

> We must fight and we must win. Now it is clear that there was a reason that the Lord sent us this war. It looks like everyone's eyes have been opened as to what the yellow nations really are militarily. After all, it can't all be blamed on our carelessness. It is time to give credit to our enemy ... All of Europe must now come together and save itself from the yellow people. Otherwise, after a time there will be no Europe under their onslaught.[87]

In part Srebrianski's statement, threatening the eclipse of Europe at the hands of a militarily-adept East, reflects his outrage that the European nations have not joined together as a group to assist Russia in the war effort. At the same time, he elevates the role of Russia as the nation called upon to unmask this danger to Europe. This notion of Russia as a savior nation with a special mission is one that runs through Russian culture and is reflected here in Srebrianski's thought. Another interesting aspect of this text is the way in which Srebrianski frames his compliment to Japan for its military successes, while simultaneously subverting the compliment. By placing Japan's military prowess within a Christian context, i.e. by implying that a Japanese victory is part of a plan created by a greater spiritual power, Srebrianski removes agency from the Japanese and diminishes their military accomplishments.

Srebrianski achieves the same end on numerous occasions in his diary with his recurrent motif that the war is punishment of the Russian people by God for their failures in living a Christian life, i.e. that for their wicked behavior, God has sent them to war, and that a weaker people, the Japanese, has been chosen to teach Russians a lesson. The effect of reiterating this motif of Russians as failed Christians is to continue to foreground and to shine a spotlight on (Christian) Russians as the major players in cosmic events, despite their sinful ways, while the (pagan) Japanese are relegated to a supporting role. The idea that God uses non-Christians as pawns in the service of the Russian Orthodox asserts the relative importance of Orthodox compared to other peoples, as well as of the Orthodox and their relationship to their God. The notion that God uses non-Christians to punish Russians straying from the Christian path is a long-embedded thread in Russian culture. For example, in the Primary Chronicle the attacks of the pagan Polovtsy on the Russians is seen as God's punishment for their sins, and the Hypation Chronicle attributes Igor's defeat to the same.[88]

In the final analysis, Srebrianski's letters offer a rich picture of one individual's experience in the Russo-Japanese War. First and foremost, the letters reflect Srebrianski's primary functions in the war, which, as a regimental military chaplain, were directed at carving out a spiritual space for his troops within the Chinese milieu to ensure that his soldiers were inspired to perform their duty in war and to prepare for eternal life. From the very first, Srebrianski honored and respected his troops, exhibiting great affection for them, praising their heroism, and weeping for the wounded and the dead. His sensitivity extended to his daily dealings with the Chinese, which reflected an active engagement with, openness to, and understanding of them on a human and personal level. While recording what he observed of their customs and habits,[89] Srebrianski provided a window into the daily lives of the Chinese and into how they dealt with war and with the presence of an occupying force.

Srebrianski's letters also convey some of the challenges and struggles he faced in the physical, emotional, and spiritual spheres. The spiritual and physical labors of war challenged him, as did what he considered to be the transgressive nature of the press and the revolutionaries, as well as the military decisions that were out of his control. These challenges were recorded in detail and with able skills of observation and expressive writing. Also of great value were the descriptions of aspects of several noteworthy battles that Srebrianski personally experienced. Srebrianski's diary captures well both the war and the author. His loyalty to his faith and to the Russian nation was not undermined by the war, despite the many challenges. In Russia, he returned to his role in the church as spiritual father and teacher, contributing to humanitarian work and the social good. His deep commitment to existing institutions propelled him to higher circles of power in Moscow that he did not seek, but that he contributed to with full commitment.

Srebrianski's subsequent writings do not reference Asia. Just as we do not know how Srebrianski imagined Asia prior to his arrival in Manchuria, we also do not know whether or how he reimagined it after the Russo-Japanese War. However, one cannot but suppose that Srebrianski's thoughts turned occasionally to the East when he prayed before the Iversk Mother of God icon. As he recounts in his diary, this icon was presented to him by the people of Orel before the war in gratitude for his contribution to building the church at the Orel railroad station.[90] Srebrianski brought this icon with him to Asia. One day during the war, the Japanese attacked the supply trains, and many items belonging to Srebrianski, including the icon, were lost. Miraculously, however, because of the inscriptions on its back, the icon was returned to Srebrianski by the Japanese.[91]

Notes

1 The transliteration system I am using is that of the U.S. Board of Geographic Names, Table 9.4, *The Chicago Manual of Style*, 14th edn (Chicago: University of Chicago Press, 1993), 346. Well-known Russian names are rendered in a form that is familiar to English speakers. The last name Srebrianski (Srebryanskiy) is written as it is commonly found in the U.S. Recently efforts have been made by scholars in Russia to "russify" the last name through the insertion of an "e"—Serebryanskiy—but the correct spelling of the name since the 1700s has been "Sre ..." and should remain historically accurate.

2 As a result of the reform of the cavalry in 1907, the 51st Chernigov Dragoon Regiment became the 17th Hussar Regiment, headed by Grand Duke Mikhail Aleksandrovich (*Pyat' protiv tridtsati*, n.p.). See *Pyat' protiv tridtsati: Istoriya 51-go dragunskogo / 17-go gusarskogo Chernigovskogo polka 1668–2018* (Orel: Molodyezhnoye bratstvo vo imya Sv. Velikovuchenika I Pobedonostsa Georgiya, 2017).

3 In this chapter, dates are given according to the source text. Srebrianski uses the Julian calendar, which was in effect in Russia during the time of the Russo-Japanese War. The Julian calendar was then thirteen days behind the Gregorian calendar used in the West.

4 For my discussion, I am using the second edition (1912). See Mitrofan Srebrianski, *Dnevnik polkovogo svyashchennika*, 2nd edn (Moscow: Pechatnja A. I. Snegirevoj, 1912). According to the foreword, the difference between the first and second editions is that the second includes photographs and restores elements that had been eliminated in the first. The complete title of the work is: *Dnevnik' iz' vremen' Russko-Yaponskoy voyny svyashchennika 51-go dragunskago (pozdnee 17-go gusarskago) Chernigovskago Yeya Imperatorskago Vysochestva Velikoy Knyagini Yelisavety Feodorovny polka Mitrofana Vasil'yevicha Srebryanskago s momenta otpravleniya polka v' Manchzhuriyu 11-go iyunya 1904 goda i po den' vozvrashcheniya yego v' g. Orel' 2-go iyunya 1906 goda.*

5 David Wells and Sandra Wilson, "Foreword," in *The Russo-Japanese War in Cultural Perspective, 1904–05*, eds. David Wells and Sandra Wilson (London: Macmillan and New York: St. Martin's Press, 1999), 1–29; here ix.

6 When this author visited the Martha Mary Convent shortly after the fall of the USSR, the staff and priests knew virtually nothing of Mitrofan Srebrianski. Since then, his place in history has been reestablished.

7 Srebrianskaya, *Prepodobnyy Sergiy*, 45, 51. See N. A. Srebrianskaya, *Prepodobnyy Sergiy Ispovednik* (Voronezh: Voronezhskiy gosudarstvennyy pedagogicheskiy universitet, 2013). Mitrofan Srebrianski's work is also valuable in comparing his

account with those of other diarists of the war, as well as of journalists from different countries covering the war.

8   Wells and Wilson, "Foreword," ix.

9   These are discussed in David Schimmelpenninck van der Oye, *Russian Orientalism: Asia in the Russian Mind from Peter the Great to the Emigration* (New Haven: Yale University Press, 2010), and David Schimmelpenninck van der Oye, *Toward the Rising Sun: Russian Ideologies of Empire and the Path to War with Japan* (DeKalb: Northern Illinois University Press, 2001).

10 The transliteration of geographical names of locations in Manchuria has presented certain challenges because it is based on the Russian found in the diary, and not on the original Chinese. The geographical names that Srebrianski, a man unfamiliar with the Chinese language, records in Russian depends completely on his interpretation of the sounds he hears. While it is possible to identify larger or more well-known locations, smaller, less familiar locations, or those that no longer exist today, present more of a difficulty. However, Srebrianski is very thorough in noting geographical names, and it is possible to identify some locations with the help of maps from the period. The sections of the diary are as follows: Chapter 1 – From Orel to Manchuria; Chapter 2 – Lyaoyan'-Shakhe; Chapter 3 – Shakhe-Inkou; Chapter 4 – Attack of Inkou; Chapter 5 – Time preceding the Battle of Mukden. Battle of Mukden and Retreat; Chapter 6 – At the Borders of Mongolia; Chapter 7 – Attacking the Japanese near Sanvaytszy village; Chapter 8 – Quiet. Peace. Return.

11 Srebrianski discusses the themes of his sermons in his diary. The text of some later sermons can be found in Srebrianskaya, *Prepodobnyy Sergiy*, 82–119.

12 He was acknowledged to have had a great cultural-moral impact on his regiment and was a talented musician and actor. See Srebrianskaya, *Prepodobnyy Sergiy*, 63, 206.

13 He wrote about his dreams (Srebrianskaya, *Prepodobnyy Sergiy*, 196–203), an article about proper behavior in church, and an article about church music.

14 Srebrianskaya (*Prepodobnyy Sergiy*, 38–44) notes that this diary is unpublished and in the hands of his relatives. She cites excerpts from the diary, including a poem that she attributes to Srebrianski. St. Seraphim of Sarov is among the most revered saints of the Eastern Orthodox Church and was particularly respected by the Russian royal family, who also attended the festivities in Sarov.

15 All italics are found in the original text, Srebrianski, *Dnevnik*, 1. All translations from Russian are mine.

16 Srebrianski, *Dnevnik*, 4.

17 Srebrianski, *Dnevnik*, 12.

18 A similar pattern emerges in Srebrianski's reaction to nature as he traverses European Russia and Siberia and moves into Manchuria. Initially he is comfortable in the natural milieu which reminds him of the Voronezh area (*Dnevnik*, 10). Later he is greatly impressed and awed by the mountains, cliffs, and rushing streams of the Siberian landscape (*Dnevnik*, 11), particularly when he travels the Great Siberian Tract (*Dnevnik*, 27–32) near Irkutsk, causing him to remark and make note of what he sees. He also feels a deep connection between nature and spirituality: "Oh, the beauty, the beauty of nature! How it elevates the soul and brings it closer to God! Officers say to me, 'When you look at your surroundings, how can you not believe?'" (*Dnevnik*, 12), and concludes, "Yes, if people always paid attention to their surroundings and searched for the truth, nature would help them a very great deal" (*Dnevnik*, 12). Srebrianski is also acutely aware of the discomforts of nature in the east, such as insects, dust, and heat and humidity.

19 The building of the railroad began in 1891. See Christian Wolmar, *To the Edge of the World* (Philadelphia: Perseus, 2013), 60.

20 During his trip across Siberia a few years earlier, John Foster Fraser includes a photo of and describes his visit to the Monastery of St. Innokentii, a missionary to China in the early nineteenth century. See John Foster Fraser, *The Real Siberia:*

Together with an Account of a Dash through Manchuria (London: Cassell, 1902), 112–17. According to Benson Bobrick, St. Stephen of Perm established a church in the Kama River Valley in 1376, where a missionary had been murdered previously, and by 1455 missionaries in the region were being supported by the military. See Benson Bobrick, *East of the Sun: The Epic Conquest and Tragic History of Siberia* (New York: Holt, 1993), 38. Further, Bobrick states that by 1586 Tyumen' had two churches, with the first monasteries also being established around this time. He points out that although originally Russia did not favor the forced conversion of natives because of the preference for tribute from them, Vitus Bering in the late 1720s suggested that natives should be converted to Orthodoxy to stabilize the Siberian region, Bobrick, *East of the Sun*, 107–8, 161. According to Yuri Slezkine, the relationship of Russia and Russians to the native peoples encompassed many issues beyond conversion to Christianity. Included among them was the idea that native peoples also required education, "laws, manners, clothes" etc. See Yuri Slezkine, *Arctic Mirrors: Russia and the Small Peoples of the North* (Ithaca: Cornell University Press, 1994), 59.

21 James Forsyth, *A History of the Peoples of Siberia: Russia's North Asian Colony 1581–1990* (Cambridge: Cambridge University Press, 1992), 31–3.

22 Srebrianski, *Dnevnik,* 19.

23 The process of migration from Russia to Siberia began in the mid-nineteenth century, increasing annually. According to Forsyth, 35,000 people per year went to Siberia in the 1880s, around 96,000 per year in the later 1890s, and "between 1906 and 1914 emigration from European Russia to Siberia became a flood. This reached its peak in the year 1908, during which 759,000 people crossed the Siberian boundary." Forsyth, *History*, 191.

24 Of the latter, Srebrianski says, "We are crossing the wide and deep Siberian Ob River. Even though we are here at the upper reaches of the river, the bridge is just a little shorter than the bridge over the Volga at Syzran'. We have started to become accustomed to the hugely long bridges and voluminous rivers, but before it was somehow a little terrifying." Srebrianski, *Dnevnik,* 17.

25 See Robert Geraci, "Russian Orientalism at an Impasse: Tsarist Education Policy and the 1910 Conference on Islam," in *Russia's Orient: Imperial Borderlands and Peoples, 1700–1917*, eds. Daniel R. Brower and Edward J. Lazzerini (Bloomington: Indiana University Press, 1997), 138–61, here 138–9. Nicholas Senn, whose recounting of his journey across Siberia was published in 1902, states that in Omsk, with 50,000 inhabitants, there were 13 Russian Orthodox churches, one Catholic church, and one Lutheran church. He states that in Krasnoyarsk, with a population of 27,000, there were 12 Russian Orthodox, one Protestant, and one Catholic church. See Nicholas Senn, *Around the World via Siberia* (Chicago: W. B. Conkey Company, 1902), 89, 92, 98. For more information on missionary work in Siberia, see Yuri Slezkine, "Savage Christians or Unorthodox Russians? The Missionary Dilemma in Siberia," in *Between Heaven and Hell: The Myth of Siberia in Russian Culture*, eds., Galya Diment and Yuri Slezkine (New York: St. Martin's Press, 1993), 15–31.

26 Jews were not permitted to settle in Siberia until the 1830s, but by the end of the nineteenth century 34,500 Jews were living there, Forsyth, *History*, 196. Jews constituted a large percentage of the population in Sretensk, Verkhneudinsk, and Kansk, which was referred to as the "Jerusalem of Siberia," Bobrick, *East of the Sun*, 328. At the end of the nineteenth century, 10 percent of the population in Russia was Muslim, Schimmelpenninck van der Oye, *Toward the Rising Sun*, 125.

27 A moleben is a service of supplication in honor of a saint.

28 Srebrianski, *Dnevnik,* 13.

29 Tim Cresswell, *Place: A Short Introduction* (Oxford: Blackwell, 2004), 27.

30 Srebrianski, *Dnevnik,* 49.

122 *Xenia Srebrianski Harwell*

31 Srebrianski, *Dnevnik*, 53.
32 Interestingly, according to legend, Ermak and his men transported a collapsible tent over the Urals to use as a field church. Bobrick, *East of the Sun*, 107.
33 Srebrianski, *Dnevnik*, 169.
34 Srebrianski, *Dnevnik*, 170.
35 Srebrianski, *Dnevnik*, 176.
36 Anne Buttimer, "Home, Reach, and the Sense of Place," in *The Human Experience of Space and Place*, eds. Anne Buttimer and David Seamon (New York: St. Martin's Press, 1980), 166–87; here 167.
37 Srebrianski, *Dnevnik*, 129.
38 Srebrianski, *Dnevnik*, 101.
39 Lorraine Dowler, Josephine Carubia and Bonj Szczygiel, "Introduction. Gender and Landscape: Renegotiating Morality and Space," in *Gender and Landscape: Renegotiating Morality and Space*, eds. Lorraine Dowler, Josephine Carubia and Bonj Szczygiel (London: Routledge, 2005) 1–15; Deutsche cited on 6.
40 Dowler, "Introduction," citing James Duncan on 39.
41 See Betsy Perabo, *Russian Orthodoxy and the Russo-Japanese War* (London: Oxford, 2017), for a discussion of the Russian understanding of holy war (6–7), of the concept of "justified war" (66–9), and of the relationship between the liturgical ceremony and the military (69–72).
42 Perabo, *Russian Orthodoxy*, 9.
43 Perabo, *Russian Orthodoxy*, 2, 11.
44 Perabo, *Russian Orthodoxy*, 10.
45 Perabo, *Russian Orthodoxy*, 12.
46 Srebrianski's first impression of the Chinese is somewhat critical. He says: "Everywhere the Chinese are dirty and sunburnt. The front part of their heads is shaven and at the back is a long braid. Hardly anyone wears a hat. They wrap their braid around their head, and the wind blows it around—a terrible sight. No less dirty [...] are the Mongols on their little horses [...]. Incidentally, I am speaking only about their outward appearance; they seem well disposed to Russians [...]" (*Dnevnik*, 36). He also finds that they look alike, work in a naked or semi-naked state, and live in crowded conditions. He notes that the train station is filthy and odoriferous, and dismissively refers to Chinese writing as hieroglyphics. He zeroes in on the disorderly cemeteries. He notices that women find it painful to walk. On the other hand, he sees similarities between Chinese villages and those in some parts of Russia, finds the dandies of the city to be like Russian dandies, and curious boys who crowd the Russians to be like children everywhere (and is later saddened that Chinese children fear the Russians). He appreciates the beauty of a fanza in Kholobtun, but notes the swampiness, the odors, and the lack of sanitation. He sympathizes with the Chinese workers who have been ordered to clean the streets and who are being beaten by other Chinese.
47 Srebrianski, *Dnevnik*, 75.
48 Srebrianski, *Dnevnik*, 52–3. Srebrianski does not indicate an awareness of the protocols of The Hague Conference and other conferences that, according to Perabo, were handed out to soldiers as the rules of behavior in wartime (*Russian Orthodoxy*, 123) and that required soldiers to leave the local civilian population alone.
49 Srebrianski, *Dnevnik*, 251.
50 Srebrianski, *Dnevnik*, 214.
51 According to Perabo, Buddhism was not widely represented in Russia (*Russian Orthodoxy*, 47) but began to be studied more seriously following the Crimean War (*Russian Orthodoxy*, 49). For a more extensive discussion of Buddhism in Russia and of the Russian Orthodox mission in Japan, see Perabo, *Russian Orthodoxy*, 50–55 and throughout her book. For statistics on the diversity of religious groups in Russia, see Perabo, *Russian Orthodoxy*, 39, 46.

52 Srebrianski, *Dnevnik*, 280.
53 Srebrianski, *Dnevnik*, 281.
54 Srebrianski had an interest in architecture in general. He was instrumental in the building of church properties in Russia, including the Martha-Mary Convent. In addition, he skillfully constructed small models of churches with his own hands, and there are photographs of him holding these models (Srebrianskaya, *Prepodobnyy Sergiy*, 186). Towards the end of his life, in exile in Vladychnya, he himself designed and built the house he lived in.
55 Srebrianski, *Dnevnik*, 81.
56 Srebrianski, *Dnevnik*, 82.
57 The idea of the ossification of Asian culture was a thread in Russian thought that originated during the time of Nicholas I, 1825–55, when the intelligentsia began to view China as a site of lethargy and stagnation. Schimmelpenninck van der Oye, *Toward the Rising Sun*, 92.
58 Srebrianski, *Dnevnik*, 286.
59 Srebrianski, *Dnevnik*, 287.
60 For an eyewitness account of the demonstrations along the railroad and the changes occurring in Russia written by a returning soldier, see Captain Vladimir Semenoff, *The Price of Blood: The Sequel to "Rasplata" and "The Battle of Tsushima,"* transl. Leonard Lewery and Major F. R. Godfrey (London: John Murray, 1910), 197–209.
61 Srebrianski, *Dnevnik,* 221.
62 Adrian Jones points out that the Russo-Japanese War recalibrated Russia's idea of itself as a powerful empire, a people with a destiny, and a modern nation. Jones, "Easts and Wests Befuddled: Russian Intelligentsia Responses to the Russo-Japanese War," in *The Russo-Japanese War in Cultural Perspective, 1904–1905*, eds. David Wells and Sandra Wilson (Great Britain: Macmillan, 1999) 134–59, esp. 135, 141. At this point in his diary, Srebrianski is not thinking in such global terms. He is specifically engaged with his troops, supports and reveres them for their sacrifices, and feels that the events in Russia are damaging to the troops at a crucial time in the war.
63 Wells and Wilson appear to substantiate the concerns expressed by Srebrianski in stating that the coverage of events in newspapers was not necessarily reliable, and that lubki and postcard cartoons also promoted unreliable information ("Introduction," 14). See Sandra Wilson and David Wells, "Introduction," in *The Russo-Japanese War in Cultural Perspective, 1904–05* (Basingstoke: Macmillan, 1999). 1–29. They also state that the genre of real and fake war documentation was robust, 15.
64 Srebrianski, *Dnevnik*, 193.
65 In his book, Vladimir Semenoff also accuses the press of failing to publish various documents and eyewitness accounts of certain battles, *Price of Blood*, 210. For example, he points his finger specifically at the newspaper *Novoe Vremya* for publishing an incomplete collection of letters written by a lieutenant who perished in the sea battle, and then doctoring those letters that were published in an effort to paint a negative picture of those involved in the war.
66 For a discussion of the reporting on the Russo-Japanese War by other nations, see Alexander M. Nordlund, "A War of Others: British War Correspondents, Orientalist Discourse, and the Russo-Japanese War, 1904–1905," *War in History* 22: 1 (2015): 28–46; Gary P. Cox, "Of Aphorisms, Lessons, and Paradigms: Comparing the British and German Official Histories of the Russo-Japanese War," *The Journal of Military History* 56 (July 1992): 389–401; Troy R. E. Paddock, "Still Stuck at Sevastopol: The Depiction of Russia during the Russo-Japanese War and the Beginning of the First World War in the German Press, *German History* 16: 3 (1998): 358–76; Kevin R. Swafford, "'In the Thick of It': The (Meta) Discourse of Jack London's Russo-Japanese War Correspondence," *Pacific Coast Philology* 50:

1 (2015): 82–102; and Michael S. Sweeney, "'The Narrative is the Thread, and Truth is a Fabric': Luigi Barzini and the Russo-Japanese War," *American Journalism* 32: 1 (2015): 41–59.
67 Srebrianski, *Dnevnik*, 193.
68 According to Srebrianskaya, as late as 1930 Srebrianski wrote that he considered the events of 1905 to have been criminal acts (*Prepodobnyy Sergiy*, 54).
69 Wells and Wilson state that in time Russia would have defeated Japan, but was undermined by poor leadership, plummeting morale, and the revolution at home ("Introduction," 13).
70 Semeneff, too, praises the soldiers and puts the blame on the leadership for failures during the war. He also complains that he is under a gag order in terms of writing to set the record straight. He points out that while he himself was silenced, the newspaper *Novoe Vremya* was under no such obligation. *Price of Blood*, 212–14.
71 Bobrick, *East of the Sun*, 369.
72 Srebrianski, *Dnevnik*, 221.
73 Bobrick, *East of the Sun*, 384.
74 *Pyat' protiv tridtsati*, n.p.
75 Srebrianskaya, *Prepodobnyy Sergiy*, 56.
76 Srebrianskaya, *Prepodobnyy Sergiy*, 65.
77 Srebrianskaya, *Prepodobnyy Sergiy*, 58.
78 Srebrianskaya, *Prepodobnyy Sergiy*, 62.
79 Srebrianskaya, *Prepodobnyy Sergiy*, 145.
80 Srebrianskaya, *Prepodobnyy Sergiy*, 147.
81 Srebrianskaya, *Prepodobnyy Sergiy*, 149.
82 Srebrianskaya, *Prepodobnyy Sergiy*, 163–6.
83 Schimmelpenninck van der Oye, *Toward the Rising Sun*, 4, 8, 9, 86, 180, 190, 202, 209.
84 Wells and Wilson, "Introduction," 3.
85 Schimmelpenninck van der Oye, *Toward the Rising Sun*, 82, 197, 209.
86 Schimmelpenninck van der Oye, *Toward the Rising Sun*, 35, 50, 197, 203.
87 Srebrianski, *Dnevnik*, 213.
88 Bobrick, *East of the Sun*, 15, 17.
89 Srebrianski normally maintained a level-headed tone regarding what he saw. Only once did he erupt emotionally at Chinese customs. This occurred after someone related to him that he had just witnessed a death sentence: "[...] right in front of the police station the heads of two young women were cut off for adultery. Their heads were thrown into the street in dirty sacks to teach passers-by about faithfulness in marriage. Srebrianski said: "This is the kind of country we find ourselves in now! And when will the Lord allow us to leave?" *Dnevnik*, 50.
90 Srebrianski, *Dnevnik*, 129.
91 Srebrianski, *Dnevnik*, 250.

7 Bad medicine

Ritual, sacrifice, and the birth of Soviet Sakha literature

Naomi Caffee

Spectators in central Moscow who attended the 2018 public festivities for Maslenitsa, a Russian Orthodox holiday marking the beginning of the season of Lent, were treated to a highly unorthodox sight: a shamanic ritual performed on an open-air stage. The shaman, outfitted in a traditional leather costume adorned with clanging bells, sat before a fire and chanted while beating on a traditional drum, in a ritual appeal to the spirits of the Higher World to intervene on behalf of the wellbeing of humankind. But this was no improvisation: in fact, the performance was a contemporary revival of *The Red Shaman,* a revolutionary 1925 work by the Sakha (Iakut) writer Platon Oiunskii. This performance by the Olonkho Sakha National Theater was one of several staged by indigenous troupes from the Russian Republics of Chuvashia, Sakha, and Mari El, who were invited by the Moscow-based Golden Mask organization to perform as part of the citywide holiday celebration.[1]

The curation of indigenous performances for this occasion, as well as the content of the Sakha troupe's performance, raises several questions about the aesthetics, history, reception, and political ramifications of indigenous self-representation in Russia. How did Oiunskii's 1925 work come to be viewed as emblematic of Sakha culture and the Sakha experience, and how did it come to occupy such a central place on a public stage in the Russian metropole? What is the relationship of Oiunskii's drama to an actual shamanic ritual, and what is the significance of shamanism in this work, both at the time of its inception and in the present day? Finally, what can the literary history behind the events depicted on the festival stage tell us about the intertwined imaginaries of Russia and its indigenous peoples? In order to find out, it is necessary to look more closely at the world of the Sakha people of northeastern Siberia in the years immediately leading up to and following the 1917 Russian Revolution.[2] This study features two writers who brought the original text of the *Red Shaman* into being under extraordinary circumstances, and in doing so, formed the genesis of the Sakha national literary tradition.

Petr Chernykh-Iakutskii (1882–1933) and Platon Oiunskii (1893–1939) were Russian-educated members of the Sakha intelligentsia who became early participants in the Soviet literary apparatus. They were born within a decade of one another in the late nineteenth century, in remote areas of the northeastern

Siberian territory that would in 1922 become the Iakut Autonomous Soviet Socialist Republic (Iakut ASSR). Their lives were marked by violence, hunger, illness, and political upheaval, which led them to continuously navigate between Sakha and Russian cultures, as well as Imperial Revolutionary and Soviet political systems.[3] They both received a Russian Orthodox parochial education prior to the 1917 Revolution, and in the years following the Revolution and Civil War, during the Soviet Union's radical program of internal nation-building known as *korenizatsiia*, they "branded" themselves as Soviet Sakha writers by joining Communist political and literary organizations and by taking up pen names that signaled their indigenous origins: "Oiunskii" is derived from *oiun*, the Sakha-language word for shaman, and "Iakutskii" is the Russian-language adjective for Sakha.[4] As writers, educators, ethnographers, and representatives of the emerging Soviet Sakha nation, Oiunskii and Chernykh-Iakutskii attempted to arrive at new modes of indigenous writing that would bridge the Sakha people's past and present, as well as the Soviet Union's metropole and periphery.[5] As such, their works of the early Soviet era fuse together elements of Sakha oral literature and ritual, the Russian literary tradition, and Marxist-Leninist ideology, sowing the seeds for what would eventually become the Stalinist directive for cultural expression: an aesthetic that was "national in form, socialist in content."[6]

However, this was not an easy synthesis. It was achieved under conditions of extreme suffering and uncertainty, which is evident in these authors' works as well as their life stories and the widely divergent ways they were incorporated into in the Sakha canon. Chernykh-Iakutskii, who died of diphtheria in 1933 after spending his final years in rapidly declining health on the outskirts of Moscow, was spared the worst of the Stalinist Terror but did not live to see the founding of the Soviet Writers' Union of Iakutiia nor to participate in its increasingly brutal literary politics throughout the 1930s. Oiunskii, on the other hand, occupied a central position in the Soviet cultural apparatus for the majority of his writing career and, like many others, eventually paid for it with his life. Hailing from a Sakha family of politically correct class background and possessing talents as a scholar and political activist as well as a poet, he fit the bill of a "national" Soviet Sakha writer more readily than Chernykh-Iakutskii, whose mixed heritage, bicultural upbringing, and Russian-language publications led to his classification as a Russian or Russophone (*russkoiazychnyi*) writer. At the same time, however, Oiunskii's ascendance to the pantheon of Sakha national writers was deferred by the Stalinist Terror: in 1938, four years into his term as the chairman of the Writers' Union of Iakutiia, he was arrested on charges of "bourgeois nationalism." He died in prison in 1939, and his works were re-introduced to the public only after his official rehabilitation in 1955.[7]

This study seeks to shed light on the textual and institutional relationship that connects these two early figures in Sakha literature, and, in doing so, to better understand the process of canon formation and the role of competing, clashing, and coinciding imaginaries at its heart. To this end, I will analyze two works that exemplify this connection: the aforementioned 1925 play by Oiunskii, *The Red Shaman*, which was translated into Russian by Chernykh-Iakutskii and the Sakha writer Aleksei Boiarov in 1930, and Chernykh-Iakutskii's own 1928 short story "Bad Medicine" ("*Strashnoe lekarstvo*").[8] These works, written on the eve of the Stalinist cultural revolution, offer a glimpse into the chaotic yet intensely productive time period in which their authors lived. The works converge on a single central thematic element: upholding violent sacrifice—enacted through culturally hybridized ritual—as necessary in order for a new world and a new Sakha people to emerge.

New rituals for a new world: Platon Oiunskii's *The Red Shaman*

Platon Oiunskii's *The Red Shaman* is a hybrid text fusing elements of Sakha oral literature with shamanic ritual and Western-style drama, re-casting indigenous traditions within a Soviet teleological framework. Linking this synthesis to his own "shamanic" poetic persona, Oiunskii wrote in his preface to the 1925 first edition that the initial drafts were composed in a shaman-like trance of revolutionary fervor following the events of 1917.[9] The finished work is the product of a transitional period in Oiunskii's career, as he was becoming a central figure in the Soviet Sakha intelligentsia and ascending the ranks as a Communist Party operative in the newly-formed Iakut ASSR. These roles immersed him in two worlds simultaneously. First was the world of the Sakha language, folklore, and traditional lifeways, as he engaged in ethnographic and philological explorations of his native culture in an effort to define and delineate the Soviet Sakha nation, equipping it with its own modern literary idiom, alphabet, and shared cultural repository. Overlapping all of this was the All-Union Soviet world, with its own customs, beliefs, language, and increasingly complex ideological, logistical, and organizational structures. These circumstances connected Oiunskii to Maksim Gor'kii, the renowned Russian writer, revolutionary, and architect of Soviet multinational literature, who had an interest in Sakha culture and personally encouraged Chernykh-Iakutskii to produce the first Russian translation of *The Red Shaman*.[10] When Chernykh-Iakutskii's Russian translation was eventually published in 1930, it achieved even more widespread visibility – and triggered a spate of negative attention towards Oiunskii that eventually culminated in his 1938 repression.[11] Thus, as a cultural artifact, *The Red Shaman* bears the marks of its long and varied process of inception. Its hybrid content and structure, along with its numerous editions, translations, and performative variations, help to stage the interaction—and violent conflict—of the worlds its author inhabited.

Oiunskii described *The Red Shaman* as adhering to episodes from the Sakha oral epic *olonkho* and noted that its overall structure was meant to correspond to a central *olonkho* theme: the hero's struggle to defend his people from a dangerous outsider.[12] The titular character of the Red Shaman, who summons revolution even as it hastens his own obsolescence and death, serves as an early literary record of the contentious relationship between Soviet visions of modernity and the simultaneous drive to celebrate and preserve indigenous cultures and lifeways. Sakha cosmology likewise forms the backdrop of the drama, as the action takes place in and among the Lower, Middle, and Upper Worlds, with the Middle World corresponding to the earthly realm populated by humans. Disrupting the common categorization of shamans into "white" and "black" along the lines of general moral intent, Oiunskii's Red Shaman takes a prerevolutionary indigenous paradigm and imbues it with Soviet cultural significance.[13] In the opening monologue, as the Red Shaman sits upon a white-and-red-checked carpet, he describes this process in terms of renewal, awakening, and rebirth:

> In the midst of a weary and worn-out world,
> Where eight fateful roads
> Run through the ravine into the ethereal distance,
> I stand, proud, fate itself.
> I am the Red Shaman. In my powerful wings
> I can cast a spell with the wind
> To the people sleeping in impotence,
> But will I be able to open their eyes?
> Will I be able to return sight to the blind?
> To kindle a bright beam of freedom,
> So that, like the dawn of rebirth,

> It would shine like the sun from behind the clouds? [Prologue, lines 1–12][14]

As the self-professed embodiment of "fate," the Red Shaman's mission is evident, and subsequent passages emphasize that it can only be realized through violence. In the world of Oiunskii's text, even the process of attaining the power to shamanize is fraught with pain and struggle on the way to symbolic death and rebirth under a new identity. It is worth pointing out that the Red Shaman's transformation echoes the process by which the Revolution led Chernykh to become "Iakutskii" and Sleptsov to become "Oiunskii." This process can be seen in a passage where the Red Shaman narrates his origin story, describing the anguished fugue commonly referred to by practitioners and scholars alike as shamanic "sickness."

> My heart was pounding, as if
> Someone pierced through it with a dagger.
> And, seeing nothing around me,
> I lay motionless in the bloody abyss.
> [...]
> My body was seized by fever and ague.
> I fainted from furious anguish.
> (pause).
> When I came to, I found out
> That while I was unconscious
> I leapt and ran the whole time,

Summoning all the spirits.
And from that time on I became a shaman [...]
[Act 1, Scene 3, lines 20-23; 42-49]

The Red Shaman's central role as an intermediary between multiple worlds is further bolstered by ethnographic details such as his elaborately ornamented shaman's coat, his shamanic tree, which enables him to attain the ecstatic state necessary for accessing the Lower and Higher Worlds and intervening between them, and the act of beating on the drum accompanied by the onomatopoetic refrain of "Dom-ere-dom-ere-dom!" Yet even as the Red Shaman mediates between the Lower, Middle, and Upper Worlds, he is tasked with a secondary axis of mediation: between past and present, traditional and modern. Oiunskii's titular character, much like Oiunskii himself, hails from the world and belief system of the prerevolutionary past but heralds a prophetic message of the paradigm shifts of the future. This message is accompanied by no small measure of ambivalence, as the Red Shaman ponders:

Can I rid them of their shackles,
Illuminate them with the logic of freedom,
Raise them up to the level of this path,
Take them to the promised land,
And as to an arrow, say: "Fly,
Wheresoever I will it!?"
By enlightening them all with the light of truth,
Will I be able to repay and praise,
Once and for all, the power that shines
Upon the great banner of labor? [Prologue, lines 48-57]

Positioned at the intersection of seemingly irreconcilable realms, the Red Shaman describes his intervention as a return, a rebalancing, a restoration of the proper cosmic order. Crucially, the ultimate goal of this intervention is to forge solidarity with the downtrodden:

I want to return life-giving happiness
to Mother Earth
And breathe a word of warm sympathy
into those who are exhausted. [Prologue, lines 90-94]

Onto this picture Oiunskii superimposes elements of revolutionary mysticism and Soviet revolutionary teleology. *The Red Shaman* is divided into four acts, corresponding to the four seasons of the year. The titular character begins his ritual call to revolution in the spring, and the drama concludes with his death in the winter. This also corresponds to the trajectory of the Russian revolutions of 1917, which began in early spring, continued through the year with the tsar's abdication and the establishment of the Provisional Government under Kerensky, and ended with the Bolshevik coup in November. The plot of Oiunskii's drama hinges on class struggle between Oros-bai, an exploitative rich villain, and the Red Shaman, as well as the simple working people the shaman is defending and attempting to arouse into revolutionary consciousness.[15] Oros-bai plans to sacrifice his own daughter to the heavenly spirit of the Higher World in order to gain absolute power over the earthly Middle World. In the end, the shaman saves the daughter's life and liberates his people by casting a spell to block the spirits' path to the Middle World and drive out Oros-bai. In doing so, however, the Red Shaman transfers the burden of sacrifice onto himself. Upon saving his people from Oros-bai while "drunk with ecstasy," he realizes he is no longer needed in the new world he has helped to bring about. Having shamanized himself into irrelevance in the drama's final act, he dutifully sacrifices himself by slashing his shamanic drum with a knife, burning the remainder of his shamanic accouterments, and dramatically collapsing on the ground near the fire.

> THE RED SHAMAN (Standing on his knees and striking the drum)
> Dom-ere-dom! Dom-ere-dom! Dom-ere-dom!
>
> (Then picks up everything, his effigy, his shaman's costume, his drum and drumstick, and throws it all into the fire.)
>
> With the universe ablaze,
> I, the militant shaman,
> have stopped shamanizing.
> Let the spirits from above and below
> Realize their fate.
> […]
> The curse will disappear!
> Shamanizing will die!
> The world will live on
> Without demons and disasters.
> (Walks away and lies on his back, exhausted.)
> [Act 4, Scene 3, lines 51-65]

Yet it is the Spirit of Fire that has the final word in this work. He pronounces the death of the Red Shaman, and indeed the death of all spiritual practice, and the drama ends with him devouring the shamanic tree in his flames, laughing ominously.

> Drunk on dreadful ecstasy,
> Our Red Shaman has died. […]
> Light will come - the haze will disappear …
> For us spirits, trouble has come! […]
> Let it not lead people into temptation!

Let the stinking smell of the Keriakh-tree
Disperse in a cloud of smoke! [...]
I am the free, proud spirit of fire!
There's a lot for me to devour!
(loudly laughing)
Haha, Haha, Haha, ha!
Haha, Haha, Haha, ha! [Act 4, scene 4, lines 3-32]

The devouring fire also has a real-world analog: it evokes the burning of icons, religious books, and shamanic artifacts during the height of anti-religious fervor at the end of the 1920s.[16] Oiunskii characterizes this destruction as reflexive and even suicidal, as it unfolds through the dramatic arc of the Red Shaman character as well as in the final monologue by the Spirit of Fire, who simultaneously forecasts the end of the existence "for us spirits" and celebrates the newfound bounty of things to devour, punctuating his statement with garish, foreboding laughter. By ending the drama in this way, Oiunskii situates ritualized violent destruction—especially that which is *self-inflicted*—as the necessary catalyst for cultural regeneration. Indeed, the work itself would be sacrificed towards this goal: it was banned not long after the publication of the 1930 translation, and Oiunskii was banned from publication entirely during the period from 1938 to 1955. Moreover, the work triggered the martyrdom of its author, who died for his efforts to preserve and promote Sakha traditional culture while also adapting it to new, ideologically acceptable forms and propagating it from within new institutional structures. Yet these same institutional structures also enabled the afterlife of Oiunskii's legacy; only in 1955, after his posthumous rehabilitation, did he take his place in the official pantheon of Sakha national literature. As a result, the character of the Red Shaman, the work as a whole, and Oiunskii himself collectively embody the clash of worldviews and imaginaries that led to the creation of the modern Sakha literary tradition. In spite of the earnest attempts by Oiunskii and his contemporaries to establish literary traditions and national cultures that were simultaneously modern, ideologically consistent, and internally coherent, works like *The Red Shaman* instead reveal geologic layers of struggle, shaped by the irreconcilable interests and violent lives of their all-too-human creators. This realization was not lost on Petr Chernykh-Iakutskii, the author of the lesser-known 1928 story "Bad Medicine" ("*Strashnoe lekarstvo*"), the title of which serves as a fitting metaphor for this process as a whole.

"Bad Medicine": death and life after *The Red Shaman*

Petr Chernykh-Iakutskii spent his entire life as an intermediary between Russian and Sakha cultures, yet in spite of, or perhaps *because* of this fact, remains a peripheral figure in the Sakha national literary canon. He was bilingual in the Russian and Sakha languages, and although he published exclusively in Russian, he listed his nationality as Iakut in official documents and began publishing under the pen name "Iakutskii" in the 1920s.[17] Chernykh-Iakutskii was born in a small village on the shores of the Sea of Okhotsk to a Sakha mother—whom he would later describe as a "simple, illiterate woman"—and a Russian Orthodox priest, who, by his account, was a violent alcoholic. His autobiographical writings reveal a troubled early life marred by poverty, illness, and domestic violence, as the family shuttled between remote rural parishes in the Russian Far East.[18] After eventually settling in Iakutsk, he received his early education at the Iakutsk Theological Seminary, although ill health forced him to drop out before graduating. In his early professional life he worked as a clerk for the Iakutsk Spiritual Consistory and published essays, short stories, and poems in local newspapers and journals, as well as a collected volume of lyric poetry, *Quiet Strings* (*Tikhie struny*) in 1909. At this time he became increasingly involved in revolutionary circles, publishing in the underground local press and eventually joining the Socialist Revolutionary party—activities which led him to be dismissed from his job and even put under police surveillance by the Tsarist authorities.[19]

Following the Revolution and Civil War, Chernykh-Iakutskii's work took a turn toward the civic, and in the early 1920s he published works with titles like "To the Working Woman" (*"Zhenshchine-rabotnitse"*) and "To the Proletariat of the World" (*"Proletariiam vsego mira"*) while also taking up a post as the editor of *Iakutskaia Pravda* and contributing to politically-oriented anthologies such as *Ogni severa* (*Fires of the North,* 1921) and *Taezhnye iskorki* (*Little Sparks of the Taiga,* 1923). Worsening health problems cut short his productivity in the mid-1920s and forecast the tone of despondency that would be found in his subsequent literary works. "I will soon die. My life is completely over," he wrote in one letter to a fellow Sakha revolutionary in the winter of 1926, describing a bedridden, isolated existence marred by asthma, chronic conditions of the esophagus and lower intestine, and severe psychological distress.[20] It was none other than Platon Oiunskii, in his capacity as the head of the Revolutionary Committee of the Iakut ASSR, who applied to have him officially classified as a "writer-invalid" and supplied with a pension, housing, clothing, food rations, and medical attention.[21] Later in 1926, Chernykh-Iakutskii used this status in order to relocate to the Moscow region for medical treatment, where he remained for the rest of his life. A brief but impactful meeting with Maksim Gor'kii in 1928 appeared to inspire his most enduring contribution to Sakha literature: his 1930 Russian translation of Oiunskii's *The Red Shaman.*

Written during this time of renewed creativity and simultaneous physical and psychological decline, Chernykh-Iakutskii's short story "Bad Medicine" explores a similar dynamic of martyrdom and ritual sacrifice as *The Red Shaman.* Here, however, revolutionary fervor gives way to despondency when an emotionally tormented Sakha man seeks out a ritual cure that results in his gruesome death. Likewise absent from Chernykh-Iakutskii's text are the symbolic ritual objects, dynamic action structured across the four seasons of the year, and the Sakha cosmology of the Lower, Middle, and Upper Worlds, which figure so prominently in *The Red Shaman*. Instead, Chernykh-Iakutskii's story is a portrait of a family in crisis, set against impressionistic descriptions of a languid, seemingly endless winter. And in contrast to the language of fire, destruction, rebirth, and universal awakening that characterize the text of *The Red Shaman*, Chernykh-Iakutskii's story dwells on immobility, helplessness, waning strength, and sleep. This shift in emphasis is visible from the story's introductory lines, which depict a somnolent, frozen taiga landscape:

> Iakut winter night...
> Everything freezing from the cold. The earth cracks open.
> The cracks in the earth snake around underfoot in a zigzag, like the tip of a bayonet. The air is transparent, resonant, like glass, like crystal. The rustling noises of the taiga are carried from far in the distance. The diamond sieve of the sky trembles and glimmers. And in the place where the icy nights of the grey ocean meet the Iakut land, the North Pole suspends a billowing gauze of flashing light. It quivers, it spills forth, it plays in all the shades of the rainbow.
> The ice and the snows sleep, the taiga and the tundra sleep. Earth and heaven sleep.[22]

Elena Rufova, a prolific contemporary scholar of Soviet Sakha literature, connects the motif of sleeping and awakening in Chernykh-Iakutskii's story to a widespread trope in Soviet literature as a whole during this time: awakening is associated with revolutionary consciousness, marking the subject's entry into the forward march of history.[23] In this case, Chernykh-Iakutskii's sleeping northern lands do not suggest delayed awakening as much as willful sedation in response to the persistent threat of violence. As the world sleeps, the frozen earth "cracks open" to resemble the tip of a bayonet; in another passage, the sound of cracking ice is compared to a gunshot (*gulko, kak vystrel'*). In the midst of this hostile environment, the story's main character, Altan, the head of the household, is kept awake by a mysterious psychosomatic malady that has its roots in his family's multigenerational oppression by a rich kulak.

> [Altan] remembered his father, a hardy, strong old man, who lived his whole life in bondage to their kulak neighbor—the *toion*. The heavy reins of life pulled on him all his long years, until a bear overtook him in the taiga. Those same reins pulled at Altan. The same bondage, in the form of an unpaid debt, lay on his shoulders.

Altan's resulting illness, echoing Chernykh-Iakutskii's own chronic health problems at the time of writing, is described as a strange type of eating disorder, equal parts physical and psychological, attributed to poor living conditions and low-quality food.

All are asleep in the household of Altan the Iakut... [...]

Only Altan himself does not sleep. A fierce malady has come upon him. It gives him no peace. It chases away his dreams. It is driving him to an early grave. Altan's throat had begun to close up—that was his terrible sickness. *As barbat* is what the Iakuts call it, a frequent visitor to households in these parts. Lack of nourishment causes it. A diet of awful flatbreads made from rye kernels, badly sifted flour, and frozen butter, taken together with hot tea, sour milk, and pine sap—this is what gives rise to the sickness.

After a failed attempt at a cure from a shaman, who unhelpfully dismisses the sickness as the intractable work of a demon, Altan's wife Matryona becomes more desperate, and she finally implores an old family friend, Nikolai, to help them. The malady she describes to Nikolai is not only a matter of Altan's health—it has also exacerbated the breakdown of traditional gender roles and family bonds, resulting in Altan's failure to live up to the expectations of a Sakha head of household. This culminates in the rejection of life itself:

I'm at my wit's end with him. He won't eat; I can't even get a crumb of food down his throat. It's terrifying to watch someone die of hunger. When we sit down to dinner, we eat, but he just sits and watches with greedy eyes. Then he goes and lies in his nook with his face to the wall and cries. And you know yourself—a Iakut man rarely cries. So it must be unbearable for him. And since we eat in front of him, I feel like I'm to blame. You start trying to talk sense into him and he gets upset, curses at you. I sometimes throw a hunk of bread into the yard and gnaw on it in secret, hiding like a thief, almost swallowing it whole. That's what's been driving me mad.

Unlike the impotent shaman, who is not even afforded an appearance in the story but is instead relegated to Matryona's secondhand account, Nikolai is in possession of secret knowledge: a ritual cure which Matryona hopes will deliver them from their suffering. Enacting this cure proves to be as meticulous as it is gruesome. When Nikolai is finally exhorted to visit Altan's household and is persuaded to share his secret knowledge, he instructs Altan to dig up the corpse of the last person in the village who suffered from the same malady, grind up her esophagus into powder, and drink the powder in a tincture. Altan does not make it that far, however, and is struck dead in the process of digging into the grave. In Chernykh-Iakutskii's description of these events, the failure of the cure seems to make time itself stand still, as sleep and death become one:

Matryona sleeps. She doesn't hear her husband get up and grab the trowel, axe, and knife. She doesn't hear the creak of the door, the sound of Altan heading out somewhere, clapping on his hat.

Matryona sleeps. She has pleasant dreams.

An hour passes by … two … three.

The Iakut winter night continues on. Everything stiffening with the cold. The stars are shining brightly. The northern lights flicker in the sky.

Heaven and earth sleep. The tundra and the taiga sleep.

And Altan sleeps. He sleeps soundly, so soundly, the uninterruptable sleep, the sleep from which there is no waking up. He sleeps near the half-dug-up grave. Near him the iron trowel, the axe, and the knife also sleep.

Altan sleeps.

Chernykh-Iakutskii portrays Altan's death as the final attainment of the slumber he wished for all along. Moreover, at this point Matryona and Altan are not the only ones sleeping: the tools intended for Altan's violent ritual, along with the whole of the Sakha natural world, the "tundra and taiga," are also asleep. Correspondingly, the revolutionary fervor that had been ubiquitous in Sakha literature, and embodied by the textual and performative phenomenon of Oiunskii's *Red Shaman,* here gives way to an expression of desperate, unceremonious demise. In Chernykh-Iakutskii's story, beliefs and symbolic systems have lost their power, and ritual objects have lost their animus, yet there is no satisfying equivalent to replace them, resulting in the "bad medicine" of the story's title. A similar change can be observed in the violent self-sacrifice undertaken by the main characters in both works. If the mission of Oiunskii's Red Shaman was to become "fate itself" and to use his shamanizing powers to force his people to awaken to a new world, for Chernykh-Iakutskii's characters, ritual becomes empty and impotent, culture is rendered meaningless, and the will to live dissipates, rendering every person and every thing inanimate. The "bad medicine" of Altan's slow suicide, marked by the breakdown of traditional bonds and the failure of ritual, heralds a new kind of sacrifice entirely—one which would become increasingly familiar to writers in the Stalin era.

Conclusion: the afterlife of sacrifice

The conclusions of these foundational works of Sakha literature prompt us to consider the nature of sacrifice and its function in connecting the texts, their authors, and their legacies across Russian, Soviet, and Sakha cultural worlds. Having undergone Russian Orthodox religious education and Soviet ideological indoctrination, in addition to harboring a lifelong interest in traditional Sakha lifeways and oral literature, both Oiunskii and Chernykh-Iakutskii were in a position to utilize cross-cultural themes of ritual and sacrifice in order to bring about a change in the consciousness of their readers, as well as to preserve their own status and livelihoods in a new political landscape. Embedded in the rapidly shifting institutional structures of the late Imperial and early Soviet era, their life stories present a familiar trajectory reminiscent of religious martyrs: they arose from humble beginnings and Russian Orthodox parochial education to baptism by fire during the Revolution, followed by rebirth as Soviet Sakha writers, and eventually, ascended to a kind of eternal life as figures in the Sakha literary canon.[24] Their interlocking personal and allegorical sacrifices, as well as the ways they came to be framed by subsequent generations, reveal modern Sakha literature to be a tradition born from destruction, but which is also primed for regeneration and resignification.

This idea is captured in Oiunskii's portentous dedication to Maksim Gor'kii in the opening lines to *The Red Shaman.*

> Maxim! You once said:
> "Never let your brave thoughts weaken,
> Never let the fire of your words burn out,
> Be strong and never lose yourself!"
> May your words ring true,
> May your wish for me come to pass!

Foreshadowing the Spirit of Fire that devours the old world at the end of the drama's final act, here Oiunskii casts the words themselves as fire, possessing the potential to destroy and create in their own kind of fateful alchemy. On the level of the text as a whole, the dedication functions as a ritualistic mode of invocation grounded in Sakha tradition but which is explicitly Soviet. Instead of the spirits of the Upper World, it is the mythic figure of Gor'kii, along with the multinational literary project he represents, who is summoned to start the "fire" of Oiunskii's genius. Thus, while the implied audience of *The Red Shaman* is the nascent Sakha proletariat, its direction of address is the Soviet metropole.

It is namely this performative gesture of Moscow-centered multiculturalism that endures in the discourse surrounding the staging of *The Red Shaman* at the 2018 Moscow Maslenitsa festival. In an interview with Sakha News about the motivations and impact of the indigenous performances, one government official of the Sakha Republic remarked that even amid Moscow's own diverse cultural offerings, "ethnic and national performances take first priority for audiences." The director of the Sakha National Dance Theater added that "we are glad to fulfill our mission of presenting our unique culture to the wider Moscow audience."[25] Meanwhile, an interview with a Moscow spectator serves as a reminder of the longstanding economic ties between center and periphery, driven by extractive industries, underlying the celebration of indigenous cultures: "All I ever knew about Iakutiia was that diamonds are mined there. It turns out that's not the only thing they have to be proud of."[26] Viewing the Moscow staging of *The Red Shaman* in light of the work's turbulent history reveals the intersecting worlds at the heart of the Sakha literary canon and national culture, characterized as much by violence and "bad medicine" as by awakening and resilience. In this we might speculate that Gor'kii's wish for Oiunskii, as imagined by Oiunskii in his opening dedication to *The Red Shaman,* did indeed come to pass.

Notes

1 *I would like to thank colleagues at North-Eastern Federal University in Yakutsk, Professors Oleg Sidorov and Elena Rufova, for their assistance in the early stages of this project.

   The Russian Federation consists of several different types of administrative units called federal subjects. Republics (as distinct from krais, oblasts, autonomous oblasts, autonomous okrugs, and federal cities) are granted the greatest degree of autonomy, possessing their own constitutions, governments, and language-use rights. For more information on the Maslenitsa festival, see "Krasnyi shaman" potriaset voovrazhenie moskvichei," *Sakha News: informatsionno-analiticheskii portal*, February 13, 2018, http://www.1sn.ru/205700.html. Descriptions of the other performances in the program are available on Golden Mask's official website, Goldenmask.ru: https://www.goldenmask.ru/proj_100215.html.

2 Both Oiunskii and Chernykh-Iakutskii used the endonym *sakha*, as well as the Russian-language exonym *iakut*, for self-identification in various contexts.

3 Iakutiia was the site of one of the last battles of the Russian Civil War, known as the Iakut Revolt or, in the language of early Soviet Union, the "White Bandit Uprising" (*belobanditskoe vosstanie*), in which White Army forces were defeated and driven out only in 1922. See James Forsyth, *A History of the Peoples of Siberia: Russia's North Asian Colony, 1581–1990* (Cambridge: Cambridge University Press, 1992), 253–60.

4 The history of nation-building in the Soviet Union, especially in the country's non-Russian republics, has been the topic of several landmark studies in recent years including Terry Martin's *Affirmative Action Empire: Nations and Nationalism in the Soviet Union* (Ithaca: Cornell University Press, 2001) and Francine Hirsch's *Empire of Nations: Ethnographic Knowledge and the Making of the Soviet Union* (Ithaca: Cornell University Press, 2005). The linguistic and literary components of this sweeping project form the subject of studies such as Lenore Grenoble's *Language Policy in the Soviet Union* (Dordrecht: Kluwer Academic Publishers, 2003) and Kathryn Schild's "Between Moscow and Baku: National Literatures at the 1934 Congress of Soviet Writers" (Ph.D. diss., University of California, Berkeley, 2010). Key contributions to this body of scholarship from the late Soviet era are Chingiz Guseinov's *Formy obshchnosti sovetskoi mnogonatsional'noi literatury* (Moscow: Mysl', 1978) and *Etot zhivoi fenomen: sovetskaia mnogonatsional'naia literatura vchera i segodnia* (Moscow: Sovetskii pisatel', 1988).

5 A detailed history of the organization is available in John and Carol Garrard, *Inside the Soviet Writers' Union* (London: I.B. Tauris, 1990); for a discussion of the organization's ideological mandate, as articulated at the First Congress of Soviet Writers in Baku in 1934, see Kathryn Schild, "Between Moscow and Baku."

6 Although this mandate was later developed and put in place by an array of Soviet cultural authorities, the words are Stalin's own, from a speech to the Sixteenth Party Congress in 1930. I. V. Stalin, *Marksizm i natsional'no-kolonial'nyi vopros* (Moscow: Partizdat, 1934). See also Erik van Ree, *The Political Thought of Joseph Stalin: A Study in Twentieth Century Revolutionary Patriotism* (London and New York: Routledge, 2003).

7 Vinokurov-Ursun, et al. *Soiuz pisatelei Iakutii* (Iakutsk: Bichik, 2009). Repression under the charge of "bourgeoise nationalism" was an all-too-common fate for the early generations of revolutionary intelligentsia from national minority groups, particularly during the years of the Stalinist Terror. See Martin, *Affirmative Action Empire*, 24; 424. For a thoroughly researched Russian-language biography of Oiunskii, see Oleg Sidorov, *Platon Oiunskii* (Moscow: Molodaia gvardiia, 2016).

8 According to the Sakha literary scholar Elena Rufova, the story is likely to have been composed in 1928, since the earliest draft of the Russian-language text exists

in Chernykh-Iakutskii's notebook of the same year. Elena Rufova, email to the author, August 20, 2019. The story was first published in a Sakha translation by S. Tolbonova: Chernykh-Iakutskii, P. "Ynyryk emp," *Kyhyl yllyk* no. 5–6 (1934): 41–54; no. 1 (1935): 46–61. The Russian original was published in editions of Chernykh-Iakutskii's collected works in 1945, 1954, and 1982.

9 E. Sidorov discusses this in the commentary to *Krasnyi Shaman,* his recent Russian-language translation of *The Red Shaman* (Iakutsk: Iakutskii gosudarstvennyi universitet, 2004), 3. According to Oleg Sidorov, Oiunskii's contemporaries vividly recalled how he would recite excerpts of the work at informal gatherings, sometimes becoming so rapt that it was unclear whether he was merely reciting poetry or attempting to actually shamanize. Early drafts were also staged for local agit-prop theater. *Platon Oiunskii* (2016), 127. Elsewhere Oleg Sidorov identifies a real-life analogue to Oiunskii's main character: the shaman and performer Nikolai Protasov, who famously gave up shamanizing during the peak of Soviet anti-religious fervor in the early 1930s and committed suicide by cutting his own throat in 1934. "Shamany—predstaviteli nebesnykh sil," *Ilin* 23, no. 2 (2001): http://ilin-yakutsk.na rod.ru/2001-2/38.htm.

10 The Sakha writer A. F. Boiarov, Chernykh-Iakutskii's co-translator for the 1930 Russian edition of *The Red Shaman,* notes in his preface that Gor'kii actually published his first enthusiastic impressions of the work in a public address to the First Congress of Siberian Writers, which was then published in *Pravda*. Oiunskii, *Krasnyi shaman,* 1930, 9. In this speech Gor'kii professes: "Not knowing the languages of the Buryat and the Iakut (*sakhalar*), I could nevertheless understand the amazing feeling laid out by Iakut poets unknown to me, the authors of the poem "Kysyl Oiun." *Pravda,* April 20, 1928. During his visit to the Soviet Union in the summer of 1928, Gor'kii held official meetings with writers and culture workers from many of the Soviet Union's national minority groups. At the time he was living in Italy in the midst of an eight-year period of exile, and he would return permanently to the Soviet Union only in 1930. Dmitrii Bykov discusses the trip, as well as Gor'kii's public persona and role in the Soviet literary canon, in *Byl li Gor'kii?* (Moscow: Molodaia Gvardiia, 2017), 232–6. Regarding Gor'kii's influence on the development of Soviet Sakha literature specifically, see L. M. Morozova and V. F. Afanas'ev, *Gor'kii i Iakutiia* (Iakutsk: Iakutskoe knizhnoe izdatel'stvo, 1968).

11 Oleg Sidorov gives a detailed account of the internal political and ideological struggles among the Sakha intelligentsia underpinning the criticism Oiunskii received for *The Red Shaman.* One notable denouncement by Nikolai Mordinov-Amma Achchygyn condemns the work on grounds of "archaism, symbolism, shamanism, mysticism." *Platon Oiunskii,* 122–3.

12 A. V. Lukina, "Analiz poema 'Krasnyi shaman' P. Oiunskogo v issledovaniiakh I. V. Pukhova," *Siuzhetologiia i siuzhetografiia* 1 (2016): 93–4. In his prologue to the 1930 Russian translation of *The Red Shaman,* Oiunskii explicitly mentions the Sakha legends he draws from, and maps the folkloric tropes directly onto Marxist-Leninist ideology—in this case, the struggle to overturn feudal inequalities and cultural backwardness. *Krasnyi shaman,* 12–5.

13 For information about the world history of shamanic practices, including extensive material on "shamanic sickness" and distinctions between "black" and "white" shamans across multiple cultures, see Mircea Eliade, *Shamanism: Archaic Techniques of Ecstasy,* translated by Willard R. Trask, Bollingen Series LXXVI (New York: Pantheon Books, 1964). Focusing on the Siberian context, see Andrei Znamenski, *The Beauty of the Primitive: Shamanism and Western Imagination* (Oxford University Press, 2007); John Grim, *The Shaman: Patterns of Siberian and Ojibway Healing,* The Civilization of the American Indian Series (Norman: University of Oklahoma Press, 1983); and Anna Reid, *The Shaman's Coat: A Native History of Siberia* (London: Weidenfeld & Nicolson, 2002). Another excellent source of information is a

compendium of Russian-language scholarship on shamanism, translated into English and compiled by Andrei Znamenski: *Shamanism in Siberia: Russian Records of Indigenous Spirituality* (Dortrecht: Kluwer Academic Publishers, 2003).

14 All quotations are from the 1930 Russian-language translation by A. F. Boiarov and Peter Chernykh-Iakutskii, cross-referenced with the 1925 Sakha-language original. All translations are my own unless otherwise indicated.

15 Andrei Znamenski analyzes these episodes from *The Red Shaman* along with other contemporaneous literary works in the context of 1920s Soviet ethnographic enthusiasm and 1930s anti-religious fervor in *The Beauty of the Primitive: Shamanism and Western Imagination,* 328–42.

16 Znamenski, *The Beauty of the Primitive,* 328–42.

17 Elena Rufova, *Tvorchestvo P. N. Chernykh-Iakutskogo v kontekste literaturnogo protsessa Iakutii nachala XX veka* (Novosibirsk: Nauka, 2014), 33–4.

18 Chernykh-Iakutskii's autobiographical writings were discovered in the personal archive of the historian Grigorii Popov (1887–1942). They were edited and published with introductory notes by Liudmila Zhukova in "Nakhodka v lichnom archive G. A. Popova k biografii poeta P. Chernykh-Iakutskogo," *Iakutskii Archiv* 1 (2007): 108–13.

19 Grigorii Tarskii, *Petr Chernykh Iakutskii: ocherk zhizni i tvorchestva* (Iakutsk: Iakutskoe knizhnoe izdatel'stvo, 1964), 17–19.

20 Correspondence from Chernykh-Iakutskii to Mikhail Vinokouroff, 25 February 1926. Alaska State Library, Vinokouroff collection MS81, Box 15, Folder 3.

21 Rufova, *Tvorchestvo P. N. Chernykh-Iakutskogo,* 87.

22 All quotations are from Peter Chernykh, *Izbrannoe* (Iakutsk: Iakutskoe gosudarstvennoe izdatel'stvo, 1945), 149–62. Translations are my own.

23 Rufova, *Tvorchestvo P. N. Chernykh-Iakutskogo,* 109–11.

24 The connection between Bolshevism, religious martyrdom, and eschatology is the subject of a recent study by the historian Yuri Slezkine, *The House of Government* (Princeton: Princeton University Press, 2018). Drawing on a wealth of correspondences, memoirs, and public rhetoric from high-ranking Soviet officials, Slezkine draws comparisons between the Bolsheviks and millenarian religious sects from various historical periods, leaving significant implications for the study of Soviet national literatures.

25 "Krasnyi shaman" potriaset voovrazhenie moskvichei," *Sakha News,* 2018.

26 "Krasnyi shaman".

8 Heroism or colonialism?

China and the Soviet imagination of Manchuria in *Port Arthur*

Zhen Zhang

The postwar space of Manchuria is as dynamic in its contested realities as it is open to cultural, historical, and political imaginations. A textual imagination of Manchuria could speak as loud, if not more lucid, than unprocessed facts and realities. The historical novel *Port Arthur* (*Port-Artur*), as a fictional form of historiography, rewrites the Russo-Japanese War (1904–05) with historical precision and panoramic scope, using real names of geographical locations, historical figures, and naval battles. The novel not only finds its way into the Soviet shrine of literary masterpieces by winning the Stalin Prize in literature in 1946 but also reaches a large amount of readers through multilingual translations, official promotions, and unrestricted circulation. Despite its instantaneous popularity and immediate success within the socialist bloc, the novel was simultaneously controversial in its imaginations of Manchuria, especially its political implications and its pejorative portrayal of the Chinese. Revisiting the defeat of the Russian Imperial Navy in the Russo-Japanese War after the triumph over the Japanese in the Second World War is less a gesture to salute to the valor of the Soviet army than a nostalgic imagination to reconnect to the Russian imperial past in Manchuria. The questions arise when we compare the textual imaginations of Manchuria as represented in the novel with the realities of the Manchuria during the Russo-Japanese War: Do not the full-blown patriotic voice and the absence and demonization of Chinese in the novel have colonial overtones, considering the fact that the war actually happened within the Qing sovereignty? Is a displaced heroism not a disguised form of colonialism?

Zhou Enlai (1898–1976), the premier of the People's Republic of China from 1949 to 1976, was the first person to raise doubts of imaginations of Manchuria as shown in the novel and to see the potential danger of the Soviet encroachment of the sovereignty of newly founded People's Republic in reality. His reading provides a glimpse into the dynamics of the foreign policies between the People's Republic of China and the Soviet Union in the 1950s and, more importantly, the self-positioning of China in the bipolar world after the Second World War. However, this work and its reception in China have rarely been discussed in English-language scholarship. In this chapter I showcase historical realities and the consequences of the Russo-Japanese rivalry in Manchuria at the beginning of the twentieth century and reception of the novel in Soviet Union, before mapping out Zhou Enlai's critical engagement with the novel followed by a close analysis of the novel. I argue that the critical reading of *Port Arthur* in China reinforces an alternative view of the Soviet Union in the time of the "honeymoon period" between China and the Soviet Union in the 1950s, changing from the benevolent ally during the Second World War to an imperial threat in formation. Such a view contributed critically, if circumstantially, to a repositioning and reshaping of China's foreign policy in the 1950s—turning China from being a country belonging solely to the socialist camp led by the Soviet Union to a country that has a shared history of colonialism and imperialism with many other Afro-Asian countries. This foreshadows China's involvement in the Bandung Conference in 1955, the Non-Aligned Movement, and ultimately the Sino-Soviet Split towards the end of the 1950s.

Whose Manchuria? The realities and consequences of the Russo-Japanese War

It is almost indisputable that the Russo-Japanese War of 1904–1905 was an imperialist one in the sense not only that Russia and Japan were two competing global powers in northeast Asia, one weakening and the other rising, but also that the war was fought on Chinese territory without Chinese consent. The war, involving both land and naval battles, happened near Port Arthur, aka Lüshun 旅順 in Chinese naming convention. The port of Lüshun, located in Liaoning Peninsular in the northeast part of China, was significant geopolitically: it was both a port that connects China to the international waters shared by Korea, Japan, and Russia, and the southern entry into the hinterlands of Manchuria. To a large extent, the war fought at Port Arthur and its adjacent waters was as significant in its scale and intensity of the confrontation as in its global impact on the trajectory of world history. The scale of the actual warfare and mobilized resources were so great that the editors of *The Russo-Japanese War in Global Perspective: World War Zero*, went as far as to claim that "Although historians commonly refer to Europe's Great War of 1914–18 as the First World War, this volume contends that in many ways the modern era of global conflict began a decade earlier with armed confrontation between Russia and Japan."[1] In addition, the consequences of the war went far beyond the region of northeast Asia. Historian Rotem Kowner claims that "If the Russo-Japanese War carries any global significance it lay not in its origins in the actual warfare, in the diplomatic alliances, or in financial support obtained during the war, but in its repercussions. ... the war affected the stability of Europe, Russia in particular, the equilibrium between the United States and Japan, and the territorial status quo in northeast Asia."[2] The victory of the Japanese over a major European power, Russia, not only gave Japan the entry ticket to Manchuria and the world of great powers but also brought about sweeping and disastrous social unrest in Russia, power realignment in Europe, rising global political significance of the United States, and national awakening of the Euro-American colonial world, not to mention enduring humiliation for all echelons of Qing society.

The rivalry between Russia and Japan over Manchuria began years before the war broke out. The weak Qing Empire was forced to open more of its ports and markets after its defeat by France in 1885 and Japan 1895. Manchuria, with its abundance of natural resources, human capital, and weakened Chinese control, became an open space for economic interests and political domination. In this region, Japan and Russia were the two major, if not the only, players.[3] After the defeat in the First Sino-Japanese War (1894–95), the Qing Empire was forced to sign the Treaty of Shimonoseki (1895), which included recognition of the independence of Korea; ceding of the Liaoning Peninsula, Taiwan, and Penghu to Japan; and payment in the form of great fines to Japan as a result of losing the war. The consequence of this war was evident: Japan would have influence over the nominally independent Korea and certain territories of the Qing Empire. However, the Western powers refused to let Japan have everything it desired. Six days after the signing of the treaty, Russia, France, and Germany demanded that Japan withdraw from the Liaoning Peninsula, including Lüshun (the so-called Triple Intervention), for they also had great interest in the northeast part of Qing territory.

As a result, the Russian Empire further expanded its imperial power to Manchuria. Instead of waging war against China directly like Japan, Russia expanded its imperial presence mainly through railway networks. In 1897, Russians started to rebuild the fort of Lüshun to support its Pacific fleet, and they started to build the Chinese Eastern Railway (CER) in Manchuria, linking Russia's Far East to the seaports on the Liaoning Peninsula, with the newly established city of Harbin as the intersection.[4] The railway made Manchuria *de facto* a territory under Russian influence, if not *de jure* a protectorate of the Russian Empire. According to Felix Patrikeeff and Harold Shukman's account, the Russian railway networks functioned more as political domination of Manchuria than mere as usurping commercial interests. As they claimed, "[Russian railway projects] were by far the most ambitious in terms of their physical scale and extent, and most audacious in their political scope."[5] Furthermore, these projects "brought with them unprecedented forms of military and political privileges that the Russian government felt were commensurate with its need to protect its concessions."[6] Russians even had a political concept to legitimize the Russian imperial presence in Manchuria:

> Russian involvement in Manchuria was the creation of a unique concept, the *polosa otchuzhdeniya*, meaning something like 'separation strip' or 'exclusion strip.' On the one hand, this was a logical political form, allowing the Russians to protect their valuable railway by granting absolute rights to land a few metres on either side of the line. On the other hand, even when this modest concession was multiplied by the length and extent of the railway line, the outcome would be a fair amount of territory that had been handed over to the Russians. Moreover, as with Harbin and the other centres of population along the line, the ceded land had a way of bulging and expanding Russian presence.[7]

In the name of protecting the railway from destruction by the Boxers, Russia stationed a sizable army in Manchuria that remained there until the end the Russo-Japanese War in 1905. After the war, Russia's interests based on the CER were transferred to Japan, which paved the way for Japan's imperiled land expansion in northeastern China.

The impact of the Russo-Japanese War was not only regional but also global. First of all, the war brought about a series of repercussions to East Asia. Japan's victory over a major Western imperial power was a takeoff point for Japanese imperialism. As Peter Duss has argued, the Russo-Japanese War, as opposed to the Japanese opening of Korea in 1874 and the Sino-Japanese War of 1894–1895, was the takeoff point for Japanese imperialism,[8] claiming that "Russo-Japanese War marked the takeoff point of Japanese imperialism— the historical moment when a position on the Asian mainland and hegemony in East Asia became a fundamental national commitment."[9] The reasons for such a position were threefold: first, that "the victory over Russia established Japan as the peer of the other imperialist powers in East Asia;" second, that "Japan's new position was an inflated sense of Japan's strategic military needs;" and third, that "the victory over Russia and the postwar settlement was to create a pervasive popular imperialism."[10] The Japanese side's growing military confidence and expansive optimism generated by the victory was in sharp contrast with Russian sentiments, which was clouded with defeat, dishonor, and disillusionment with the imperial rule. The news of defeat outside the empire was a rude awakening for the Russian Empire.

To use Rotem Kowner's words, for Russia the impact of the war was "both concrete and psychological."[11] The war functioned as a catalyst for Russian society, bringing in social unrest like the Russian Revolution in 1905, financial crisis and an aggregated opposition to the very political system of autocracy.[12] For Qing society, the war between Russia and Japan in the Chinese territory was not only a mere contempt for the Qing sovereignty but also an unprecedented humiliation for the Chinese educated echelons at large. Qing rulers were forced to take more radical measures for modern reform, and a sense of Chinese nationalism was on the rise. The reform started shortly after the Boxer Rebellion was further accelerated and intensified and expanded into many sectors of the Chinese society: the civil service examination system which had existed for more than 1300 years was officially abolished; a modern education based on the Japanese model was introduced and Chinese students were sent to study in Japan; military modernization was accelerated; anti-Qing nationalists started to accumulate forces.[13]

Other than the immediate players in the war, the ramifications of the conflict could be felt within Western powers and the colonial world. The victory of Japan over Russia destabilized the balance of power in Europe and pushed political realignment between these powers.[14] And for the colonial world, the impact of the fact that a non-European power could defeat a major European power by adopting modern technology was far-reaching. The colonial population became increasingly disillusioned by colonial rule sought self-identification; the more radical parts of the population even saw this event as a "portent for their own prospects of breaking free of colonial rule and taking the course of modernization on the Japanese model."[15] After the war, the old world order was destabilized and the energy unleashed from the realignment of power structures ultimately led to The First World War a decade later.

Reading of *Port Arthur* in the Soviet Union: displaced heroism as colonialism

Despite the complex reality in Manchuria before and after the war as described above, *Port Arthur* simplified the narrative of the war to give readers the impression that Russia was defending its own territory from the Japanese attack. In the name of heroism, Port Arthur and its adjacent waters, and Manchuria implicitly, was taken uncritically to be part of Russian territory under the threat of Japanese invasion. The colonial presence of Russia in Manchuria was erased from the narrative and replaced by heroism of the Russian soldiers. Such a viewpoint was not simply a fiction by an individual writer but to a large extent it was endorsed by author himself and even sanctioned by the Soviet authority after the Second World War. I argue that this officially endorsed heroism, however sensational a term it may sound, is none other than a displaced term for colonialism in this particular context.

The novel was written by Aleksandr Nikolaevich Stepanov (1892–1965). In his autobiography, written after to the publication of the whole work in the mid-1950s, the author not only once again paid tribute to the heroism of distinguished generals and common soldiers, but also circumstantially reaffirmed the colonial status of Port Arthur. According to his short autobiography, Stepanov came from a family with a strong military tradition: his father was an artillery scholar (*uchenyi artillerist*), and he had been exposed to military tales and books of battle scenes since his childhood. He himself worked as a combat commander (*stroevoi komandir*) during the First World War and started to keep a diary. In 1921 he was concussed as a result of the suppression of the Kronstadt Rebellion and could not work for a long time; he relocated himself to Krasnodar, working as an engineer and a university instructor.[16] As regards the intention and sources of writing *Port Arthur*, he claims,

> In the year of 1932 I was badly ill and for many years I was chained to the bed. Being used to working my whole life, I suffered a lot from the compelled idleness. And I could not work as an engineer anymore. In front of me stood an agonizing question: what is to be done? And for long sleepless nights when before my eyes reminiscences of past days went by in long strings, especially the unforgettable details of the heroic defense of Port Arthur arose distinctly and brightly, which I had to go through even in my youthful years. The pictures of unparalleled heroism and courage of private soldiers and lower officials, the bright examples of several honorable generals (*chesnykh generalov*) and admirals, Makarov,

Kondratenko, Belii, and the black-hearted betrayal behavior (*chernaia predatel'skaia deiatel'nost'*) of Stessel', Fok, and others surfaced in my memory. Gradually I wished to write down all of it, and talk about unrenowned heroes—simple people, who showed devotion to the motherland (*predannost' rogine*) with their own blood on the distant hills of Arthur.

I proceeded to work. Lying in bed, I started to write down my reminiscences with my pencil. But soon I was convinced that a lot of things had been forgotten, and there were many things that I could not understand, and I knew even less about the factual conditions of the matters in the besieged fortress. I had to study historical materials, read through a lot of books, and familiarize myself with archival sources. However, all these efforts turned out to be not sufficient. There were not enough meetings with living people who participated in the heroic defense; I wanted to liven up and complement the materials with their tales. I was lucky enough to meet with a bunch of interesting people, who told me many valuable, bright, and totally forgotten episodes that happened in the days of siege of Port Arthur.[17]

These passages suggest that the author intended to dedicate the novel to the heroism of the Russian defense of Port Arthur. He used the word *rodina* to describe Lüshun without a second thought: *rodina* is a highly patriotic word that can be roughly translated as motherland, or home country. This short autobiography was inserted at the very beginning of the text published by State Publishers of Artistic Literature in 1955; the author must have been aware of the colonial history of Lüshun[18] and its subsequent official repatriation to China after 1949. However, he failed to mention that this so-called heroism was first of all wrapped in a larger historical reality, that is, Russian colonialism in northeast China at the turn of the century.

The author was not alone in having this colonial view of Manchuria. To a large extent it represented the official view of Soviet on the matter of Manchuria after the Second World War. The novel reached a large number of readers in the Soviet Union and it was circulated widely throughout the Soviet Union. The novel was published in 1940 and again in 1942, both in Krasnodar, and then in 1944 it was published in large numbers for a national audience. It was then reissued seventeen times to a total of over a million copies in dozens of languages, and turned into a play and a screenplay.[19] Furthermore, the novel won the Stalin Prize of the first order in 1946, shortly after the end of the Second World War, in which the Soviets fought against and defeated the Japanese troops in northeast Asia.

The timing of the Stalin Prize in literature showcased the officially endorsed view of the postwar order of Lüshun and northeast China at large—to potentially reclaim the land that used to be affiliated with the Russian Empire. The Stalin Prize was itself both aesthetic and ideological. In his careful analysis of the selection process in the Soviet postwar cultural landscape in the 1940s and 1950s, Oliver Johnson confirms that the final decision-making process was overseen by the Politburo, perhaps even Stalin himself despite its complex and sometimes whimsical selection process by the prize committee.[20] It is impossible to gauge how extensive Stalin's personal intervention was in this particular case. However, the novel would not have won the prize if it were not something Stalin himself approved. The gesture of acknowledgment, the defeat of Russia by the Japanese forty years earlier, is like a memorial reclamation of the lost territory, invoking the sentiments of patriotism and self-defense. The heroism, no matter how outstanding it was, was predicated on the presupposition that Lüshun was and continued to be a Russian-Soviet territory. And this uncritical restaging of imperial and colonial Russian heroism in a Soviet publication affirmed, rather than challenged, the colonial heroism of Russia's imperial past.

Zhou Enlai's Reading of *Port Arthur*: forging a postcolonial sovereignty

Zhou Enlai read *Port Arthur* (*Lüshun Kou* 旅順口) while on the train to meet Stalin in 1950.[21] At the point of boarding the train, Zhou was still unsure of the future relations between Soviet Union and the newly-established China, and his mission was to back up Mao using his diplomatic and negotiation skills; at this point Mao had been in Moscow for a few days waiting to meet with Stalin but no actual results had been yielded. A treaty had been signed between Chiang Kai-shek and Joseph Stalin and the fate of that treaty was still uncertain: Mao wanted the previous treaty to be annulled in favor of a new one, while the Soviet side was still ambivalent despite Mao's personal presence in Moscow. During the transition of power in China, the fate of northeast China remained uncertain; after the Second World War, northeast China was occupied by Soviet troops and military presence could easily be turned into making it an administrative republic of the Soviet Union. It is in this historical and geopolitical reality that Zhou embarked on the train in Beijing, unsure of what kind of challenges to be expected upon his arrival in Moscow.

On the Beijing to Moscow train, Zhou first got hold of the novel and revealed his harsh resentment of it. It is impossible to find the exact words Zhou used to describe his feelings about the novel, but according to the memoir of He Qian (1921–98), Zhou's secretary, who was on the same train, Zhou was totally dismayed by it, saying that it was "absolutely nonsense: how come this kind of book wins the Stalin Prize. You see, not everything in Soviet Union is correct and good."[22] Such a negative commentary remained his reading for the following years.

The second time Zhou referenced the novel was in conversation with his military secretary Lei Yingfu (1921–2005) in the winter of 1950 after his trip to the Soviet Union. The commentary was more nuanced than his first encounter. According to the account of Lei Yingfu, the conversation between the two started from the realities of the Korean War and moved to the defense of Liaoning Peninsula and the novel was brought up as a relevant topic. Zhou shared his reading with Lei:

It is really a bad novel. Some parts of the novel are unbearable. First, this book advocates Tsarist Russia's war of invasion and plunder. Second, this theme of this book goes totally against Lenin's teaching; when Lüshun was fallen, Lenin made clear in one of his pieces that that was a war of reactionary plunder (*lueduoxing fandongxing de zhanzheng*). Third, the book is at its best in demonizing Chinese: in it Chinese people are either spies and profiteering merchants, or prostitutes and liars. It is really insulting to have Chinese being described like this. Fourth, the hero Makarov that the book praises someone who merely does some technical repair and minor reform in the Tsarist corrupted military. This lower-rank official was probably a bit better than the utterly corrupted generals. But he totally embraces Tsarist reactionary system and policies of aggression. What worth does it have to praise such a person?[23]

The third time Zhou commented on the novel was in a more official setting. According to the writing of Ma Jia, in 1956 Zhou had a semi-official meeting with around thirty Chinese writers and artists in Ziguangge, Zhongnanhai, in which he brought up the novel himself and again expressed his distaste for it, saying,

The novel *Port Arthur* advocates Russia's chauvinism and sings praises for Tsarist war of invasion. In the book Kondratenko is never a hero but a tool that Tsarist Russia used to invade China's Lüshun. In his *The War in China*, Lenin mentions that European capitalists' evil hands reach China and invade China's Lüshun. Tsarist Russia and Japan fight for Lüshun; both are invaders. In the book there is not a single Chinese who is good. This is a great distortion of the Chinese people.[24]

In addition, Zhou makes a reference to current politics,

As you know, Khrushchev came to visit China not long ago. We visited Lüshun and Dianyan battery. He wanted to honor those Tsarist generals like Kondratenko and proposed to build a monument. I refused him immediately. Lüshun is Chinese territory and cannot be the site for memorialization of Tsarist invaders.[25]

Zhou's fourth reference was directed towards Chinese generals based in Lüshun in 1973. The comment happened shortly after his meeting with the President of the Republic of Congo, Marien Ngouabi (1938–77), and his wife in Dalian. According to Ding Jindong,[26] who accompanied him during his trip to Lüshun, Zhou restated his aversion to the novel using similar arguments, indicating the novel's defensive narrative of Tsarist Russia's imperial aggression in China and demonization of Chinese people. Zhou also used the occasion to comment on history,

Lüshun Kou navy base is a beautiful base: here the scenery is enchanting. Contemplating on the beautiful nature, one should never forget the things that happened a hundred years ago. One really should not forget the trauma and sufferings that the Russo-Japanese War brought to the Chinese people. To reflect on that history, it still has far-reaching meaning for today.[27]

Despite the different circumstances and timings of these references, in every instance, Zhou was making an effort to invoke the Soviet text. The Russian text, a case of advocating a chauvinistic heroism and a colonial mapping of China and the Chinese, as Zhou has pointed out many times, was put on trial.

Zhou no doubt was well aware of the fictionality of the Russian text; it was a historical novel after all. However, Zhou chose to read it as though it were not fiction but historical evidence of increased Soviet chauvinism. He suspended the fictional world that was created by the author and looked for the historicity, that is, an outer text that the text itself inevitably failed to adhere to. Zhou, not being a "professional" literary critic, was less concerned about the literariness of the text than about the factual prejudices within it.[28] What he had in mind were the implications for the everyday internal and external politics he oversaw. The instances of invoking the novel twice in 1950 and once in both 1956 and 1972 had their idiosyncratic indexes in terms of the capricious Sino-Soviet political relations of the past century; the common thread of those idiosyncrasies that Zhou wanted to emphasize was China's sovereignty over Lüshun. Zhou's reading, seeing the novel as the Other, created a counternarrative, antithesis of the novel. By creating an anti-discourse discourse, Zhou was carefully forging a new identity for China, a postcolonial sovereign China, distancing itself gradually from the socialist camp headed by the Soviet Union in the postwar world order.

Port Arthur as colonial space and Chinese as colonized subjects

Zhou, of course, did not put his thoughts into written words. But his reading regarding the narrative of this well-received Soviet novel is evident: even though the novel engages with a particular historicity in Russian historiography, the novelistic rewriting of the historiography must be contested; instead of making an effort to acknowledge imperial Russia's unjust conquest of Lüshun prior to the Russo-Japanese War, the narrative reinforces a colonial view of China under the mask of Russian military heroism. Now it is my task to look into the working schemata of the textuality: working alongside Zhou's thesis, I argue that the text substitutes the historicity of Lüshun with a colonial vision. Zhou did not specifically use the word 'colonialism'. My reading engages in this term extensively.

The narrative of the novel, by way of reimagining the port of Lüshun, the battle scenes, and Chinese people, establishes a colonial vision of China. I am using "colonial vision" broadly in this context. I am not saying the novel itself engages in the topic of Russian colonialism in China directly, but the novel as a form of narrative invites readers to mentally map China in a controlled way. We see the widely used tropes of colonial narrative: the normalization and naturalization of the colonial status quo, in which the colonized land is barely populated by natives; the heroes are the colonizers protecting the land from other invaders; and the colonial subject is largely neglected, stereotyped, and demonized.

In the narrative, the cites of Lüshun, Dalian, and Manchuria are, implicitly and explicitly, taken for granted to be Russian spaces, and China on the other hand is uncritically rendered as a space for Russian domination. Furthermore, there are almost no descriptions of the traces of their colonial history, that is, occupation by Tsarist Russia. In addition, the native Chinese are almost totally absent from the depiction of these spaces except for some limited references which are trivialized and unimportant.

From the beginning to the end of the novel, the port of Lüshun, or the colonial name as is used in the novel, Port Arthur, is naturalized as a Russian city as if it had permanently existed as such and therefore never been part of China. The novel opens like this:

> This was on January 26, 1904. Port Arthur, and the drab, bleak, rocky hills surrounding it, were lit up by the slanting rays of the setting sun. A light breeze was blowing, sweeping away the snow that still lay in the hollows here and there.
>
> Animation unusual for a weekday reigned in the port and the town. This evening the officers of the Pacific Fleet were giving a ball to celebrate the birthday of Maria Ivanovna, the wife of Admiral Stark, the Fleet Commander. It seemed as though the entire Russian population of Kwantung had gathered in Port Arthur that day to witness the festivities and to catch a glimpse of the naval officers in their resplendent uniforms and of the high society folk in their smart and fashionable clothes. No less a personage than Admiral Alexeyev, the Viceroy of the Far East, was to attend the ball with his brilliant staff.[29]

The introduction of the port city is highly controlled and imbued with colonial mentality. The very first two paragraphs first use real historical dates (January 26, 1904) and geographical location (Port Arthur) and then move to a depiction of nature (breeze, snow, hollows) before introducing the inhabitants of the space (officers, admirals, and family members). The transition from the natural beauties of Lüshun in the first paragraph to Russian dwellers in the space in the second paragraph is so smooth and natural that it is almost impossible to imagine that this space has anything to do with China. The implication is that the Russian population is simply indigenous. Also, the author uses festivities and the theme of family to accentuate a cultural-familial link between the space and the dwellers in that space. As indicated in the second paragraph, the purpose of the gathering is to "celebrate the birthday of Maria Ivanovna, the wife of Admiral Stark, the Fleet Commander," which attracts "the entire Russian population of Kwantung" and "high society folk" and "Admiral Alexeyev, the Viceroy of the Far East." This familial celebration turns into a cultural event of ritualistic bond—it is as if a Russian cultural tradition is naturalized and localized. The implicit message that emerges from such a depiction is that Russians who have established everyday rituals are native to this Port Arthur. The jovial festivities cover up the violence of occupation and territorial conquest.

Apart from naturalizing the colonial locality at the beginning of the novel, there are places in the narrative that more directly reference China as spaces of domination and conquest in contrast to Lüshun, implicitly conceived as a Russian territory that must be protected. When General Stessel hears about Japan's sudden attack of the Russian naval base, for a moment he is totally flabbergasted. His wife, Vera Alexeyevna, finds a way to calm him:

> The outbreak of war with Japan did not disturb her very much. With her husband she had gone through the recent Chinese campaign, which had brought Stessel glory, high rank, decorations, valuable trophies from the palaces of Peking, and the reputation of a hero.
>
> ...
>
> "Calm yourself, Anatole. Remember the Chinese campaign. After all, the Japs are like the Chinese; you yourself have told me that dozens of times. You will be at the head of our Russian troops again, and great glory awaits you. Pull yourself together. ..."
>
> The General gradually calmed down, kissed his "Chief of the Household Staff" and in his loud, parade-ground voice, told his orderly to bring him his greatcoat.[30]

Stessel's fear is assuaged by the direct reference to the China's weakness. Instead of seeing Japan's attack as a looming threat, Vera sees it as an opportunity to gain further glory. Vera's logic is clear: since Stessel has so easily won glory from the plunder of Beijing, there is no reason to fear the Japanese, because Chinese and Japanese are the same. The three-step equation (Chinese equals weakness and is conquerable; Chinese equals Japanese; Japanese is weak and conquerable) serves as a placebo for Stessel. The constant of this equation is their shared mental map of China, a conquerable China. China and Lüshun seems to stand against each other, though implicitly. China is out there for conquest and Lüshun is under attack from the Japanese. Stessel becomes the speaker for and protector of the city of Lüshun, and his confidence comes from his Chinese campaign; here China and Lüshun are implicitly contrasted, similarly to the contrast between Japan and Lüshun. Lüshun is clearly not seen as a Chinese city, as Stessel makes himself clear when he mobilizes the troops to the port:

> Stessel, looking haggard after a sleepless night, inspected the regiments, congratulated the men on the opening of hostilities, and exhorted them to conduct themselves like Suvorov's "wonderful heroes," *not to disgrace their country* [italics added], but to beat the Japanese to the joy of the Little Father, the Tsar.[31]

Suvorov is invoked to serve as the role model for the defense. Aleksandr Suvorov (1729–1800) is a historical figure, famous for his imperial military campaigns against the Poles, the Turks, and the French and who won numerous battles during these campaigns; he was a critical figure in the territorial expansionism associated with Catherine the Great (1729–96). Stessel uses Suvorov to implicitly justify the conquest of Lüshun and explicitly to encourage the soldiers to fight against the Japanese. The implication is that just like Suvorov's heroic campaign in Europe, the campaign against the Japanese is also heroic. "Not to disgrace their country" is the clear evidence that Stessel's vision of Lüshun is that it is without question, Russian territory. One might say that Stessel is not the positive hero in the novel; but his negativity as the novel conveys it is not his imperial conquest of Lüshun but rather his compromised attitude in defending Lüshun in comparison to the more determined hero Kondratenko. Stessel is rendered as negative precisely because he, instead of fighting to the end, compromises too much in his negotiations with the Japanese.

In terms of the sovereignty of Lüshun, the positive hero Kondratenko is unswervingly colonial. This is the speech Kondratenko makes during the siege Lüshun by the Japanese:

> "We are cut off from the army in Manchuria and from Russia, and we are not likely to be relieved soon," he said. "We are holding a small plot of Russian soil and the town of Port Arthur. It is *our own, a Russian town* [italics added], for we spent millions of the people's money and an enormous amount of labor in building it. We erected the forts and batteries. Furthermore, our fleet is in Port Arthur. If the Japanese get right up to the port they'll wreck the fortress and the town, and try to capture the fleet. Consequently, we must hold the enemy here, as long as possible. You must defend your positions with the utmost determination. Our country is keenly watching the course of the war and expects you to defend Port Arthur to the last. Let us devote all our efforts, our lives, if need be, to justify the confidence our Tsar places in us, and uphold worthily the glory of Russian arms in the Far East. For you, brave lads and heroes, for our Tsar, and for our beloved country, I cry: hurrah!"[32]

As Stepanov states in his bibliography, Kondratenko is the positive hero that the novel tries to praise. Kondratenko's heroism comes less from his military commands than from his high-spirited patriotism and uncompromised position in defending the port against Japanese attack. From here we see that in the name of heroism and self-defense, the novel naturalizes the colonial status of Lüshun.

Similar to the city-fortress of Lüshun, Dalian and Jinzhou also fall into the category of colonial space. Dalian is described as governed by a corrupted Russian, Vassili Vasilievich Sakharov, who collaborates with a Chinese profiteer/Japanese spy: "The same evening, in Dalny, the largest port in the Kwantung Province, the City Governor, Army Engineer in Reserve Vassili

Vasilievich Sakharov, was sitting in his study in the company of Nikolai Ivanovich Ti Fong-t'ai, a Christian Chinese, his partner in numerous commercial undertakings."[33] The administrative names "City Governor" and "Kwantung Province" legitimize the colonial presence of Russia, erasing the precolonial historicity. In addition to legitimization by administrative naming, the city of Jizhou is described as a city under Russian domination by symbolic gendered relations between master and servants:

> The chief of Kinchow Garrision, Lieutenant Gorbov, Commander of the Mixed Company of the Fifth Regiment, had his quarters in a Chinese fanza near the north gates. They found the Lieutenant sitting on the carpet-covered floor, strumming a guitar and humming a sad love song, and sipping vodka from a tumbler. Two very young Chinese girls were standing in the corner gazing with awe and fright at the "Russian Captain."[34]

In this description, Jinzhou's occupation by Russian troops is symbolically captured in the language of gender: a masculine military Russian commander is contrasted with "two very young Chinese girls," who "were standing in the corner gazing with awe and fright at the 'Russian Captain.'" The imagery of male Russian domination over female Chinese servants is symbolic of the order in Jinzhou. That is, the feminized Chinese are under the male surveillance and control of Russians. This is a colonial narrative through symbolism. Furthermore, Manchuria is cognitively mapped as a colonial locality in a different manner from the previous locations. In the novel, Manchuria instead of being a place that has its own history and people, is prefixed with Russian and postfixed with army—Russian Manchurian Army. Manchuria is gazed at from and filtered through a colonial eye. Other than such naming, we do not detect any more narratives of people, living conditions, or natural surroundings in Manchuria. Manchuria is as if an empty space with only the name of Russian Manchurian Army—a typical colonial naming strategy.

In addition to the colonial narrative of the Chinese space, the novel also presents Chinese people as colonial subjects. The first instance of such colonial mapping of the Chinese people expresses itself in the neglect of any extensive narration of Chinese communities in this occupied area. The novel stretches more than a thousand pages, but there is almost no extensive portraiture of the Chinese people, their attitudes towards the war, or different aspects of their communities. The largest portion of the novel is filled with detailed depiction of the direct confrontations between the Russians and the Japanese on the sea and on land, including fleet maneuvers, conversations switching back and forth between generals, and the battle scenes—the narration is an imagined restaging of the minute-by-minute actions during each Russo-Japanese confrontation.

This is not to say that there is no reference at all to the Chinese, but the very limited depiction of Chinese people lacks any detail. In other words, they are only be gazed from a distance. Here the colonial gaze is an ideology held by the colonizers: the colonized have no individuality, no developed personalities, but are only a dehumanized and voiceless mass. Here the Chinese are similarly spectralized, meaning that they are dehumanized, dispensable; they do not speak, they do not have a collective voice, but only a negligible image. This is the reaction of Stessel when the city hears about the Japanese attack:

> After settling with the battalion Stessel went back to the railway station. Noticing that there were Chinese among the passengers he immediately issued the order: "Throw the Chinese out of the train and see they don't get on again. Let them get out of Port Arthur the best way they can!"[35]

The Chinese are colonial subjects: not equal to the Russians in the city in times of crisis. As regards the civilians in the city, Russians have access to use the railway to evacuate the city, the Chinese do not.

In addition, during the war the Chinese are not treated as human beings: they are part of nature, a backdrop for the genuine confrontations between the two military powers:

> A shell dropped among the Chinese junks anchored close together near the shore. A big conflagration ensued. The Chinese reed sails burned like dry straw, emitting dense clouds of smoke. The fire quickly spread from one junk to another and soon all were burning fiercely. In the glare of the flames the Chinese crews could be seen jumping into the water and swimming to the shore.[36]

Here the Chinese civilians are under the telescope gazed by the Russian conquerors. Under the colonial gaze, they are not part of the game, other than being played by the heroic rivalry between the Russians and Japanese.

Colonial victimization: the defeat of Russia, a Chinese fault?

The colonial narrative also expresses itself in the stereotyping of the Chinese as spies and one of the major forces that bring about Russia's defeat in the war. In his seminal essay "On Violence," Frantz Fanon described the colonist's narrative of victimization of the colonized: "As if to illustrate the totalitarian nature of colonial exploitation, the colonist turns the colonized into a kind of quintessence of evil."[37] In this context, the "treacherous" Chinese become the source of evil, the source of Russian defeat.

In the postscript attached to the novel, the author jumps out of the fictionalized historical narrative of the Russo-Japanese War in Lüshun and provides his authorial comments on the war itself. The author attributes Russia's defeat by Japan in 1904 to the failure of General Stessel to fight to the end and his inability to acknowledge the strength of the Japanese military. As regards the reasons for Russia's failure in the war, the author says,

On January 2, 1945, an official parade was held in Port Arthur to celebrate the fortieth anniversary of the fall of the fortress. At this parade General Ota, the commandant of the fortress, delivered a speech in the course of which he said that *Samurai courage and bravery alone* [italics added] had not been enough to capture the fortress. *"Sincere" relations* [italics added] between General Nogi and Stessel were also needed for this. Thus, forty years later, the Japanese themselves admitted that it was *Stessel's treachery* [italics added] that enabled them to capture the Russian fortress which had been cut off on land and sea.[38]

The "treachery" and "sincere relations" the author references are Stessel's, yet only on the surface; beneath the surface it is Chinese espionage that ultimately leads to Russian defeat. Readers will soon find out that his "treacherous" deeds are due to Chinese espionage.

In the novel the author singles out two major examples of espionage which lead to the failure of the Russians in the war. The first episode describes a young Chinese girl's "treacherous" work of smuggling out information for the Japanese, and the other involves Ji Fengcai's "treacherous" effort to bribe and corrupt the Russian generals. Both of these episodes are short in length in comparison with the description of the battles in the frontiers, but the message of these two short insertions are profound. The two episodes suggest to the reader that defeat was not the fault of the Russian soldiers but instead to Chinese collaboration with the Japanese.

The first episode involves Japan's sudden attack and Russia's first major defeat, which cost the life of General Makarov and sinking of many Russian ships. In the narration, the first two "Chinese" persons' espionage activities are clearly the direct reason for the Russian defeat. The appearance of the Chinese seems to interrupt the narrative and similarly interrupts Russian wartime preparation for the Japanese attack. The narration focuses on internal conflicts between the navy leadership and the army leadership, the leadership dictated by the appointed Kwantung aristocratic governor and the local generals, between the college-educated engineer and the working-class sailors and the artillerymen. However, the contradictions, disputes, misunderstanding, and arguments are directed only against their common enemy, the Japanese; these confrontations can be easily ameliorated or postponed to an unforeseen future. But the image of the Chinese people lurks beneath the surface of the Russians' heroic and strategic battle against the Japanese and poses not only a pause in the narrative time but also, more explicitly, a threat to the Russian victory over the Japanese.

Kong Xiang and a nameless beggar interrupt the narrative as follows. This artificial insertion of the character serves only the purpose of implying direct consequences of Kong Xiang's espionage—major losses in the Russian fleet. The first appearance of Kong Xiang comes with her mistress Riva, a Jewish prostitute who is in love with Lieutenant Dukelsky. Riva is introduced to the readers without any preamble, and readers find it quite out of place within the verbose description of Japan's attacks and Russia's reactions prior to this episode and the introduction of the young, college-educated engineer Zvonarev and his gradual involvement later in the story. And even from an overall view of the novel the character of Riva is quite out of place. Her life story is only briefly introduced: an Odessa native; she was carried away by "the general stream of businessmen, adventures and speculators that flowed to the Far East"[39] and met the poker-lucky Dukelsky in the steamship *Vladimir*; he ransomed her from her "Madame" and brought her to Lüshun.[40] The only reason for this character, from my perspective, is to introduce Kong Xiang and her spying activities. Kong Xiang is introduced as Riva's Chinese maid; Kong Xiang is a typical example of a colonial subject who is subjugated to the structure of the master language but who does not necessarily speak the master's language properly and needs to be disciplined:

> She then proceeded with her toilet. At the sound of a silver bell ornamented with dragons, a small, slender girl, looking like a Chinese doll, entered the room and making repeated curtsies wished her mistress good morning in very broken Russian. ...
>
> A column of black smoke that rose from the railway station, accompanied by the roar of an explosion, revealed the truth to her.
>
> "Somebody's shooting!" she exclaimed in fright.
>
> "Japs! Japs! Make war for Looshia!" lisped the Chinese girl.
>
> "War! What do you mean, you ninny?" demanded Riva.
>
> "Japs, he fightee in de night-time," answered the girl.
>
> "Why didn't you tell me that at once, you little idiot?" demanded Riva angrily. "There's a war on, but you remain as dumb as an idol. When shall I knock some sense into that stupid head of yours? You bring me all sorts of tittle-tattle, but when war breaks out you say nothing about it!"[41]

Using a bell to summon Kong Xiang, Riva, as the master, calls her servant "little idiot," "stupid head," and "dumb as an idol." Here we see in classic colonial terms, Kong Xiang depicted as a colonial subject who cannot speak the colonizer's language fluently and who must bear the mistress's blame in silence. And such a silence is read as intellectual inferiority by the colonizer-master. This negative image of Kong Xiang only gets worse when readers find out in a few pages that she is a spy working for the Japanese. We find Kong Xiang listening to the conversation while she serves Lieutenant Dukelsky and Georgie, a friend of Dukelsky; as a result she obtains the number and names of battleships that are damaged by the Japanese attack and smuggles out this valuable information to the Japanese:

> Kung Siang went to her tiny room and there, taking out a sheet of paper, a slab of Indian ink and a brush, sat down to write a note in ideographs. ... The girl ran back to the kitchen, snatched up a large hunk of bread, stuffed the paper on which she had been writing into it and

returned to the yard. She beckoned the Chinese beggar to the kitchen door and there conversed with him a long time in Chinese. During the conversation the names of all the Russian ships which had been damaged were mentioned.[42]

This puts the Japanese ahead of the Russians in terms of intelligence. We see in the following pages that Japanese fleets seem to know the timing and which Russian fleets (weak and damaged ones) to attack. Kong Xiang's spying activity is repeated on page 223 and this time it brings about the major defeat of the Russians.

Furthermore, when Riva is emotionally defeated by the death of her lover Dukelsky, she cannot go through with the funeral, dedicated as it is to the dead Russian sailors and commanders. Then, we see Kong Xiang among the Russian generals in a domestic setting, Riva's chamber once again, accompanied by naval officers, collecting information from their conversation:

> While Riva was seeing her guests off to the quayside, Kung Siang found time to run and see the old Chinese beggar who had been to the house before. After exchanging a few brief sentences with him she hastened home, but the Chinese, grunting and groaning, hobbled away in the direction of Tea Valley. ...
>
> Half an hour later Admiral Togo knew exactly the time when the Russian torpedo boats were to put out, the course they were to take, and the fact that the fleet was putting to sea in the morning. All the Japanese ships were withdrawn from the region of the Sanshantao Islands, and the squadron of light cruisers and torpedo boats received orders to lie in wait for the Russian torpedo boats on their return, at the approaches to Port Arthur.[43]

For the next thirty pages or so the narrative resumes the battle scenes, strategies, and conversations on the topic of commanding from both sides. However, as a result of Kong Xiang's espionage, we know that Russian fleets are fatally defeated and the primary commander, a positive hero the novel praises, Makarov, is killed during the battle. This marks the end of the first part of the novel.

Kong Xiang's spying operations result in advancing Japanese intelligence, which leads finally to Russia's first major defeat, although we learn later on in the novel that Kong Xiang's accomplice, the Chinese beggar He Changxi, is in fact the Japanese General, Baron Tanaka. The general portraiture of Chinese is to be noted: they are like Kong Xiang, collaborators with the Japanese.

Kong Xiang is the only spy; the other major Chinese character is a businessman turned spy, Ji Fengtai, who exercises his affluence to corrupt the Russian generals, Stessel included, on a personal level, so that they let down their guard. The insertion of this episode also interrupts the the narrative flow and likewise discredits the Chinese businessman Ji Fengtai for his espionage against the Russians. Differently from Kong Xiang's activities, Ji exercises his economic power over Stessel's political-diplomatic decisions. He is introduced

to the readers as the most powerful and resourceful businessman in Dalian—
he has a russified name, "Nikolai Ivanovich Ti Fong-t'ai;" he is a "Christian
Chinese" and a partner of Sakharov "in numerous commercial undertakings."[44] We find him having a conversation with the city governor of
Dalian, Vassili Vasilievich Sakharov:

> "You've done me brown, Nikolai Ivanovich!" the City Governor was
> saying reproachfully. "You have bought all my houses and establishments
> for a mere song. Taking advantage of my embarrassment, you are strip-
> ping me to the skin!"
> The Chinese gave him a sly glance out of his slanting eyes and,
> adjusting the uncomfortable European coat that he was wearing,
> answered with a bland smile:
> "The man who can cheat you hasn't been born yet, Vassili Vasilievich!
> Not everybody can build a city and a port costing hundreds of millions of
> rubles and make a fortune of ten million on it. The whole of the Far East
> rings with your fame. To have such an income and not to have had a single
> Senate investigation! You are the wizard and magician of Kwantung!"[45]

We see here that Ji is blamed for his purchase of Sakharov's properties in
Dalian. He fits squarely into the stereotype of the dishonest profiteer. From
the continuing conversation, we find that Ji has taken over Sakharov's properties in Dalian for a relatively cheap price because the Japanese are soon to
occupy the city. Ji has a Russian passport, but he has no ideology whatsoever
except for making money, and he is not loyal to Russia:

> "But you are a Russian subject too."
> "But not an officer. Merely a merchant, ready to pay taxes to anybody
> in the world in order to get out of fighting."[46]

As a Russian subject, Ji seems unable to be assimilated into the Russian
patriotic norm. Instead, he serves his new Japanese master by providing
information from the Russian side. He offers to protect Sakharov's business
interest in exchange for information:

> "Let's split the difference. Make it four and half, but on this condition: I
> must be kept informed of all that's going on in Port Arthur."
> "But suppose it's besieged?"
> "There's no siege that money can't break through."
> "In return you will keep me informed about all my affairs in China,
> Korea and Japan, won't you?"[47]

Then Ji instructs Sakharov to bribe all levels of officials in Lüshun by
exploiting their particular weaknesses. His instructions of how to bribe the
officials are extremely detailed and customized:

Tauts, the Chief of Police of Port Arthur. A hundred rubles per month, not a kepeck more. If he starts any blackmailing business, whisper a word into the car of Vera Alexeyevna Stessel—and make her an appropriate gift, of course—and she'll soon put that rascal in his place. She must have gifts worthy of her station—Chinese antiques of gold and silver, precious stones, and feminine ornaments, but no money, not under any circumstances. The value of the gifts to be commensurate with the services rendered. As for the General—not even a hint, of course. The fool would flare up and give the whole show away. Colonel Vershinin, the Commissar of the Port Arthur City Council, is just a blockhead, and therefore honest. You can get him by letting him have for next to nothing things that he needs, such as a length of cloth for a greatcoat, underlinen, handkerchiefs, scent—incidentally, he is very fond of scent.[48]

We see how meticulous Ji is. And the conversation continues further, it enters into the realm of military secrets. Ji reveals his cooperation with the Japanese. He almost threatens Sakharov not to behave other than listening to his orders:

"You, Vassili Vasilievich, must bear this in mind when you are in Port Arthur. Every step you take will be immediately reported to us and properly appraised."

"Is that a threat?"

"God forbid. Merely a friendly warning," said Ti Fong-t'ai with a broad smile.[49]

In the following seven hundred pages we see the back and forth of detailed account of the war scenes. However, Sakharov, as instructed by Ji, uses his economic influence over Vera Alekseeva and many other officers. Sakharov's cabinet: he bribes the innocent Wan Liu with Japanese clothes, combs, and other feminine goods; due to illness, Sakharov gives all his documents and associations with the Chinese side to Fok; Fok tries to match Duke Gan Ji Mu Luo Fu with Wan Liu through Vera Alekseeva, but Wan Liu declines the offer; Fok becomes the new deputy of the Chinese inside the Russian circle; Mr. Xu makes agreement with Fok.[50] And finally we learn that General Stessel is surrounded by corrupt officials, bought out by Sakharov, and remotely controlled by Ji. Sakharov, Fok, Reis, and Vera Alekseeva are all corrupt Russians without whom Stessel would not likely compromise with the Japanese. But the novel insinuates this: the Chinese businessman Ji Fengtai is the tail end of corruption, the source of compromise, and the ultimate reason for Russia's defeat.

The two episodes showcase that the image of the Chinese is that of a spy, a spy who works for Japanese in the homeland. The image of spy, I argue, is a typical colonial narrative of colonized subjects. This is not the first time that the Chinese are described as spies during the 1904 Russo-Japanese War. The modern Chinese writer and thinker Lu Xun (1881–1936) also mentions an episode of a Chinese person being recognized as a spy, this time one who works for Russians and is executed by the Japanese. This story is documented in his "Preface to A Call to Arms," *Nahan Zixu*, in which Lu Xun shares his student experience while he is in Japan and the following story is widely circulated and interpreted in many different ways:

> I do not know what advanced methods are now used to teach microbiology, but at that time lantern slides were used to show the microbes; and if the lecture ended early, the instructor might show slides of natural scenery or news to fill up the time. This was during the Russo-Japanese War, so there were many war films, and I had to join in the clapping and cheering in the lecture hall along with the other students. It was a long time since I had seen any compatriots, one day I saw a film showing some Chinese, one of whom was bound, while many others stood around him. There were all strong fellows but appeared completely apathetic. According to the commentary, the one with his hands bound was a spy working for the Russians, who was to have his head cut off by the Japanese military as a warning to others, while the Chinese beside him had come to enjoy the spectacle.[51]

Here, Lu Xun is a witness of Chinese subjects within Japan during the war between empires. The Chinese subject, as presented in the classroom within the empire, is similarly spectralized; he is a "spy working for the Russians" and had "to have his head cut off by the Japanese military as a warning to others," and the colonized whole "had come to enjoy the spectacle." The Chinese here are described as not having a sense of identity, not having any sense of kinship among themselves. This is precisely the logic of colonialism: the dominated subjects have no language to speak for themselves—they are not supposed to have an identity of being Chinese but only be interpolated as nameless spies. The Chinese can either be spies working for the Japanese (Kong Xiang and Ji Fengtai) or spies working for the Russians (the beheaded and nameless Chinese)—they simply cannot be Chinese working for the Chinese on Chinese territory.

Conclusion

The Sino-Soviet Split was not only one of the most important historical events of the twentieth century but also one of the key events of the Cold War. Scholars have shed light on the reasons for the split between the two Marxist and Leninist states from various perspectives. Especially since the collapse of the Soviet Union and opening of China in the 1980s, historians have had more access to archival documents that were not available during the height of the Cold War. As a result, recent studies on this topic have diverged from the speculative historiography as it had been during the Cold War period. Looking at the world-historical event from a distance, scholars broke new ground for this old topic: Lorenz Lüthi situates the Sino-Soviet Split within the framework of ideological rivalry between Moscow and Beijing[52] while Jeremy Friedman sees the clash of the two countries rooted in two competing revolutionary models in world revolution.[53] However, as multifaceted and resourceful as these narratives could be on the question of the Sino-Soviet Split, they tend to see Khrushchev's denunciation of Stalin at the Twentieth Congress of the Communist Party of the Soviet Union (CPSU) in 1956 as the starting point of the deterioration between Moscow and Beijing. In this article, I question the "suddenness" of the split. I find that the Sino-Soviet coalition was never as strong as one had imagined: historical tensions had been building up prior to the final split. China was mindful of Russia's imperial past even when the two countries were close in the early 1950s.

In this chapter, I looked into the power relations of Manchuria before and after the Russo-Japanese War and the imagination of Manchuria as represented in the novel *Port Arthur*. Following Zhou Enlai's reading of the book, I provide my own analysis. My reading centers on the word "colonial," which is a word Zhou did not actually use, butnevertheless implied. The historical novel, when rewriting the historicity of 1904 after the Second World War in 1946, still inscribes a colonial vision of northeast China in two aspects: (1) Port Arthur as colonial space and Chinese as colonized subjects; (2) colonial victimization of the Chinese. Such a crossing out of the novel ~~Port Arthur~~, proposed by Zhou in at least four different occasions, emphasizes the visibility of the colonial past of Lüshun. I argue that Zhou Enlai's criticism of *Port Arthur* was an early indication of a deepening mistrust towards the Soviet Union. This anticipates China's identity as a postcolonial sovereignty, distancing itself from the socialist led Soviet Union while at the same time projecting a possible discursive alliance with other postcolonial states in Asia and Africa. This, I would argue, foreshadows the upcoming Bandung Conference.

Notes

1 *I would like to thank the following colleagues: participants at the conference "Asia in the Russian Imagination" held at University of Utah's Asia Center on March 23–24, 2018 and two anonymous reviewers of this article for their comments and critique, and Matthew Romaniello, Jane F. Hacking, Jeff Hardy for their careful editing and valuable comments. I would like to especially thank Sheldon Lu for pointing me to the Soviet novel *Port Arthur* in the first place.

   John W. Steinberg, Bruce W. Menning, David Schimmelpenninck Van Der Oye, David Wolff, Shinji Yokote, "Introduction," in *The Russo-Japanese War in Global Perspective: World War Zero* (Leiden: Brill, 2005), xix.

2 Rotem Kowner, "Between a Colonial Clash and World War Zero: The Impact of the Russo-Japanese War in a Global Perspective", in *The Impact of the Russo-Japanese War*, ed. Rotem Kowner (New York: Routledge, 2007), 4–5.

3 The United States and Britain are equally interested in Manchuria. For a detailed discussion, please see Felix Patrikeeff and Harold Shukman, *Railways and the Russo-Japanese War: Transporting War* (New York: Routledge, 2007), 37–8.

4 Russia's aggression and expansion in Manchuria is based on a secret treaty signed by Li Hongzhang on behalf of the Qing Empire and Alexey Lobanov-Rostovsky on behalf of the Russian Empire in 1896 in Moscow. The Sino-Russian Secret Treaty gives Russia military, economic, and administrative access to the vast land of Northeast China.

5 Patrikeeff and Shukman, *Railways and the Russo-Japanese War*, 33.

6 Patrikeeff and Shukman, *Railways and the Russo-Japanese War*, 34.

7 Patrikeeff and Shukman, *Railways and the Russo-Japanese War*.

8 Such a position is controversial. Counterposing Peter Duss's position, Rotem Kowner claims that the Russo-Japanese War did not cause any significant change in the course of Japanese imperial expansion. For a detailed discussion, please see Rotem Kowner, "The War as a Turning Point in Modern Japanese History." in *The Impact of the Russo-Japanese War*, ed. Rotem Kowner (New York: Routledge, 2007), 29–46.

9 Peter Duss, "The Takeoff Point in Japanese Imperialism," in *Japan Examined: Perspectives on Modern Japanese History*, ed. H. Wray and H. Conroy (Honolulu: University of Hawai'i Press, 1983), 154.

10 Duus, "The Takeoff Point," 155–6.

11 Kowner, "Between a Colonial Clash and World War Zero," 7.

12 For a detailed discussion of the impact on Russian society, please refer to Abraham Ascher, *The Revolution of 1905*, vol. 1: *Russia in Disarray* (Stanford: Stanford University Press, 1988); John Bushnell, "The Specter of Mutinous Reserves: How the War Produced the October Manifesto," in *The Russo-Japanese War in Global Perspective: World War Zero*, eds., John W. Steinberg, Bruce W. Menning, David Schimmelpenninck van der Oye, David Wolff, Shinji Yokote (Leiden: Brill, 2005), 333–48; Jan Kusber, "Soldiers' Unrest Behind the Front after the End of the War," *Rethinking the Russo-Japanese War, 1904–05:* Vol. 1, *Centennial Perspectives*, ed. Rotem Kowner (Folkestone: Global Oriental, 2007).

13 Harold Z. Schiffrin, "The Impact of the War on China," in *The Impact of the Russo-Japanese War*, ed. Rotem Kowner (New York: Routledge, 2007), 169.

14 Matthew S. Seligmann, "Germany, the Russo-Japanese War, and the Road to the Great War," in *The Impact of the Russo-Japanese War*, ed. Rotem Kowner (New York: Routledge, 2007), 109–23.

15 Kowner, "Between a Colonial Clash and World War Zero," 19.

16 A. Stepanov, "Avtobiografiia," 3. All translations from the Russian are my own.

17 Stepanov, "Avtobiografiia," 4.

18 The author must have been aware of Lenin's criticism of the Russian autocracy. Lenin claimed that "It was the Russian autocracy and not the Russian people that started this colonial war, which has turned into a war between the old and the new bourgeois worlds. It is the autocratic regime and not the Russian people that has suffered ignoble defeat." Vladimir I. Lenin, "The Fall of Port Arthur," in *Lenin Collected Works*, vol. 8, trans. Bernard Isaacs and Isidor Lasker (Moscow: Foreign Languages Publishing House, 1962), 47–55.

19 A. N. Stepanov co-authored the screenplay with the screenwriter I. F. Popov (1886–1957).

20 Oliver Johnson, "The Stalin Prize and the Soviet Artist: Status Symbol or Stigma?" *Slavic Review* 70: 4 (2011): 831.

21 The novel Zhou Enlai had was the Chinese translation. The translation of *Port Arthur* was published by Foreign Language Books Publishing Bureau in Moscow in 1947. The Chinese translation was done by Chen Changhao (1906–67) with the pseudonym Cangmu. Chen Changhao was none other than the renowned Political Commissar (*zhengwei* 政委) of the Fourth Red Army (*hongsi fangmian jun* 紅四方面軍). The translation was conducted and finished during his years in Moscow shortly after the end of the Second World War, along with his translation of

   Selected Works of Lenin (*Liening wenji* 列宁文集) and a compilation of the first
   Russo-Chinese dictionary (*ehua cidian* 俄華辭典).
22 Shi and Chen, *Zhou Enlai de Gushi* 周恩来的故事, 349.
23 Lei, "Yinrongwanzai Enhaiyoumeng 音容宛在 恩海尤蒙."
24 Ma, *Zuguo*.
25 Ma, *Zuguo*.
26 Ding Jindong used to be the head of the Lüda Garrison Headquarters.
27 Ding, "Zhou Enlai," 23.
28 I am using the word "professional" sarcastically. Reading is an inalienable gift of
   human being and should never become professional.
29 Stepanov, *Lüshun Kou*, 7–8. The translation comes from the English translation of
   this work, Stepanov, *Port Arthur*, 9.
30 Stepanov, *Lüshun Kou*, 18; *Port Arthur*, 17.
31 Stepanov, *Lüshun Kou*, 24; *Port Arthur*, 21.
32 Stepanov, *Lüshun Kou*, 471; *Port Arthur*, 351.
33 Stepanov, *Lüshun Kou*, 341; *Port Arthur*, 259.
34 Stepanov, *Lüshun Kou*, 297; *Port Arthur*, 227.
35 Stepanov, *Lüshun Kou*, 38; *Port Arthur*, 33.
36 Stepanov, *Lüshun Kou*, 319; *Port Arthur*, 243.
37 Frantz Fanon, "On Violence," *The Wretched of the Earth*, trans. Richard Philcox
   (New York: Grove Press, 1961), 6.
38 Stepanov, *Lüshun Kou*, 1058; *Port Arthur*, 784.
39 Stepanov, *Lüshun Kou*, 44; *Port Arthur*, 37.
40 Stepanov, *Lüshun Kou*, 45; *Port Arthur*, 38.
41 Stepanov, *Lüshun Kou*, 40–41; *Port Arthur*, 35.
42 Stepanov, *Lüshun Kou*, 46–7; *Port Arthur*, 39.
43 Stepanov, *Lüshun Kou*, 223; *Port Arthur*, 171.
44 Stepanov, *Lüshun Kou*, 341; *Port Arthur*, 259.
45 Stepanov, *Lüshun Kou*, 341; *Port Arthur*, 259.
46 Stepanov, *Lüshun Kou*, 342; *Port Arthur*, 260.
47 Stepanov, *Lüshun Kou*, 343; *Port Arthur*, 260.
48 Stepanov, *Lüshun Kou*, 343; *Port Arthur*, 261.
49 Stepanov, *Lüshun Kou*, 345; *Port Arthur*, 262.
50 Stepanov, *Lüshun Kou*, 807.
51 Xun Lu, "Preface to the First Collection of Short Stories," in *Selected Stories of Lu
   Hsun*, trans. Yang Hsien-yi and Gladys Yang (New York: W. W. Norton, 2003), 2–3.
52 Lorenz Lüthi enlarges upon the role of ideology on the Sino-Soviet Split, dismissing other explanatory frameworks. For a detailed discussion, please see Lorenz
   Lüthi, *The Sino-Soviet Split: Cold War in the Communist World* (Princeton: Princeton University Press, 2008).
53 In his recent research, Jeremy Friedman sees the Sino-Soviet Split as the clash
   between two competing revolutionary programs in the global stage of revolution,
   Soviet Union as anti-capitalist and China as anti-imperialist, both vying for leadership in the decolonized states. For a detailed discussion, please see Jeremy
   Friedman, *Shadow Cold War: The Sino-Soviet Competition for the Third World*
   (Chapel Hill: University of North Carolina Press, 2015).

Part III
Realities

9 Welfare and work

Reintegrating "invalids" into Soviet Kyrgyzstan after the Great Patriotic War

Michael J. Corsi

In the Soviet Union after the conclusion of the Second World War, welfare and work became complementary institutions; the existence of one presupposed the operation of the other. In the interwar period, socialist propaganda crystallized the tremendous value of labor in the minds of party members and citizens alike. During the Soviet industrial drive of the 1930s, for example, Nikolai Bukharin expressed to the central press his conviction that "our heroes and heroines are people of labor," emphasizing the dissoluble association between the efforts of Soviet working men and women with the progressive development of socialist society.[1] Commitment to socially-productive labor, at least according to the rhetoric of Bolshevik revolutionaries, was therefore one of the strongest measures of individual merit in this period. From the perspective of the Soviet Union's returning post-World War II wartime population—consisting of those individuals who would come to acquire the decisive "invalid" label—the reception of welfare was, therefore, inexorably tied to their obligation to work.

One of the greatest challenges the Soviet government had to meet upon the conclusion of the Second World War was the reintegration of its wartime invalid population back into society. In the context of war, the term *invalid* referred to any person who belonged to a group that was eligible for state benefits due to incapacities they suffered as a result of their military service; it did not share the derogatory connotation that comes with the English-language use of the word. Soviet medical experts defined invalidity as "a loss of working capacity," but maintained that such loss had to be either extremely long-term or permanent.[2] Individuals who were temporarily barred from social labor due to afflictions such as infection or minor injury did not fall within the category of invalidity. However, elsewhere in the Soviet Union "invalidity" took on various shades of meaning. For example, the state exercised an entire subsidiary concentration on psychological invalidity, concerned with how to define and control the mentally disabled.[3]

Many of the veterans who filtered back into the Soviet heartlands had been physically injured in Russia's Great Patriotic War. Over 27 million soldiers and civilians had lost their lives in the conflict, and historians of the war in Russia estimate that millions more had returned home who were either shell-shocked, psychologically traumatized, physically handicapped, or some combination of them all.[4] Mark Edele, for example, claims that anywhere between 10 and 19 percent of Russia's surviving soldiers were considered to be "war invalids," and of this group 2.6 million had been medically discharged and were officially recognized as being "permanently disabled."[5] Provision of welfare to these individuals thus became a top priority for ministry officials concerned with their successful social reintegration.

Some of the earlier research on institutional insurance, mostly published in the 1950s and 1960s, has commented on the tendency of Soviet public relief efforts to assist only the most productive members of society, excluding those individuals whom authorities considered to be the least capable of meaningful contribution to society at large. Analyses of this kind, however, have focused heavily on statistical interpretations of the Soviet state budget. Gaston Rimlinger, for example, in his examination of trade union benefits, argued that "[w]ith the exception of minor benefits, like layette or nursing grants, the entire benefit structure is strongly incentive-oriented, in the sense that the benefit amounts depend on previous earnings and length of service, and eligibility is related to both age and years of total, and sometimes continual, service."[6] Rimlinger's argument gives the impression that Soviet ministers allocated welfare entirely in accordance with strict economic definitions of "service" to the state, independent of any overarching political considerations. There were, of course, specific criteria to which ministers in charge of welfare were held when deciding who was to be rewarded and how much those recipients were to receive. Such a purely economic perspective, however, provides historians with an overly numerical explanation of the rationale behind welfare distribution without much consideration of how Soviet social and ideological policy also influenced decision-making in this regard.

Recent arguments have examined the phenomenon of Soviet social service more comprehensively, and have provided convincing evidence debunking these earlier claims. In the first place, as Stephen Kotkin has argued, "Industrialists," urban planners, and government officials struggling to fulfill official quotas were "often concerned about obtaining a reliable, docile supply of labor, and social reformers, crusading for what they took to be the best way to minimize social costs and maximize social benefits, shared a logic, even if their aims often appeared divergent."[7] Furthermore, Kotkin maintains that in fact it was these seemingly "unproductive" members of society who were to receive welfare from the state in the event of "death, disability, sickness, old age, pregnancy and childbirth, or unemployment, for working people and family members."[8] Unfortunately, at the union-wide level, ministry officials only imperfectly implemented such universalist aspirations. As historian Donald Filtzer has pointed out, the Ministry of Health in the postwar period was consistently bogged down by the "splintering of health-care provision" which led to "bureaucratic parochialism."[9] For example, hoarding of government resources had a negative impact on the functioning of Soviet sanatoria and rest homes. The disorganization caused by sub-ministerial resource competition produced an inevitably unequal provision of public services.

Other scholars have argued that the provision of social assistance to the most impoverished members of society cultivated a unique and effective kind of paternalism between the Stalin regime and ordinary people, which helped to bolster both the cult of personality surrounding Stalin himself as well as the level of faith everyday Soviet citizens were willing to put into the state and government.[10] Myth and propaganda in the Soviet Union was not always directed toward apotheosizing the exclusive and seemingly ineffable image of the Party. Rather, much more vehement were efforts to showcase the talents and capabilities of the Soviet common person, regardless of his or her social or political station, and how the transition from a pre-socialist to a socialist society had been smoothly facilitated by cooperation with the new leadership. The invalids returning home after the conclusion of the War were one such group through which this transition took place.

Because of their outlying geography, distance from the main centers of Soviet industrial production, and the tendency Soviet authorities had to exile malcontents and other unwanted peoples there, the union republics of Central Asia provide historians with a clear example of places where manpower was scarce and the incorporation of invalids into the Soviet workforce more direct. Scholars of Central Asian history in particular have demonstrated how the Soviet Union placed intensive labor demands on agriculture in Kazakhstan and Transoxiana during the pre-war years. David Christian, for example, has pointed out how Soviet policy in Central Asia in the 1930s was dominated by "mobilizational demands," reduced emphasis on *korenizatsiia,* the spread of Russian as the primary language of bureaucracy, translation of documents into Cyrillic, and the introduction of large-scale economic projects devoted to activities like cotton production and irrigation.[11] Such socio-economic considerations in the region prioritized elevating the value of collective labor to the utmost importance. Indeed, Central Asia, particularly the fertile lands of the Kazakh steppe, became increasingly important to the Soviet economy in the postwar years, supplying an overwhelming amount of cotton, wheat, oil, and, after the Virgin Lands program of the 1960s, food to the Soviet imperial core.[12] Ultimately, interference in Central Asian affairs was not successful in culturally integrating the territory into the Soviet sphere to a lasting degree, and Marxist-Leninist principles of the importance of service to society failed to supplant the more firmly entrenched Islamic mores of Uzbekistan, Kazakhstan, and Kyrgyzstan.[13] However, ideology did influence the way Soviet authorities themselves evaluated the importance of social labor as connected to the reintegration of postwar invalids.

In particular, the Kyrgyz Soviet Socialist Republic (Kyrgyz SSR) experienced a massive influx of displaced war invalids in the years following the conclusion of the Great Patriotic War, and the ways in which the government chose to respond to them is telling of the general reaction to invalid reintegration throughout the Soviet Union. In Soviet Kyrgyzstan, care for returning invalids became the responsibility of the Kyrgyz Ministry of Public Welfare (*Ministerstvo Sotsial'nogo Obespecheniia Kirgizskoi Respublikii,* hereafter, the

Kyrgyz MSO), which, by 1947, had over 28,342 invalids to manage.[14] Thereafter an entire industry of welfare management for incoming invalids emerged. This welfare certainly provided some semblance of relief to the victims of the War as well as to their families. However, underneath the charity provided by the state, below all of the material goods, pensions, and education offered to invalids, the overriding objective of the Kyrgyz SSR was the procurement of work and the expectation of invalids to fulfill their duties within the Soviet workforce. Public welfare was consequently palimpsest in nature; it existed both as a genuine economic and material boon to war victims as well as a mechanism of social imposition which was placed upon them. As Yuan Gao has pointed out elsewhere in this volume, "trauma" could be made to appear as a "personal, even national triumph," if only it could be contextualized in the right kind of narrative. In the case of twentieth-century Soviet Kyrgyzstan, postwar invalidity was turned into an opportunity for productivity by just such a narrative, one which praised the reintegration of socially-responsible veterans and the benefits of hard work.

Welfare

The Second World War brought more material and human destruction to the Soviet Union than to any other combatant in the conflict. By 1945, millions of soldiers and civilians had been killed on the eastern front. Across the Soviet Union, the destruction caused by fighting left no part of the domestic economy untouched. The Nazi war machine had destroyed thousands of Soviet towns and villages, tens of thousands of schools, libraries, factories, and bridges, more than half of the country's railway tracks, and over 6 million buildings. In addition, the countryside suffered an unprecedented loss of livestock: 7 million horses, 17 million cattle, 20 million pigs, and 27 million sheep and goats were killed as a result of the German invasions.[15] Cities across the empire lay in ruins. The city of Rostov, to take only one example, was the largest Soviet city that had come under occupation by Nazi forces, and had been occupied twice, once in 1941 and again in 1942. The consistent bombardment of the city, coupled with indiscriminate gunfire in the streets, the massacres of Rostov's Jewish population, and the deportation of women and children to German labor camps, left thousands in the city dead and thousands more displaced.[16] Estimates for the total number of civilians and soldiers who had been killed in the conflict vary, but it is safe to assume that the Soviet Union lost anywhere between 25 to 30 million people as a result of both the fighting itself and the starvation that gripped cities in the aftermath of occupation. This number does not account for that demographic of victims that historian Chris Bellamy has referred to as having left an "invisible legacy," including the millions of soldiers and civilians left psychologically traumatized, injured, or physically mutilated.[17] These people subsequently became "invalids" upon their return home, and it fell to the all-union and local governments to facilitate their reintegration.

At the all-union level of distribution, Soviet policies of welfare management reflected the same expectations of productivity that directed ministers' decisions in the individual republics. At the highest level of the executive, the first deputy chair of the Soviet Sovnarkom, Vyacheslav Molotov, issued decrees dictating how lower-level ministers were to divide their overall resources to assist the functioning of the Soviet Union's welfare industries. Molotov, along with his co-council member Ia. Chadaev, had been commenting on the state of the Soviet Union's welfare apparatus from as early as 1942. The Sovnarkom passed resolutions which outlined how efficaciously Soviet industries had fulfilled their material distribution quotas from previous years (the reports invariably concluding that they fell under government expectation), and how resources would be distributed to local ministries from that point forward in order to improve their output. For example, in 1942 Molotov passed Resolution no. 74, which called for an "improvement in the work of the prosthetic industry."[18] In order to increase the number of items such as canes, bandages, and wheelchairs being produced across the Union, Resolution no. 74 required ministries in each of the union republics to provide raw materials for the construction of prostheses, and that the People's Commissariat of Public Welfare of the USSR (Narkomsobes) help train experts—doctors, engineers, and other "highly qualified specialists"—to oversee the work being done in local workshops across the empire.[19] Molotov and other Sovnarkom members intended resolutions of this type to increase the total availability of material assistance across all of the union republics in the postwar years. And their efforts seem to have paid off, especially at a time when the proportion of those in need of state welfare had significantly risen across the board—by 2.5 times in the RSFSR, 3 times in the Belorussian Soviet Socialist Republic, and 4.5 to 5 times in places like Armenia, Turkmenistan, and Kazakhstan.[20] As V. A. Acharkan, chief of the Soviet Labor Research Institute, noted in his report on the state of welfare distribution after the war: "At the end of 1946, for the unemployed pensioners in the cities and working settlements, pensions had been significantly increased through the passage of the decree (*ustanovleniia*) on 'bread benefits' (*khlebnoi nadbavki*) to a considerable degree."[21] Such "benefits" in the form of pensions, bread, vegetables, cattle, prostheses, and invalid homes, became the staple items of Soviet welfare across all of the union republics.

In the Kyrgyz SSR, one of the defining characteristics of the provision of welfare was that it was complicated. As an organized apparatus—one that culminated in a highly stratified and preordained execution of state authority—the bureaucracy of public aid, coupled with the carrying out of Ministry orders, existed as a duality between top and bottom, those with their fingers on the highest echelons of power and the public officials entrusted to perform their duties at the ground level. Its internal coherence reflected the same kind of utilitarian expectations of those who parsed out welfare as by those who received it. The convoluted network of ministries, departments, and government officials that issued decrees and acted on behalf of Kyrgyzstan's disabled population constituted an unequal hierarchy, and the decisions that were passed down from one government organ to another did not always do so linearly, or effectively. At the top was what Kyrgyz officials referred to as the "Presidium of the Supreme Soviet of the Kyrgyz SSR" (*Prezidium Verkhovnogo Soveta Kirgizskoi SSR*), which itself deferred to the authority of the USSR, typically through the Narkomsobes or Sovnarkom. From there, orders were passed on to the Kyrgyz MSO, which would subsequently issue directives to the leading subsidiary departments in the various regional oblasts—from Frunze to Osh to Issy-Kul'.[22] Such an organization was intended to emulate the most cherished Soviet ideals of high centralization and efficiency. However, particularly at the lower levels of the governmental hierarchy, the successful implementation of the various decrees (*postanovleniia*) put forth by the Kyrgyz MSO required a high degree of lateral participation, and the cooperation of the various artels (*artelei*), collective farms, cooperatives, local ministries, public servants, and factory workers which were expected to actually execute these orders was highly unreliable.

In the eyes of state ministers, the invalid in Soviet Kyrgyzstan was first and foremost a person in need; his or her identity was defined by the nature and quantity of support received, with his or her capacity for reintegration into Kyrgyz society subject to an evaluation of how well he or she put that support to use. The invalid became an object which demanded the purposeful and consistent engagement of all sectors of society. The question of the invalid's well-being stretched from center to periphery, from the officials working out of the Kyrgyz MSO to the various local kolkhozes the invalid had returned to. The rationale behind this notion was made palpable in the official discourse.

First, there were the duties of the general community; the 1948 report to the Presidium, authored by Minister Chaikun, clearly delineated a portion of the burden of responsibility: "In the function of rendering material support to invalids of the Great Patriotic War, the work and the general support of the collective farms acquires special significance for the families of the war victims."[23] An informative note passed by the Kyrgyz MSO to the Presidium chairperson, comrade Kulatov, in 1947, had required that "In the duty of improving the material-living conditions of the invalids of the Great Patriotic War," a provisional base was to be set up in each kolkhoz for the rendering of immediate assistance to those in need.[24] Care for the disabled became a *collective* affair, the responsibility for determining how effectively said assistance would reach the needy becoming the duty of the entire community. Accountants from the Kyrgyz MSO had already conducted in all of the Kyrgyz oblasts a "ten-day collection of means" (*dekadnik sbora sredstv*), and this had been allied with the creation of a general fund of public support for the kolkhozes.[25] From this general fund poured the collective efforts of the Kyrgyz working men and women. It took the form of money, various market produce, heads of cattle, manufactured products and garments for daily wear, shoes, boots, fuel, coal, renovations to living quarters, and the provision of individual gardens and other plots of land.[26] According to the official report, over ten thousand invalids and their family members benefited from the generosity and hard work of their friends and neighbors.

Second, there was the responsibility of the state, and assistance at this level could take several difference forms. Direct assistance included pensions, the provision of material assistance to the collective farms, and the construction of housing for invalids. The provision of pecuniary assistance to the poor and other in-need elements of society (*nuzhdaiushchiisia*) was a strategy employed by Soviet authorities. By 1948, the distribution of pensions had become a rigorously monitored and controlled process. Money in particular moved from the general provisional fund owned and operated by the Kyrgyz MSO across the country, entering the pockets of beneficiaries via a plethora of interconnected yet functionally independent organizations—the state banks, the post, the kolkhozes, and so on. The Ministry relied on the cooperation of these various lateral institutions to collectively protect, manage, and release the money to thousands of invalids. For example, throughout 1947 and the first quarter of 1948, the pensions that the Kyrgyz MSO had paid to invalids throughout the entire republic totaled just over 56 million rubles.[27] Just under 25,000 invalids received these rubles from 1947 to 1948, totaling approximately 2,200 rubles per person. Given that this would presumably be an invalid's only source of income, these numbers further emphasize the state's contribution to Kyrgyzstan's disabled peoples.[28]

Such a system was bound to be ridden with problems, and the delivery of pensions was poorly managed and very often truant. Various regional, oblast', and state commissions, located in every district of the republic, were responsible for assigning pensions to invalids of the Great Patriotic War. Although the records do not provide exact numbers for how often these commissions were supposed to meet, Ministry officials noted that, for example, in the Taldy-Suisk region of the Issy-Kul' oblast', the commissions had met only three times since the beginning of January, and in Novo-Voznese-novsk meetings took place once per month.[29] The reports complained that the commissions were meeting "irregularly," heavily implying that officials expected them to meet more frequently than had been the case in Issy-Kul'. Furthermore, ministers noted that these commissions were never fully staffed. When petitions were reviewed, they were only ever incompletely considered, and on multiple occasions the decision of the commission was delivered well in violation of the established period for doing so.[30] In some cases, protocols for the assignment of pensions might reach the ministry without any of the commission members having actually signed the paperwork.

Complications at the distributive level also prevented invalids from promptly receiving their assistance. Thus, in December of 1947, invalids in all of the Kyrgyz oblasts were inconvenienced as a result of lower-level mismanagement. Such read the informative report delivered by A. Niiazaliev, minister of social welfare for the Kyrgyz MSO, to Comrade Kulatov of the Presidium: "The payment of the pension was carried out in an untimely manner, per the fault of the district workers, such as the post offices and *Gosbank*." As a consequence, the residents of Dzhalal-Abadski, Toktogul, and the Ala-Bukinska districts were delayed the reception of over 101,000 rubles.[31]

Welfare from the state also came in the form of material assistance. The Kyrgyz MSO regularly provided goods to each of the country's 1,617 kol-khozes, which were subsequently distributed to invalids and to the families of individuals who had been killed in the war. In 1947 alone, through the Kyrgyz MSO general fund for mutual assistance, 471,254 rubles were donated to the collective farms. Further aid came in the form of 2,698 centers (100kg) of grain, 159 centers of various other products, 52 heads of large cattle, and 232 heads of smaller cattle.[32] The nature of cumulative material assistance provided to the invalids was such as to ensure they could only ever make use of it via its distribution and function in the kolkhozes. Boots, tools, grain, heads of cattle, materials such as coal and other fuel for industry and manufacture—all of these items directly played into the state's desire to increase the productivity of the collective and increase the capacity for individual work to a maximum.

Even seemingly individual-oriented aid was tied to the functioning of the kolkhoz, such as the provision of invalid housing. In the first place, the designation of new invalid homes was a punctiliously regulated form of assistance; the quality and locations of housing available and the invalid demographics to which they were to be allotted was a statistical and highly calculated process. Ministry accountants allocated housing based on the precise movement of invalids themselves back into the country, how these invalids could be situated into one or another preordained category of disability type (for example, those who were included in the 1939 register, those who had lived in the houses during the war years without being transferred out of them, those who had already died, etc.), on age group, and other specially reserved criteria. Staffing at the houses was rigorously monitored. Many of the well-off invalid homes were specially equipped with a full range of doctors, medical personnel, and special labor-instructors to ensure that invalids were healthy enough to con-tribute to the maintenance of the collective farms. The ministry reports con-tained information concerning the employment of invalids into positions of "useful labor"—invalids who worked in the workshops (*v masterskikh*), in other "labor processes" (*trudprotsessakh*), in the home, and by other occupations not covered in the official reports.[33]

The allocation of invalid housing was organizational, purposeful, and productive—its end result, the creation of a class of invalids that was to become attached to that very particular genus of welfare itself. In Soviet Kyrgyzstan, the housed-invalid became particularly well attuned to his own responsibilities in the collective, and this was precisely because of how his own reception of state-sponsored welfare situated him into a condition of economic dependency; the Kyrgyz MSO did not mete out welfare impar-tially. See, for example, the notes of one senior accountant for the adminis-tration of Invalid Home No. 1 to the department at the Frunze oblast' (*Frunzeiskomu oblsobesu*): "Invalid Home No. 1 has a rural, subsidiary plot of land (*khoziaistvo*) with a connected pasture, the purpose of which is to provide to invalids *the opportunity* to use the remainder of their possible labor, on the one hand, and to improve the cultural-living standards of their life, on the other [emphasis added]."[34] To receive a home was to receive land, to receive land was to work, and to work was to receive an opportunity to improve oneself, as went the rhetoric of Kyrgyz (and Soviet) public welfare. The greater portion of the reports made by the various organs of government acting on behalf of the Kyrgyz MSO utilized the language of "improvement" (*uluchshenie*), "material-living conditions" (*materialno-bytovye usloviia*), and "training" (*obuchenie*) when discussing the desired ramifications of welfare on the future development of Kyrgyzstan's invalids. The invalid's identity thereafter became ever more classified, his or her position in society more clearly defined by the assistance he or she received and the work he or she was expected to carry out.

Work

Throughout Soviet Kyrgyzstan an evaluation of invalid work potential was taking place behind the backs of disabled peoples everywhere; the decrees, orders, informative reports, requests, inquiries, messages, and other mediums of high government bureaucracy in which this evaluation was happening set in motion an apparatus of power that medical authorities held over state invalids. Through this constantly recycled discourse the invalid became an object of intense scrutiny, fixated upon by state authorities concerned with creating better definitions of identity and with increasing human productivity. Across the Soviet Union, disabled peoples were fighting hard to demonstrate that they possessed as much merit to be considered just as "Soviet" as their able-bodied neighbors. The surest way to demonstrate one's utility in Soviet society (and thereby to join the ranks of the theoretically empowered proletariat) was to contribute one's productive forces, to enter the workforce. This was true, for example, for the deaf, as historian Claire Shaw has recently attested: "For many deaf people, sign language was a path to Sovietness—a means to become workers, to overcome backwardness, and to gain independence and agency—and in the 1950s and 1960s this hybrid deaf-Soviet identity became prominent."[35] But for the invalid who received a particular form of welfare from the state, assistance itself became a tool by which Soviet authorities could assign individuals into desirable categories of labor. The specific forms that invalid welfare took established a degree of permanence and rigidity concerning how the disabled person could survive upon returning home; ministry officials had ensured that the duality between work and life was such as to make the conditions of the latter dependent and inflexibly attached to the obligations of the former. What came to define the invalid after he or she had received their allotted welfare from the state was the degree to which he or she would be capable of performing certain forms of work, the nature and extent of the training the state would have to invest in these individuals in order to ensure that the execution of work would satisfy ministry demands, and how effectively said work had improved their social level.

At the highest government offices, officials maintained consistent attention to the training and employment of the disabled population; the success of social welfare was most often associated with the extent to which production quotas had been reached, as well as the year to year statistical improvements in the employment rate of the various sectors of the Soviet service industry. Merit and reward were predicated on productivity and efficiency. Observe the comments made by Minister Chaikun in his 1948 memo to the Presidium: "The working invalids of the Great Patriotic War demonstrate examples of [great] self-demanding work (*proiavliaiut obraztsy samotviorzhenoi raboty*), but only in the Frunze oblast' 517 people are Stakhanovites of production."[36] If the Stakhanovite invalids in the Frunze oblast' served as the model that the rest of Kyrgyzstan's returning wartime population was expected to follow, then this work ethic would most easily be achieved in those occupations that the Kyrgyz authorities deemed conducive to invalid workplace productivity. Furthermore, for Chaikun, the Frunze oblast' was the *only* place that possessed Stakhanovite workers, and this of course meant that the rest of the Kyrgyz invalid population had some serious catching up to do.

Support from the Kyrgyz MSO went most directly to the training of individuals which would enable them to adopt new occupational identities. That cohort of accountants, bookkeepers (*schiotvodov*), shoemakers, chauffeurs, electricians, lathe operators (*tokarei*), specialists of animal husbandry (*zootekhnikov*), machinists (*slesarei*), photographers, mechanics, sewers (*shveinikov*), fieldhands (*polevodov*), and others emerged as the new invalid working class.[37] It fell to a new body of occupational specialists whom the Kyrgyz MSO had directed to provide adequate training to these invalids, to provide courses for them, and to ensure their technical development and the quality of their finished products. An entirely new industry emerged out of all major regions of the Kyrgyz SSR, one in which invalid productivity was of paramount importance. For example, in 1947 alone, these instructors had successfully trained 21 accordion players, 4 watchmakers, 87 tradespeople (*torgov. rabotnikov*), 89 specialists of animal husbandry, and a whole host of unique and variegated local laborers.[38] The "training or retraining" (*obuchenie i pereobuchenie*) these invalids received was not restricted either to the town or countryside; it was predicated on skill, efficiency, and personal capability to serve as a contributing member of society. Failure to produce productive invalid workers was met with serious reprisal. The Kyrgyz MSO consistently maintained data that documented all regional ministries that had failed to completely fulfill proposed plans for training and workplace requalification. Among these included the Ministry of Automotive Transport, the Ministry of Food, the Ministry of Health Care, the Ministry of Textile Production, the Ministry of Finance, the Kyrgyz Cooperative Union, the Frunze Instrumental Factory, and other smaller factories in the oblast'.[39] Even at the level of the Kyrgyz MSO itself, certain individuals responsible for the prevention of invalid job placement could be held accountable. For example, on the direction of officials in the Ministry of Public Welfare, some invalids were denied access to employment. Eventually, certain other member of the Kyrgyz MSO brought these charges to the attention of the higher party organs, to which they directed relevant materials to the Procurator. For their interference, these officials were ultimately prosecuted in a court of law.[40]

Even in the provision of certain material assistance specifically beneficial to physically impaired invalids, the systematization of Soviet welfare was such as to realign all facets of regional organization to the perpetual fight for increased work and production. The manufacture and distribution of prosthetics acquired especial significance in the postwar years; the establishment and maintenance of the factories and distribution teams that made up this emergent industry profoundly adjusted the urban architecture and regularities of daily life. Let us take the example of the old elementary school which stood on Voroshilov street in the Frunze oblast'. In 1942 this school was decommissioned and the building was transformed into the primary prosthetics factory for the Frunze oblast'. The task of making prosthetics thereafter consistently improved. By 1947, the prosthetics factory reported that it had satisfied the state plan for the production of prosthetic-orthopedic products by 110.5 percent; it prepared and distributed 2,009 [general] prosthetics to consumers, 2,105 pairs of orthopedic shoes/braces (*ortobuvi*), 1,967 prosthetic legs (*par obuvi na protezy*), and at the same time undertook repairs of other orthopedic shoes and prosthetics in the specialized prosthetic-orthopedic repair workshops—those present in the Frunze, Perzhevalsk, and Osh oblasts.[41] The increased demand on the manufacture of invalid products placed a complimentary demand on the productive forces of industries throughout Soviet Kyrgyzstan. For example, in 1947, the Ministry of the Automotive Industry was required by the Soviet of the Union of Ministries to provide twenty tri-axial motorcycles to the Kyrgyz MSO. These motorcycles were to be provided to "invalids of the Great Patriotic War, missing both lower limbs," in order to improve their material well-being and workplace flexibility.[42] Unfortunately, by 1948 the Kyrgyz MSO had still not received the requested parts.

The directors, factory managers, and other individuals responsible for the provision of welfare to invalids, too, fell under intense scrutiny, and again, this was because Kyrgyz MSO officials believed such welfare to be beneficial to invalid reintegration into the workplace. "Patronage," and the failure to adequately provide it, was usually couched in the rhetoric of "the improvement of material-living conditions," its success measured according to a high standard of how many new jobs had been created. Criticism fell on certain department heads for whom "the question of job employment for invalids of the Great Patriotic War was of no special significance," particularly because in their respective oblasts these individuals were almost perpetually away on business trips or recreational vacations. The failure of certain factory managers to provide an adequate supply of patronage was a consistent point of contention, and in 1948 the Kyrgyz MSO minister N. Barakhtianskii reported to Razzakov that in Frunze, the sheepskin coat factory, the motor vehicle repair factory, the brickmaking factory, the "Kirkontora" factory (*Kirkontora "zagotskot" zavod*), and others had failed in their duties to maintain job availability or provide other forms of patronage to Kyrgyzstan's invalids.[43] Where city managers and factory owners fell short, the altruism from the local kolkhozes could make up. Thus, in September, to "the most needy of the invalids" (*ostronuzhdaiushchimsia invalidam*), the rural managers of the Issy-Kul kolkhozes were "of one spirit" (*edinodushno*) and accepted the responsibility of caring for and maintaining Kyrgyzstan's needy population.[44] The responsibility for reintegrating invalids was always a putatively *collective* affair, and, as such, the individuals responsible for their well-being took part in the simultaneous redefinition of their own positioning within Soviet society. Furthermore, by reentering the workforce, invalids themselves were being situated into a larger community of laboring citizens. This eliminated aspects of their identity which might have served to set them apart from their fellows, either as culturally Kyrgyz or medically incapacitated, and incorporated them into the larger socialist citizenry.[45] Invalidity did not preclude social collectivity.

Just what was the result of this collective charity for the individual and family? The fickle and unreliable nature of the welfare system was such as to ensure that in certain cases individual invalids would remain victims. Thus, the members of one "Kyrgyz brigade"—A. Putalov, Taimasov, and Karpenko—who were responsible for traveling the countryside and assessing the efficacy of the implemented Kyrgyz MSO welfare directives bore some bad news regarding the unfortunate families that the kolkhozes had failed to protect. Such was the case for the Varvara Bezrukova, widow of one of the many fallen soldiers of the Great Patriotic War, in the "New Life" kolkhoz during the winter of 1947–48. To stave off the starvation of her and her family during the worst portions of the winter months, Varvara was given a "one-time assistance of some damp peas and cereal waste products" by the kolkhoz, and her situation at the time of the report was such that at least 100 kilograms of wheat had been kept from her, rendering her family devoid of any bread with which to feed themselves.[46] Similar circumstances greeted the Reshetnikovs, a family of the same kolkhoz, for whom the collective refused to even provide enough supplies to prevent their yard from going fallow or their apartment from crumbling down around them.[47] In the town of Przhebalsk the family of the fallen soldier Arkhipov—three young children with an elderly mother— were evicted from their apartment and forced to live in a partially destroyed barn (*v polurazrushennom sarae*) during the winter months. These individuals and more joined the growing statistics that made up Kyrgyzstan's displaced and impoverished demographic—those invalids and their families for whom welfare was not as forthcoming as the Ministries may have intended. They were joined by the despair of the children, all 990 of them by 1948, who went without adequate clothing or enough pairs of shoes, the nearly 1,200 families who did not have enough fuel to warm their lodgings in the wintertime, and the 423 families whose apartments were in dire need of repairs.[48]

Although government directives may have focused nearly exclusively on the value of invalid work, the need to fill workplace vacancies, or the expectation of an idealistic and exponential increase in industrial productivity, one should nevertheless recognize the impact played by those objectives of Soviet social welfare not directly associated with issues of economy—those of definition, classification, and deployment. From the perspective of the state, the invalid assumed a new identity, one which brought him or her back into society and established his or her individual fate as a *collective* responsibility. This was as true for the victims of the First World War as the Second, and we may therefore better appreciate the insight of historian Alexandre Sumpf on the social condition of Russia's post-World War I invalids: "During the war, the body and the soul were national: to be mutilated or amputated was not only an individual accident, but it was moreover a public affair, consequent of the commitment of the entire nation in the army. This opinion did not recognize (*L'opinion ne voit pas*) an individual fate, but [rather] the pieces of a collective destiny that made soldiers die ..." or, by extension, return to their own communities disabled, forever changed.[49] Furthermore, "The status of the invalid was thus constructed at the crossroads of several different areas of expertise, at the center of which the medical discourse predominately sat."[50] As Steve Barnes has demonstrated in his study of the Gulag, the definitive characteristic of the Soviet prison system could not be limited to its economic productivity alone. Instead, the Gulag served as a site where the moral reconfiguration of prisoners achieved its highest realization; inmates were subjected to morale and political education, the careful recrafting of the criminal identity and the persistent belief in his or her "redeemability," and the way that the products of the inmate's forced labor was used as an image that could be flaunted as evidence of his individual reform.[51] The Gulag—as with the invalid home, the creation of urban invalid industry, or the ubiquitous distribution of social welfare—was the apparatus in which the new Soviet individual could be created. It was a place for the definition of identity, for the readjustment of individual values, for the practice of ideologically-reinforced behavior, and for the assumption of a new role in life.

That Barnes's focus lies on the Gulag in Karaganda reveals the extent to which Central Asia served not only as a site for the forced exile of thousands of Soviet citizens but also as place of experimentation, alteration, and self-ascriptive rediscovery. As in Soviet Kazakhstan, Kyrgyzstan was just isolated enough to allow local authorities to practice a form of socialism that best fit conditions specific to Kyrgyz sensibility; the invalid was one such object of experimentation that permitted a mixture of Kyrgyz individuals with specific socialist values. These values touched upon the importance that socialist ideology placed on the reformative aspects of labor to recreate the individual. Hard work made better citizens, and the responsibility of Kyrgyzstan's returning veterans to reenter the workforce served to homogenize them with the other members of Soviet society. In this way, the policies for reintegrating Kyrgyzstan's invalids can be seen to have imposed an identity on them that equalized them with workers anywhere else, one which was not culturally-defined but rather a product of their alignment with the collective values of an ideal socialist citizenry.

For authorities in the Kyrgyz MSO, at least insofar as they were connected to the distribution of welfare to invalids, this identity came predominately to be associated with work. Why else would the first page of the newest informative report, this time sent to the chairman of the Union of Ministries of the Kyrgyz SSR, Comrade Razzakov, be concerned first and foremost with those invalids who, by February of 1948, still had not found employment? Throughout the country, from Frunze to Issyk-Kul to Tallask to Osh, exactly 1,654 disabled individuals were still jobless.[52] 1,654 individuals were still surviving off the charity of the state without recontributing any of their own productive capabilities to the upkeep of their own society. If the invalid was a working person, then his or her failure to obtain adequate employment, particularly so long after their migration back into the heart of the Soviet Union, was reflective of the failure of socialism, both in its inability to provide work to individuals capable of some kind of productive labor as well as in providing for the needy in society in every way possible. The reasons for their lack of employment—that they were unable either due to physical or other health ailments, that working projects in their area had been scrapped, that they had been refused work by local committees, that too few invalids had migrated out from the center of the city to ensure equal opportunity for everyone—were carefully documented by Ministry officials. These officials recorded the numbers of incoming invalids and anticipated their movements and future job prospects.[53]

These circumstances reveal the reflective, Janus-like nature of Soviet welfare with even more clarity. In their report to the higher Ministries and the Presidium, the brigade representatives took it upon themselves to assure their superiors that in certain other Kyrgyz oblasts and towns—Frunze, the Pokrovskii neighborhood, etc.—adequate measures had been taken to meet government directives, to provide welfare to the needy, and to close the gap between unemployed and employed invalids. The report ended on a mixed note—three new invalid homes had been constructed, two apartments had been renovated, and 62 children had been provided with new clothing. However, in certain oblasts some children still went without shoes, and the kolkhozes continued to face shortages of construction materials such as timber and glass for their "next construction [projects]."[54] Just as the welfare provided to an invalid served as a reflection of the work he or she was expected to carry out, so too the perpetuation of a work ethic that was incontrovertibly fixated on the "next" task at hand reflected the general success of Soviet social security. And of course, in the general welfare of the collective was reflected every individual tragedy.

Conclusion

In the Soviet Union, to be an invalid meant that one was *disabled*, and the understanding of "disability" by all sectors of Soviet society, from practitioners of medicine to everyday citizens, was in and of itself highly versatile and easy to modify. It was contingent upon ever-expanding criteria by which society perceived the relative usefulness of an individual based on his or her productive capacity. Being an invalid, however, also took on a social dimension. Invalids in the Soviet Union became objects of scrutiny; individuals who adopted the "invalid" identity became for most people separate categories of representation in the social consciousness, upon which entirely different, if not arbitrary, measures of value came to be placed. The opinions and characterizations of invalidity were many, and at times quite confused, as was the jurisdiction under which the right to such judgment was held. When it served their purposes, doctors and other Soviet officials could observe and make comments about invalids as objects of compassion. Golfo Alexopoulos, for example, has discussed the benefits that having an invalid family member could possess for incarcerated Russian citizens. Appeals to the Soviet Amnesty Commission were made much more effective, and the incarcerated person more likely to receive a pardon, if they had a disabled family member who depended on them. Furthermore, disabled persons themselves were released in such high proportions that "prisoners were faking illnesses or hacking off fingers in order to obtain early release as invalids."[55] Individuals attached to this identity throughout the Soviet period eventually came to occupy a position stratified with a peculiar kind of social significance, one which transformed the "invalid" from an object of singular dependence to that possessing a particular kind of use.

Therefore, it comes as no surprise that the government officials tasked with rehabilitating invalids returning to Soviet Kyrgyzstan after the Second World War thought of them no differently from the disabled population in any other part of the country. The decrees and informative reports that officials working out of the Kyrgyz MSO passed reflected the desire to homogenize Kyrgyzstan's invalid population with the rest of Soviet society. They did this by attaching the postwar responsibilities of the invalid population to those socialist principles that championed the goodness of collective labor. In doing so, officials had hoped to transform the invalid's identity to better fit the universal expectations of society; the state came to recognize disabled peoples no longer in terms of incapacity but rather as equally contributive members of the socialist community. In this way, Kyrgyzstan serves as a model case study because it demonstrates just how typified the ideology of state had become by the late-Stalinist period, at least at the executive level.

As the transformation of invalid identity began to reorient these individuals into the social sphere, invalids acquired an attendant duty to society, a responsibility to work and to be productive that was very much conditional to one's membership within the socialist community. As with so much else in the Soviet Union, this utilitarian focus concerning the position of the invalid in Soviet society allowed both medical professionals as well as government officials to generate expectations regarding the relative usefulness of the returning invalid's work and life, to develop new institutions dedicated to successfully integrating these people back into postwar Soviet society specifically in the manner set forth by their own predeterminations, and to cast judgment on the relative success or failure of their ability to fulfill these expectations. There were certainly differences in the ways in which officials handled welfare in Soviet Kyrgyzstan compared with other union republics. However, at the level of executive action, the motivations of Soviet party members were more or less consistent across the empire. In the Soviet Union, productivity and contribution to the workforce were the goals of the postwar reintegration of invalids, ancillary provision of social welfare, the method.

Notes

1 Quoted in David Brandenberger, *Propaganda State in Crisis: Soviet Ideology, Indoctrination, and Terror under Stalin, 1927–1941* (New Haven: Yale University Press, 2011), 92–3.
2 A. D. Glazunov, *L'goty Invalidam Voiny* (Moscow: Iuridicheskaia Literatura, 1970), 11–12.
3 See for example Julie V. Brown, "Societal Responses to Mental Disorders in Prerevolutionary Russia" in *The Disabled in the Soviet Union: Past and Present, Theory and Practice*, eds., William O. McCagg and Lewis Siegelbaum (Pittsburgh: University of Pittsburgh Press, 1989). On schizophrenia and other psychological disorders, see David Joravsky, "The Stalinist Mentality and the Treatment of Schizophrenia" in *The Disabled in the Soviet Union: Past and Present, Theory and Practice*, eds. William O. McCagg and Lewis Siegelbaum (Pittsburgh: University of Pittsburgh Press, 1989), 119–49; on the increasing focus on perversion in the late-Imperial law and medical professions see Laura Engelstein, *The Keys to Happiness: Sex and the Search for Modernity in Fin-de-Siècle Russia* (Ithaca: Cornell University Press, 1992); on the prevalence of infanticide during the Soviet period, see Sharon Kowalsky, *Deviant Women: Female Crime and Criminality in Revolutionary Russia* (DeKalb: Northern Illinois University Press, 2009).
4 Chris Bellamy, *Absolute War: Soviet Russia in the Second World War* (New York: Alfred A. Knopf, 2007), 2.
5 Mark Edele, *Soviet Veterans of World War II: A Popular Movement in an Authoritarian Society, 1941–1991* (Oxford: Oxford University Press, 2008), 82.
6 Gaston V. Rimlinger, "The Trade Union in Soviet Social Insurance: Historical Development and Present Functions," *ILR Review* 14: 3 (1961): 397–418, especially 401.
7 Stephen Kotkin, *Magnetic Mountain: Stalinism as a Civilization* (Berkeley: University of California Press, 1995), 20.
8 Kotkin, *Magnetic Mountain*, 20.
9 Donald A. Filtzer, *Soviet Workers and Late Stalinism: Labour and the Restoration of the Stalinist System after World War II* (Cambridge: Cambridge University Press, 2002), 109–10.
10 Joonseo Song, "Rule of Inclusion: The Politics of Postwar Stalinist Care in Magnitogorsk, 1945–1953," *Journal of Social History* 43: 3 (2010): 663–80.
11 David Christian, *A History of Russia, Central Asia, and Mongolia* (Malden, MA: Blackwell Publishers, 1998–2018), 410–11. Also, see Elizabeth E. Bacon, *Central Asians under Russian Rule: A Study in Cultural Change* (Ithaca: Cornell University Press, 1980).
12 Sally N. Cummings, *Understanding Central Asia: Politics and Contested Transformations* (New York: Routledge, 2012), 46–7.
13 See William Fierman, *Soviet Central Asia: The Failed Transformation* (Boulder: Westview Press, 1991).
14 Central State Archives of the Kyrgyz Republic (TGAKR), f. 511, op. 1, d. 7, l. 13.

15 Frederick L. Schuman, *Russia since 1917: Four Decades of Soviet Politics* (New York: Alfred A. Knopf, 1957), 278.

16 For a more complete picture of Soviet Rostov during the war, see Jeffrey W. Jones, *Everyday Life and the "Reconstruction" of Soviet Russia during and after the Great Patriotic War, 1943–1948* (Bloomington: Slavica Publishers, 2008), 16–39.

17 Bellamy, *Absolute War*, 2.

18 TGAKR, f. 1682, op. 3, d. 18, l. 57.

19 TGAKR, f. 1682, op. 3, d. 18, l. 57.

20 V. A. Acharkan, *Obespechenie veteranov truda v SSSR*, (Moskva: Izdatel'stvo "Nauka", 1965), 89.

21 V. A. Acharkan, *Obespechenie*, 46.

22 Frunze was the official name of the Kyrgyz capital from 1926 until the collapse of the Soviet Union in 1991. Thereafter the name was changed to Bishkek.

23 TGAKR, f. 511, op.1, d. 7, l. 17.

24 TGAKR, f. 511, op. 1, d. 7, l. 35.

25 TGAKR, f. 511, op. 1, d. 7, l. 35.

26 TGAKR, f. 511, op. 1, d. 7, l. 35–6.

27 TGAKR, f. 511, op. 1, d. 7, l. 84.

28 I would like to thank Jeff Hardy for his input on these numbers, as he helped me to verify the accuracy of these approximations.

29 TGAKR, f. 511, op. 1, d. 7, l. 84–85.

30 TGAKR, f. 511, op. 1, d. 7, l. 85.

31 TGAKR, f. 511, op. 1, d. 7, l. 39.

32 TGAKR, f. 511, op. 1, d. 7, l. 17–19.

33 TGAKR, f. 1682, op. 2, d. 24, l. 3–7. This information comes from the report made by the accountant for the Frunze oblast' covering the year 1939.

34 TGAKR, f. 1682, op. 2, d. 24, l. 52.

35 Claire Shaw, "Deafness and the Politics of Hearing," in *Russian History through the Senses: From 1700 to the Present*, eds., Matthew P. Romaniello and Tricia Starks (New York: Bloomsbury, 2016), 211.

36 TGAKR, f. 511, op. 1, d. 7, l. 14.

37 In 1948 alone, 2,410 were successfully integrated into these and other occupations. TGAKR, f. 511, op. 1, d. 7, l. 15.

38 TGAKR, f. 511, op. 1, d. 7, l. 33.

39 TGAKR, f. 511, op. 1, d. 7, l. 34.

40 TGAKR, f. 511, op. 1, d. 7, l. 14–15.

41 TGAKR, f. 511, op. 1, d. 7, l. 16.

42 TGAKR, f. 511, op. 1, d. 7, l. 18.

43 TGAKR, f. 511, op. 1, d. 7, l. 175.

44 TGAKR, f. 511, op. 1, d. 7, l. 176.

45 Frances Bernstein, for example, has discussed how the Soviet prosthetic industry served a similar purpose after the Second World War. Prostheses allowed for the concealment of physical deformities soldiers had suffered and a reclamation of their pre-war masculinity. This served both to eliminate the shameful vestiges of the brutality of the war and better homogenize Soviet invalids with other, non-deformed members of society. See Frances Bernstein, "Prosthetic Manhood in the Soviet Union at the End of World War II," *Osiris* 30: 1 (2015): 113–33.

46 TGAKR, f. 511, op. 1, d. 7, l. 183.

47 TGAKR, f. 511, op. 1, d. 7, l. 183.

48 TGAKR, f. 511, op. 1, d. 7, l. 184.

49 Alexandre Sumpf, "Un droit à la rehabilitation? Le statut légal des invalides russes de la Grande Guerre, 1912–1927," *Le mouvement social* 257 (October–December 2016): 149.

50 Sumpf, "Un droit à la rehabilitation?" 150.

51 Steve Barnes, *Death and Redemption: The Gulag and the Shaping of Soviet Society* (Princeton: Princeton University Press, 2011), 49.
52 TGAKR, f. 511, op. 1, d. 7, l. 172.
53 TGAKR, f. 511, op. 1, d. 7, l. 173.
54 TGAKR, f. 511, op. 1, d. 7, l. 187.
55 Golfo Alexopoulos, "Exiting the Gulag After War: Women, Invalids, and the Family," *Jahrbücher für Geschichte Osteuropas, Neue Folge* 57: 4 (2009): 567.

10 Urbanization, language vitality, and well-being in Russian Eurasia

Lenore A. Grenoble

Contact between speakers of Russian and other languages in Eurasia is long-standing and well-documented historically, dating to centuries ago to early colonization and increasing over time. The Russian expansion across Eurasia began in the fifteenth century; by the 1700s contact with even the most eastern Siberian peoples on Kamchatka was well-established; by the early 1900s, a Russian trading post was founded in the very far northeast in Anadyr, Chukotka, a distance of over 6,000 kilometers from Moscow, as the crow flies (see Figure 10.1).[1] Russian colonialism involves expansion, annexing contiguous territories, resulting in a region disproportionate to the rest of the country in terms of land mass and population. In imperial Russia, the lands lying east of the Urals and extending to the far north-eastern outposts of Eurasia were seen as a source of revenue, with the local indigenous peoples supplying tribute in the form of fur, an important trade commodity for the Russian conquerors. Throughout the Soviet period this overall view of colonialism was further extended, at times in sync and at times in conflict with Soviet ideologies, with major industrial development and resettlement of the area by people from western and central parts of the USSR. But there is clear continuity from imperial times until today: Siberian Eurasia has served as an economic supplier and primary asset for Russia, with little investment in infrastructure for local peoples. To put this in a broader context:

> The entire territory to the east of the Ural Mountains accounted for 52 percent of the imperial landmass, 7.5 percent of the overall population, and 19 percent of the Empire's exports in 1897; these figures grew to 57 percent, 10.5 percent, and 46 percent respectively in the USSR in 1985. In 2014, Muscovy's colony covered 75 percent of the nation's territory, was inhabited by 20.5 percent of its population, and provided between 76 and 78 percent of exports. If Siberia stopped supplying commodities today, Russia's exports would be smaller than Hungary's. With more than 55 percent of its federal revenues in some way derived from the use and export of natural resources, *Russia is in the unusual situation of feeding off a settler colony that itself remains poor and underdeveloped.* (my emphasis)[2]

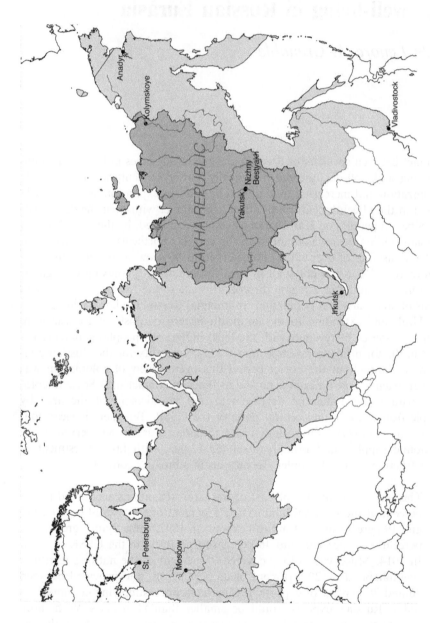

Figure 10.1 Map of Sakha

In this chapter I address the impact of the status of indigenous peoples in Eurasia as colonized peoples living in a poor, underdeveloped settler colony, a peripheral territory which continues to supply the geopolitical center in the western, European parts of the Russian Federation, the core of Russia. Urbanization and immigration are rapidly changing the demographics of Russian Eurasia and transforming this peripheral territory. This chapter illustrates the impact of urbanization on indigenous language vitality and well-being as exemplified in the Sakha Republic, a top-level political division of the Russian Federation, located in north-eastern Eurasia. The Sakha Republic provides an excellent place for studying their effects as it represents a significant portion of Russian-Asian territory with a dynamic population.

One of the factors driving language shift is urbanization. This is a wide-spread phenomenon in the Arctic, bringing with it major changes in lifestyle and introducing cultural tension.[3] While young people often prefer an urban lifestyle, many indigenous peoples reject it: Inuit cultural identity for many continues to be strongly connected to spending time out on the land, hunting, fishing, trapping, and camping.[4] Indigenous peoples who maintain a traditional lifestyle and are connected to the land show higher language retention rates, both in terms of language transmission as well as the preservation of different linguistic domains (such as those linked to traditional knowledge or cultural practices). Urbanization fosters a shift to urban culture, assimilation to the majority language, and, correspondingly, a host of social problems for indigenous peoples. Urbanization is already taking place at a particularly rapid rate in the Arctic, changing the very way of life of the local populations.[5]

There are few studies of urban language usage among Arctic indigenous groups. Instead, research has focused on studying them in villages, even though urbanization is a major factor in their lives. It is important to understand how these radical changes in the surrounding region are influencing indigenous Arctic languages and cultures, the dynamics of language contact, and, in particular, the relationship between language vitality and well-being. In this paper I discuss urbanization and its impact on indigenous peoples in north-eastern Siberia, focusing on language in the Republic of Sakha (Yakutia) as both a diagnostic (or *indicator*) of social and cultural vitality, and as a tool for resilience and a resource for well-being. Using data from the Sakha Republic on urban and rural language vitality and usage, I present a theoretical model for understanding the relations between these social and linguistic factors, adapting a model of well-being from Dodge et al. to combine with the notion of linguistic vitality, discussed in more detail below.[6] The model treats language as one of a complex system of interacting behaviors. Changes to another node or in the language node itself can have an impact on overall social well-being. Disruption to an existing network occurs within a time frame and, the longer the disruption, the more likely is major social disruption. One implication is that sustainability cannot be reduced to simple cause-and-effect relationships between socio-cultural variables.

I present an overview of urbanization in the Russian Federation with a focus on the current situation in the Sakha Republic and changing demographics there. This is followed by a discussion of the multiethnic and multilingual profile of Sakha, and a Model of Well-Being. Language is an important protective factor and resource for offsetting the stressors on indigenous populations. For discussion of the linguistic effects of multilingualism, language contact and shift, see Kantarovich, Chapter 11 (this volume), which focuses on the Chukchi and Sakha languages. Details about the experimental methods used in this project can be found in Grenoble et al. (2019).[7]

Urbanization in the Russian Federation and the Soviet legacy

The overall global trend is toward increasing urbanization. As of 2017, approximately 74 percent of the total population in the Russian Federation was urban according to data from the World Bank. The situation in Siberia and the Russian Far North warrants specific discussion, however. In order to understand the current situation in Sakha, as elsewhere in the Russian Federation, it is important to understand the lasting effects of Soviet policies in the region. Industrialization of the Sakha Republic began in the Soviet period, with deliberate, centralized planning that moved people to the region for development purposes. People were moved from the European parts of the USSR to Siberia because of these policies, rather than for independent economic or social reasons. These were considered hardship posts, and people were forcibly relocated by state policies, with added economic incentives, in part to make up for the increased cost of living.

No discussion of resettlement to the region would be complete without mention of the Soviet practice of deporting political prisoners to Siberia and the Far North. The Soviet penal system, or Gulag, was a carryover of Tsarist policies of forced labor camps (*katorga*), but the deportations of prisoners numbered in the millions and reshaped the region. The industrial development of Siberia was not just a "byproduct" of Soviet labor camps, but beginning in 1929, it was an explicit goal of the camps: prisoners were sent to remote places in Siberia to industrialize them in order to extract natural resources, move defense industries further from the West, and fortify the Far Eastern borders against invasion.[8] Some modern industrial cities, such as Magadan and Norilsk, were founded and built by prison labor.

And they have left an indelible imprint on society on a more personal level. Even today, in my own fieldwork in Sakha I meet people who are the descendants of prisoners, or who worked in Soviet prisons, or work in the modern Russian prisons. Indigenous peoples have stories of encounters with the inmates; one (indigenous) elder told me how a friend in her village went to watch a boat of incoming prisoners and saw her own husband among them. The net result was massive interior migration within the USSR simply because of these policies, and people ended up being in cities in isolated (and very cold) regions. In a nutshell, internal migration was forced for both ideological and economic reasons, with people ending up in cold, remote cities with poor transportation and no infrastructure. The cost of living in Russia's Far North is four times higher than the rest of the country, and the far northern cities depend heavily on state subsidies for the basic requirements of living, food and fuel. These are regions that would not be densely populated today without deliberate social engineering, given the harsh climate conditions. For example, in January, the mean average temperature in Yakutsk is -45C/-49F; Moscow is considerably warmer with a mean temperature of -10C/14F. By way of comparison, the January mean temperature in Winnipeg is -19C/-2F; standard steel structures "rupture on mass scale" with temperatures at -37C/-35F, i.e., warmer than Yakutsk in January.[9]

Furthermore, Soviet policies resulted in the delineation of "boundaries of social divisions of labor" along ethnic lines, so that the urban centers were populated by workers who had immigrated from elsewhere in the USSR, and the local indigenous peoples were largely excluded from these centers and the industrial labor force.[10] This further separated indigenous from non-indigenous peoples, and relegated the former to the periphery, geographically and socially. This has left a lasting imprint on society in Siberia. Since the 1990s, a number of demographic changes have helped to reshape this core/periphery dichotomy: (1) the massive emigration of settlers back to more European parts of Russia and radical drop in overall population immediately following the collapse of the Soviet Union; (2) the subsequent increased internal migration of Sakha and minority indigenous peoples within the Sakha Republic; and (3) the immigration of both permanent and seasonal workers from other parts of the former USSR to Sakha.

Case study: The Republic of Sakha (Yakutia)

Sakha is the largest subnational governing body in the world with three time zones spanning a total of 1,190,555 square miles (or 3,083,523 square kilometers), making it approximately six times the size of France. The total population of Sakha is 958,528 people (all figures from the 2010 All-Russian Census). It has one of the coldest climates of the inhabited regions of the world, with average low temperatures in January of -35C (-30F); the coldest recorded temperatures outside of Antarctica are in Sakha, with Omyakon setting a record low in 1933 of -67.7 C (-89.9 F) (data from World Meteorological Organization). Thus, not surprisingly, the Republic is sparsely populated, with less than one person per square mile (0.80/square mile, or 0.31/km^2).

Sakha is ethnically diverse, and in contrast to much of the Russian Federation, ethnic Russians are not the majority: here they constitute 36.9 percent of the population. 48.7 percent of the population is ethnic Sakha (a Turkic people), and the remaining is a mixture of other ethnic groups (e.g. Ukrainians, Tatars) who have immigrated to the region, and a small but significant number of indigenous peoples. It is also multilingual. Russian is the national language and widely used throughout the Republic, and Sakha is the local majority language. There are numbers of speakers of more recent immigrant languages, and a smaller number of speakers of languages indigenous to the region.

Urbanization in Sakha

The Sakha Republic has seen significant demographic changes due to industrialization, migration, and a combination of economic and political factors. As elsewhere in the Russian Far North, the total population of Sakha decreased in the years immediately following the break-up of the Soviet Union, with a decline of approximately 12 percent from 1989 to 2002. Although it has not returned to its previous high, it has slowly but steadily risen since then, as seen in the data provided in Table 10.1:

Table 10.1   Total population in Sakha Republic

Year	1989	2002	2010	2018
Population	1,081,408	949,280	958,528	964,330

Source: Federal State Statistics Service Russia

The initial decline is due to out migration to more European parts of Russia, and the subsequent increase largely represents immigration from Central Asia and the Caucasus (and not an increase in birth rates). At the same time, there has been significant population change in the cities and urban settlements in Sakha. There are only nine cities in the Republic with a population of greater than 10,000, and just one with a population of over 70,000, the capital Yakutsk. These population trends are given in Table 10.2:[11]

Table 10.2 lists all cities in the Sakha Republic with a population of 10,000 or higher as of January 2018, as estimated by the Federal State Statistics Service of Russia, along with Nizhny Bestyakh, one of the only three cities or urban settlements that has shown a population increase since 2002 (together with Yakutsk and Viljujsk). It highlights several interesting facts about the overall

Table 10.2   Population change in cities and urban settlements

		2002	*2010*	*2018*
1.	**Yakutsk**	229,951	269,691	311,760
2.	Nerjungri	66,269	61,747	57,009
3.	Mirnyj	39,981	37,188	35,223
4.	Lensk	24,558	24,966	23,479
5.	Aldan	24,715	21,275	20,595
6.	Ajchal	15,782	13,727	13,683
7.	Udachnyj	15,698	12,613	11,676
8.	**Viljujsk**	9,776	10,234	11,095
9.	Zhataj	8,405	9,504	10,089
	Nizhny Bestyakh	3,327	3,518	4,152

Source: Federal State Statistics Service Russia

demographics and population trends in Sakha. First, almost a third of the entire population of the Republic is concentrated in the capital. The difference in size between it and the second largest city (Neryungri) is striking. Approximately 51 percent of the population of this vast region lives in just nine cities.

The areas that are growing are of particular interest. While the remainder of this chapter focuses on Yakutsk, it is still important to discuss the two other towns which show a population increase. Viljujsk is a Sakha-dominant city. There are no available data on the ethnic make-up of the city itself, but we can extrapolate from data on the Viljujsk region (*ulus*) from the 2010 All-Russian Census, with a reported 83.1 percent of the population ethnic Sakha, and only 12.5 percent Russian (old.sakha.gov.ru-node-16400).

Nizhny Bestyakh is of particular interest within the context of understanding the current dynamics of Yakutsk. It is located 30 kilometers from the capital on the opposite side of the Lena River (see Figure 10.2). The village is accessible by ferry in warmer months and by a winter road over the river when it is frozen; this winter route was opened on 25 December 2017. There are plans underway for constructing a bridge across the river to make it accessible year-round to and from Yakutsk.

A rail stop of the same name lies ten kilometers south of Nizhny Bestyakh; it is the final station of the Amur-Yakutsk rail line. Since 2014 it has been open to freight trains and thus has been a major transportation and shipping center, supplying the city of Yakutsk and beyond. Shipping to Nizhny

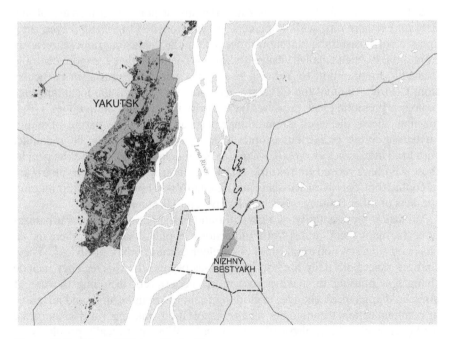

Figure 10.2 Map of Nizhny Bestyakh

Bestyakh has been increasing: the Sakha Government reported that a total of 527,600 tons of agricultural materials in a ten-month period (January-October 2017) through this station alone.[12] All indications are that the role of this town as a center for shipping will continue to grow, and not just by rail. The port in Nizhny Bestyakh currently processes 20,000 tons of freight annually, but its capacity will expand to 500,000 tons per year by 2021. Moreover, full passenger rail service is expected in 2019, which will open the town to a greater influx of people. City planners in the Sakha Republic anticipate that Nizhny Bestyakh will become a suburb town of Yakutsk, with a population of 15,000–20,000.

At present, more than the population increase, Nizhny Bestyakh is of great interest because it is a center of immigration from other regions. There are no available data on the current ethnic make-up of its population, but in 2013 data indicated a mixed population of Sakha and Russians, together with peoples immigrating primarily from Central Asia and the Caucasus: Uzbeks, Kyrgyz, Chechens, Armenians, and others.[13] Sixty-eight percent of the population are described as Russian speakers (*russkoiazychnoe*), and 30 percent as "indigenous"; this likely refers to ethnic Sakha who are classified as indigenous by the Sakha government. Nizhny Bestyakh has not been a place where high numbers of indigenous minorities live.

Urbanization in Yakutsk

Yakutsk, the capital of Sakha, has had the largest population increase of any Russian northern city, with 43 percent growth from 1989 to 2010;[14] even rural areas in north-eastern Sakha show movement of the indigenous population away from more isolated smaller villages to larger settlements that are more centrally located.[15] Immigration to Yakutsk from other parts of Eurasia, in particular from Central Asia and the Caucasus, has radically changed the local language ecologies, presenting new pressures on minority indigenous communities. Urbanization affects the levels of multilingualism as well as the nature of multilingualism. While indigenous peoples living in rural settings may be in contact with local indigenous groups, Russians (or Russian language), and Sakha people, those who have moved to Yakutsk, and to medium-sized cities (Neryungri) are in contact not only with Russians and Sakha (Yakut) but also with immigrant speakers of other languages (such as Kyrgyz and Ukrainian).

Yakutsk is representative of a general trend in the Republic toward urbanization. In many rural areas with indigenous populations today, there is an increased range of non-rural types of employment and urban lifestyles.[16] These changes affect both daily life and interactions beyond the village. They include changes in housing to make homes more modernized, including the use of household appliances, changes in clothing to more urban fashion, and advances in communication technologies and transportation, making rural areas more readily accessible, both physically and virtually. While historically people living in villages were forced to depend on subsistence hunting and herding for food, improved access to urban distribution centers has made marketable goods more readily accessible. This has naturally had an impact on traditional lifestyles. In sum, rural areas are becoming less rural and more urban-like.

Urbanization and indigenous peoples in Yakutsk

Soviet policies for industrializing the Russian Far North resulted in a core urban area, with indigenous peoples relegated to the periphery in rural settlements; they were both geographically and socially marginalized. Things changed with the break-up of the Soviet Union and the economic changes that came with it. The large-scale industrial urbanization of Siberia could not survive in a post-Soviet era and market economy, and an immediate result was a decline in population due to emigration and higher mortality rates. However, the indigenous peoples largely did not leave their homelands, but rather, there was increased internal migration. Much of this was movement into cities, rather than to other rural areas, a migration triggered by new employment opportunities. For example, economic changes in the 1990s in Chukotka led to greater indigenous populations in larger settlements, driven by the higher standards of living, more reliable supply sources and simply more jobs in Siberian cities.[17] Within the Sakha Republic, the numbers and percentages of indigenous peoples living in cities has consistently risen since the 1989 census was taken, as shown in Tables 10.3 and 10.4:

Table 10.3 Indigenous population in Sakha, Urban vs. Rural, 1989–2002

| | 1989 | | | | | 2002 | | | | |
| | Total | Urban | | Rural | | Total | Urban | | Rural | |
		No.	%	No.	%		No.	%	No.	%
Evenki	14,428	2,411	16.7	12,017	83.3	18,232	4,221	23.2	14,011	76.8
Even	8,668	1,909	22.0	6,759	78.0	11,657	3,569	30.6	8,088	69.4
Yukaghir	697	196	28.1	501	71.9	1,097	426	38.8	671	61.2
Dolgan	408	35	8.6	373	91.4	1,272	156	12.3	1,116	87.7

Source: Burtseva et al. 2014

Table 10.4 Indigenous Population in Sakha, 2010

People	Total	Urban	Rural	Percentage urban
Evenki	21,008	5,486	15,533	26.1%
Even	15,071	5,077	9,994	33.7%
Yukaghir	1281	559	722	43.6%
Dolgan	1906	260	1,646	13.6%
Chukchi	670	262	408	39.1%

Source: All-Russian 2010 Census

The most recent census data on urban trends date to 2010, given in Table 10.4. The table shows an increase across all groups since 2002, and an even more marked increase since 1989; coupled with an overall increase in the population of each group, there has also been an increase both in the numbers of peoples living in cities, and the percentage of the total population. Evenki, for example, have nearly doubled in terms of the numbers of urban dwellers, and Even have increased by about two and half times.

The raw numbers are significant in terms of the actual population, in particular when such small groups are involved. It means that the experience of indigenous peoples living in urban (or urbanized) areas has changed over the last thirty years, in that many are less isolated today and also more likely to be in daily contact with speakers of Russian. Crucially, it is not the case that the indigenous peoples live in particular neighborhoods or areas within Yakutsk. Rather, they are scattered throughout the city and thus do not form local communities where they interact face-to-face on a daily basis within their local neighborhood without traveling to some other part of the city. The numbers of indigenous peoples are small, and they are relatively dispersed, so there are no micro-level speech communities. Moreover, because their numbers are so small, they find strength in unity. There are festivals and celebrations in Yakutsk that celebrate the indigenous minorities collectively. These are of great celebration and are effective in creating a shared sense of indigenous pride. They create opportunities for groups of people to gather in one place, but the lingua franca for these groups is Russian, even though songs and poems will be performed in the local indigenous language. Communication with the audience is primarily in Russian, with the symbolic use of greetings and introductions in a local language.

This is in contrast to areas that have been more recently settled by immigrants from Central Asia, who are more likely to settle together in specific neighborhoods or regions, creating localized speech communities. The lingua franca outside of these neighborhoods is Russian; in response to an informal survey of produce merchants in the city of Yakutsk, all reported using Russian (and not Sakha) in the workplace with customers, but speaking their native language within their neighborhoods. In areas with dense populations, such as Nizhny Bestyakh. Kyrghyz can be heard spoken in the local stores by customers. The net result is that the indigenous peoples who have migrated to urban centers are even further minoritized.

Multilingualism in the Sakha Republic

Although sparsely populated, the Sakha Republic is multilingual, and home to speakers of a number of different ethnic groups, autochthonous and historical immigrants, along with recent settlers. Some of the latter are permanent, and others more transient, including migrant workers. There are two majority languages in the Republic, Russian and Sakha. Both are official languages according to the *Language Law of the Republic of Sakha (Yakutia)*, ratified on

October 16, 1992, with the more recent changes ratified on May 30, 2017. Article 2 of the Law guarantees people of any group the right to use their language. The law makes the Sakha language the official state (*gosudarstvennii*) language of the Republic (Article 3), while also declaring Russian a state language, and the language of interethnic communication (or *iazyk mezhnatsional'nogo obshcheniia*; Article 5). The law further recognizes Even, Evenki, Yukaghir, Chukchi and Dolgan as official languages in those regions where the peoples live, with equal status as the state languages.[18] The two Yukaghir varieties, Tundra (or Northern, ISO 639-s ykg) Yukaghir and Kolyma Yukaghir (also called Forest or Southern Yukaghir, ISO 639–3 yux), although closely related, are classified by linguists and the speakers themselves as distinct languages. Thus, within the context of the Sakha Republic, we need to consider a set of languages with different statuses: Russian and Sakha, both official but unequal, and what are technically six local languages. However, all statistics for both the Yukaghir peoples and languages present them as one, and the census data reflect this practice.

Russian is the national language and is used in all aspects of life. It is the primary language of the government, mass media, education and, critically, in national standardized tests that are required by law at different educational levels. Sakha is the second majority language; the highest concentration of Sakha speakers is in rural areas, and some villages and towns are Sakha dominant. Sakha is a member of the Turkic language family and thus genealogically unrelated to Russian, and quite different from it structurally. There are a number of lexical borrowings from Russian to Sakha, but the languages are in no way mutually comprehensible. Although both are written in the Cyrillic alphabet, there are some additional letters in Sakha for sounds that are not found in Russian.

The Sakha language has four main dialects: central, north-eastern, north-western, and Vilyuy dialects; the standard language is based on the central dialect. The dialects are mutually intelligible, but there are some significant differences in the phonology and lexicon; it is generally acknowledged by Sakha people in Yakutsk that the language is spoken "better" in the *ulus*, a term used in Sakha today to refer to agricultural municipal districts where the population is predominately ethnic Sakha and linguistically Sakha-dominant (underscoring its historical use in Turkic and Mongolic languages to refer to an ethnic group).

Sakha is widely used in daily and social life among the Sakha people. Historically, it was the language of wider communication in the Republic and was often spoken by smaller indigenous groups and even the Old Believer populations (who are ethnically Russian) as a means of interethnic communication. In mixed marriages, children tended to learn Sakha, which was socially dominant. The language, however, is ranked vulnerable, although an estimated 93 percent of ethnic Sakha know their language, and it is the regional language of the Republic of Sakha (Yakutia). Bilingualism is widespread, with 89 percent of ethnic Sakha speaking Russian; lower in rural areas. It has largely been replaced by Russian as L2 for speakers of other languages in the Republic and for some ethnic Sakha. In the last few decades of the Soviet era, use of Sakha was actively repressed and its use declined. There is a rise of Sakha language vitality, in particular among young people, but many Sakha in Yakutsk are alarmed by the growth of Russian as the dominant lingua franca, and the pervasive use of Russian and English on the internet.[19] In particular people point to the impact of YouTube on language use, even in Sakha-dominant villages, as there is little to no content in the Sakha language. Children of all ages are reported to spend considerable time on YouTube. Sakha parents are further concerned about a lack of Sakha-immersion schools in Yakutsk.[20]

In addition to Sakha, five indigenous languages are officially recognized in the Sakha Republic. The only official data for the numbers of speakers is at the national level, and again dates to the 2010 census (Table 10.5). Note that these numbers are widely recognized as high. First, they reflect self-reporting of both ethnicity and ethnic language use, and both numbers are probably inflated. Second, as is the case in endangered language populations elsewhere, the majority of speakers are elderly, and children have a tendency not to learn their ancestral tongue. Thus, the overall trend in numbers of speakers declines as older speakers pass away and are not replaced by younger ones. This is unquestionably the case for all minority indigenous languages in Russia Eurasia. Table 10.5 provides at best a snapshot view of census data for the Russian Federation as a whole in 2010:

Table 10.5   Minority indigenous languages

	Ethnic population	*Number of speakers*	*Percentage of total*
Evenki	38,396	5,656	12.5%
Even	21,830	5,656	26%
Chukchi	15,908	5,095	32%
Dolgan	7,885	1,954	13%
Yukaghir	1,603	370	12.5%

Source: 2010 All-Russian Census

There is, however, data available on the minorities living in Yakutsk itself. Again, the data are current only from 2010, and there has been considerable immigration to Yakutsk from the Commonwealth of Independent States since that time. These peoples come with knowledge of their language and use it. By and large they do not acquire Sakha, making Russian the lingua franca. Table 10.6 gives the total population of Yakutsk by ethnic group, including the two majority groups (Russian and Sakha), the official indigenous minorities, and those populations with more than 1000 peoples. Note that not everyone declared their ethnicity in the 2010 census; of a total population of 295,564, nearly 10,000 did not.

Table 10.6   Ethnicities in Sakha Republic

	Number	Percentage [21]
Majority		
Sakha (Yakut)	140,272	49.2
Russian	113,624	39.8
Indigenous minorities		
Evenki	2,870	0.01
Even	2,176	0.0076
Dolgan	189	
Chukchi	59	
Yukaghir	211	
Other, over 1,000		
Ukrainian	3,935	0.0137
Kyrgyz	3,004	0.01
Buriat	2,573	< 0.01
Armenian	2,328	< 0.01
Tatar	2,017	< 0.01
Uzbek	1,952	< 0.01
Tadzhik	1,860	< 0.01
Totals		
Total declared	285,191	
Total	295,564	

Source: 2010 All-Russian Census

Only Sakha and Russians represent significant populations within Yakutsk, although again, the numbers of certain immigrants have increased since 2010. (There is a visible Kyrgyz presence in the city, in particular among merchants. Informal interviews conducted in summer 2018 identified a large number of ethnic Kyrgyz who had moved to Yakutsk or neighboring areas for commerce.) Critically, the numbers of indigenous minorities are negligible and insufficient to constitute a speech community in a large city like Yakutsk, where individuals are invisible in the larger population.

Language and well-being in the Russian Arctic in the aftermath

Colonialism, the changes triggered by the collapse of the Soviet empire, and the subsequent social and economic restructuring of the country have had serious effects on indigenous peoples in Eurasia; taken together, the long-term result has been trauma, historical and contemporary. Although the impact of the Soviet system is unique for indigenous peoples in the Russian Federation, the northern peoples share many traits with indigenous peoples elsewhere in the world, and in particular in other Arctic regions, where the living conditions are comparable. It is thus instructive to examine the position of indigenous peoples in the Republic of Sakha within the broader context of Arctic indigeneity. Moreover, one of the consequences of the end of Soviet control was an opening up of relations between indigenous peoples in Eurasia and other countries, and in particular across the Arctic. This has led to a strengthening of ties between peoples, joint initiatives, and a repackaging of identity in Eurasia:[22] people who were considered the "small peoples of the North" (*malye narody severa*) in the Soviet period are now the "small-numbered indigenous peoples" (*malochislennye korennye narody*) and often refer to themselves as specifically "Arctic," as part of a pan-Arctic indigenous community.

There has been considerable discussion of the notion of well-being in the Arctic and how to consider Arctic life for indigenous peoples from the standpoint of well-being. As a working model of well-being, I follow the definition in Dodge et al.'s study of well-being as "a balance point between an individual's resource pool and the challenges faced."[23] They depict well-being as a balancing act on a see-saw, as illustrated in Figure 10.3. Stable well-being is thus defined as having the psychological, social and physical resources needed to meet whatever challenge or challenges, be they psychological, social and/or physical.

Each time an individual meets a challenge, the system of challenges and resources comes into a state of imbalance, as the individual is forced to adapt his or her resources to meet this particular challenge.[24] The basic idea behind this model is that when people have more challenges than resources, the see-saw dips, as does their well-being.

Stressors

A number of challenges face indigenous peoples in the Sakha Republic. These are too many for full discussion here, and I single out just a few. In Russian Eurasia as elsewhere, historical trauma resulting from colonization is known

Figure 10.3 Model of well-being
Source: Dodge et al. (2012, 230).

to contribute to youth suicide, alcoholism and high rates of mental health issues.[25] Multiple studies have shown that the rates of Hepatitis B are significantly higher in ethnic Sakha and Evenki populations than in other non-indigenous peoples (or "settlers") living in the same areas. Similarly, cancer rates for indigenous peoples in the Russian Federation are higher, with Evenki populations twice as high, and rates for people in Chukotka are four times higher than the comparative settlers.[26]

Urbanization is a known stressor and chronic stress itself is a major negative factor. Chronic stress has had a serious negative impact on the health of urban indigenous women in Canada.[27] Indigenous peoples who have adapted to harsh climate conditions do not handle the stress of urbanization, and the concomitant man-made social and environmental factors, as well. Rapid urbanization and cultural and economic change in Siberia have put tremendous stress on indigenous minorities there.[28]

Resources and social indicators

A set of *Indicators* for evaluating well-being in the Arctic was developed by the Arctic Social Indicators project (or ASI-I).[29] This work built on previous analyses by the United Nations Human Development Index and the Arctic Human Development Report so as to identify a core set of domains for evaluating Arctic well-being. Indicators were determined to be useful aids for planning, informing policy, and for guiding decisions and actions, in addition to being valuable simply in building awareness of current conditions and trends over time. Indicators are used by some groups to predict change, while other groups use them to promote change. In developing the indicators, they specifically attempted to identify measurable variables. The indicators were further adapted and expanded in Arctic Social Indicators II (ASI-II)[30] to include the following: (1) cultural vitality; (2) contact with nature; (3) fate control; (4) material well-being; (5) education; and (6) health.

For our purposes, cultural vitality is of greatest relevance, as it is defined in the report as the percentage of a population that retains and speaks their ancestral language. The indicators can be tied to what are labeled *protective factors* for Aboriginal communities in Canada.[31] These are factors that are useful in maintaining and improving health, and in reducing risk. In the model of well-being presented here, protective factors are resources that individuals and communities can bring to bear in stressful situations to tip the balance toward coping. These are defined by McIvor et al. (2009) who group them into six categories: (1) land and health; (2) traditional medicine; (3) literature on traditional medicine makes direct links to land; (4) language and culture; (5) spirituality; and (6) traditional foods. As these categories suggest, there is a negative correlation between well-being and an urban lifestyle, which disrupts ties to the land, access to traditional spiritual places, food and medicine.

Happiness among Australian Aboriginals shows a positive relationship between language use and well-being: "even after controlling for a range of socio-economic variables, living on one's homelands/ traditional country and undertaking harvesting activities is associated with a higher level of self-reported happiness for indigenous Australians. *So too were learning an Indigenous language and participating in Indigenous cultural activities*" (my emphasis).[32]

Studies of well-being among Australian Aboriginal populations have shown that living a decentralized lifestyle away from urban centers improves health. People living on the land exhibit lower mortality rates and lower rates of cardiovascular disease. "Conventional measures of employment, income, housing and education did not account for this health differential."[33] This study does not specifically consider the effects of language and culture, but other studies have shown that traditional activities, such as hunting, fishing, berry picking, are linked to the land, as are story-telling and religious practices. In Siberia, traditional shamanist/animist practices are closely linked to the land and to language.

Language as a protective resource

A significant number of studies, in particular in Australia and Canada, indicate a positive correlation between indigenous (Native/Aboriginal) language use and well-being across the board.[34] The positive mental and social effects are perhaps not as surprising as the physical ones, with a decrease in depression and substance abuse in indigenous populations who use their language, as opposed to comparison groups that do not. Decreased suicide rates may be the most compelling evidence for language as a protective factor. Hallett, Chandler and Lalonde surveyed 150 Aboriginal communities in British Columbia and found that knowledge of the indigenous language varied inversely with suicide rates.[35] This study carefully examined a set of markers of cultural continuity, which were operationalized as including a degree of self-governance, access to traditional lands, health care delivery, cultural facilities, education, and child protection. They controlled for these factors, and found that those Aboriginal groups (or "bands" in the Canadian context) that lack markers of cultural continuity have higher rates of youth suicide and school drop-out rates. Specifically, they found that in communities with less than 50 percent of the people reporting knowledge of the language, the suicide rate was 96.59 per 100,000; it dropped to 13.00 in 100,000 in those communities with 50 percent or more knowledge of the Native language. In the handful of communities where a majority of the band members reported a conversational knowledge of Native language, youth suicide rates effectively dropped to zero; they were six times higher in bands where less than half of the members reported conversational knowledge.[36] In sum, more knowledge of the language means less suicide, and less knowledge correlates strongly with more youth suicide.

Beyond the psychological and social advantages, an increasing number of rigorous studies demonstrate that use of language has a positive impact on physical well-being (or health), with indigenous populations showing lower rates of obesity, diabetes, and cardiovascular disease when they have access to their language. Diabetes rates are inversely correlated with indigenous language retention: of 31 Canadian First Nations communities surveyed in Alberta, Oster et al.[37] found lower rates of adult-onset (Type II) diabetes in those communities with higher rates of indigenous language use.

Conclusion

The overall impact of urbanization and immigration from other regions on the indigenous minorities in Yakutsk requires detailed study. It is clear that their overall language ecologies have changed dramatically over the last twenty years. Historically, they lived in small settlements, often in close proximity to other indigenous groups. They were often plurilingual, societies, using multiple indigenous languages. Sakha was the local lingua franca, and people were closely connected to the land and to their own cultural practices. This has changed radically, with urbanization resulting in people living with many neighbors but few who are indigenous, living an urban lifestyle and using Russian on a daily basis. While indigenous peoples have moved from the geographic periphery to the urban center, they are still often marginalized in Yakutsk society, and experience a range of stresses related to this displacement.

The colonial past of Imperial Russia and the Soviet Union has left indigenous populations with historical trauma. Their stress is exacerbated by the development practices of the Soviets in Siberia as a whole, and in the area of focus here, the Sakha Republic. Had the region been developed under market conditions, the local demographics, settlement structure and infrastructure would be very different than they are today.[38] The readjustments to lifestyle that were necessitated by the collapse of the artificial Soviet economy have been felt by indigenous and non-indigenous inhabitants, with extensive relocations of peoples and reorganization of their daily lives. All indicators suggest that speakers of minority indigenous languages, and even speakers of the local majority language Sakha (Kantarovich, this volume) are under pressure. The combined effect of the colonial legacy and post-Soviet urbanization has been language shift.

There is a shared set of stressors across indigenous communities, overall happiness and well-being strongly correlate with access to language and culture. The Model of Well-Being presented here indicates that building a set of protective factors can provide a set of resources to people under stress, and more research is needed to see how language in Eurasia can be leveraged as a protective factor Although such studies have been conducted in North America and Aboriginal Australia, there is every reason to think that they would apply in the Russian Arctic as well, and indicate the important potential of language for well-being.

Notes

1 Research on this project was funded by the Guggenheim Foundation and the Humanities Division of the University of Chicago. James Forsyth, *A History of the Peoples of Siberia: Russia's North Asian Colony 1581–1990* (Cambridge: Cambridge University Press, 1992).

2 For broad discussion, see Vladislav Inozemtsov, "The New Old Russia," *American Interest* 13: 3 (2018): 49–50.

3 Susan. A. Crate, Bruce C. Forbes, Leslie King, and Jack Kruse, "Contact with Nature," in *Arctic Social Indicators I (ASI-I)*, eds., Joan Nymand Larsen, Peter Schweitzer, and Gail Fondahl (Copenhagen: Nordic Council of Ministers, 2010), 109–27; Rasmus O Rasmussen, ed., *Megatrends*, TemaNord 2011: 527 (Copenhagen: Nordic Council of Ministers, 2011).

4 Peter Schweitzer, Peter Sköld and Olga Ulturgasheva, "Cultures and identities," in *Arctic Human Development Report II: Regional Processes and Global Linkages*, eds., Joan Nymand Larsen and Gail Fondahl (Copenhagen: Nordic Council of Ministers, 2014), 105–50; Edmund Searles, "Placing Identity: Town, Land, and Authenticity in Nunavut, Canada," *Acta Borealia: A Nordic Journal of Circumpolar Societies* 27: 2 (2010): 151–66.

5 Susan A. Crate, "Investigating Local Definitions of Sustainability in the Arctic: Insights from Post-Soviet Sakha Villages," *Arctic* 59: 3 (2016): 294–310; Julie Cruikshank and Tatiana Argounova, "Reinscribing Meaning: Memory and Indigenous Identity in Sakha Republic (Yakutia)," *Arctic Anthropology* 31 (2000) 96–119; Susanne Dybbroe, Jens Dahl, and Ludger Müller-Wille, "Dynamics of Arctic Urbanization," *Acta Borealia* 27: 2 (2010): 120–24.

6 Rachel Dodge, Annette P. Daly, Jan Huyton, and Lalage D. Sanders, "The Challenge of Defining Wellbeing," *International Journal of Wellbeing* 2: 3 (2012): 222–35.

7 Lenore A. Grenoble, Jessica Kantarovich, Irena Khokholova, and Liudmila Zamorschikova, "Evidence of Syntactic Convergence among Russian–Sakha Bilinguals," *Suvremena Lingvistika* 45: 87 (2019): 41–57.

8 Fiona Hill and Clifford Gaddy, *The Siberian Curse: How Communist Planners Left Russia Out in the Cold* (Washington, D.C.: Brookings Institution Press, 2003), 211.

9 Hill and Gaddy, *The Siberian Curse*, 216.

10 Dekabrina M. Vinokurova, "Migration in the Cities of Sakha Republic (Yakutia): Temporal-Social Aspects," *Anthropology & Archeology of Eurasia* 56: 3–4 (2017): 257.

11 Place names are spelled according to conventions in the English language media (rather than straight transliteration of Russian Cyrillic) to facilitate identification. Many place names also have alternates in the Sakha language.

12 *Novosti*, "Za 10 mesiatsev cherez stantsiiu Nizhnii Bestiakj dostavleno i pererabotano 527.6 tys. ton gruzov," November 3, 2017, https://www.sakha.gov.ru/news/front/view/id/2831428; accessed September 20, 2018.

13 Sakha Government, "Geograficheskaia i istoricheskaia spravka o naslege," data accessed February 9, 2103, and archived at https://www.webcitation.org/ 6EMAfiysh.

14 Timothy Heleniak, "Boom and Bust. Population Change in Russia's Arctic Cities," in *Sustaining Russia's Arctic Cities. Resource Politics, Migration and Climate Change*, ed. Robert W. Orttung (New York: Berghahn, 2017), 84.

15 Vera Kuklina and Natalia Krasnoshtanova, "The Urbanization of Indigenous Peoples of Northeastern Siberia," in *New Mobilities and Social Changes in Russia's Arctic Regions*, ed. Marlene Laruelle (New York: Routledge, 2017), 111.

16 Kuklina and Krasnoshtanova, "Urbanization of Indigenous Peoples," 106; 110–11.

17 Lee Huskey, "Globalization and the Economies of the North," in *Globalization and the Circumpolar North*, eds., Lassi Neinine and Chris Southcott (Fairbanks: University of Alaska Press, 2010), 76.

18 "v mestakh prozhivaniia ètikh narodov i ispol'zuetsia naravne s gosudarstvennymi iazykami" (Article 6, *Language Law of the RS[Y]*).

19 Jenanne Ferguson, "Language has a Spirit: Sakha (Yakut) Language Ideologies and Aesthetics of Sustenance," *Arctic Anthropology* 53: 1 (2016): 95–111.

20 See Kantarovich (this volume) for an analysis of language use among university students in Yakutsk.

21 Percentage of population is calculated only for those who have declared their ethnicity, not for the absolute total.

22 See, for example, Lenore A. Grenoble and Carl Chr. Olsen (Puju), "Language and Well-being in the Arctic: Building Indigenous Language Vitality and Sustainability," *Arctic Yearbook 2014*.

23 Rachel Dodge, Annette P. Daly, Jan Huyton, and Lalage D. Sanders, "The Challenge of Defining Wellbeing," *International Journal of Wellbeing* 2: 3 (2012): 230.

24 Marion Kloep, Leo B. Hendry, and Danny Saunders, "A New Perspective on Human Development," *Conference of the International Journal of Arts and Sciences* 1: 6 (2009): 337.

25 See Michael J. Kral, "Suicide and Suicide Prevention among Inuit in Canada," *The Canadian Journal of Psychiatry* 61: 11 (2016): 688–90 and references therein.

26 For discussion and references, see Tatiana E. Burtseva, Tatiana E. Uvarova, Mikhail I. Tomsky and Jon Ø. Odland, "The Health of Populations Living in the Indigenous Minority Settlements in Northern Yakutia," *International Journal of Circumpolar Health* 73 (2014): 257–8.

27 Anita Benoit, Jasmine Cotnam, Janet Raboud, Saara Greene, Kerrigan Beaver, Art Zoccole, Art, Doe O'Brien-Teengs, Louise Balfour, Wei Wu, and Mona Loutfy, "Experiences of Chronic Stress and Mental Health Concerns among Urban Indigenous Women," *Archives of Women's Mental Health* 19: 5 (2016): 809–23, doi: 10.1007/s00737-016-0622-8.

28 Andrew I. Kozlov, Galina Vershubsky, and Maria Kozlova, "Stress under Modernization in Indigenous populations of Siberia." *International Journal of Circumpolar Health* 62: 2 (2003): 158–66; Mark V. Sorensen, James J. Snodgrass, William R. Leonard, Thomas W. McDade, Larissa A. Tarskaya, Kiundiul I. Ivanov, Vadim G. Krivoshapkin, and Vladimir P. Alekseev, "Lifestyle Incongruity, Stress and Immune Function in Indigenous Siberians: The Health Impacts of Rapid Social and Economic Change," *American Journal of Physical Anthropology* 138: 1 (2009): 62–9.

29 Joan Nymand Larsen, Peter Schweitzer, and Gail Fondahl, eds., *Arctic Social Indicators* (Copenhagen: Nordic Council of Ministers, 2010).

30 Joan Nymand Larsen, Peter Schweitzer, and Andrey Petrov, eds., *Arctic Social Indicators II: Implementation* (Copenhagen: Nordic Council of Ministers, 2014), 36.

31 Onowa McIvor, Art Napoleon, and Kerissa Dickie, "Language and Culture as Protective Factors for At-Risk Communities," *The Journal of Aboriginal Health* 5: 1 (2009): 6–26.

32 Nicholas Biddle and Hannah Swee, "The Relationship between Wellbeing and Indigenous Land, Language and Culture in Australia," *Australian Geographer* 43: 3 (2012): 226.

33 Kevin G. Rowley, Kerin O'Dea, Ian Anderson, Robyn McDermott, Karmananda Saraswati, Ricky Tilmouth, Iris Roberts, Joseph Fitz, Zaimin Wang, Alicia Jenkins, James D. Best, Zhiqiang Wang and Alex Brown, "Lower than Expected Morbidity and Mortality for an Australian Aboriginal Population: 10-year Follow-up in a Decentralised Community," *The Medical Journal of Australia* 188: 5 (2008): 286.

34 Katherine Capone, Nick D. Spence, and Jerry White, "Examining the Association between Aboriginal Language Skills and Well-being in First Nations Communities," *Aboriginal Policy Research: Health and Well-Being Vol. IX*, eds., Jerry P.

White, Julie Peters, Peter Dinsdale, and Dan Beavon (Toronto: Thompson Educational Publishing, 2011) 57–78; Michael J. Chandler and Christopher E. Lalonde, "Cultural Continuity as a Hedge Against Suicide in Canada's First Nations," *Transcultural Psychiatry* 35 (1998): 191–219; Onowa McIvor, Art Napoleon, and Kerissa Dickie, "Language and Culture as Protective Factors for At-Risk Communities," *The Journal of Aboriginal Health* 5: 1 (2009): 6–26; Richard T. Oster, Angela Grier, Rick Lightning, Maria J. Mayan, and Ellen L. Toth, "Cultural Continuity, Traditional Indigenous Language, and Diabetes in Alberta First Nations: A Mixed Methods Study." *International Journal for Equity in Health* 13: 92 (2014), doi: 10.1186/s12939-014-0092-4; Kevin G. Rowley, Kevin G., Kerin O'Dea, Ian Anderson, Robyn McDermott, Karmananda Saraswati, Ricky Tilmouth, Iris Roberts, Joseph Fitz, Zaimin Wang, Alicia Jenkins, James D Best, Zhiqiang Wang and Alex Brown, "Lower than Expected Morbidity and Mortality for an Australian Aboriginal Population: 10-year Follow-up in a Decentralised Community," *The Medical Journal of Australia* 188: 5 (2008): 286; Courtney Parker, Courtney, and John Ahni Schertow, "Preserving Language Key to Overcoming Native Suicide Epidemic." *Intercontinental Cry (IC)*, 2016.

35 Darcy Hallett, Michael J. Chandler and Christopher E. Lalonde, "Aboriginal Language Knowledge and Youth Suicide," *Cognitive Development* 22 (2007): 392–9.

36 Hallett, Chandler, Lalonde, "Aboriginal Language Knowledge," 396–8.

37 Oster et al., "Cultural Continuity."

38 Hill and Gaddy, *The Siberian Curse*; Timothy Heleniak, "Migration in the Arctic," *Arctic Yearbook* (2014), 18–19.

11 Evolving language contact and multilingualism in Northeastern Russia

Jessica Kantarovich

Despite the vastness and desolateness of northeastern Russia, the region has long been the site of repeated cultural contacts among different indigenous ethnic groups. Evidence of these contacts is present in similarities in the mythology and material culture of these groups, as well as, notably, the spread of certain economic practices such as reindeer herding in the tundra and whaling along the coast. We know, for example, that the Chukchis adopted reindeer herding from the Tungus people and later learned whaling from the Yupiks once they migrated to the coast.[1] Like other Turkic peoples, the Sakha originally exclusively practiced horse husbandry, before some northern Sakha took up fishing and reindeer herding, likely also due to contact with the Tungus.[2] Nevertheless, for centuries, the indigenous groups managed to preserve certain distinct cultural practices as well as their own languages.

The social ecology of this region, and Siberia more broadly, changed dramatically with the beginning of Russian colonization. Russian efforts were motivated primarily by the promise of resources in the vast wilderness to the east, particularly in the form of furs. These furs became a required tribute (*yasak*) to the tsar from the indigenous peoples of the region, who often abandoned their own sustenance hunting practices in favor of sable hunting in order to meet the ever-increasing demand among the Russian nobility. The result was not only the plundering of the ecological diversity of Siberia, but the complete disruption of the traditional economies of its residents.

Nevertheless, the "small peoples of the north," as they came to be called, were largely able to preserve their cultures and ways of life throughout the imperial period. The interruption of cultural transmission would not begin until the Soviet period, when authorities took painstaking efforts to reorganize the nomadic lifestyles of these peoples into something more "civilized." What the imperial and Soviet periods have in common is the conceptualization of the Russian northeast, and of its indigenous residents, as desperately in need of Russian oversight and care. As Slezkine notes, Russia's circumpolar peoples have been "seen as the most consistent antipodes of whatever it meant to be Russian:" as such, in their view it became necessary to adopt them into Russian society, not just to neutralize the threat they posed but also for their own good.[3]

This molding of the Siberian peoples into what Russian authorities imagined they should be—less backward and barbaric—is particularly apparent in the language policy of the Soviet period. Russians played a very direct role in shaping the Siberian indigenous languages into something that was more recognizable to them: standardized and written rather than simply oral (using a single Cyrillic alphabet to capture the unrelated languages' distinctive inventories of sounds). The initial efforts by Soviet scholars to create educational materials for languages that were easily acquired in childhood may have merely been well-intentioned paternalism—certainly, they were not as overtly destructive as later laws which would greatly restrict the use of these languages at all. Yet, the Soviets made it clear that these languages could not simply be let alone to exist as they were, and that at the very least they should be rendered secondary in a Russian-speaking society. In this effort, they were radically successful.

The societal effects of the loss of indigenous language diversity due to Russian colonization (and the subsequent push for industrialization and urbanization in the northeast) are examined by Grenoble in Chapter 10 of this volume. She notes that language shift not only profoundly threatens the preservation of indigenous cultures but also is tied intimately to the well-being of indigenous people and can serve as a predictor for quality of life. The work here investigates some of the cognitive effects that colonization produces among shifting speakers, to the extent that we can observe such effects via changes in the grammatical patterns of the languages as they are used by modern speakers. I focus on two Siberian languages, Sakha and Chukchi, arguing that the linguistic changes to these languages in the modern era are of a markedly different sort than the kind that can be reconstructed during their long, pre-colonial history.

Russian and Siberian contact in the linguistic context

Siberia and the Russian Far East have historically been fairly linguistically diverse, once comprising at least 40 distinct languages from nine different language families: Uralic, Turkic, Mongolic, Tungusic, Chukotko-Kamchatkan, Aleut-Inuit-Yupik, Ket, Nivkh, and Ainu.[4] This list does not include non-autochthonous languages that are presently spoken in the area, such as Slavic languages (Russian and, to a lesser extent, Ukrainian), Chinese, and Central Asian languages spoken by recent economic migrants to the Republic of Sakha. Most of the indigenous languages were still being spoken at the time Russians first arrived in Siberia in the seventeenth century; however, the situation has changed considerably within the last few decades, with many of the Siberian languages ceasing to be spoken in favor of Russian, which is economically and socially more dominant. Table 11.1 presents the number of self-reported speakers of the more populous indigenous languages of Siberia, across the entire country. Note that these numbers are likely to be inflated, as speakers tend to over-report their linguistic proficiency in categorical surveys or else conflate ethnicity with language.

Table 11.1 captures the linguistic dominance of Russian: almost all of the people surveyed by the mandatory census (99.4 percent) are at least bilingual in Russian, with the numbers being highest among younger generations. While multilingualism can be reconstructed among Siberians prior to Russian contact, the present situation represents a dramatic change in the linguistic ecology of the region: practices such as trade, exogamy, and conquest among the indigenous groups would certainly have promoted the adoption of new languages, but there has never before been a single, dominant ethnic group across the entire region.

Thomason and Kaufman first proposed that linguistic contact can be of two types: language maintenance or language shift.[6] These types are characterized by the outcome of contact between two or more speaker populations, where "contact" is simply defined as people interacting with one another's languages, whether by overhearing another language, learning to speak it at any level of proficiency, or even interacting with written forms of the language. In language maintenance, the languages continue to be spoken by their respective populations, with some speakers also acquiring the language of contact (resulting in bi- or multilingualism). In language shift, one of the languages in contact ceases to be spoken, because that group has either ceased to exist (in cases where the population disappears, such as due to disease or warfare), or more commonly, has adopted a more dominant language for social, political, or economic reasons. Multilingualism is also encountered in situations of language shift but it is unstable, with initial generations of speakers learning the dominant language but ultimately ceasing to transmit their original language to their children.

Studies of language contact are additionally interested in how the grammars, sound systems, and lexicons of languages are modified by multilingual

Table 11.1 Self-reported speakers of indigenous Siberian languages compared to Russian in 2010)[5]

Language	Number of Speakers (% of Respondents)
Russian	137,494,893 (99.4%)
Chukchi	5,096
Even	5,656
Evenki	4,802
Ket	213
Koryak	1,665
Nenets	21,926 (0.02%)
Nivkh	198
Yakut (Sakha)	450,140 (0.33%)
Yukaghir	370
Yupik	508

settings. Language maintenance and language shift can produce highly similar types of changes, though these changes often have different trajectories depending on the intensity of the contact between populations. In language maintenance scenarios where contact is superficial (such as trade or other transactional relations), the languages involved may be minimally affected, possibly adopting words or expressions from one another. As contact and the degree of bilingualism intensifies, we may start additionally to see grammatical changes (changes in syntax and morphology, i.e., the structure of sentences and words). In language shift, the types of changes that occur in the languages depends on the relative size of the shifting population, and how quickly the transition to the new language occurs. If shift occurs quickly, without intervening generations of bilingual speakers who are semi-proficient in their ancestral language, the language being lost may not exhibit any grammatical changes before it disappears. Similarly, if the shifting speakers quickly and adequately learn the dominant language, or if there are not that many shifting speakers relative to the number of people already using the dominant language, there will also be few grammatical changes in the dominant language.

The crux of this particular theory of linguistic contact is that the social ecology of the languages—who uses them with whom, and in which contexts—determines their fate, rather than any facts about the languages themselves.[7] Other theories of linguistic contact propose that aspects of the languages' grammars, such as the degree of similarity between the languages in contact or their relative complexity for second language learners, determine how likely they are to be adopted by new speakers and the types of changes that occur in the languages themselves. Such factors may indeed interact with sociopolitical factors; however, the latter are paramount in predicting whether a language will continue to be used in a certain setting.

As we will see in the case of northeastern Siberia, languages which were once dominant are now themselves giving way to Russian; this is entirely the result of ecological factors, not anything inherent in the structure of these languages. On the whole, the two main languages that are investigated in this work—Sakha and Chukchi—exhibited patterns consistent with a language maintenance scenario until about the 1950s. Since then, the situation has rapidly evolved into widespread language shift to Russian.

Investigating changes in language use in the Republic of Sakha and Chukotka

The research project described here[8] focuses on understanding changes in the ecologies of language use in two regions: the Republic of Sakha (Yakutia) and the Chukotka Autonomous Okrug (also simply called Chukotka). These two regions were selected in part because they present an interesting contrastive case study of two locally dominant languages: Sakha (Yakut) in the Republic of Sakha and Chukchi in Chukotka. Sakha is recognized as an administrative language of Yakutia alongside Russian; however, Chukchi is not an official language of Chukotka. In addition to Sakha, Yukaghir (Uralic) and Tungusic languages (e.g., Even and Evenki) are spoken in the Republic. Yukaghir, Koryak (Chukotko-Kamchatkan), and Siberian Yupik (Aleut-Inuit-Yupik) are spoken in Chukotka.

It is readily apparent from census data that most speakers of these languages, with the exception of Sakha, are bilingual in Russian and that language shift is taking place. A major goal of the project is to determine which factors have led to language shift in certain situations and not others, and whether there are certain factors that promote the continued use of minority languages alongside more prestigious or more economically viable languages. For example, how has the transition from "traditional" ways of life (such as reindeer herding, hunting, fishing) to urbanization impacted the use of the indigenous languages? Additionally, while there is undeniably an overarching process of shift to Russian taking place, the interactions among the other languages have been less well-researched. Both Sakha and Chukchi have previously functioned as *lingua francas* in their respective regions, and there are still speakers (many of them older) who are multilingual, speaking their minority language in addition to Sakha/Chukchi and Russian.

Finally, the project also aims to examine the effects of the present contact situation on the structure of the languages as they are being used today, particularly in the domains of syntax and morphology. Language shift and the resulting decrease in proficiency of the average speaker has been shown to coincide with certain types of changes in the receding language. Commonly, the language shows signs of reduction and simplification: speakers have difficulty recalling how to use certain lexical items and grammatical constructions, particularly those not used in the dominant language, and simplify complicated (that is, irregular) morphological patterns.[9] The changes that occur in the receding language due to the effects of language loss differ from "healthy" language change (that is, changes that occur in a language that does not cease to be spoken) in their regularity. It is not the case that linguistic differences in the speech of shifting speakers are necessarily shared among the entire speech community, nor is it the case that the same speaker will consistently produce the same non-standard feature. The study described herein is therefore examining a system in flux: the changes we identify have only begun to appear among speakers of the languages, and may not ever become stable features of either Chukchi or Sakha as a whole.

The Sakha language in the Republic of Sakha

As I noted earlier, we have limited information about the population dynamics of northeastern Siberia prior to the arrival of Russian explorers in the seventeenth century. The origins of the Sakha people are still a matter of modern research—while they likely traveled north from the southern steppes, it is unclear when they arrived in the region that would become the Sakha Republic.[10] At the time of initial Russian contact, the Sakha had already established a presence around the northern bend of the Lena River (the area that is now the city of Yakutsk). The Sakha language itself provides some clues about which other groups the speakers came into contact with before settling along the Lena River. While Sakha is unmistakably a Turkic language, it displays some differences from other Turkic languages that are likely due to Tungusic and Mongolic influence that predates Russian contact. Linguistic and genetic data also suggest that the Sakha assimilated Tungus, Samoyeds, and Yukaghirs in the region.[11] Contact between Sakha and Tungus peoples seems to have been particularly strong, as it produced the Dolgans, who speak a language very close to Sakha but with considerable Tungusic influence. (Forsyth claims that the Dolgans are actually Tungus with extensive Yakut admixture.)[12]

During the first two centuries of Russian contact, most of the existing Siberian languages continued to be robustly spoken (linguistic maintenance). A notable exception is Itelmen, or Kamchadal, which is distantly related to Chukchi and began to disappear long before other neighboring languages. Kamchatka, where most Itelmens lived, was subject to minimal control by the Russian imperial government, and as a result Itelmens suffered considerable abuse by local officials and Russian Cossacks.[13] Violence and epidemics took a large toll on the Itelmen population: by 1820, there were only 1900 Itelmens left in the region (down from 7000 a century prior), and by the end of the nineteenth century only 58 percent of Itelmens were monolingual, with complete shift to Russian having taken place in southern Kamchatka.

The Sakha language was exceptional in a different sense: perhaps in part because many Sakha were sedentary and had already developed agriculture and animal husbandry around the Lena River, their language was the sole Siberian language to take root in town life.[14] In other settlements in the region, Russian dominated daily and political life. Within Yakutsk, many Russians even adopted the Sakha language during the nineteenth century.[15] Although the Sakha resisted Russian conquest and the fur tax (*yasak*) that was imposed on them by the Russian government, they eventually displayed a willingness to coexist with the Russians. There was early miscegenation between the Russians and Sakha, and the Sakha were early adopters of Russian cultural practices, such as patronymics.[16]

Thus, despite the fact that Russians were firmly entrenched in Yakutsk during this time, the Sakha continued to be dominant both economically and linguistically: they were successful traders and the Sakha language became a *lingua franca* used by Tungus and Yukaghirs throughout eastern Siberia, from Yenisei to Sakhalin.[17]

Throughout the twentieth century the Sakha have successfully maintained their language, especially in comparison with other languages in the Republic, such as Even, Evenki, and Yukaghir. In the early twentieth century the Sakha were the largest ethnic group in Yakutia, and Sakha continued to function as a *lingua franca*. They also developed a robust body of literature despite several disruptive language reforms, including an overhaul of the orthography in 1939 and the beginning of compulsory education in Russian in 1938.

By the 1970s, Sakha continued to be well-maintained and remained the primary language of instruction in the first eight years of school, with textbooks available in Sakha in technical subjects such as math, science, and history. However, during this period we start to see the minority indigenous languages of the region lose ground to Sakha. The 1979 Russian census indicated that:

- Out of 5763 Evens surveyed, only 44 percent claimed Even as their native language, while 53 percent claimed fluent command of Russian as either their first or second language and 70 percent said they spoke Sakha
- Out of 11,584 Evenkis in the Republic, 85 percent said Sakha was their native language, compared to only 11 percent who said it was Evenki
- Out of 525 Yukaghirs, 30 percent claimed Russian as their native language, and 23 percent claimed Sakha

Due to the fact that the Russian census requires individuals to claim just one ethnicity, this data likely does not capture many individuals with mixed Sakha heritage. (Children of mixed Sakha-indigenous marriages always chose to be registered as Sakha.) This may suggest that the Sakha language dominated within even ethnically homogenous families, or that few such families were to be found.

Based on our interviews with students of Even and Evenki heritage at the North-Eastern Federal University in Yakutsk, these trends have continued: in mixed Sakha-Even/Evenki families, children may learn Sakha but almost never learn Even or Evenki. This was also the case within the family of a Chukchi woman with whom we spoke in Yakutsk. While she herself did not speak Sakha, her husband and their children did, and their only shared language was Russian (that is, her children did not learn Chukchi).

Indeed, several speakers we interviewed in Yakutsk—including those who were ethnically Sakha and those who belonged to an indigenous minority group—expressed that Sakha is well-maintained, especially when compared to Yukaghir or the Tungusic languages. Chukchi is hardly spoken in the city of Yakutsk, and most Chukchi speakers within the Republic of Sakha live in settlements in the northeast, closer to Chukotka. Multilingualism in this region is quite high, with some speakers knowing as many as five languages.[18] These speakers pointed to the ubiquity of Sakha throughout the city—on signage, spoken by different age groups in the street—as well as to the availability of Sakha media (television and theater) and education. Some Sakha people we have spoken with, however, expressed reticence about these claims about the vitality of their language. Although primary education in the Sakha language is available in Yakutsk, there is limited space in these programs. Similarly, while there is much more television programming in Sakha than the minority languages, Russian unquestionably dominates the airwaves, particularly when it comes to children's programming.

Chukchi in the Republic of Sakha and Chukotka

It is generally believed that the Chukchis originated in the tundra west of the Anadyr River basin and eventually migrated to the northeast,[19] where the Russians first encountered them in 1644.[20] The Chukchis are generally divided into two groups, that are distinct culturally and (to a lesser extent) linguistically: the tundra Chukchis, who were nomadic reindeer herders, and the maritime Chukchis, who lived along the coast and practiced fishing and whaling. Strong social ties were maintained between these two groups,[21] however the tundra Chukchis largely outnumbered the maritime Chukchis.[22] The two groups also differed in terms of the other ethnic populations they regularly had contact with: the tundra Chukchis had greater contact with Yukaghirs, while the maritime Chukchis had close ties with the Yupik people along the coast.[23]

At the time of initial Russian contact, the Chukchi people already dominated the Far North East economically. Dunn suggests this was because the Chukchis herded reindeer year-round and did not depend on supplementing their goods with hunting.[24] Chukchi became the *lingua franca* within the region,[25] due in part to this economic dominance as well as their practice of refusing to use other groups' languages in trade.[26] The Chukchis were also significant players in the whaling economy in the Bering Sea alongside the Russians, Americans, and Yupiks. The coastal economic situation was conducive to considerable language mixing. Using written records, De Reuse reconstructs the existence of several distinct trade jargons used in this coastal setting and aboard whaling vessels.[27] These include jargons based on Chukchi (which even the Americans learned),[28] ones based on English (which would have been used mainly within ship crews),[29] and ones based on Yupik, which would have been heavily influenced by Chukchi.[30]

Even as the Russians encroached on the region, the Chukchis rapidly expanded into territory belonging to other groups, from the extreme northeast south along the coastline. They typically assimilated other Chukotkan peoples to the south, such as Koryaks, Alutors, and Kereks, who all spoke languages closely related to Chukchi. It is also clear that the Chukchis had already expanded into Yupik and Yukaghir territory. The Chukchis were already living alongside (and had likely also assimilate some) Yupiks at the time of Russian contact; some evidence for this comes from Chukchi place names of obviously Yupik origin:

Table 11.2 Chukchi place names with their Yupik etymologies[31]

Yupik	Chukchi
Imtuk	Imtun
Egheghaq	Regian
Ugriileq	Wugrel
Avan	Ivunmon
Qiwaaq	Khyuven
Tasiq	Techin
Ingleghnaq	Ilkegen
Ungaziq	Unil
Napaqutaq	Nepyakhut

Meanwhile, it is known that Chukchi expansion west and south into Yukaghir territory in the tundra continued for several centuries after Russians arrived in the Anadyr region—Russian officials even fielded complaints about Chukchi aggression from Yukaghirs, though they had little success in responding to them.[32] As the Chukchis moved into Yukaghir territory they assimilated many of them through intermarriage.[33] (These earlier patterns of cultural mixing are still very apparent to Chukchis and Yukaghirs today, who report that Yukaghirs in the early twentieth century often knew Chukchi better than their native language, and that many "Chukchi" speakers were actually ethnically Yukaghir.)

How Yukaghir and Chukchi may have impacted one another linguistically is presently an open question. The best-studied linguistic effects of the cultural mixing in Chukotka during this time are between Chukchi and Yupik, with most scholars agreeing that the effects of Chukchi on Yupik are greater than the reverse. The Yupik effects on Chukchi are mainly restricted to words the Chukchis borrowed for new animals they encountered in the coastal environment, as well as words for the new trades they picked up. Examples include *puwreq* 'beluga whale,'[34] *kupren* 'net' (from Yupik *kuuvragh-*), and *menemen* 'bait' (from *managh-*).[35] These borrowings appear to be restricted to the maritime variety of Chukchi—speakers of tundra varieties often do not recognize words of Yupik origin.[36]

Meanwhile, the effects of Chukchi on Yupik are more significant, and include borrowed words from a variety of categories, including (somewhat surprisingly) words for coastal flora and fauna, which would have replaced existing Yupik words. Yupik also extensively borrowed interjections and adverbs from Chukchi, such as the following:

Table 11.3 Particles borrowed into Yupik from Chukchi[37], [38]

Chukchi	Central Siberian Yupik	Gloss
qənwer	qinwam	'finally'
rəpet	ripatł	'even'
lureq	luraq	'probably'
enmec	inmis	'already'
ewər	iwin	'if'
panena	paninaŋ	'after all'
weler	waran	'although'
iŋqun	inqun	'in order to'
ənqom	inkam	'then, following that'
wətku	witku	'if only'
qeciqun	qisiqun	'apparently'
wenləgi	wanłigi	'all the same'

As Comrie notes, the borrowing of these words is likely the catalyst for a grammatical change in Siberian Yupik compared to the related Yupik and Inuit languages spoken in North America: the American languages express adverbial relations such as these by adding morphology to the verb, not through the use of separate words.[39]

Some linguists have argued for much more significant structural effects in Chukchi due to Yupik influence; for example, Fortescue suggests that Chukchi developed ergative case (a special marker only for subjects of transitive verbs, but not subjects of intransitive verbs) due to this contact. However, any significant changes in Chukchi from Yupik are likely to be fairly recent (intensifying in the seventeenth century, when contact would have intensified), and are likely to be restricted to the maritime variety, so it is not clear whether the widespread pattern of ergative case should be attributed to Yupik influence.

Referring back to the possible categories of language contact described in the introduction, the historical situation involving Chukchi and its neighboring languages is largely a situation of language maintenance. The changes in Chukchi and Yupik are consistent with a situation where speakers of the two languages were in sustained contact, with one language (Chukchi) being more dominant than the other, but with both languages continuing to be spoken. Although there were certainly smaller communities of Yukaghirs, Yupiks, and other Chukotkans who shifted to speaking Chukchi when they were assimilated by Chukchi territorial expansion and intermarriage, irreversible loss of these languages does not begin until the twentieth century.

As we turn our attention to the effects of Russian on Chukchi, it is important to recognize that although the Chukchis, like the Sakha, were regionally dominant, the social ecology (especially with respect to Russians) of this extreme northeast region was rather different. The Chukchis strongly resisted Russian colonization and were among the only groups that never submitted to paying *yasak* to Russian authorities.[40] In fact, while many of the indigenous groups suffered tremendous population losses due to warfare and disease in the centuries following Russian contact, the Chukchi population flourished during the 18th century, their numbers increasing from 6000 to 8000–9000.[41] It is likely that their geographical isolation (as well as the difficulty in tracking a group that remained nomadic until the twentieth century) insulated them from Russian control and, in turn, the abusive practices that took a toll on the population of other ethnic groups in the north.

By the same token, however, the continued nomadic lifestyles of the Chukchis and a lack of centralized leadership likely contributed to their failure to establish a presence in town life and made their languages more susceptible to loss through rapid modernization under the Soviets. For these and a host of other historical reasons, the Chukchis and other peoples of the north would ultimately be organized into "autonomous regions" (*okrugs/ oblasts*) or designated as *krais*, which have less administrative power than republics such as Yakutia. This extends also to modern language policy, as the "republic" status allows for languages other than Russian to function as official administrative languages in the region.[42] This difference in administrative designation also certainly goes a long way toward explaining the continued maintenance of Sakha relative to the other languages of the northeast.

The acceleration of language shift among Siberian indigenous groups begins with the introduction of problematic Soviet language policies and social restructuring in the first half of the twentieth century. The early Soviet attitude towards these groups can most generously be described as paternalistic, motivated by the perception of the northern peoples as backwards and in need of guidance to become civilized. During this early period (1917–1929) the goal of the Committee of the North (which consisted mainly of Soviet bureaucrats and some scholars) was ostensibly to encourage native autonomy;[43] there were some efforts during this time to encourage the creation of literary languages for the native peoples of the north so that they could be educated in their own languages.[44] However, all encouragement of autonomy (and recognition of the unique needs of different northern groups) vanished during the Stalin period: steps were taken to eliminate nomadism and the clan system of many indigenous groups. This system was replaced with forced reorganization into collectives (*soviets*), which seldom took the natives' own territorial designations into account.[45] Although both tundra and maritime Chukchis initially strongly resisted collectivization,[46] they were ultimately forcibly relocated into settlements throughout Chukotka during the period between 1953–1967.[47] Unsurprisingly, this is also the period when we start to see language shift among the Chukchis. Speakers born during this period are regarded by our consultants to be the last generation of fully fluent speakers.

The greatest disruption to linguistic and cultural transmission was the notorious *internat* boarding school system, in which indigenous children were removed from their families for most of the year to be educated in Russian. In many cases, children in these schools were forbidden from speaking their native languages (or even eating native foods). Although the indigenous people received an education at these schools, they were also taught that their culture (including their traditional ways of life) was not worth acquiring, and as a result failed to master their native languages and skills.[48] The *internat* system also had the inadvertent effect of escalating urbanization: young people could not participate in the traditional economies of the villages and relocated to cities in increasing numbers in the 1980s and 1990s. During Dunn's research in Anadyr (the most populous city in Chukotka) in the 1990s, he noted that it was rare to hear Chukchi spoken, even among older speakers who knew the language. However, language retention at this time seemed to be better in villages, where it was still possible to find fluent speakers as young as 30.[49] A recent, comprehensive survey of Chukchi language use in Chukotka and the Sakha Republic discovered one fluent speaker born in 1984 (35 years old at the time of publication), who, as expected, is a nomadic herdswoman.[50] Otherwise, this survey found that speakers who are presently in their 30s and 40s tend to have only a passive understanding of the language. This is consistent with the perception among our Chukchi consultants in Sakha, who claimed that the youngest proficient speakers would likely be in their 50s and older. They also echoed the claims about expedited language loss in cities, mentioning that the best remaining younger speakers are likely to be those who still live in villages and occasionally herd with their parents.[51]

Overall, this presents a bleak outlook for the vitality of the Chukchi language and points to a process of language shift that is well underway, with children no longer fully acquiring it[52]. Chukchi is presently considered an endangered (or at least a threatened) language[53], meaning that it is at risk of being lost in the near feature without serious intervention. This has also meant that we have had to approach our study of Chukchi and Sakha slightly differently. It is still relatively easy to locate proficient speakers of Sakha, even in cities, and therefore possible to collect data from a large group of participants. However, it is not possible to perform any kind of broad statistical analysis on Chukchi because there are simply not enough speakers who have sufficient knowledge of the language to participate in the experiment tasks.

The following section outlines the particular methodology that was used to assess Sakha and Chukchi language use and to elicit speech in a controlled setting.

Methodology

Research is planned at a number of field sites in the Republic of Sakha and Chukotka to contrast urban and rural settings. To date, pilot studies of Sakha and Chukchi have been carried out in Yakutsk, the capital of the Republic of Sakha and the largest growing city in the region,[54] with a population of approximately 270,000 as of 2010.[55]

The methodology used was designed to target two areas: language use and the social/ecological factors that condition it, and any structural changes in the languages. For the first goal, we administered a formal questionnaire that asked participants about their linguistic background: which languages they speak, which languages members of their immediate and extended family speak, and in which contexts and with which interlocutors they use the languages. Participants were also asked to assess their own proficiency in the languages they spoke (how well they could read, write, speak, and understand the language). The questionnaire also collected biographical information about the participants and their immediate family: dates of birth, hometowns, and education levels. In some cases, it was necessary to conduct more informal oral interviews, particularly with older speakers who would have difficulty reading and concentrating on a lengthy document. In other cases, we opted not to use a questionnaire in order to preserve our consultants' trust: as I discuss in the following sections, the minority populations of Siberia have a fraught history with the Russian government and are often understandably wary of filling out formal documents. In these cases, the speakers were able to guide the discussion and described specific experiences with their languages.

The research participants were also asked to complete two types of tasks in order for us to collect examples of their speech: a structured experiment where they were given pictures and words and asked to construct sentences using those words, and a more freeform activity where they were shown a series of pictures and asked to tell a story. In the experiment, the words were given in a recognizable dictionary citation form: speakers were expected to put the words in the appropriate order and use the appropriate inflectional morphology (i.e., modifying the citation forms for the correct case, tense, and 3rd person agreement). Table 11.4 gives an example of one of the stimuli; these words were provided to participants alongside a picture of a man extending a fish to a young boy.

In Sakha, the expected typical word order for a declarative sentence is Subject – Object – Verb; however in Russian it is Subject – Verb – Object. If the word order in Sakha has changed due to bilingualism with Russian, we expect to see instances of the verb occurring in the second position in the sentence. The situation is slightly more complex in Chukchi: unlike English, for example, Chukchi has a relatively free word order, where words in different roles can occur anywhere in the sentence. It is also possible to exclude either the subject or the object because they are otherwise indicated in the form of the verb. Russian-like sentences with Subject – Verb – Object order are fairly rare in naturalistic speech;[56] thus, although such sentences are possible, a greater incidence of them among Chukchi speakers who are bilingual in Russian may point to structural changes due to Russian influence.

In the story task, the sequence of images shows a boy and his dog going fishing; the boy falls out of his boat and the dog pulls him to safety. All of the Sakha participants were given this task, and our primary Chukchi consultant also told two longer narratives based on two children's books: one about the friendship between a little girl and a bear, and the other about a lost polar bear.

The following two sections summarize our findings for the two case studies. First, I discuss the results of the Sakha pilot study and present evidence of early structural changes due to language shift. Then I describe the results of the Chukchi study, and finally I contrast the two and describe how they inform an ecological approach to the study of language contact.

Study results: Sakha

The results of our formal questionnaire and linguistic experiment confirm that there is reason to think that the current status of Sakha is unstable, and that we may be seeing the early signs of language shift among young, urban

Table 11.4 Example of experimental stimuli

Sakha words	Chukchi words
bier 'to give'	*pelak* 'to leave'
baluk 'fish (nominative)'	*əneen* 'fish (absolutive)'
er 'man (nominative)'	*ətləgən* 'father (absolutive)'
uol 'boy(nominative)'	*ekək* 'son (absolutive)'

speakers. This investigation was conducted with 30 students at the North-Eastern Federal University in Yakutsk, all of whom identified as ethnic Sakha. The students had grown up in different parts of the Republic, but all of them spoke proficient Russian and did not have trouble interacting with the researchers in Russian. (This is unsurprising, as education at the university level in Sakha is conducted in Russian. A future goal of the project is to replicate these tasks with a more diverse pool of participants.)

The proficiency self-assessment revealed that although Sakha is still quite robust among this age group (19–24), a number of the speakers in our sample did not believe themselves to be fully fluent in the language. Of the 30 students surveyed, two spoke no Sakha at all (and only knew Russian). Two out of the 28 students who did claim to speak Sakha said they experienced some difficulty with the language, and five said they were only able to speak but could not read or write. In comparison, all 30 speakers spoke Russian, with only one expressing any difficulty with Russian.

The primary domain for Sakha use among these speakers was at home with family (especially grandparents), although many also said they used the language with friends and throughout daily life in the city. Meanwhile, Russian was the dominant language at the university and online, particularly in interactive spaces such as online gaming. Some information about tendencies in mixed families also emerged from the questionnaire data. In cases where only one parent spoke Sakha (and the other parent spoke either Russian only or Russian and Even/Evenki), the speaker was Russian-dominant or else knew very little Sakha. This represents a change compared to the pattern in the 1970s, where children in these families were very likely to learn Sakha.[57]

Some clear differences emerged in the responses to the questionnaire among the students who had grown up in Yakutsk compared to those who had grown up in less populated towns and villages. As expected, the speakers who had grown up in an urban setting were the least proficient and used Sakha in the fewest domains. Speakers from Yakutsk tended to acquire Russian and Sakha simultaneously from birth, whereas speakers who had grown up elsewhere usually only spoke Sakha until they started learning Russian in primary school (around age 7 or 8).

In general, the students seemed to be good at gauging their own proficiency—that is, the students who expressed some doubts about their Sakha ability were the ones who were most likely to make errors in their speech when they performed the two research tasks. Some speakers did in fact display nonstandard word order in their speech: instead of the expected Subject – Object – Verb order, they produced the more Russian-seeming Subject – Verb – Object order. There were also occasional errors in inflectional morphology, with speakers producing the wrong noun case or the wrong form of the verb. Typically, these forms lacked the necessary additional morphology to trigger a change in meaning: speakers were simply reading from the list of words we had provided them. Both of these types of errors are present in the following sentence:

(1) ɟaxtar   oŋoror   **kɯɯs**   tʃaj
woman (nom.)   makes   girl (nom.)   tea
Intended meaning: 'The woman makes tea for the girl'

The underlined word, the verb, is in the wrong position in the sentence (we expect it at the very end). The bolded noun has been given in its uninflected (nominative) form; however, the nominative should only be used for the subject of the verb, not the indirect object. The expected form of this sentence is:

(2) ɟaxtar   **kɯɯska**   tʃej   oŋoror
woman (nom.)   girl (dat.)   tea   makes
'The woman makes tea for the girl.'

Note that the verb is at the end, and the word 'girl' is now in the dative case (indicated through the appending of *-ka*).

Overall, however, dysfluencies such as these were rare among these speakers, suggesting that the grammatical systems of these speakers are still intact and we are not yet seeing significant contact-induced change due to Russian influence or major linguistic loss due to shift.

Study results: Chukchi

Our pilot study focused on surveying ethnic Chukchis living in Yakutsk and, when possible, carrying out the same tasks from our work with Sakha speakers. I am aware of fewer than a dozen Chukchis living in the city and have informally interviewed four speakers. (All of these speakers were much older than the Sakha students and since there was a possibility that our work would address sensitive topics, it did not seem appropriate to administer a formal questionnaire.) So far, only one of these speakers has participated in the linguistic tasks—this speaker is fully fluent and spoke Chukchi at home when she was growing up, and later specialized in Chukchi at university. Another of these speakers was an elderly woman who was also completely fluent and had also received formal Chukchi education. The other two speakers self-identified as less proficient: one speaker, the daughter of the elderly woman, is currently learning Chukchi as a second language in adulthood, and the other has not spoken much since childhood, though she still tries to read in Chukchi.

All of the speakers are acutely aware of the fact that the Chukchi language is disappearing, and lament that the interest in documenting and preserving the language (among both foreign linguists and ethnic Chukchis) developed so late. Despite this growing interest, our consultants are not optimistic about the future of their language and point to numerous obstacles to using Chukchi on a regular basis. A major issue in Chukchi language use is the lack of a speech community, especially in Yakutsk. Some speakers attempt to practice Chukchi through participation in large WhatsApp group chats; however, it seems that there is little actual conversation happening in these groups. One of our participants said that the group functions more to exchange cultural media, such as videos or news articles, and Chukchi language use does not usually go beyond talking about the weather. Language ideology—how speakers feel about the status and value of the languages in the local ecology—also emerged as a significant theme in our interviews. While speakers might believe that Chukchi is an important part of their culture, they do not think it is practical to devote time to studying it as a second language over more economically beneficial languages such as English.

The linguistic changes we expect to encounter in this type of situation are significant: all speakers of Chukchi, regardless of ability, likely also speak Russian to an extent, and for most speakers Russian is their dominant language. Thus, we expect even the fluent speakers to have some Russian influence in their speech, and we expect the less proficient speakers to have significant errors or gaps in their grammatical systems.

The fluent speaker who participated in our linguistic tasks did not show signs of major, systemic changes across the two main dimensions we considered in our Sakha study: word order and case marking. For example, throughout ten minutes of uninterrupted speech (while telling the girl and bear story), the speaker demonstrated a variety of word orders, as expected, and had a moderate preference for placing the verb at the end of a sentence. She did not have a particularly high rate of Subject – Verb – Object sentences, which is what we had predicted would be the case under Russian influence. The speaker also consistently (and correctly) used different case forms throughout the story. These results do not necessarily mean that there have been no contact-based changes in her speech, but may mean that potential changes are more subtle or sporadic, or affect different aspects of her language.

It is worth noting that there were patterns in this speaker's language that illustrate another typical dimension of language shift: problems that arise for fluent speakers who do not have a community with which to practice their language. The process of losing or forgetting language across a speaker's lifetime, called attrition, can often produce similar effects on grammatical structure as never having fully learned the language.[58] While this Chukchi speaker did not have any trouble producing full sentences, she would occasionally make corrections to things she had said or have difficulty remembering specific nouns or verbs. One strategy the speaker had when she could not remember a verb was to use the "proverb" in Chukchi. In the same way that one can substitute a pronoun for a noun, the Chukchi pro-verb *req-* is used in place of a verb and means "did so."[59] While technically grammatical, the use of this verb is not informative unless discussing a known activity. For the following sentence, for example, the speaker later supplied the verb she had meant to use (*mənumekewənet* 'I will gather them'):

(3) am   opopə   cinit   əmelʔo   mən**req**ewənet
    well   okay   myself   all   I.will.do.so.to.them
    'Well okay, I will do it to all of them myself'

These tendencies do not mean that the speaker's grammatical system has actually changed. Attrition is distinct from errors due to incomplete learning of a language in that speakers should be able to recover features of the language they have lost, with enough practice. However, this type of phenomenon illustrates that linguistic loss can occur even among fully proficient speakers in situations of language shift. This is a particularly problematic issue for linguists who document endangered languages with the goal of revitalizing them (that is, teaching them to new generations of speakers and establishing a new speech community), as these efforts often come when there are only a few elderly speakers remaining.

Conclusion

Sakha and Chukchi are two languages which were *lingua francas* in the years leading up to and following the arrival of Russians in Siberia. However, these languages have had dramatically different outcomes in the modern era. Although Sakha may presently be under threat from Russian in cities, the language is still robustly spoken throughout the Sakha Republic. The same cannot be said of Chukchi, whose most fluent speakers are over the age of 30. While children outside of major cities such as Yakutsk speak Sakha as their primary language until they go to school, this does not appear to be the case for Chukchi children except when they are involved in traditional cultural activities such as reindeer herding, hunting, and fishing.

Despite the one-time dominance of both languages, it is clear that historical factors have also contributed to the modern differences in retention between Chukchi and Sakha. The Sakha became a sedentary group with a centralized population much earlier than the Chukchis, who remained scattered across a wide geographic area. The Sakha were also able to become a fixture of town life at a time when Chukchis remained largely nomadic, passing through settlements such as Anadyrsk to trade or else to raid them. During the Soviet period, the Sakha were allowed to rear their own children, while Chukchi children were removed from their parents and educated in boarding schools, where they received no instruction (and were often prohibited from) speaking their native language.

The two groups also differ in terms of language standardization: the Sakha were able to play a direct role in the development of their orthography and a shared literary language, which is still used extensively. In comparison, the Chukchi literary language was developed by Russian scholars and has not been adopted by non-educated speakers.[60] Furthermore, although claims about dialectal variation in Chukchi are often dismissed by researchers, several of our consultants have reported finding the literary language inaccessible to them because it differs dramatically from how they speak on a day-to-day basis (the literary language is largely based on the maritime variety of Chukchi, spoken along the coast in Chukotka, while our speakers were tundra Chukchis mainly from the Kolymskoe region of Yakutia). These facts further reduce speakers' ability to engage with an already limited body of literature. Finally, the Chukchi language has no special status in Chukotka like Sakha does in Yakutia; there is therefore even less incentive to teach and master Chukchi.

It may be valuable to consider these two languages in light of their differing treatment under Russian colonialism and, indeed, how the speakers of each would have figured in the Russian imagination. The Sakha were part of a settled society that was somewhat familiar to Russians compared to the nomadic Chukchis who fiercely resisted all semblance of Russian culture. Restricting native language use has long been a tool of colonization, not merely to repress native identity and culture but to fundamentally alter the subjugated people's values and relationship to history and the world.[61] By suppressing the Chukchi language, perhaps Russian authorities sought to do what they failed to through the use of physical force: assimilate the Chukchis into Russian society.

These two case studies also affirm that a social approach to the study of language contact and bilingualism is essential in understanding the linguistic variation and change that results from these scenarios. The stability of a language is largely a product of the local ecology and is subject to change. Even if that language is a *lingua franca*, its dominance is drawn from the political or economic dominance of its speaker group. As these power dynamics evolve, so too can the status of the language.[62] Political restructuring under Russian governance and the political advantages afforded by knowledge of Russian have been the main contributing factors in the reduced status of these languages, rather than any intrinsic facts about the languages themselves. The relative linguistic complexity of the languages, for example, does not account for changes in the rates of their use. Chukchi might be considered more complex from a morphological standpoint (as a polysynthetic language, it encodes sentence meaning through many morphemes in a single word, rather than separate words); however, speakers of comparatively simpler languages, such as English, were able and willing to learn it when the Chukchi people were economically eminent.

So far the discussion has presented a somewhat dire prognosis for these languages, especially Chukchi. It is important to note that the two situations we have considered are still in flux. Possible language shift in Sakha is still in a nascent form and only appears to be a threat in urban areas. Language shift in Chukchi has not yet progressed to an irreversible stage, as there are still several generations of speakers for young learners to interact with if given the opportunity. Excepting a 2019 study of Chukchi language use, much of the information about the status of the Chukchi language within Chukotka is almost 20 years old, and the current situation may be more promising than in Sakha, where the population of Chukchis is considerably smaller.[63] (In Chukotka, there is some primary school education available in Chukchi, as well as journalism and some television programming.) It is possible that the cultural awakening among the Chukchis might have the effect of promoting language learning and reversing the linguistic and psychological results of Russian colonization. This is a question that we must leave for future inquiry.

Notes

1 James Forsyth, *A History of the Peoples of Siberia: Russia's North Asian Colony, 1581–1990* (Cambridge: Cambridge University Press, 1992).
2 Forsyth, *A History of the Peoples of Siberia*, 63.
3 Yuri Slezkine, *Arctic Mirrors: Russia and the Small Peoples of the North* (Ithaca: Cornell University Press, 2006), ix.
4 Source: Arctic Council Indigenous Peoples Secretariat, online map.
5 2010 All-Russia Census.
6 Sarah G. Thomason and Terrence Kaufman, *Language Contact, Creolization, and Genetic Linguistics* (Berkeley: University of California Press, 1988); and Sarah G. Thomason, *Language Contact: An Introduction* (Washington, DC: Georgetown University Press, 2001).
7 Salikoko S. Mufwene, *The Ecology of Language Evolution* (Cambridge: Cambridge University Press, 2001).
8 This project is currently ongoing and is funded by NSF BCS 1761551, and has previously received funding from the Humanities Division Council at the University of Chicago. University of Chicago Professors Ming Xiang and Lenore Grenoble, also an author in this volume, are the co-PIs. Liudmila Zamorshchikova of the North-Eastern Federal University in Yakutsk served as the main project coordinator in Sakha. I am currently a graduate student researcher on the project. The pilot studies were carried out by Grenoble and Kantarovich.
9 Nikolai Vakhtin and Ekaterina Gruzdeva, "Language Obsolescence in Polysynthetic Languages," in *The Oxford Handbook of Polysynthesis*, ed. Michale Fortescue, Marianne Mithun, and Nicholas Evans (Oxford: Oxford University Press, 2017); and Maria Polinsky, "Cross-linguistic parallels in language loss," *Southwest Journal of Linguistics* 14, nos. 1 & 2 (1995): 87–123.
10 Forsyth, *A History of the Peoples of Siberia*, 55.
11 Forsyth, *A History of the Peoples of Siberia*, 56; and Brigitte Pakendorf, "Contact in the prehistory of the Sakha (Yakuts): Linguistic and genetic perspectives" (Ph. D. diss., Universiteit Leiden, 2007).
12 Forsyth, *A History of the Peoples of Siberia*, 56.
13 Forsyth, *A History of the Peoples of Siberia*, 142.
14 Forsyth, *A History of the Peoples of Siberia*, ch. 3.
15 Forsyth, *A History of the Peoples of Siberia*.
16 Forsyth, *A History of the Peoples of Siberia*, 62.
17 Forsyth, *A History of the Peoples of Siberia*.
18 Vasili Robbek, "Language Situation in the Sakha Republic (Yakutia)," in *Bicultural Education in the North: Ways of Preserving and Enhancing Indigenous Peoples' Languages and Traditional Knowledge*, ed. Erich Kasten (Münster: Waxmann Verlag, 1998), 113.
19 Willem J. De Reuse, *Siberian Yupik Eskimo: The Language and Its Contacts with Chukchi* (Salt Lake City: Utah University Press), 1994.
20 John Michael Dunn, "A Sketch Grammar of Chukchi" (B.A. Honors thesis, Australian National University, 1994), 1.
21 John Michael Dunn, "A Grammar of Chukchi" (Ph.D. diss., Australian National University, 1999).
22 Forsyth, *A History of the Peoples of Siberia*, 297–8.
23 Dunn, "A Grammar of Chukchi."
24 Dunn, "A Grammar of Chukchi."
25 Nikolai Vakhtin, "Endangered Languages in Northeast Siberia: Siberian Yupik and other Languages of Chukotka," in *Bicultural Education in the North: Ways of Preserving and Enhancing Indigenous Peoples' Languages and Traditional Knowledge*, ed. Erich Kasten (Münster: Waxmann Verlag, 1998), 163.

26 Willem J. De Reuse, "Chukchi, English, and Eskimo: A survey of jargons in the Chukotka area," in *Language Contact in the Arctic: Northern Pidgins and Contact Languages*, eds., Ernst Håkon Jahr and Ingvild Broch (Berlin: Mouton de Gruyter, 1996), 48.
27 De Reuse, "A survey of jargons in the Chukotka area."
28 De Reuse, "A survey of jargons in the Chukotka area," 48.
29 De Reuse, "A survey of jargons in the Chukotka area," 58.
30 De Reuse, "A survey of jargons in the Chukotka area," 49.
31 Igor Krupnik and Michael Chlenov. *Yupik Transitions: Change and Survival at Bering Strait, 1900–1960* (Fairbanks: University of Alaska Press, 2013).
32 Forsyth, *A History of the Peoples of Siberia*, 80–81.
33 Forsyth, *A History of the Peoples of Siberia*, 81.
34 Dunn, "A Grammar of Chukchi."
35 De Reuse, *Siberian Yupik Eskimo*.
36 Dunn, "A Grammar of Chukchi," and also confirmed by my own fieldwork.
37 Bernard Comrie, "Language contact in northeastern Siberia (Chukotka and Kamchatka)," in *Language Contact in the Arctic: Northern Pidgins and Contact Languages*, eds., Ernst Håkon Jahr and Ingvild Broch (Berlin: Mouton de Gruyter, 1996), 38.
38 Georgij A. Menovščikov, *Grammatika jazyka aziatskix èskimosov* (Leningrad: Nauka, 1967), 270–71.
39 Comrie, "Language contact in northeastern Siberia," 39.
40 Forsyth, *A History of the Peoples of Siberia*.
41 Forsyth, *A History of the Peoples of Siberia*, 150.
42 The Constitution of the Russian Federation.
43 Forsyth, *A History of the Peoples of Siberia*, 265–6.
44 Forsyth, *A History of the Peoples of Siberia*.
45 Forsyth, *A History of the Peoples of Siberia*, 296–9.
46 Forsyth, *A History of the Peoples of Siberia*, 338.
47 Forsyth, *A History of the Peoples of Siberia*, 367.
48 Forsyth, *A History of the Peoples of Siberia*, 400.
49 Dunn, "A Grammar of Chukchi."
50 Maria Pupynina and Yuri Koryakov, "Chukchi-Speaking Communities in Three Russian Regions: A 120-Year Story of Language Shift," *Sibirica* 18: 2 (July 2019): 78–124.
51 Working with such speakers is a planned component of our research project in the next several years.
52 Vakhtin, "Endangered Languages in Northeast Siberia," 159.
53 Simons and Fennig, "Chukchi."
54 Timothy Heleniak, "Boom and bust: Population change in Russia's Arctic cities," in *Sustaining Russia's Arctic Cities: Resource Politics, Migration and Climate Change*, ed. R.W. Orttung (New York: Berghahn, 2017), 84.
55 2010 All-Russia Census.
56 Dunn, "A Grammar of Chukchi," 81.
57 However, it should be noted that this is only a modest tendency based on a small sample, and additional work with minority groups outside Yakutsk is necessary.
58 Monika S. Schmid, *Language Attrition* (Cambridge: Cambridge University Press, 2011).
59 Dunn, "A Grammar of Chukchi."
60 Dunn, "A Grammar of Chukchi," 9, also reported by our consultants.
61 Ngũgĩ wa Thiong'o, *Decolonising the Mind: The Politics of Language in African Literature* (London: J. Currey, 1986).
62 Thomason, *Language Contact*, 24.
63 Pupynina and Koryakov, "Chukchi-Speaking Communities."

Selected Bibliography

Andreeva, Elena. *Russia and Iran in the Great Game: Travelogues and Orientalism.* London: Routledge, 2007.

Ascher, Abraham. The Revolution of 1905, vol. 1: *Russia in Disarray.* Stanford, CA: Stanford University Press, 1988.

Austin, Paul M. *The Exotic Prisoner in Russian Romanticism.* New York: Peter Lang, 1997.

Avery, Martha. *The Tea Road: China and Russia meet across the Steppe.* Beijing: China Intercontinental Press, 2003.

Baddeley, John F. *Russia, Mongolia, China. Being Some Record of the relations between them from the beginning of the XVIIth Century to the Death of Tsar Alexey Mikhailovich A.D. 1602–1676,* 2 vols. London: Macmillan, 1919.

Bailey, Scott C. Matsushita. "A Biography in Motion: Chokan Valikhanov and His Travels in Central Asia." *Ab Imperio* 1 (2009): 165–190.

Baron, Nick. "New Spatial Histories of Twentieth Century Russia and the Soviet Union: Surveying the Landscape," *Jahrbücher für die Geschichte Osteuropas* 55 (2007): 375–400.

Bassin, Mark. *Imperial Visions: Nationalist Imagination and Geographical Expansion in the Russian Far East, 1840–1865.* New York: Cambridge University Press, 1999.

Bassin, Mark. "Inventing Siberia: Visions of the Russian East in the Early Nineteenth Century." *The American Historical Review* 96: 3 (June 1991): 763–794.

Bassin, Mark, Christopher Ely, and Melissa K. Stockdale, eds., *Space, Place, and Power in Modern Russia.* DeKalb: Northern Illinois University Press, 2010.

Bassin, Mark, Sergey Glebov, and Marlene Laruelle, eds., *Between Europe and Asia: The Origin, Theories, and Legacies of Russian Eurasianism.* Pittsburgh: University of Pittsburgh Press, 2015.

Blanchard, Ian. *Russia's Age of Silver. Precious-metal Production and Economic Growth in the Eighteenth century.* London: Routledge, 1989.

Boikova, E. V. *Rossiiskie voennye issledovateli Mongolii (vtoraia polovina XIX – nachalo XX veka).* Moscow: Institut vostokovedeniia RAN, 2014.

Breyfogle, Nicholas B., Abby Schrader, and Willard Sunderland, eds., *Peopling the Russian Periphery: Borderland Colonization in Eurasian History.* New York: Routledge, 2007.

Brooks, Jeffrey. *When Russia Learned to Read: Literacy and Popular Literature, 1861–1917.* Evanston: Northwestern University Press, 2003.

Brower, Daniel R. "Imperial Russia and Its Orient: The Renown of Nikolai Przhevalsky." *The Russian Review* 53: 3 (1994): 367–381.

Brower, Daniel R. and Edward J.Lazzerini, eds., *Russia's Orient: Imperial Borderlands and Peoples, 1700–1917*. Bloomington: Indiana University Press, 1997.

Damashek, L. M., and A. V. Remnev, eds., *Sibir' v sostave Rossiiskoi imperii*. Moscow: Novoe literaturnoe obozrenie, 2007.

Diment, Galya and Yuri Slezkine, eds., *Between Heaven and Hell: The Myth of Siberia in Russian Culture*. New York: St. Martin's Press, 1993.

Eden, Jeff. *Slavery and Empire in Central Asia*. Cambridge: Cambridge University Press, 2018.

Etkind, Alexander. *Internal Colonization: Russia's Imperial Experience*. Cambridge: Polity Press, 2011.

Forsyth, James. *A History of the Peoples of Siberia: Russia's North Asian Colony, 1581–1990*. Cambridge: Cambridge University Press, 1992.

Foust, Clifford M. *Muscovite and Mandarin: Russia's Trade with China and Its Setting, 1727–1805*. Chapel Hill: University of North Carolina Press, 1969.

Friedman, Jeremy. *Shadow Cold War: The Sino-Soviet Competition for the Third World*. Chapel Hill: The University of North Carolina Press, 2015.

Gibson, James R. *Feeding the Russian Fur Trade: Provisionment of the Okhotsk Seaboard and the Kamchatka Peninsula, 1639–1856*. Madison: University of Wisconsin Press, 1969.

Glebov, Sergey. *From Empire to Eurasia: Politics, Scholarship, and Ideology in Russian Eurasianism, 1920s – 1930s*. DeKalb: Southern Illinois University Press, 2017.

Grant, Bruce. *The Captive and the Gift: Cultural Histories of Sovereignty in Russia and the Caucasus*. New York: Cornell University Press, 2009.

Green, Nile, ed., *Writing Travel in Central Asian History*. Bloomington: Indiana University Press, 2014.

Grenoble, Lenore. *Language Policy in the Soviet Union*. Dordrecht: Kluwer Academic Publishers, 2003.

Grim, John. *The Shaman: Patterns of Siberian and Ojibway Healing*. The Civilization of the American Indian Series. Norman: University of Oklahoma Press, 1983.

Guseinov, Chingiz. *Etot zhivoi fenomen: sovetskaia mnogonatsional'naia literatura vchera i segodnia*. Moscow: Sovetskii pisatel', 1988.

Guseinov, Chingiz. *Formy obshchnosti sovetskoi mnogonatsional'noi literatury*. Moscow: Mysl', 1978.

Hill, Fiona and Clifford Gaddy. *The Siberian Curse: How Communist Planners Left Russia out in the Cold*. Washington, DC: The Brookings Institution, 2003.

Hokanson, Katya. *Writing at Russia's Border*. Toronto: University of Toronto Press, 2008.

Iadrintsev, Nikolai M. *Sibir' kak koloniia*. St. Petersburg: Tipografiia M. M. Stasiulevicha, 1882.

Jones, Ryan Tucker. *Empire of Extinction: Russians and the North Pacific's Strange Beasts of the Sea*. Oxford: Oxford University Press, 2014.

Kationov, Oleg Nikolaevich. *Moskovsko-Sibirskii trakt i ego zhiteli XVII-XIX vv*. Novosibirsk: Izd. NGPU, 2004.

Khodarkovsky, Michael. *Russia's Steppe Frontier: The Making of a Colonial Empire, 1500–1800*. Bloomington: Indiana University Press, 2002.

Kivelson, Valerie. *Cartographies of Tsardom: The Land and its Meanings in Seventeenth-Century Russia*. Ithaca: Cornell University Press, 2006.

Kowner, Rotem, ed. *The Impact of the Russo-Japanese War*. New York: Routledge, 2007.

Kotkin, Stephen and David Wolff, eds., *Rediscovering Russia in Asia: Siberia and the Russian Far East*. Armonk, NY: M.E. Sharpe, 1995.

Lantzeff, George V., and Richard A.Pierce. *Eastward to Empire: Exploration and Conquest on the Russian Open Frontier to 1750*. Montreal: McGill-Queen's University Press, 1973.

Layton, Susan. *Russian Literature and Empire: Conquest of the Caucasus from Pushkin to Tolstoy*. Cambridge: Cambridge University Press, 2005.

Lim, Susanna Soojung. *China and Japan in the Russian Imagination, 1685–1922: To the Ends of the Orient*. New York: Routledge, 2013.

Lüthi, Lorenz. *The Sino-Soviet Split: Cold War in the Communist World*. Princeton: Princeton University Press, 2008.

Martin, Virginia. *Law and Custom in the Steppe: the Kazakhs of the Middle Horde and Russian Colonialism in the Nineteenth Century*. Richmond, Surrey: Curzon, 2001.

Monahan, Erika. "Moving Pictures: Tobol'sk 'Traveling' in Early Modern Texts." *Canadian-American Slavic Studies* 52 (2018): 1–29.

Morozova, L. M. and V. F. Afanas'ev. *Gor'kii i Iakutiia*. Iakutsk: Iakutskoe knizhnoe izdatel'stvo, 1968.

Patrikeeff, Felix and Harold Shukman. *Railways and the Russo-Japanese War: Transporting War*. New York: Routledge, 2007.

Perdue, Peter. *China Marches West: The Qing Conquest of Central Eurasia*. Cambridge: Belknap Press of the Harvard University Press, 2005.

Ram, Harsha. *The Imperial Sublime: A Russian Poetics of Empire*. Madison: University of Wisconsin Press, 2003.

Randolph, John and Eugene M.Avrutin, eds., *Russia in Motion: Cultures of Mobility, 1850 to the Present*. Urbana: University of Illinois Press, 2012.

Reid, Anna. *The Shaman's Coat: A Native History of Siberia*. London: Weidenfeld & Nicolson, 2002.

Remnev, Anatolii Viktorovich. *Rossiia Dal'nego Vostoka: Imperskaia geografiia vlasti XIX – nachala XX vekov*. Omsk: Izdatel'stvo Omskogo gosudarstvennogo universiteta, 2004.

Rufova, Elena. *Tvorchestvo P. N. Chernykh-Iakutskogo v kontekste literaturnogo protsessa Iakutii nachala XX veka*. Novosibirsk: Nauka, 2014.

Schimmelpenninck van der Oye, David. *Russian Orientalism: Asia in the Russian Mind from Peter the Great to the Emigration*. New Haven: Yale University Press, 2010.

Schimmelpenninck van der Oye, David. *Toward the Rising Sun: Russian Ideologies of Empire and the Path to War with Japan*. DeKalb, IL: Northern Illinois University Press, 2006.

Sidorov, Oleg. *Platon Oiunskii*. Moscow: Molodaia gvardiia, 2016.

Sladkovskii, M. I. *Istoriia torgovo-ekonomicheskikh otnoshenii narodov Rossii s Kitaem (do 1917 g.)*. Moscow: Nauka, 1974.

Slezkine, Yuri. *Arctic Mirrors: Russia and the Small Peoples of the North*. Ithaca: Cornell University Press, 1994.

Smith, Alison K. "Movement and the Transformation of Siberia in the Eighteenth Century," *Sibirica* 16: 2 (2017): 44–67.

Stanziani, Alessandro. *Bondage: Labor and Rights in Eurasia from the Sixteenth to the Early Twentieth Centuries*. New York: Berghahn Books, 2014.

Stephan, John J. *The Russian Far East: A History*. Stanford: Stanford University Press, 1994.

Sunderland, Willard. *The Baron's Cloak: A History of the Russian Empire in War and Revolution*. Ithaca: Cornell University Press, 2014.

Tolz, Vera. *Russia's Own Orient: The Politics of Identity and Oriental Studies in the Late Imperial and Early Soviet Periods*. Oxford: Oxford University Press, 2011.

Treadgold, Donald. *The Great Siberian Migration: Government and Peasant in Resettlement from Emancipation to the First World War*. Princeton: Princeton University Press, 1957.

Widdis, Emma. *Visions of a New Land: Soviet Film from the Revolution to the Second World War*. New Haven and London: Yale University Press, 2003.

Withers, Charles. *Placing the Enlightenment: Thinking Geographically About the Age of Reason*. Chicago: University of Chicago Press, 2007.

Wolff, David, Steven G.Marks, Bruce W.Menning, DavidSchimmelpenninck van der Oye, John W.Steinberg and Shinji Yokote, eds., *The Russo-Japanese War in Global Perspective: World War Zero*. Leiden: Brill, 2006.

Wray, Harry and Hilary Conroy, eds., *Japan Examined: Perspectives on Modern Japanese History*. Honolulu: University of Hawai'i Press, 1983.

Znamenski, Andrei. *The Beauty of the Primitive: Shamanism and Western Imagination*. Oxford and New York: Oxford University Press, 2007.

Znamenski, Andrei. *Shamanism in Siberia: Russian Records of Indigenous Spirituality*. Dortrecht: Kluwer Academic Publishers, 2003.

Index

Figures are indexed in *Italic* page numbers, Tables in **Bold** page numbers